Lecture Notes in Computer Science 9679

Commenced Publication in 1973
Founding and Former Series Editors:
Gerhard Goos, Juris Hartmanis, and Jan van Leeuwen

More information about this series at http://www.springer.com/series/7408

Georgia M. Kapitsaki
Eduardo Santana de Almeida (Eds.)

Software Reuse: Bridging with Social-Awareness

15th International Conference, ICSR 2016
Limassol, Cyprus, June 5–7, 2016
Proceedings

 Springer

Editors
Georgia M. Kapitsaki
University of Cyprus
Nicosia
Cyprus

Eduardo Santana de Almeida
Universidade Federal da Bahia
Salvador, Bahia
Brazil

ISSN 0302-9743   ISSN 1611-3349   (electronic)
Lecture Notes in Computer Science
ISBN 978-3-319-35121-6   ISBN 978-3-319-35122-3   (eBook)
DOI 10.1007/978-3-319-35122-3

Library of Congress Control Number: 2016938412

LNCS Sublibrary: SL2 – Programming and Software Engineering

Printed on acid-free paper

This Springer imprint is published by Springer Nature
The registered company is Springer International Publishing AG Switzerland

Preface

The 15th International Conference on Software Reuse (ICSR) took place in Limassol, Cyprus, during June 5–7, and was hosted by the University of Cyprus. ICSR is the main premier event in the field of software reuse research and technology. The main goal of ICSR is to present the most recent advances and breakthroughs in the area of software reuse and to promote an intensive and continuous exchange among researchers and practitioners.

The specific theme of the 2016 conference was "Software Reuse: Bridging with Social-Awareness." Developers' social networks are gaining ground recently with software engineers participating in different fora collaborating and exchanging ideas and expertise. Software reuse needs to utilize, but also strengthen, this new form of synergies that can be built among engineers. The ICSR special theme aimed to bring this aspect in software reuse by raising social awareness, strengthening the existing platforms and tools, and utilizing the vast software information that exists in developers' social networks.

Responding to the call for papers, which expanded beyond the theme to other important areas, such as software evolution and reuse and software product line techniques, a total of 51 papers were submitted by authors from different organizations and institutions around the world. All papers underwent a thorough review process with the participation of at least three members from the Program Committee for each paper. In several cases, the independent reviews were followed with a discussion to consolidate the results, steered by the program chairs. As a result, 21 high-quality papers were selected as full research papers with an acceptance ratio of 41 %, while four papers were accepted as short research papers. Through a separate call for tool demonstrations, a total of four demonstration papers were selected.

The accepted papers cover different areas of software engineering, where software reuse plays an important role, such as software product lines, domain analysis and modelling, software tools, and business aspects of software. ICSR 2016 provided a complete view on the advancements in the area of software reuse in the last years for interested researchers and practitioners.

The program chairs wish to thank all authors for their contributions to a successful conference. Special thanks to General Chair George A. Papadopoulos, to Doctoral Symposium Chair Maurizio Morisio, to Workshops and Tutorials Chair Tommi Mikkonen, and to Tools Chair Frederik Kramer for their valuable work, as well as to all members of the Program Committee for their invaluable support.

June 2016

Georgia M. Kapitsaki
Eduardo Santana de Almeida

Organization

Organizing Committee

General Chair

George Angelos Papadopoulos   University of Cyprus, Cyprus

Program Co-chairs

Georgia M. Kapitsaki   University of Cyprus, Cyprus
Eduardo Santana de Almeida   Federal University of Bahia, Brazil

Doctoral Symposium Chair

Maurizio Morisio   Politecnico di Torino, Italy

Workshops and Tutorials Chair

Tommi Mikkonen   Tampere University of Technology, Finland

Tool Demonstrations Chair

Frederik Kramer   Otto-von-Guericke-Universität Magdeburg,
     initOS, Germany

Contents

Software Product Lines

Applying Incremental Model Slicing to Product-Line Regression Testing.... 3
  Sascha Lity, Thomas Morbach, Thomas Thüm, and Ina Schaefer

Automated Composition of Service Mashups Through Software Product
Line Engineering.. 20
  Mahdi Bashari, Ebrahim Bagheri, and Weichang Du

Feature Location in Model-Based Software Product Lines Through
a Genetic Algorithm 39
  Jaime Font, Lorena Arcega, Øystein Haugen, and Carlos Cetina

Carrying Ideas from Knowledge-Based Configuration to Software Product
Lines... 55
  *Juha Tiihonen, Mikko Raatikainen, Varvana Myllärniemi,
  and Tomi Männistö*

Tax-PLEASE—Towards Taxonomy-Based Software Product Line
Engineering 63
  Ina Schaefer, Christoph Seidl, Loek Cleophas, and Bruce W. Watson

Business Aspects of Software Reuse

A Method to Support the Adoption of Reuse Technology in Large Software
Organizations 73
  Luiz Amorim and Manoel Mendonça

A Practical Use Case Modeling Approach to Specify Crosscutting Concerns ... 89
  Tao Yue, Huihui Zhang, Shaukat Ali, and Chao Liu

An Approach for Prioritizing Software Features Based on Node Centrality
in Probability Network..................................... 106
  Zhenlian Peng, Jian Wang, Keqing He, and Hongtao Li

VCU: The Three Dimensions of Reuse 122
  *Jörg Kienzle, Gunter Mussbacher, Omar Alam, Matthias Schöttle,
  Nicolas Belloir, Philippe Collet, Benoit Combemale, Julien DeAntoni,
  Jacques Klein, and Bernhard Rumpe*

Reuse vs. Reusability of Software Supporting Business Processes 138
  Hermann Kaindl, Roman Popp, Ralph Hoch, and Christian Zeidler

Component-Based Reuse

A Case Study on the Availability of Open-Source Components for Game
Development 149
  Maria-Eleni Paschali, Apostolos Ampatzoglou, Stamatia Bibi,
  Alexander Chatzigeorgiou, and Ioannis Stamelos

RAGE Reusable Game Software Components and Their Integration into
Serious Game Engines. 165
  Wim van der Vegt, Enkhbold Nyamsuren, and Wim Westera

Reusable Secure Connectors for Secure Software Architecture 181
  Michael Shin, Hassan Gomaa, and Don Pathirage

Reuse-Based Software Engineering

Concept-Based Engineering of Situation-Specific Migration Methods. 199
  Marvin Grieger, Masud Fazal-Baqaie, Gregor Engels,
  and Markus Klenke

Leveraging Feature Location to Extract the Clone-and-Own Relationships
of a Family of Software Products 215
  Manuel Ballarin, Raúl Lapeña, and Carlos Cetina

AIRES: An Architecture to Improve Software Reuse. 231
  Rosana T. Vaccare Braga, Daniel Feloni, Karen Pacini,
  Domenico Schettini Filho, and Thiago Gottardi

Pragmatic Software Reuse in Bioinformatics: How Can Social Network
Information Help?. 247
  Xiaoyu Jin, Charu Khatwani, Nan Niu, Michael Wagner,
  and Juha Savolainen

Software Reuse Tools

Feature Location Benchmark for Software Families Using Eclipse
Community Releases. 267
  Jabier Martinez, Tewfik Ziadi, Mike Papadakis,
  Tegawendé F. Bissyandé, Jacques Klein, and Yves Le Traon

Java Extensions for Design Pattern Instantiation 284
  André L. Santos and Duarte Coelho

Towards a Semantic Search Engine for Open Source Software 300
  Sihem Ben Sassi

Detecting Similar Programs via The Weisfeiler-Leman Graph Kernel. 315
Wenchao Li, Hassen Saidi, Huascar Sanchez, Martin Schäf,
and Pascal Schweitzer

Domain Analysis and Modelling

Metamodel and Constraints Co-evolution: A Semi Automatic Maintenance
of OCL Constraints. 333
Djamel Eddine Khelladi, Regina Hebig, Reda Bendraou, Jacques Robin,
and Marie-Pierre Gervais

A Model Repository Description Language - MRDL. 350
Brahim Hamid

Reverse-Engineering Reusable Language Modules from Legacy
Domain-Specific Languages. 368
David Méndez-Acuña, José A. Galindo, Benoit Combemale,
Arnaud Blouin, Benoit Baudry, and Gurvan Le Guernic

A Framework for Enhancing the Retrieval of UML Diagrams. 384
Alhassan Adamu and Wan Mohd Nazmee Wan Zainoon

Tool Demonstrations

Puzzle: A Tool for Analyzing and Extracting Specification Clones in DSLs . . . 393
David Méndez-Acuña, José A. Galindo, Benoit Combemale,
Arnaud Blouin, and Benoit Baudry

FeatureIDE: Scalable Product Configuration of Variable Systems 397
Juliana Alves Pereira, Sebastian Krieter, Jens Meinicke,
Reimar Schröter, Gunter Saake, and Thomas Leich

Recalot.com: Towards a Reusable, Modular, and RESTFul Social
Recommender System. 402
Matthäus Schmedding, Michael Fuchs, Claus-Peter Klas, Felix Engel,
Holger Brock, Dominic Heutelbeck, and Matthias Hemmje

CORPO-DS: A Tool to Support Decision Making for Component Reuse
Through Profiling with Ontologies 407
Savvas Loumakos and Andreas S. Andreou

Author Index 411

Software Product Lines

Applying Incremental Model Slicing to Product-Line Regression Testing

Sascha Lity[1]([✉]), Thomas Morbach[1], Thomas Thüm[2], and Ina Schaefer[2]

[1] Institute for Programming and Reactive Systems, TU Braunschweig, Braunschweig, Germany
{s.lity,t.morbach}@tu-braunschweig.de
[2] Institute of Software Engineering and Automotive Informatics, TU Braunschweig, Braunschweig, Germany
{t.thuem,i.schaefer}@tu-braunschweig.de

Abstract. One crucial activity in software product line (SPL) testing is the detection of erroneous artifact interactions when combined for a variant. This detection is similar to the retest test-case selection problem in regression testing, where change impact analysis is applied to reason about changed dependencies to be retested. In this paper, we propose automated change impact analysis based on incremental model slicing for incremental SPL testing. Incremental slicing allows for a slice computation by adapting a previous slice with explicit derivation of their differences by taking model changes into account. We apply incremental slicing to determine the impact of applied model changes and to reason about their potential retest. Based on our novel retest coverage criterion, each slice change specifies a retest test goal to be covered by existing test cases selected for retesting. We prototypically implemented our approach and evaluated its applicability and effectiveness by means of four SPLs.

Keywords: Software product line · Model-based testing · Regression testing · Model slicing

1 Introduction

Testing is a necessary and challenging activity during software development [15]. Testing a *software product line* (SPL) [31], i.e., a family of similar software systems sharing a common platform and reusable artifacts, is even more challenging. Due to the huge number of potential variants, testing each variant individually is often infeasible. Besides the standard testing problem finding failures in (variable) software artifacts, SPL testing also focuses on the detection of erroneous interactions of variable artifacts [27]. Existing SPL testing techniques [13,23,28,30] reduce the overall testing effort, e.g., by testing only a subset of variants [19]. However, each variant is still tested individually without

---

This work was partially supported by the German Research Foundation under the Priority Programme SPP1593: Design For Future – Managed Software Evolution.

G.M. Kapitsaki and E. Santana de Almeida (Eds.): ICSR 2016, LNCS 9679, pp. 3–19, 2016.
DOI: 10.1007/978-3-319-35122-3_1

taking the commonality and obtained test results into account as common in regression testing [42].

In prior work [25,26], we proposed incremental SPL testing combining the concepts of model-based [37] and regression testing [42] including the reuse of test artifacts and test results. Based on delta-oriented modeling [9] specifying the commonality and variability of variants by means of change operations called deltas, variant-specific test artifacts, such as the test suite, are incrementally adapted. Starting with a core variant, each subsequent variant is tested based on its tested predecessor. Here, a crucial task is the decision whether a reusable test case should be retested to validate that already tested behavior is not unintentionally affected by changes. In our prior work, this retest decision is to be performed manually. To cope with this well-known *retest test-case selection problem* [42] in regression testing, change impact analysis techniques are required.

Slicing [4,41] is a promising analysis technique to automate this retest decision [8]. Existing approaches apply slicing in a white-box regression testing setup [1,7,14]. In line with our prior work [25,26], we focus on model-based regression testing, where we have no access to source code. Therefore, state-based model slicing techniques [4] allow for model-based change impact analysis and, hence, to reason about the retest of test cases [21,36]. Based on a given model element used as slicing criterion, a behavioral specification, such as a finite state machine, is reduced comprising solely elements affecting the criterion. Thus, a modified slice indicates changed dependencies regarding the criterion. In prior work [24], we proposed incremental model slicing for delta-oriented SPLs. When stepping from a variant to its subsequent one, we reuse the applied model changes specified by deltas to incrementally adapt already existing slices for same slicing criteria. As further result, we capture the differences between two subsequent slices as slice changes useable to reason about the impact of model changes.

In this paper, we adapt and apply our incremental slicing as change impact analysis technique *to automate retest decisions in incremental SPL testing*. Hence, we investigate the impact of model changes to common behavior between subsequent variants. We capture the obtained slice differences representing new/changed dependencies in respective slice changes, e.g., potential artifact interactions to be retested. The slice changes are used *to define a new coverage criterion facilitating the retest decision*. Therefore, we select reusable test cases for re-execution and further use test-case generation for generating new retest test cases to ensure coverage. We prototypically *implemented and evaluated our approach by means of four SPLs* to validate its applicability and effectiveness.

2   Foundations

Delta-Oriented Software Product Lines. Delta modeling [9] is a modular and flexible variability modeling approach already applied to various types of SPL development artifacts, e.g., finite state machines [26]. Differences between variants are explicitly specified by means of transformations called *deltas*. Based on a given *core model* M_{core} modeling a *core variant* $p_{core} \in P_{SPL}$, deltas $\delta \in \Delta_{\mathcal{M}}^{SPL}$ are

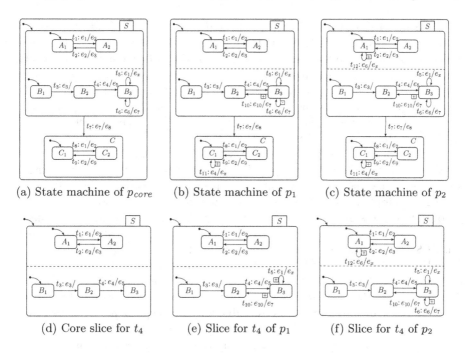

(a) State machine of p_{core} (b) State machine of p_1 (c) State machine of p_2

(d) Core slice for t_4 (e) Slice for t_4 of p_1 (f) Slice for t_4 of p_2

Fig. 1. Example of delta modeling [9] and incremental model slicing [24]

defined transforming M_{core} into the model M_i of variant $p_i \in P_{SPL}$. By P_{SPL}, we refer to the set of all valid variants of an SPL, whereas $\Delta_{\mathcal{M}}^{SPL}$ denotes the set of all deltas for P_{SPL} and model domain $\mathcal{M}$, here, *finite state machines* (FSM). A delta δ specifies change operations, such as additions (*add e*) or removals (*rem e*) of elements. For each $p_i \in P_{SPL}$, a predefined set of deltas $\Delta_{p_i} \subseteq \Delta_{\mathcal{M}}^{SPL}$ exists subsequently applied in a predefined order to automatically generate M_i. For the specification of changes between arbitrary variants, we are able to derive *model regression deltas* $\Delta_{p_{i-1},p_i}^{\mathcal{M}} \subseteq \Delta_{\mathcal{M}}^{SPL}$ to encapsulate the differences between two variants by incorporating their delta sets $\Delta_{p_{i-1}}$ and Δ_{p_i}. We refer the reader to prior work [25, 26] for the construction of model regression deltas.

Example 1. Consider the sample core state machine shown in Fig. 1a. Based on the delta set $\Delta_{p_1} = \{\delta_1 = (\text{add } t_{10}), \delta_2 = (\text{add } t_{11}), \delta_3 = (\text{rem } t_6)\}$ denoted by either + (add) or − (rem), the core is transformed into the state machine of p_1 depicted in Fig. 1b. For p_2, we apply the delta set $\Delta_{p_2} = \{\delta_1, \delta_2, \delta_4 = (\text{add } t_{12})\}$. To step from p_1 to p_2, we derive the model regression delta $\Delta_{p_1,p_2}^{FSM} = \{(\text{add } t_{12}), (\text{add } t_6)\}$ by incorporating the deltas captured in Δ_{p_1} and Δ_{p_2}.

Incremental Model-Based SPL Testing. Model-based testing [37] defines processes for automatic test-case generation based on test models. A *test model* tm, e.g., a finite state machine, specifies the behavior of a *system under test* in terms of *controllable inputs* and *observable outputs*. A system behaves as

expected if it reacts to inputs with expected outputs. To validate the conformance, test cases are derivable from the test model. A *test case tc* corresponds to
a test model path defining a sequence of controlled inputs and expected outputs.
For guiding the test-case generation, *adequacy criteria*, e.g., structural coverage
criteria like *all-transitions* [37], where each transition of the test model must be
traversed by a test case, are used to define a set of *test goals* $TG = \{tg_1, \ldots, tg_n\}$.
For each test goal, at least one test case must be generated to be collected in a *test
suite* $TS = \{tc_1, \ldots, tc_m\}$. For SPLs, these *test artifacts* exist for each $p_i \in P_{SPL}$
captured in variant-specific test artifact sets $TA_{p_i} = \{tm_{p_i}, TG_{p_i}, TS_{p_i}\}$.

In prior work [25,26], we proposed incremental SPL testing, where variants
are subsequently tested. To exploit the reuse potential of test artifacts during
testing, we adopt the concept of delta modeling to define regression deltas for the
set of test artifacts. Hence, we are able to adapt the variant-specific test artifacts
when stepping from p_{i-1} to p_i under test. Furthermore, we categorize the test
suite TS_{p_i} similar to regression testing [42] in sets of new $TS_N^{p_i}$, reusable $TS_{Re}^{p_i}$,
and obsolete test cases $TS_O^{p_i}$. *New test cases* are generated for yet uncovered
test goals of p_i. *Reusable test cases* were generated in prior testing steps and are
also valid for p_i. *Obsolete test cases* are not valid and removed from TS_{p_i} of p_i.
Obsolete test cases are potentially reusable for a subsequent p_j under test and,
thus, remain recorded in a shared artifact repository. From $TS_{Re}^{p_i}$, we manually
select test cases $TS_R^{p_i} \subseteq TS_{Re}^{p_i}$ for retesting that already tested behavior is not
influenced as intended also known as retest test-case selection problem [42].

The testing workflow is defined as follows. We start by testing p_{core}, i.e., we
apply standard model-based testing [37]. The obtained test suite and test results
are stored in a shared test artifact repository reused and updated by subsequent
testing steps. By stepping from p_{i-1} to p_i, we apply the following:

1. Compute test artifact regression deltas based on delta sets $\Delta_{p_{i-1}}$ and Δ_{p_i}.
2. Apply regression deltas to adapt the reusable test artifacts.
3. Categorize test cases to obtain test suites $TS_{Re}^{p_i}$ and $TS_O^{p_i}$.
4. Apply test-case generation for uncovered test goals to obtain $TS_N^{p_i}$.
5. *Analyze change impact of applied model changes.*
6. *Select reusable test cases to be retested captured in $TS_R^{p_i}$.*
7. (Re-)Test variant p_i and record results.

Afterwards, we select the next variant p_{i+1} to be tested until no variants remain.
In Sect. 3, we present how Steps 5 and 6 are automated by applying change
impact analysis techniques, i.e., incremental model slicing.

Example 2. We use the core from Example 1 as test model for p_{core} and focus
on all-transition coverage. A test case tc_1 is generated for transition t_6 also
covering t_1, t_2, t_3, and t_4. To step to p_1, we adapt the core test artifacts to TA_{p_1}
based on Δ_{p_1} also representing the regression delta $\Delta_{p_{core}, p_1}^{FSM}$. The test model is
transformed as shown in Fig. 1b. $TG_{p_{core}}$ is adapted by removing t_6 and adding
t_{10} and t_{11}. The test suite is adapted such that tc_1 is obsolete and removed as
well as new test cases for t_{10} and t_{11} are added. To step to p_2, the test artifacts
are adapted similarly, whereas tc_1 becomes reusable again and is added to $TS_{Re}^{p_2}$.

Incremental Model Slicing. Slicing was first proposed by Weiser [41] for static analysis of procedural programs. Meanwhile, slicing is also adapted for the analysis of state-based models, e.g., finite state machines. Such *model slicing* [4,18,20] allows for a model reduction by abstracting from model elements not influencing a selected element, e.g., a transition, used as slicing criterion c. A reduced model is called *slice* and preserves the execution semantics compared to the original model w.r.t. the criterion c. We focus on *backward slicing*, where a slice comprises elements influencing the criterion c determined based on (1) *control* and *data dependencies* between elements, and (2) to ensure model well-formedness, e.g., element reachability and model connectedness. Backward slicing investigates which elements have potential influences on a slicing criterion and, thus, indicates retest potentials when changed influences are determined.

In prior work [24], we combined model slicing and delta modeling to analyze delta-oriented SPLs. A slice $Slice_{p_i}^c$ for a criterion $c \in C_{p_i}$ of variant p_i is incrementally computed by exploiting the model changes specified in the model regression delta $\Delta_{p_{i-1},p_i}^{FSM}$. By C_{p_i}, we refer to the set of all slicing criteria of p_i. The incremental computation is defined by $incr_{Slice} : C_{SPL} \times \Delta_{FSM}^{SPL} \times SLICE_{C_{SPL}} \rightarrow SLICE_{C_{SPL}}$ where $C_{SPL} = \bigcup_{p_i \in P_{SPL}} C_{p_i}$ and $SLICE_{C_{SPL}}$ denotes the set of all slices of the current SPL. Starting with the prior slice $Slice_{p_j}^c$ for criterion c, the regression delta is applied to change the slice completed by standard model slicing. If there is no prior slice, we apply standard model slicing to compute a new slice reusable for subsequent variants. In addition, we directly determine the differences, i.e., *slice changes*, between the prior and current slice captured in a *slice regression delta* $\Delta_{Slice_c}^{p_j,p_i}$. The slice changes indicate the impact of applied model changes to the slicing criterion referring to behavior to be retested and, therefore, facilitate automated retest decisions as proposed in the next section.

Example 3. Consider the core slice for t_4 capturing all its influencing elements shown in Fig. 1d. Based on Δ_{p_1} from Example 1, the core is transformed into model p_1. As those model changes have influences on t_4, we recompute its slice and derive the slice regression delta $\Delta_{Slice_{t_4}}^{p_{core},p_1} = \{(add\ t_5), (add\ t_{10})\}$ shown in Fig. 1e. By stepping to p_2, the model changes also results in slice changes for $Slice_{p_2}^{t_4}$.

3 Automated Retest Decisions Based on Slice Changes

Change Impact Analysis. By stepping from p_{i-1} to p_i under test, the test model regression delta $\Delta_{p_{i-1},p_i}^{FSM}$ captures all changes between the test models. Each change has an impact on already tested behavior common in both variants. To investigate whether these impacts have unintended side effects, e.g., based on unintended artifact interactions, the potentially affected behavior should be retested by re-executing reusable test cases $tc_j \in TS_{Re}^{p_i}$ of p_i. The identification of affected behavior and the selection of reusable test cases is performed manually in our incremental SPL testing strategy [25,26]. For automation, we apply our incremental slicing technique [24] as change impact analysis. Based on obtained slice changes indicating changed dependencies and their side effects to already tested behavior, we automate the retest decision.

For the successful application of incremental model slicing as change impact analysis technique, we require (1) a set of slicing criteria suitable to investigate the change impact, (2) a set of meaningful dependencies, and (3) model regression deltas specifying the test model changes between subsequent variants under test. Similar to test-case generation, where test goals are used to guide the generation process, we use test goals as slicing criteria for (1), as changes may influence their corresponding behavior. We focus on all-transition coverage, i.e., a well-known structural coverage criteria used for test-case generation [37], such that each transition serves as a slicing criterion. As in prior work [24], we focus on the control dependencies proposed by Kamischke et al. [20] for (2). To fulfill (3), the required model regression deltas are provided by the incremental testing strategy.

Furthermore, the order in which variants are tested influence the result [3,16] as the derived model regression deltas and, thus, the result of the change impact analysis may differ. We omit the investigation of the best testing order, i.e., an order of variants allowing for maximal test artifact reuse and minimal retest decisions, and leave it for future work. We assume that a certain testing order is given starting with the core variant. However, to incorporate the testing order for change impact analysis, we identify three potential application scenarios for the derivation of slice changes as follows, where each scenario specifies which prior slice for a given slicing criterion is to be selected for adaptation to reason about change impact. For a slicing criterion contained in a test model for the first time, we start with a new slice.

1. **Least Slice Difference** – By stepping to the next variant, we select one of prior computed slices for the same slicing criterion, i.e., a transition contained in both variants, such that the resulting slice changes are minimized. To select a suitable slice, all prior computed slices must be stored and an additional analysis is required. The determination of a suitable slice, e.g., by analyzing the core and all deltas defined for already tested variants, is left open for future work. Due to a potential change minimization, a reduction of retest decisions and a reduction of test cases to be retested is achievable.

2. **Last Variant** – For a slicing criterion, we check whether a slice to be adapted exists in the prior variant p_{i-1}. If a prior slice exists, we obtain slice changes for the slicing criterion. Otherwise, a new slice has to be computed and no retest decision can be made. In such a case, either all reusable test cases covering the slicing criterion should be retested or none of the test cases are re-executed leading to possible missed failures. A new slice may be used as basis for incremental slicing in the subsequent variant p_{i+1} under test.

3. **Previous Slice** – Similar to the prior scenario, we check for a slicing criterion if a previous slice to be adapted exists. In contrast, we select the last computed slice for the corresponding criterion of an already tested variant p_j under test, where the respective test model element was contained. Thus, we ensure the

determination of slice changes if existing, resulting in retest decisions to be made for the current variant p_i under test.

We do not choose the *Least Slice Difference* scenario as it requires an additional analysis effort, i.e., a crucial factor for change impact analysis, and the slice selection to achieve minimized slice changes is an open question left for future work. We further do not choose the *Last Variant* scenario as we are interested in retest decisions to be made in every variant. The scenario does not ensure retest decisions as for some slicing criteria the last variant under test does not contain a required slice to be adaptable. In this paper, we focus on the *Previous Slice* scenario following the incremental idea by providing retest decisions based on slice changes for each variant under test. Depending on a given testing order, the scenario, however, may result in redundant decisions for some slicing criteria in subsequent variants under test. To select already computed slices, we store each new/adapted slice in a shared slice repository.

Based on the *Previous Slice* scenario, we apply incremental slicing for change impact analysis as follows. The incremental testing strategy starts with the test of p_{core}. As p_{core} is the first variant under test, no retest potentials arise and we solely compute for all test goals used as slicing criteria the first slices such that $\forall tg \in TG_{p_{core}} : incr_{Slice}(tg, \emptyset, \epsilon) = Slice^{tg}_{p_{core}}$ holds. By the second parameter $\emptyset$, we refer to the empty model regression delta not existing for the core, whereas the third parameter ϵ represents that no prior slices exist for the slicing criterion tg. These slices build the basis of the change impact analysis for the next variants. For the remaining variants to be tested, we apply our analysis after the test-case generation step for covering not yet covered test goals such that

$$\forall tg \in TG_{p_i} : \begin{cases} incr_{Slice}(tg, \emptyset, \epsilon) = Slice^{tg}_{p_i} & \text{if } \neg\exists Slice^{tg}_{p_j}, j < i \quad (1) \\ incr_{Slice}(tg, \Delta^{FSM}_{p_{i-1}, p_i}, Slice^{tg}_{p_j}) = Slice^{tg}_{p_i} & \text{if } \exists Slice^{tg}_{p_j}, j < i \quad (2) \end{cases}$$

holds. For each test goal of a variant p_i under test, one of the two cases is valid. In case (1), the test goal and, thus, the respective model element is contained in a test model for the first time. That is, no prior slice exists in the shared slice repository to be adaptable for analyzing the change impact. For the test goal, a new slice is computed and stored for subsequent testing steps. In case (2), we have access to a prior slice of the test goal to be adaptable based on incremental model slicing. In addition to the adapted slice, we obtain the slice regression delta $\Delta^{p_j, p_i}_{Slice_{tg}}$ as result facilitating retest decision to be made.

A slice regression delta captures additions/removals of test model elements of the updated slice. Both, additions and removals represent changed behavioral influences on the respective slicing criterion, i.e., test goal, caused by the applied model changes. Those changed influences may indicate potential sources of errors to be (re-)tested, e.g., due to unintended artifact interactions. In contrast, an empty slice regression delta implies that no changed influences exist and, thus, no retest potentials arise for the corresponding test goal.

To reason about the retest of test cases, we require a scale by means of an expressive criterion based on these slice changes. Coverage criteria are promising scales as they are already applied in various scenarios, e.g., all-transition coverage for test-case generation [37]. Hence, we define a new coverage criterion to control the retest decision as described in the next paragraph.

Example 4. Consider Examples 2 and 3 again. For p_{core}, we compute for each test goal a respective slice, e.g., the slice for t_4 depicted in Fig. 1d. By stepping to p_1, all test artifacts are adapted and for each test goal, a slice is either created from scratch or updated by applying the incremental slicing, in which we use the slices of the core as basis. For instance, compared to the base slice of t_4, its updated slice comprises two new elements as shown in Fig. 1e indicating new dependencies for t_4 to be tested. By stepping to p_2, the slice of t_4 is again updated. Furthermore, the slice of t_6 computed for p_{core} is now updated to investigate the applied model changes as the element was not contained in p_1.

Retest Coverage Criterion. Similar to the definition of model-based coverage criteria, where test model elements, e.g., transitions are used as test goals [37], we combine slicing criteria with their slice changes to define a novel *retest coverage criterion*. A *retest test goal* $rtg_l = (e_k, tg) \in TG_R^{p_i}$ is defined as a pair of test model elements such that tg represents a slicing criterion of p_i for which a slice regression delta $\Delta_{Slice_{tg}}^{p_{i-1}, p_i}$ exists, and e_k corresponds to one of the following cases:

1. A state/transition added to the slice $Slice_{p_i}^{tg}$ via $\Delta_{Slice_{tg}}^{p_{i-1}, p_i}$.
2. A source/target state of a transition removed with $\Delta_{Slice_{tg}}^{p_{i-1}, p_i}$ still contained in the current test model.

Retest test goals are defined for Case 1 to (re-)validate newly introduced dependencies between element e_k and slicing criterion tg. For Case 2, retest test goals are specified to validate that removed behavior represented by a removed transition is not remained in the variant implementation under test, and that new dependencies build due to the removal are implemented as expected. With $TG_R^{p_i}$, we refer to the retest test goal set of the variant p_i under test.

   To cover a retest test goal $rtg_l \in TG_R^{p_i}$ by a test case tc, both, e_k and tg must be traversed by the test model path of tc. Test case tc specifies a representative execution of the current variant validating that no unexpected behavior is implemented based on the new dependencies between both elements. Similar to model-based coverage criteria, for each retest test goal $rtg_l \in TG_R^{p_i}$, at least one test case must exist for its coverage. An empty retest test goal set indicates that no retest decisions are to be made.

Example 5. We use the slice changes for t_4 obtained in Example 4 by stepping from p_{core} to p_1 as basis to define respective retest test goals. The set $TG_R^{p_1}$ comprises two retest test goals $rtg_1 = (t_5, t_4)$ and $rtg_2 = (t_{10}, t_4)$ to be covered by (reusable) test cases. In p_2, we similarly derive for t_4 the retest test goal $rtg_3 = (t_6, t_4)$.

Retest Test-Case Selection and Generation. To validate that changes do not unintentionally influence already tested behavior when stepping to a subsequent variant under test, we require the selection of reusable test cases to be retested. Based on a set of retest test goals $TG_R^{p_i}$ for a variant p_i, we are able to make retest decisions. Therefore, each retest test goal $rtg_l \in TG_R^{p_i}$ must be covered by at least one (reusable) test case. We identify three coverage scenarios as follows:

1. *New Test Cases* – By adapting the test model based on a model regression delta, new model elements e_k may be added for the first time, i.e., all prior tested variants do not comprise e_k. Those elements will also be contained in slices for the first time resulting in retest goals $rtg_l = (e_k, tg)$ not coverable by reusable test cases. For this type of retest test goals, we check whether newly added test cases $tc \in TS_N^{p_i}$ are selectable to cover retest test goals.
2. *Reusable Test Cases* – By stepping to a subsequent variant, some elements e_k may again be added to the current model via the model regression delta, i.e., e_k was already contained in a prior test model. Those elements will again be contained in slices resulting in retest goals $rtg_l = (e_k, tg)$ covered by reusable test cases to be selected for retest. For this type of retest test goals, we check whether reusable test cases $tc \in TS_{Re}^{p_i}$ are selectable for retest.
3. *New Retest Test Cases* – Some retest test goals may not be covered by the current test suite. All test cases are defined by a certain test model path which must traverse the element combination specified by a retest test goal for its coverage. We apply test-case generation to derive new *retest test cases* covering the remaining retest test goals. The newly generated retest test cases are added to the variant-specific test suite also reusable for subsequent variants under test. For this type of retest test goals, we generate new test cases $tc \in TS_{R,N}^{p_i}$ for covering the remaining uncovered retest test goals.

The selected reusable test cases $TS_R^{p_i}$ and the generated retest test cases $TS_{R,N}^{p_i}$ are captured in a *retest suite* $TS_R^{p_i} = TS_R^{p_i} \cup TS_{R,N}^{p_i}$ for variant p_i under test.

The resulting test suite $TS_{p_i} = TS_N^{p_i} \cup TS_R^{p_i}$ for p_i comprising all new and retest test cases is executed to (re)test p_i. The test suite may contain redundant test cases, e.g., by means of test goal coverage, and, thus, be still optimizable to further reduce the testing effort. To minimize the set of executed test cases, test suite minimization [42] is applicable, which is, however, out of our scope. After test case execution, all new and updated test artifacts, e.g., slices and test cases, are stored in the shared test artifact and slice repository. The incremental testing process is either finished or selects the next variant to be tested.

Example 6. To cover the retest test goals from Example 5, we select a reusable test case, i.e., generated for p_{core}, covering t_5 and the retest test goal rtg_1. In contrast, as t_{10} is a new transition not contained in a prior variant, we generate a new test case for t_{10} to cover rtg_2. For covering rtg_3 in p_2, we again select a reusable test case, i.e., the test case for t_6 defined in Example 2. To cover the new retest test goal $rtg_4 = (t_{12}, t_4)$ in p_2, we generate a new retest test case.

4 Evaluation

Prototype. Our approach is realized as ECLIPSE[1] plug-ins to facilitate its extendability in future work. We use the CAISE-tool eMoflon[2] for the model-driven development based on respective meta models defined in the ECLIPSE modeling framework.[3] We applied FeatureIDE[4] for feature modeling and to derive the set of valid feature configurations generated in default order, i.e., by incrementing the number of features contained in a configuration after covering all potential combinations of the current number of features. Furthermore, our approach requires the generation of test cases to cover (retest) test goals during testing all variants. For test-case generation, we apply CPA/TIGER[5] an extension of the symbolic model-checker CPA/CHECKER[6] for the language C. Therefore, we realized a transformation from our event-based models to C-Code by encoding the event handling based on respective variables and their restricted access.

Subject Product Lines. For evaluation, we apply our approach to our example and to three existing SPLs already served as benchmarks in the literature [10]. These systems are (1) a *Wiper* SPL comprising variable qualities of rain sensors and wipers, (2) a *Vending Machine* SPL with optional selection of various beverages, and (3) a *Mine Pump* SPL describing a pump control system with variable water level handling and an optional methane detection facility. We chose these systems as each has unique characteristics, e.g., the mine pump SPL is specified by parallel regions mainly synchronized by internal variables and events, whereas the wiper subsystems communicate via internal events. Based on the set of dependencies containing only control and not data dependencies, the slicing and the change impact analysis is affected by the different system characteristics.

Results. For the evaluation of our approach and its prototypical implementation, we derive two research questions to be answered:

RQ1. Is incremental model slicing *applicable* as change impact analysis to reason about retesting of test cases in incremental SPL testing?
RQ2. Do we achieve a gain in *effectiveness* from the slicing-based retest testcase selection compared to retest-all [42]?

As already explained in Sect. 3, for the evaluation set-up, (1) we focus on all-transition coverage [37], (2) transition test goals are used as slicing criteria, (3) we choose the set of control dependencies proposed by Kamischke et al. [20], and (4) we select the *Previous Slice* scenario for the derivation of slice changes.

---

[1] https://eclipse.org/.
[2] http://www.emoflon.org/emoflon/.
[3] https://eclipse.org/modeling/emf/.
[4] http://wwwiti.cs.uni-magdeburg.de/iti_db/research/featureide/.
[5] http://forsyte.at/software/cpatiger/.
[6] http://cpachecker.sosy-lab.org/.

Table 1. Results of change impact analysis and retest test-case selection

SPL	$|P_{SPL}|$	∅ Test Goals (Transition/Retest)	∅ Test Cases (New/Reuse/Obsolete)	∅ Retest (Select/New)	∅ Retest All
Example	3	24.0 (14.3/9.6)	17.0 (8.0/7.6/1.3)	4.6 (1.6/3.0)	7.6
Wiper	8	63.6 (17.5/46.1)	71.1 (14.1/33.5/23.5)	32.5 (21.0/11.5)	33.5
Mine pump	16	106.2 (33.5/72.7)	51.7 (4.6/26.3/20.8)	16.3 (13.5/2.8)	26.3
Vending machine	28	108.8 (15.4/93.4)	92.2 (5.2/16.0/70.9)	18.2 (14.6/3.6)	16.0

In Table 1, our results of the change impact analysis and the retest test-case selection are summarized denoted by average values of test goals and test cases. For change impact analysis, we consider the number of retest test goals referring to the impact of applied model changes between subsequently tested variants. As we can see, the three existing SPLs have a high number of retest test goals compared to their approximate model size represented by the number of transition test goals. Thus, the applied model changes have a large impact on common behavior detected based on our incremental slicing. For instance, the vending machine SPL has 93.4 retest test goals compared to 15.4 transition test goals on average, where we have a maximum of 208 retest test goals for variant p_{11} and a minimum of 27 for p_2. This difference is mainly caused based on the exchange of the offered beverages representing the main behavior of a vending machine variant, whereas the exchange of the payment currency has a rather small impact. Another crucial factor for the high number of retest test goals is the testing order. In the given default order, the exchange of beverages is alternating and, therefore, results in lots of model changes with a large impact on common behavior between variants. A different order may reduce these changes and also their impact to be retested. Similarly, for the wiper and the mine pump SPL, the testing order as well as the behavior of some features alternating added or removed from the variants result in high number of retest test goals.

By comparing the number of retest test cases generated and selected with our approach to retest-all, we see at first sight that our approach and retest-all executes similar numbers of test cases for the vending machine and the wiper SPL. Solely for the mine pump SPL and the running example, we achieve a reduction of test cases to be retested (16.3/4.6) against retest-all (26.3/7.6). However, based on a more precise consideration of the vending machine and wiper results, we see that this average values are of course influenced by the number of retest test goals. In those variants, where we have a high number of retest goals, e.g., for variant p_{11} (208) of the vending machine SPL, we require more covering test cases (34) with our approach in contrast to retest-all (20) as retest-all does not ensure our retest coverage criterion. But, for variants with a small number of retest goals, e.g., for variant p_4 (28) of the wiper SPL, we require less test case (26) than retest-all (51). Hence, our retest decisions depend also on the testing order as well as the added/removed behavior of some features as described above. Again, another testing order may improve also the results of the vending machine and wiper SPL for the retest test-case selection.

Summarizing, our results show the applicability of our approach (**RQ1**). Based on incremental slicing, we are able to detect the impact of applied model changes when stepping to subsequent variants captured by retest test goals. The determined retest test goals are then used to select test cases to be retested, where we obtain positive results in the reduction of test suite size to be enhanced by investigating testing orders in future work.

To answer **RQ2**, we evaluate the fault detection capability of our approach compared to retest-all [42] by means of a set of faults to be detected. Unfortunately, for the SPLs under consideration, we do not have such a set of real faults. As no faults exist, we utilize simulated ones derived by incorporating the changes applied to a test model when stepping to a subsequent variant. Therefore, we take changes captured in the model regression deltas into account, where added transitions as well as source and target states of removed transitions which are still contained in the test model are used for fault generation. We combine those elements with other transitions from the test model to define faults representing erroneous artifact interactions caused by changes and their impact on common behavior. For the evaluation, we generate for each variant a set of simulated faults. We randomly select 10 % of the faults from this set to obtain a random data set on which test cases are executed to validate the fault detection. Depending on the size of the original variant-specific fault set, we derive a maximum of different random data sets to investigate the fault detection capability.

In Table 2, our results for the fault detection capability are summarized denoted by average values of undetected (alive) and detected (dead) faults. As we can see, our approach has for all four SPLs a good fault detection rate and performs better compared to retest-all. We obtained the best results for the vending machine SPL, where almost all faults are detected (0.08 alive) by our determined retest suites. But, this result must be relativized when considering the results shown in Table 1. On average, we select more test cases as retest-all allowing for a better chance to detect faults. However, for those variants, where we select less test cases than retest-all, we still have a better detection rate. For the wiper SPL, we select slightly less test cases compared to retest-all, where only three of the eight variants under test increase the average values. Thus, our approach allows for a good detection rate with a reduced set of test cases to be retested. This is supported based on the results of the mine pump SPL. Here,

Table 2. Results of the approach effectiveness compared to retest-all

SPL	∅ Faults	# Fault Sets	Size Fault Sets	Approach ∅ Alive/∅ Dead	Retest-all ∅ Alive/∅ Dead
Example	17	22	7	0.11/6.89	2.84/4.16
Wiper	69	22	7	1.05/5.95	3.05/3.95
Mine pump	136	54	17	3.79/13.21	5.11/11.89
Vending machine	73	30	10	0.08/9.92	0.96/9.04

we obtained a good detection rate with reduced variant-specific retest suites (cf. Table 1).

Summarizing, our approach shows a better fault detection capability compared to retest-all (**RQ2**). For all SPLs, we detect more faults than retest-all, where in the worst cases our approach detect and miss at least the same numbers of faults. The undetected faults mainly belong to artifact interactions seeded in model parts, where changes had no impact and are ignored by our approach.

Threats to Validity. For our approach and its evaluation, the following threats to validity arise. Due to varying interpretations of a systems' behavior, test modeling may result in different models to be used for model-based testing processes. This problem exists in general for model-based testing [37] and is not a specific threat for the delta-oriented test models of the four SPLs. To cope with this threat, we compared our re-engineered models with the original documented models [10] to ensure that both instances specify the same behaviors.

The non-existence of faults is a potential threat. For evaluating the effectiveness, we require the existence of faults detectable during test-case execution. Therefore, we derived simulated faults representing potential erroneous artifact interactions. We further select several randomly chosen fault sets to obtain varying data sets for each variant under test. In future work, we want to use a model-based mutation testing framework [2] for fault generation and apply the approach on real SPLs with an existing fault history.

We evaluated our approach by means of four SPLs with different system characteristics. Based on the obtained results showing a gain in effectiveness, we propose the assumption that our obtained results, up to a certain extent, are generalizable to other SPLs as well. However, we must investigate this assumption by performing more experiments with more complex systems. In addition, all four SPLs are modular event-based systems, i.e., the behavior is specified based on several subsystems, which are synchronized and controlled via events. To find the barrier for which systems our approach does not fit, we must include other types of systems in future experiments.

The choice of the coverage criterion used for test-case generation is a relevant factor influencing the obtained test suites. We focused on all-transition coverage, whereas more complex criteria exists to be considered in future experiments.

In this paper, we apply only control dependencies for the slicing computation due to our prior work [24]. As next step, we integrate also data dependencies and more complex control dependencies [4] allowing for a more fine-grained change impact analysis and, therefore, to ensure a more conclusive retest decision.

The testing order is also a threat. We applied the default order obtained from FeatureIDE, but other testing orders may influence our results. An investigation of the best testing order optimized for incremental SPL testing is required to be used for future evaluations to consolidate the achieved positive results.

The choice of the test-case generator may represent a threat. Depending on the applied generator, the obtained test suites may differ and, thus, the selection of test cases to be retested. However, our approach is independent of a specific test-case generator only required for providing test cases.

The neglection of factors such as time required for change impact analysis or test-case execution cost may be threats. The analysis time is a crucial factor for a successful retest test-case selection. Likewise, testing costs are important as there are solely limited testing budgets/resources available. We will perform a comprehensive evaluation in future work, where the analysis time is measured as well as limited testing resources are taken into account.

5 Related Work

We discuss related work regarding SPL regression testing as well as the application of slicing for change impact analysis. For a discussion concerning related (1) variability-aware slicing approaches, e.g., conditioned model slicing for annotated state machines [20], and (2) incremental slicing techniques, e.g., to support software verification [40], we refer to our prior work on incremental slicing [24].

SPL Regression Testing. Existing techniques realize SPL regression testing in the industrial context [13,33,34], for product-line architectures [11,22,29], for sample-based testing [32], as well as to allow for incremental testing [5,6,12, 25,26,38,39]. Uzuncaova et al. [38] propose one of the first incremental strategies for SPL testing, where test suites are incrementally refined for a variant under test. Baller et al. [5,6] present multi-objective test suite optimization for incremental SPL testing by incorporating costs and profits of test artifacts. Varshosaz et al. [39] present delta-oriented test-case generation, where delta-oriented test models facilitate test-case generation by exploiting their incremental structure. Compared to our approach, where test cases are selected for retest, those techniques focus on the determination and optimization of SPL test suites. Dukaczewski et al. [12] propose an adaption of our previous work [25,26] for incremental requirements-based SPL testing. In contrast, we focus on finite state machines facilitating a more fine-grained reasoning about behavioral change.

Slicing for Change Impact Analysis. Mainly white-box regression testing approaches exist applying slicing for change impact analysis [1,7,8,14,17,35]. Agrawal et al. [1] propose three types of slices for a test case comprising its executed program statements, where a modification of at least one of these statements indicates a retest. Jeffrey and Gupta [17] adopt this technique and define a prioritization of test cases to be re-executed. Bates and Horwitz [7] present slicing on program dependence graphs and reason about retest based on slice isomorphism. Gupta et al. [14] propose program slicing to identify affected def-use pairs to be retested by selected test cases. Tao et al. [35] present object-oriented program slicing for change impact analysis by incorporating the logical hierarchy of object-oriented software. We refer to Binkley [8] for an overview of program slicing techniques applied for change impact analysis. In contrast to those techniques, our approach is applied in model-based testing and it does not cope with evolution of software, but rather with incremental testing of SPLs. In the context of model-based regression testing, Korel et al. [21], and Ural and Yenigün [36] propose retesting of test cases based on dependence analysis. Both techniques are similar to our approach, also starting their analysis based on model differences to reason about change impact. In contrast to our approach, where slices are defined for model elements, their dependence analysis is applied on the model path of a test case resulting in a different retest test-case selection.

6 Conclusion

In this paper, we proposed the application of incremental slicing as change impact analysis technique for automated retest decisions in SPL regression testing. By stepping to a subsequent variant under test, we capture differences between slices as slice changes indicating the impact of model changes, i.e., changed dependencies between model elements. Based on a novel retest coverage criterion, each slice change represents a retest test goal to be covered by reusable or newly generated retest test cases. We prototypically implemented and evaluated our approach concerning its applicability and effectiveness by means of four SPLs.

We obtained positive results to be enhanced in future work by (1) considering more elaborate control and data dependencies [4], and (2) also applying forward slicing facilitating a more fine-grained analysis and more comprehensive retest decisions. Furthermore, we plan a case study by means of a real SPL from the medical domain provided by our industrial partner, in which we also want to investigate how we can apply our approach in practice. In addition, we want to adapt our analysis technique to cope with SPL evolution. In this context, an investigation of the first application scenario for change impact analysis (cf. Sect. 3) is aspired as this scenario seems to be more preferable when SPL evolution arises.

References

1. Agrawal, H., Horgan, J.R., Krauser, E.W., London, S.: Incremental regression testing. In: ICSM 1993, pp. 348–357. IEEE Computer Society (1993)
2. Aichernig, B.K., Brandl, H., Jöbstl, E., Krenn, W., Schlick, R., Tiran, S.: Killing strategies for model-based mutation testing. Softw. Test. Verif. Reliab. **25**(8), 716–748 (2014)
3. Al-Hajjaji, M., Thüm, T., Meinicke, J., Lochau, M., Saake, G.: Similarity-based prioritization in software product-line testing. In: SPLC 2014, pp. 197–206 (2014)
4. Androutsopoulos, K., Clark, D., Harman, M., Krinke, J., Tratt, L.: State-based model slicing: a survey. ACM Comput. Surv. **45**(4), 53:1–53:36 (2013)
5. Baller, H., Lity, S., Lochau, M., Schaefer, I.: Multi-objective test suite optimization for incremental product family testing. In: ICST 2014, pp. 303–312 (2014)
6. Baller, H., Lochau, M.: Towards incremental test suite optimization for software product lines. In: FOSD 2014, pp. 30–36. ACM (2014)
7. Bates, S., Horwitz, S.: Incremental program testing using program dependence graphs. In: POPL 1993, pp. 384–396. ACM (1993)

8. Binkley, D.: The application of program slicing to regression testing. Inf. Softw. Technol. **40**(1112), 583–594 (1998)
9. Clarke, D., Helvensteijn, M., Schaefer, I.: Abstract delta modeling. In: GPCE 2010, pp. 13–22 (2010)
10. Classen, A.: Modelling with FTS: a collection of illustrative examples. Technical report P-CS-TR SPLMC-00000001, PReCISE Research Center, University of Namur (2010)
11. Da Mota Silveira Neto, P., do Carmo Machado, I., Cavalcanti, Y., de Almeida, E., Garcia, V., de Lemos Meira, S.: A regression testing approach forsoftware product lines architectures. In: SBCARS 2010, pp. 41–50 (2010)
12. Dukaczewski, M., Schaefer, I., Lachmann, R., Lochau, M.: Requirements-based delta-oriented SPL testing. In: PLEASE 2013, pp. 49–52 (2013)
13. Engström, E.: Exploring regression testing and software product line testing - research and state of practice. LIC dissertation, Lund University (2010)
14. Gupta, R., Harrold, M.J., Soffa, L.: Program slicing-based regression testing techniques. Softw. Test. Verif. Reliab. **6**, 83–112 (1996)
15. Harrold, M.J.: Testing: a roadmap. In: ICSE 2000, pp. 61–72. ACM (2000)
16. Henard, C., Papadakis, M., Perrouin, G., Klein, J., Heymans, P., Traon, Y.L.: Bypassing the combinatorial explosion: using similarity to generate and prioritize t-wise test configurations for software product lines. IEEE Trans. Softw. Eng. **40**(7), 650–670 (2014)
17. Jeffrey, D., Gupta, R.: Test case prioritization using relevant slices. In: COMPSAC 2006, vol. 1, pp. 411–420 (2006)
18. Wang, J., Dong, W., Qi, Z.-C.: Slicing hierarchical automata for model checking UML statecharts. In: George, C.W., Miao, H. (eds.) ICFEM 2002. LNCS, vol. 2495, pp. 435–446. Springer, Heidelberg (2002)
19. Johansen, M.F., Haugen, O., Fleurey, F.: An algorithm for generating t-wise covering arrays from large feature models. In: SPLC 2012, pp. 46–55. ACM (2012)
20. Kamischke, J., Lochau, M., Baller, H.: Conditioned model slicing of feature-annotated state machines. In: FOSD 2012, pp. 9–16 (2012)
21. Korel, B., Tahat, L., Vaysburg, B.: Model-based regression test reduction using dependence analysis. In: ICSM 2002, pp. 214–223 (2002)
22. Lachmann, R., Lity, S., Lischke, S., Beddig, S., Schulze, S., Schaefer, I.: Delta-oriented test case prioritization for integration testing of software product lines. In: SPLC 2015, pp. 81–90 (2015)
23. Lee, J., Kang, S., Lee, D.: A survey on software product line testing. In: SPLC 2012, pp. 31–40. ACM (2012)
24. Lity, S., Baller, H., Schaefer, I.: Towards incremental model slicing for delta-oriented software product lines. In: SANER 2015, pp. 530–534 (2015)
25. Lochau, M., Lity, S., Lachmann, R., Schaefer, I., Goltz, U.: Delta-oriented model-based Integration testing of large-scale systems. J. Syst. Softw. **91**, 63–84 (2014)
26. Lochau, M., Schaefer, I., Kamischke, J., Lity, S.: Incremental model-based testing of delta-oriented software product lines. In: Brucker, A.D., Julliand, J. (eds.) TAP 2012. LNCS, vol. 7305, pp. 67–82. Springer, Heidelberg (2012)
27. McGregor, J.D.: Testing a software product line. Technical report CMU/SEI-2001-TR-022, Carnegie Mellon University (2001)
28. da Mota Silveira Neto, P.A., Carmo Machado, I.D., McGregor, J.D., de Almeida, E.S., de Lemos Meira, S.R.: A systematic mapping study of software product lines testing. Inf. Softw. Technol. **53**, 407–423 (2011)
29. Muccini, H., van der Hoek, A.: Towards testing product line architectures. Electron. Notes Theor. Comput. Sci. **82**(6), 99–109 (2003). TACoS 2003

30. Oster, S., Wübbeke, A., Engels, G., Schürr, A.: A survey of model-based software product lines testing. In: Zander, J., Schieferdecker, I., Mosterman, P.J. (eds.) Model-Based Testing for Embedded Systems, pp. 338–381. CRC Press, Boca Raton (2011)

31. Pohl, K., Böckle, G., Linden, F.J.V.D.: Software Product Line Engineering: Foundations, Principles and Techniques. Springer, Heldelberg (2005)

32. Qu, X., Cohen, M.B., Rothermel, G.: Configuration-aware regression testing: an empirical study of sampling and prioritization. In: ISSTA 2008, pp. 75–86 (2008)

33. Runeson, P., Engström, E.: Chapter 7-regression testing in software product line engineering. Adv. Comput. **86**, 223–263 (2012). Elsevier

34. Runeson, P., Engström, E.: Software product line testing - a 3D regression testing problem. In: ICST 2012, pp. 742–746. IEEE (2012)

35. Tao, C., Li, B., Sun, X., Zhang, C.: An approach to regression test selection based on hierarchical slicing technique. In: COMPSACW 2010, pp. 347–352 (2010)

36. Ural, H., Yenigün, H.: Regression test suite selection using dependence analysis. J. Softw.: Evol. Process **25**(7), 681–709 (2013)

37. Utting, M., Legeard, B.: Practical Model-Based Testing: A Tools Approach. Morgan Kaufmann Publishers Inc., Burlington (2006)

38. Uzuncaova, E., Khurshid, S., Batory, D.: Incremental test generation for software product lines. IEEE Trans. Softw. Eng. **36**(3), 309–322 (2010)

39. Varshosaz, M., Beohar, H., Mousavi, M.R.: Delta-oriented FSM-based testing. In: Butler, N., Conchon, S., Zaïdi, F. (eds.) ICFEM 2015. LNCS, vol. 9407, pp. 366–381. Springer, Switzerland (2015). doi:10.1007/978-3-319-25423-4_24

40. Wehrheim, H.: Incremental slicing. In: Liu, Z., Kleinberg, R.D. (eds.) ICFEM 2006. LNCS, vol. 4260, pp. 514–528. Springer, Heidelberg (2006)

41. Weiser, M.: Program slicing. In: ICSE 1981, pp. 439–449 (1981)

42. Yoo, S., Harman, M.: Regression testing minimization, selection and prioritization: a survey. Softw. Test. Verif. Reliab. **22**(2), 67–120 (2007)

Automated Composition of Service Mashups Through Software Product Line Engineering

Mahdi Bashari[1(✉)], Ebrahim Bagheri[2], and Weichang Du[1]

[1] Faculty of Computer Science, University of New Brunswick, Fredericton, Canada
{mbashari,wdu}@unb.ca
[2] Department of Electrical and Computer Engineering,
Ryerson University, Toronto, Canada
bagheri@ryerson.ca

Abstract. The growing number of online resources, including data and services, has motivated both researchers and practitioners to provide methods and tools for non-expert end-users to create desirable applications by putting these resources together leading to the so called *mashups*. In this paper, we focus on a class of mashups referred to as service mashups. A service mashup is built from existing services such that the developed service mashup offers added-value through new functionalities. We propose an approach which adopts concepts from software product line engineering and automated AI planning to support the automated composition of service mashups. One of the advantages of our work is that it allows non-experts to *build and optimize* desired mashups with little knowledge of service composition. We report on the results of the experimentation that we have performed which support the practicality and scalability of our proposed work.

Keywords: Service mashups · Feature model · Software product lines · Automated composition · Planning · Workflow optimization

1 Introduction

More and more companies are now making their application services publicly available to non-affiliated developers through online platforms such as ProgrammableWeb. These services can be accessed through well-defined RESTful APIs. Many of these services are highly reliable and provide functionalities that cannot be otherwise easily implemented by smaller software development companies or end-users such as Google Maps, Zazzle and Paypal, just to name a few. Therefore, the popularity of such publicly available online services and the ease of adoption of their REST-based SOA architectures have motivated researchers and practitioners to develop tools and methods which allow end-users to seamlessly build new services by composing existing APIs [4]. Such services are often known as *service mashups*. A service mashup is a service which is composed of a number of other services and provides added-value through new functionalities.

© Springer International Publishing Switzerland 2016
G.M. Kapitsaki and E. Santana de Almeida (Eds.): ICSR 2016, LNCS 9679, pp. 20–38, 2016.
DOI: 10.1007/978-3-319-35122-3_2

The added value of service mashups is through the emergence of newer functional capabilities that were not available prior to the integration of the already existing services.

There is considerable amount of research on semi-automatic and automatic methods for composing service mashups [10]. Most of these approaches assume that the end-user is familiar with the specifics of each and every instance of services' execution and invocation criteria, i.e., their pre-requisites, input and output types and other types of execution requirements. However, when considering the fact that the objective of such work is to enable automated runtime selection and composition of services from the available service possibilities with minimal user intervention and high-availability, this becomes a noticeable shortcoming. It can prevent non-expert users who do not have the required knowledge to benefit from and use such approaches.

In order to address this issue, we follow an intuitive approach to separate the non-expert end-users from the complexities of the services by using concepts from Software Product Lines (SPL). It has already been argued in the literature that while end-users might have difficulty understanding the underlying specifics of services, they are more comfortable when dealing with higher-level representations of functionality expressed through SPL features [13]. A *feature* is often defined as an incremental prominent or distinctive user-visible functionality of a software and is therefore quite understandable for the end-users. In other words, while the end-user may not know which specific services are collectively needed to satisfy her requirements, she would know which user-visible functionalities are expected from the final product.

The integration of services and features have already been extensively investigated in the literature [13]. We specifically base our work on the model proposed by Lee and Kotonya where features are operationalized through atomic or composite services [13]. In this model, two distinct lifecycle phases are introduced: *(i)* domain engineering phase: during which appropriate services that can operationalize features are identified, and are connected to their corresponding features, and *(ii)* application engineering phase: during which the end-users select their desired features through which the right services are identified. Our work is positioned within the application engineering phase of this model and provides mechanisms for automatically composing and optimizing a service mashup based on the user-specified feature requirements.

In this paper, we provide the following concrete contributions:

- We propose an AI planning based method for automated service mashup composition which operates based on feature model configurations as the main input model for specifying user requirements and generates a WS-BPEL workflow that satisfies those requirements.
- We further propose a method for optimizing the created WS-BPEL workflow by considering the concepts of safeness and threat from the planning domain in order to inject parallelism into the generated workflow and improve its execution efficiency (e.g. reduce execution time).

The rest of this paper is organized as follows: Sect. 2 will cover the required background information and the problem statement. In Sect. 3, we will describe the details of the proposed approach. Section 4 will then provide the details of the experiments and the insights gained from them. The related work is covered in Sect. 5 and finally, the paper is concluded in Sect. 6.

2   Problem Statement and Background

The objective of our work is to enable non-expert end-users to automatically *optimially compose* publicly available services in order to satisfy the requirements without being concerned with the technical details of service composition. To achieve this objective, we rely on the integration of *services* and software product line *features*. As mentioned earlier, researchers such as Lee and Kotonya [13] have already explored and concretely investigated how services and features can be integrated. There is ample literature that builds on a two-phase lifecycle that integrates services and features in its first phase and then, in the second phase, uses the integrated model to derive a product that satisfies the end-users' desired feature selections [13]. The derived product will then be operationalized by the services that are connected to the selected features. In this paper, we assume that the first domain engineering phase of the lifecycle, i.e., the connection between services and features, has already been completed using one of the established methods in the literature [13]. Our focus will therefore be to systematically support the application engineering phase of the lifecycle. Current automated service composition methods work on inputs such as OWL-S service descriptions [10], temporal logic [5], or other languages, which are used to specify the characteristics of the desired composed service mashup. However, we are interested in an input specification model *abstract* enough to be used by non-expert end-users to specify their requirements and an output that would be *concrete* enough to be directly executable. For this purpose we use feature models as the input specification model and generate the final outcome of the composed service mashup in WS-BPEL.

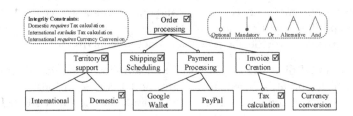

Fig. 1. A sample feature model for an order processing mashup family.

2.1   Feature Models

Feature models are among the widely used variability modeling tools used in Software Product Line Engineering (SPLE). A feature model provides a hierarchical tree structure that represents the organization of and the relation between the features. Features can be structurally related to each other through optional, mandatory, Xor-, Or-, or And-group relations. These relations express the possible variabilities of the product family. Feature models also represent crosscutting variations using integrity constraints. The use of feature models has the advantage of being understandable while having the power to represent complex variability of a family and therefore is usually used as a shared model between users and system developers in software product line engineering [14].

Figure 1 depicts a feature model for a product family that processes a purchase request and creates an invoice in different ways. The product family represented through the 'Order Processing' root node has four sub-features, namely invoice creation, shipping scheduling, payment processing, and territory support, where shipping scheduling and payment processing features are optional. Territory support sub-features are mutually exclusive. Furthermore, the selection of the 'international' feature prevents the selection of the 'tax calculation' feature and requires the selection of the 'currency conversion' due to the integrity constraints.

A feature model *configuration* is a subset of the features in a feature model which satisfies the structural and integrity constraints, and represents a viable instance of the family. Prior work has shown that a feature model configuration can be used as an effective tool for representing the end-users' requirements [14]. For example, the selection of features marked with a checkbox in Figure 1 represents a valid feature model configuration that can also be considered to be the requirements expressed by an end-user.

2.2   Business Process Execution Language (BPEL)

The Web Service Business Process Execution Language (WS-BPEL), commonly interchangeable with BPEL, is a well-known standard for the specification and execution of service-oriented business processes. In WS-BPEL, processes are built using WSDL-SOAP services and processes themselves are exposed as WSDL-SOAP web services. Control flows in WS-BPEL are expressed by structured activities and data is passed between services by sending variables as parameters. Figure 2 represents a graphical representation for a WS-BPEL code for the possible realization of the feature model configuration in Fig. 1 where features marked with checkboxes are selected. The general process for a service composition is made of hierarchical organization of activities using $<flow>$ and $<sequence>$ tags. The activities in $<flow>$ can be executed in any order or in parallel while activities in a $<sequence>$ tag should be executed in order. The synchronization between activities in a $<flow>$ tag can be done using $<link>$ tags which has been shown by yellow arrows in Fig. 2.

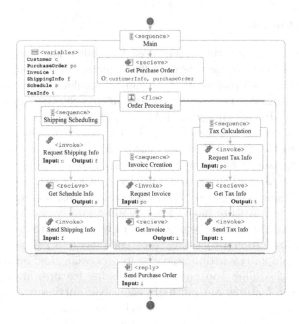

Fig. 2. Graphical representation of a possible WS-BPEL process for order processing.

The atomic activities in WS-BPEL are made of service invocations, receiving a callback for a service invocation, and a number of WS-BPEL actions or control activities which will not be considered in this paper for the sake of simplicity and without loss of generality. Each service invocation may receive some variables as input and may return one or more outputs. WS-BPEL code can be readily executed using existing WS-BPEL engines.

In the next section, we will describe our proposed automated mashup composition and workflow optimization method which receives the end-users' requirements through a feature model configuration process and automatically builds a fully executable WS-BPEL process to serve as the target service mashup.

3   Proposed Approach

In our work, an input feature model configuration serves as the end-users' requirements and it is realistically assumed that the features of the feature model configuration have already been connected to relevant services during the domain engineering phase [13]. We refer to the feature model configuration and the services connected to the features as the *domain model*. The objective is to generate a fully executable WS-BPEL process based on the domain model. Our proposed method first creates a workflow model that consists of all the features present in the domain model through an AI planning problem. The obtained workflow is then optimized and converted into WS-BPEL. In the following, we first formally define the domain model.

3.1   Domain Model Specification

We define the *domain model* to consist of five sub-models, namely feature model, service model, context model, service annotations, and feature model annotations. We start by formally defining a feature model configuration and a workflow and then define the models that connect these two together.

In order to define feature model configuration, we first need to define the feature model. A feature model can be formally defined as:

Definition 1 (Feature model). A feature model is a tuple $fm = (F, \mathcal{P}, \mathcal{F}_O, \mathcal{F}_M, \mathcal{F}_{IOR}, \mathcal{F}_{XOR}, \mathcal{F}_{req}, \mathcal{F}_{exc})$ where

- F is a set of features;
- $\mathcal{F}_O : F \mapsto F$ is a function which maps an optional child feature to its parent;
- $\mathcal{F}_M : F \mapsto F$ is a function which maps a mandatory child feature to its parent;
- $\mathcal{F}_{IOR} : F \mapsto F$ and $\mathcal{F}_{XOR} : F \mapsto F$ is a function which maps child features and their common parent feature, grouping the child features into optional and alternative groups, respectively;
- $\mathcal{P} : F \mapsto F$ is a function which maps each feature to its parent and hence we have $\mathcal{P} = \mathcal{F}_O \cup \mathcal{F}_M \cup \mathcal{F}_{IOR} \cup \mathcal{F}_{XOR}$;
- $\mathcal{F}_{req} \subset F \times F$ is a set of requirement relations which represents dependency between features.
- $\mathcal{F}_{exc} \subset F \times F$ is a set of exclusion relations between features which represents pair of features that both can not be selected in a valid feature model configuration.

Consequently, a feature model configuration is defined as follows:

Definition 2 (Feature model configuration). A feature model configuration is a set $C \subseteq F$ where

- if $f \in C$ then $\mathcal{P}(f) \in C$
- if $f' \in C$ and $(f, f') \in \mathcal{F}_M$ then $f \in C$
- if $f, f' \in F$ and $f'' = \mathcal{P}(f) = \mathcal{P}(f')$ and $(f, f''), (f', f'') \in \mathcal{F}_{XOR}$ then $f \in C \Rightarrow f' \notin C$
- $f, f' \in F$ and $(f, f') \in \mathcal{F}_{req}$ then $f \in C \Rightarrow f' \in C$
- $f, f' \in F$ and $(f, f') \in \mathcal{F}_{exc}$ then $f \in C \Rightarrow f' \notin C$.

In order to operationalize a feature model configuration in a SOA model, the orchestration of features implemented using services needs to be implemented in a workflow. A workflow specifies the sequence of interactions between the services. Our objective is to first develop a workflow from a feature model configuration and then convert that into WS-BPEL. We define a workflow based on a service specification as:

Definition 3 (Service). A service specification $s = (I, O, O_c)$ is a triple where

- I is a set of entities that the service accepts as input when invoked.
- O is the set of entities that the service returns as output after being invoked.
- O_c is the set of entities that is received in service callback.

Definition 4 (Workflow). A workflow is a triple $w = (E, N, \mathcal{E})$ where

- E is a set of entities which can be used as input or output in the operations of the workflow. Each entity $e \in E$ has a type.
- N is a set of operation nodes which can be:
  - *An invocation node* is a triple $(s, \mathcal{I}, \mathcal{O})$ where $s \in S$ represents the invoked service and $\mathcal{I}$ and $\mathcal{O}$ specify the mapping relation between workflow entities, and input and output of the services.
  - *A receive node* is a pair $(s, \mathcal{O}_c)$ where $s \in S$ represents the invoked service which has resulted in callback and $\mathcal{O}_c$ specifies the mapping relation between workflow entities and the outputs of service callback.
- $\mathcal{E} \subset N \times N$ shows directed edges between operation nodes such that for each $n, n' \in N$, $(n, n') \in \mathcal{E}$, the operation of node n should be performed before n' in the execution process.

In order to be able to automatically make a transition from a feature model to a workflow, we define a *context model*, which represents the environment in which the service mashup will operate in. Relations between the feature model, services and the context model are represented with annotations on these models. These annotations are used for creating a workflow from the feature model configuration. We formally define a context model as:

Definition 5 (Context model). A context model is a triple $c = (c_T, c_E, S)$ where

- c_T denotes *context types*, which is a tuple $(\Theta, \Phi, \mathcal{F})$ where
  - Θ is a set of data types
  - Φ is a set of fact types
  - $\mathcal{F} : \Phi \mapsto \Theta \times .... \times \Theta$ is a function which specify the data type of entities that each fact type is defined on.
- c_E is *context entities* which is a pair $(E, \mathcal{T})$ where
  - E is a set of entities that exist in the context
  - $\mathcal{T} : E \mapsto \Theta$ is a function which defines the type of each entity
- S is *context state* which is a set $S \subset \Phi \times E \times .... \times E$ such that for each fact $f = (\phi, e_1, ..., e_i) \in S \Rightarrow (\phi, \mathcal{T}(e_1), ..., \mathcal{T}(e_i)) \in \mathcal{F}$ and shows the facts which are true in that context.

In our context model definition, *context entities* are similar to object instances passed between functions, and *context types* are used for strictly specifying entity types. Furthermore, the context model also consists of the *context state*, which is defined by *facts*. Facts can express the relationship between zero or more context entities. Let us elaborate on this using Fig. 3. In this example, c and *po* are two context entities, which are of customer and purchase order types, respectively. Furthermore, the fact *ordered(c, po)* expresses that customer c has ordered the purchase order *po*. This fact is represented using fact type *ordered* which relates an entity of type customer to an entity of type purchase order. We will explain in the following how the context model information will be used to annotate features.

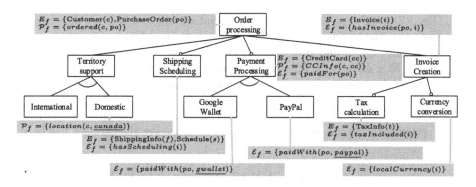

Fig. 3. An annoated feature model for the order processing family.

Based on the context model, each feature in the feature model needs to be annotated with three sets: *(i)* the set of entities that are required by a service consisting of this feature; *(ii)* the set of facts that should be true in the current state of the context model in order for the service that consists of this feature to safely execute, and *(iii)* the set of facts that will become true in the context model once a service that consists of this feature is executed. These annotations can be formally defined as:

Definition 6 (Feature model annotation). The annotation for feature model fm is a function $\mathcal{A}_{FM}$ which maps each feature f in the feature model to a triple $(E_f, \mathcal{P}_f, \mathcal{E}_f)$ where

- $E_f \subset E$ is the set of entities that must exist in a context model in order to execute any service mashup with feature f.
- $\mathcal{P}_f \subset \Phi \times E \times .... \times E$ is the set of facts which should be true in the context model in order to execute a service mashup with feature f.
- $\mathcal{E}_f \subset \Phi \times E \times .... \times E$ is the set of facts that will be true in the context model after executing a workflow with feature f.

Figure 3 shows the annotations for our order processing feature model. As seen in the figure, for each feature, $E_f, \mathcal{P}_f, \mathcal{E}_f$ are defined as needed. For instance, the figure shows that for the 'Invoice Creation' feature to be included in the goal service mashup, a context entity i of type *Invoice* needs to be present in the context model. Furthermore, when the service mashup consisting of the 'Invoice Creation' feature is executed, the fact $hasInvoice(po, i)$ will become true as an effect, which means purchase order entity po will have an invoice entity i.

In addition to feature model annotations, we also annotate the services in a similar vein. The annotation of services with pre-conditions and post-conditions (effects) has been already widely used in the literature [10] and we adopt a similar strategy.

Definition 7 (Service annotation). A service annotation for service s is a tuple $\mathcal{A}_s = (\mathcal{P}_I, \mathcal{Q}_I, \mathcal{R}_I, \mathcal{P}_C, \mathcal{Q}_C, \mathcal{R}_C)$ where

- $\mathcal{P}_I, \mathcal{P}_C \subset \mathcal{P} \times \mathcal{IO} \times .... \times \mathcal{IO}$ are the facts that should be true over the entities interacting with the service (including inputs, output, callback output) in order to invoke the service and receive any callback.
- $\mathcal{Q}_I, \mathcal{Q}_C \subset \mathcal{R} \times \mathcal{IO} \times .... \times \mathcal{IO}$ are the facts that become true over the entities interacting with the service after the service is invoked or the callback has been received.
- $\mathcal{R}_I, \mathcal{R}_C \subset \mathcal{R} \times \mathcal{IO} \times .... \times \mathcal{IO}$ are the facts that become false over the entities interacting with the service after the service is invoked or the callback has been received.

For example in the service *Request Shipping Info* in Fig. 2, assuming the input *customerInfo* is of type customer, the output *shippingInfo* is of type shippingInfo, and the callback output *shippingSchedule* is of type schedule in the context model, one could define the annotations for this service as $\mathcal{Q}_I = \{hasShippingInfo(customerInfo, shippingInfo)\}$, $\mathcal{Q}_C = \{hasShippingSchedule \ (customerInfo, shippingSchedule)\}$, and the other annotation sets would be empty. This annotation means after the invocation of this service the value of the output would be the shipping information for the input customer and after receiving the callback the value of the callback output would be the shipping schedule for the input customer.

In our model, the feature and service annotations serve as a bridge between the feature and service spaces and allow us to automatically compose a service mashup based on the end-users' feature selections.

Problem Statement. Given a context model type c_T, a feature model fm, a feature model configuration C, a feature model annotation $\mathcal{A}_{FM}$, a set of services S, and their corresponding annotations $\mathcal{A}_S$, the goal is to find a workflow w using services in S which satisfies the requirements of feature model configuration C.

3.2   Proposed Solution

We propose to formalize the above problem statement as a planning problem and provide a solution through AI planning. The AI planning model would be concretely defined by the initial context state as the starting point of the planner and the expected context state as the goal of the planner. Therefore, we need to formalize how the initial context state, expected goal state and the service invocations can be defined with an AI planning context to generate a workflow.

We adopt the widely used STRIPS planning specification model to provide our problem formalization, which can easily be converted to a Planning Domain Definition Language (PDDL) model. A planning problem in STRIPS [7] can be defined as below:

Definition 8 (Planning problem). A planning problem is a triple $p = (S_{initial}, S_{goal}, A)$ where:

- $S_{initial}, S_{goal}$ are the initial and goal states. These states are represented by a set of atomic facts,

- A is the set of available actions. This set includes all the actions that can be done in order to change the state. Each action $a \in A$ is a tuple $(I, F_{pre}, F_{add}, F_{del})$ where
  - I is the set of parameters that an action takes.
  - F_{pre} is the set of atomic facts which should be in a state in order for that action to be applicable in that state (i.e. action a is applicable in state S where $F_{pre}(a) \subseteq S$).
  - F_{add} is a set of facts which are added to a state after the action has been applied to the state.
  - F_{del} is a set of facts which are deleted from the state after the action has been applied to the state. Therefore, if S_{succ} be the state after applying action a to state S then $S_{succ} = S - F_{del}(a) \cup F_{add}(a)$.

Definition 9 (Planning problem solution). Sequence $s = <a_1, ..., a_i>$ is a solution to planing problem $p = (S_{initial}, S_{goal}, A)$ if

- a_1 is applicable on state $S_{initial}$;
- for each $1 < j \leq i$ action a_j is applicable in state S which has been resulted by consecutive application of action $a_1, ..., a_{j-1}$ on the initial state $S_{initial}$;
- consecutive application of actions $a_1, ..., a_i$ on initial state $S_{initial}$ will result in a state S such that $S_{goal} \subseteq S$.

In the proposed method, we formalize the problem as a method for finding a workflow expressed through a sequence of service invocations and callbacks, which results in the expected context state and satisfies the requirements expressed in the configured feature model.

Generating Initial and Goal States. Initial and goal states of the planner are built by aggregating the annotations of the feature model configuration, which represents the end-users' requirements. For a feature model configuration C, initial and goal states for planning problem $p = (S_{initial}, S_{goal}, A)$ would be:

- $S_{initial} = \bigcup_{f \in C} \mathcal{P}_f$
- $S_{goal} = \bigcup_{f \in C} \mathcal{E}_f$

Generating Actions. In our planning model, actions are considered to be the service operations that can be executed in the final service mashup. These actions are invocations of different services or receiving callbacks. Each of these actions affects the context state.

- **Invocation.** An invocation of service $s = (I, O, O_c)$ with annotation $\mathcal{A}_s = (\mathcal{P}_I, \mathcal{Q}_I, \mathcal{R}_I, \mathcal{P}_C, \mathcal{Q}_C, \mathcal{R}_C)$ can be defined as an action $a_{invoke}(s) = (I, F_{pre}, F_{add}, F_{del})$ where
  - input of the action is $I = I \cup O \cup O_c$
  - $F_{pre} = \mathcal{P}_I$
  - $F_{add} = \mathcal{Q}_I$ and a predicate showing that service s callback is pending $(callbackPending(s))$ if it has a callback
  - $F_{del} = \mathcal{R}_I$

```
1: function OPTIMIZE(workflow w = (E, N, ℰ))
2: repeat
3:    W ← {}
4:    for all e = (n₁, n₂) ∈ ℰ do
5:       ℰ' ← ℰ ∪ {(n', n₂) s.t. (n', n₁) ∈ ℰ}
6:             ∪{(n₁, n') s.t. (n₂, n') ∈ ℰ} − {(n₁, n₂)} :
7:       w' ← (E, N, ℰ')
8:       if SAFE(w') then
9:          W ← W ∪ {w'}
10:      end if
11:   end for
12:   w ← SELECT(W)
13: until TERMINATIONCONDITION(w)
14: return w
```

Algorithm 1. Pseudo-code for workflow optimization.

– **Callback** is of service $s = (I, O, O_c)$ with annotation $\mathcal{A}_s = (\mathcal{P}_I, \mathcal{Q}_I, \mathcal{R}_I, \mathcal{P}_C, \mathcal{Q}_C, \mathcal{R}_C)$ can be defined as an action $a_{callback}(s) = (I, F_{pre}, F_{add}, F_{del})$ where
   • input of the action is $I = I \cup O \cup O_c$
   • $F_{pre} = \mathcal{P}_C \cup \{callbackPending(s)\}$
   • $F_{add} = \mathcal{Q}_C$
   • $F_{del} = \mathcal{R}_C \cup \{callbackPending(s)\}$

Workflow Creation. Now that the planning goal and planning problem domain are concretely defined, a planner can be used in order to find a solution for the planning problem. The solution will be a sequence of actions which takes us from the initial context state to the expected context state. Based on the solution of the above planning problem $s = <a_1, ..., a_i>$, a workflow $w = (E, N, \mathcal{E})$ can be built where:

– The workflow entities set $E = \bigcup_{f \in C} E_f$.
– The operation node set $N = n_1, ..., n_i$ is made from the action sequence where n_j is built based on a_j where the service for the operation is the corresponding service for that action. Similarly, the assigned input and output for the operation node are corresponding entities assigned to action parameters.
– The edge set E is $\{(n_{j-1}, n_j)$ such that $1 < j \leq i\}$ which means the operation nodes should be executed in the order specified in the action execution.

Workflow Optimization. Although the generated workflow can be used to generate WS-BPEL code, given that the AI planners produce strictly sequential plans, the generated workflow would not benefit from potentially more efficient and valid plans which use parallel execution of operations when possible. Using parallelism in a service workflow can significantly affect the efficiency of the

```
 1: function SAFE(workflow w = (E, N, ℰ))
 2: for all  n ∈ N do
 3:    for all  p ∈ 𝒫(n) do
 4:       safeCausalLinkFound ← false
 5:       for all  n' ∈ N do
 6:          if AFTER(w, n', n) and p ∈ 𝒬(n') then
 7:             if ¬THREATEXISTS(w, n, n', p) then
 8:                safeCausalLinkFound ← true
 9:             end if
10:          end if
11:       end for
12:       if ¬safeCausalLinkFound then
13:          return false
14:       end if
15:    end for
16: end for
17: return true
```

Algorithm 2. Pseudo-code for examining safeness of a workflow.

composed service [20]. Therefore, once a plan is generated by the AI planner, we take an additional step to optimize the workflow.

Workflow optimization can be performed by consecutive removal of the edges in the workflow which do not affect the *safeness* [15] of the workflow. The details of our method for optimization has been shown in Algorithm 1. In the main loop in the algorithm (Lines 2–13), the edges are removed consecutively until the termination condition (Line 13) is met. In each iteration of the loop, each edge in the workflow is examined (Line 4) to see whether the workflow stays safe even after the removal of that edge or not (Line 8). If so, the edge is added a set W (Line 9). The new workflow after removal of an edge would be a revised workflow which would not include the removed edge but instead new edges are added to preserve the connectivity of the workflow. This is done by adding edges from the start node of the removed edge to the immediate nodes after the end node of the removed edge and similarly the immediate nodes before the start node and the end node of the removed edge (Lines 5–6). This ensures that the order of execution for the nodes before and after stay the same. After all edges are examined, the best workflow is selected from the set W and the current workflow is replaced by that workflow (Line 12).

The definition of SELECT and TERMINATIONCONDITION depends on the optimization method which has been selected. The definition for SAFE which is responsible for examining the safeness of a workflow has been defined in Algorithm 2. The definition of this function has been inspired by the safeness condition in partial order planning [15]. In this function, the main loop iterates over all operation nodes of the workflow (Lines 2–16) and its immediate inner loop iterates over all facts that is required to be true as the precondition of the node (Lines 3–15). For each precondition fact p of each node n, this algorithm iterates

---

1: **function** THREATEXISTS(workflow w, node n, node n',fact p)
2: **for all** $n'' \in N$ **do**
3:    **if** $\neg$AFTER(w, n'', n') or $\neg$AFTER(w, n, n'') and $p \in \mathcal{R}(n'')$ **then**
4:       **return** *true*
5:    **end if**
6: **end for**
7: **return** *false*

Algorithm 3. Pseudo-code for examining existence of threat to a causal link.

over all the nodes in the workflow (Lines 5–11) in order to find an operation node n' which makes that fact true and is executed before node n (Line 6). The relation between node n' and n is called causal link for p. If such a node is found, it is examined if a *threat* to that causal link exists (Line 7). If there is no threat to the causal link between two nodes, a safe causal link has been found (Line 8). If there exists no safe causal link for a precondition fact of a node (Line 12), the workflow is not safe.

A threat exists for a causal link when there exists an operation node that can be executed between the two nodes of the causal link and makes the fact of the causal link false. The function which examines a causal link for possible threat has been shown in Algorithm 3. This algorithm works by iterating over all nodes in the workflow and analysing if it can pose a threat to the causal link (Lines 2–6). A node can be considered a threat to a causal link if it does not execute before the start node or after the end node of the causal link and makes the related fact to that causal link false (Line 3).

Although the optimization process keeps the workflow safe, it does not ensure that the workflow has the same preconditions and effects. A small modification can be done in the input workflow in order to ensure that workflow preconditions and effects remain the same during and after the optimization. This modification adds a new start operation node with no precondition and workflow preconditions as the effects to the beginning of the workflow and an end operation node with no effect and with expected effects as the preconditions to the end of the workflow. Considering that the optimization will not affect preconditions, it can be easily proven that if the start and end nodes are removed from the workflow after optimization, it will satisfy the expected preconditions and effects.

In order to make the derived workflow executable, it needs to be converted into WS-BPEL. In WS-BPEL, each flow is defined by a *<process>* tag which is made of the *<variables>* tag and a set of actions organized with *<sequence>* and *<flow>* tags. Actions in the flow tag can be executed in parallel while actions in the sequence tag should be executed sequentially. Often more than one WS-BPEL code can satisfy user's goals. Here, we adopt the method used in [18] for creating an efficient WS-BPEL code from the created workflow. This method takes as input a workflow represented as a directed graph and generates an efficient WS-BPEL representation.

4   Experiments

In order to perform experiments, we have developed a fully integrated toolset that supports our proposed approach. In our implementation, we have used OWL as the representation language for the context model as suggested in [10], OWL-S for representing services and their annotations [9], and SA-FMDL format for representing the feature model and its annotations [2]. For planning, the FF planner [9], which is a fast PDDL planner is used and for optimization a greedy implementation is used that chooses an action with the best immediate gain. Our experiments were performed on a machine with Intel Core i5 2.5 GHZ CPU, 6 GB of RAM, Ubuntu 14.04, Java Runtime Environment v1.8.

4.1   Workflow Generation

The main focus of our experiments with regards to workflow generation is the assessment of the scalability of the proposed method in terms of its running time. We evaluate the efficiency of the method from two perspectives:

- **Experiment 1.1 (Scalability in terms of services repository size):** How does the workflow generation time increase as the number of services in the repository grows?
- **Experiment 1.2 (Scalability in terms of feature model configuration size):** How does the workflow generation time increase as the size of the feature model configuration grows?

In order to run the experiments, three models were required: context model, services and their annotations, feature model and its annotations.

Context Model: We have developed an OWL ontology for the context model with 30 entity types and 600 fact types. This context model is used to annotate the services and the feature model.

Services and Their Annotations: In order to generate the services and their annotations, we developed a random OWL-S service description generator which creates service description with inputs, outputs, precondition, and effects randomly picked from our context model. This OWL-S service description generator is highly customizable with different service model characteristics (e.g. number of inputs, outputs, precondition, and effects). Three service repository sets have been created where services in the repositories of different sets have different numbers of precondition and effects. In our experiments, we used 3, 6, and 9 as the number of preconditions and effects. Each of these repository sets has 10 different repositories of sizes between 1,000 to 10,000. Totally, 30 different service repositories have been created.

Feature Model and Its Annotations: We used the SPLOT feature model generator to generate a feature model with 1,000 features. In order to annotate this feature model, a customized feature model annotation generator is developed which randomly picks annotations from the context model and assigns them

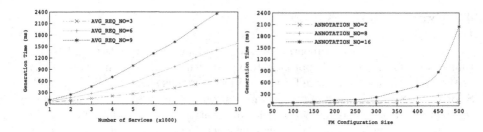

Fig. 4. Workflow generation time in terms of service repository and FM conf. size.

to the features of the feature model. Using this annotation generator, three different annotation sets were created for the feature model where the number of annotations for each feature was 2, 8 and 16. In the first experiment, a feature model configuration with 50 features is selected and the time to generate the workflow using service repositories of different sizes is measured. This operation is done repeatedly 20 times with different feature model configurations of the same size and the average time for generating the workflow is calculated. This experiment is repeated for all three repository sets. Figure 4 (left) shows how the workflow generation time increases with the increase in the size of the service repository. As it can be seen from the figure, the increase in time is linear and does not significantly increase with the increase in the number of services in the repository and remains practical (around 2.4 s for 9,000 services).

In the second experiment, the service repository with 1,000 services and an average sum of precondition and effects of 6 is selected. In this setting, the time for generating workflows for feature model configurations of different sizes is measured. The feature model configuration is generated by a tool which gets a feature model and desired number of features in the configuration and returns a random valid feature model configuration with that size. For each configuration size, 20 different configurations is generated. For each number of annotations, the average time required for generating the workflow is calculated for different configurations. Figure 4 (right) shows the average workflow generation time with different feature model configuration sizes for different number of annotations. As seen in the figure, the generation time remains linear for various configuration sizes when the number of annotations are 2 and 8 per feature. However, when the number of annotations are increased to 16, the generation time becomes exponential and shows rapid increase. It is important to note that (i) even with the increase, the time is manageable for practical purposes, i.e., 2 s for 1,000 services and 500 requirements. (ii) Literature suggests that the number of annotations is typically in the range of 5–6 annotations per feature [1], in which case, the performance of the generation algorithm is linear.

4.2   Workflow Optimization

The focus of the second set of experiments is on the investigation of the scalability of the optimization method. We explore the optimization method scalability when

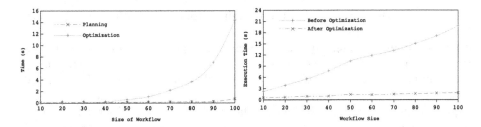

Fig. 5. Workflow optimization and execution time in terms of workflow size.

the size of workflow increases. In addition, we explore whether the optimization method is able to decrease the time-to-completion of the service mashup.

- **Experiment 2.1 (Optimization scalability in terms of workflow size):** How does the workflow optimization time increase with the increase in the size of workflow (in terms of growth in the number of workflow nodes)?
- **Experiment 2.2 (Effectiveness of the optimization in terms service mashup time-to-completion):** How much does the time-to-completion of a service mashup is decreased as a result of the optimization?

In order to run this experiment the models from the previous experiment were used. The service repository with 1,000 services and an average number of preconditions and effects of 6 were employed. The services were annotated with random time-to-completion with a normal distribution $\mathcal{N}(200\,\text{ms}, 50)$.

For the first experiment, 20 different configurations in each workflow size category is randomly selected and the average time for workflow generation and optimization is calculated. Figure 5 shows how workflow generation and optimization time increases as the size of workflow grows. This shows that the workflow optimization method is considerably slower than the planning method. However, given the fact that the optimization method is only a one time task, its benefits in terms of reducing the time-to-completion is noticeable.

In the second set of experiments, the objective is to measure whether the optimization method has been to generate workflows that have a lower time-to-completion (execution time) or not. For this purpose, the time-to-completion of the generated workflows were calculated both before and after the optimization. Figure 5 shows the result of the optimization. As seen in the figure, the time-to-completion of a workflow increases as the size of the workflow increases. However, the optimization method has been able to maximize parallelism in the workflow such that there is no noticeable growth with the increase in the workflow size. For instance, for a workflow with 100 activities, which on average take 20 s prior to optimization, the optimization method has been able to reduce the time-to-completion to 1 s.

5   Related Work

Our work is positioned among considerable other research on service composition using AI planning methods. Given the fact that planners usually take initial and goal states as the way to define the planning problem, adopting this approach for modeling the expected outcome of a service composition is quite intuitive. Therefore, many existing approaches specify the expected outcome using a planner input language or a model that is easily convertible to a planner input [10,12]. For example, in [12], an XML dialect of PDDL is used to define the expected service specification. However, specification of requirements in those languages requires expert knowledge. In order to facilitate the design of service mashups in some approaches, the concrete service mashup is generated from the abstract process created by the user using some GUI interface. For example in [16], users drag and drop required components of their service mashup into a canvas and create the flow by connecting these components using arcs where this process is facilitated using semantic annotations for components. Such approaches still rely on the users for designing the logic of the service interactions. Another way used for specifying service requirements is through natural language specifications. For example in [8], an approach is proposed where a composite service is created based on a request in natural language using semantic annotation of the components. Although natural language seems an easy to use method of specifying requirements, it does not provide the user with a tangible model of functionalities which makes it confusing to use and unreliable. Feature models provide a tangible way to represent functionalities and have been used to represent service families. However, existing automated approaches only suggest methods which customize the services [1,3]. For example, Baresi et al. [3] use aspect-orientation in WS-BPEL to activate/deactivate aspects in WS-BPEL code of the service composition in order to customize it.

WS-BPEL allows sequential as well as parallel invocation of services. However, most AI planning methods come up with total-ordered sequential composition of services [20]. For example in [6], a planner is used to find the goal service composition which is sequential although WS-BPEL is used to represent the composition. Some of the other automated service composition methods generate compositions which take advantage of parallelism [11,20]. For example in [20], service composition is modeled as a tree search problem where the goal is to find a service composition with maximum parallelization. In another example [11], the service composition problem is modeled as a sub-graph search in a service dependency graph where the goal is to find a composition which satisfies its functional requirements as well as optimizing different quality attributes such as parallelism. However, enabling parallelisim is embedded in the composition process of these methods. In order to compose services with parallel execution, [19] suggests that partial-order planning methods need to be used. However, none of the existing service composition methods use partial-order planning because existing partial-order planners are significantly less efficient than total-order planners [17]. We suggest that enabling parallelism in the workflow can be viewed as an optimization problem. The idea of optimizing a total-order plan in order to take advantage of parallelism has been explored in the planning area [21]. However, it has not been used in the context of service composition. Our approach uses the ideas from the planning domain to propose an optimization model where different optimization methods can be used in order to enable parallel execution of operations in a workflow.

6   Conclusion

In this paper, we propose a method for the automated composition of service mashups. The service mashup composition process is operationalized through a novel approach that combines the modeling power of software product line feature models with AI planning techniques. The novelty of our work is in that end-user requirements are expressed as feature model compositions, which have been shown to be understandable by end-users. We automatically transform the feature model composition into a viable executable workflow through the mapping of the feature space into the AI planning domain. Given the fact that AI planning techniques only generate strictly sequential plans, we further develop an algorithm to optimize the developed workflow through the introduction of parallelism. The final outcome of our approach is an optimized executable business process represented in WS-BPEL format. Through our experiments we have shown that our work is scalable and is also able to efficiently produce workflows that are optimized using parallelism.

References

1. Asadi, M., Mohabbati, B., Groner, G., Gasevic, D.: Development and validation of customized process models. J. Syst. Softw. **96**, 73–92 (2014)
2. Bagheri, E., Asadi, M., Ensan, F., Gasevic, D., Mohabbati, B.: Bringing semantics to feature models with SAFMDL. In: Proceedings of CASCON 2011, pp. 287–300. IBM Corporation (2011)
3. Baresi, L., Guinea, S., Pasquale, L.: Service-oriented dynamic software product lines. Computer **45**(10), 42 (2012)
4. Benslimane, D., Dustdar, S., Sheth, A.: Services mashups: the new generation of web applications. IEEE Internet Comput. **5**, 13–15 (2008)
5. Bertoli, P., Pistore, M., Traverso, P.: Automated composition of web services via planning in asynchronous domains. Artif. Intell. **174**(3), 316–361 (2010)
6. Chafle, G., Das, G., Dasgupta, K., Kumar, A., Mittal, S., Mukherjea, S., Srivastava, B.: An integrated development environment for web service composition. In: ICWS 2007, pp. 839–847. IEEE (2007)
7. Fikes, R.E., Nilsson, N.J.: Strips: a new approach to the application of theorem proving to problem solving. Artif. Intell. **2**(3), 189–208 (1972)
8. Fujii, K., Suda, T.: Semantics-based dynamic web service composition. Int. J. Coop. Inf. Syst. **15**(03), 293–324 (2006)
9. Hoffmann, J., Nebel, B.: The FF planning system: fast plan generation through heuristic search. J. Artif. Intell. Res. **14**, 253–302 (2001)
10. Hristoskova, A., Volckaert, B., Turck, F.D.: The WTE framework: automated construction and runtime adaptation of service mashups. Autom. Softw. Eng. **20**(4), 499–542 (2013)
11. Jiang, W., Zhang, C., Huang, Z., Chen, M., Hu, S., Liu, Z.: Qsynth: a tool for QoS-aware automatic service composition. In: ICWS 2010, pp. 42–49. IEEE (2010)
12. Klusch, M., Gerber, A., Schmidt, M.: Semantic web service composition planning with OWLS-XPlan. In: AAAI Fall Symposium on Semantic Web and Agents (2005)
13. Lee, J., Kotonya, G.: Combining service-orientation with product line engineering. IEEE Softw. **27**(3), 35–41 (2010)

14. Lee, K., Kang, K.C., Lee, J.J.: Concepts and guidelines of feature modeling for product line software engineering. In: Gacek, C. (ed.) ICSR 2002. LNCS, vol. 2319, pp. 62–77. Springer, Heidelberg (2002)

15. McAllester, D., Rosenblatt, D.: Systematic nonlinear planning. In: Proceedings 9th National Conference on Artificial Intelligence (AAAI-91), Anaheim, CA. pp. 634–639 (1991)

16. Ngu, A.H.H., Carlson, M.P., Sheng, Q.Z., Paik, H.Y.: Semantic-based mashup of composite applications. IEEE Trans. Serv. Comput. **3**(1), 2–15 (2010). iD: 1

17. Nguyen, X., Kambhampati, S.: Reviving partial order planning. In: Proceedings of the 17th International Joint Conference on Artificial Intelligence, vol. 1, pp. 459–464. Morgan Kaufmann Publishers Inc. (2001)

18. Ning, G., Zhu, Y., Lu, T., Wang, F.: BPELGEN: an algorithm of automatically converting from web services composition plan to BPEL4WS. In: ICPCA 2007, pp. 600–605. IEEE (2007)

19. Peer, J.: Web Service Composition as AI Planning - A Survey. University of St. Gallen, Switzerland (2005)

20. Rodriguez-Mier, P., Mucientes, M., Lama, M.: Automatic web service composition with a heuristic-based search algorithm. In: ICWS 2011, pp. 81–88. IEEE (2011)

21. Siddiqui, F.H., Haslum, P.: Plan quality optimisation via block decomposition. In: Proceedings of the Twenty-Third International Joint Conference on Artificial Intelligence, pp. 2387–2393. AAAI Press (2013)

Feature Location in Model-Based Software Product Lines Through a Genetic Algorithm

Jaime Font[1,2(✉)], Lorena Arcega[1,2], Øystein Haugen[3], and Carlos Cetina[1]

[1] SVIT Research Group, San Jorge University, Zaragoza, Spain
{jfont,larcega,ccetina}@usj.es
[2] Department of Informatics, University of Oslo, Oslo, Norway
[3] Department of Information Technology,
Østfold University College, Halden, Norway
oystein.haugen@hiof.no

Abstract. When following an extractive approach to build a model-based Software Product Line (SPL) from a set of existing products, features have to be located across the product models. The approaches that produce best results combine model comparisons with the knowledge from the domain experts to locate the features. However, when the domain expert fails to provide accurate information, the semi-automated approach faces challenges. To cope with this issue we propose a genetic algorithm to feature location in model-based SPLs. We have an oracle from an industrial environment that makes it possible to evaluate the results of the approaches. As a result, the proposed approach is able to provide solutions upon inaccurate information on part of the domain expert while the compared approach fails to provide a solution when the information provided by the domain expert is not accurate enough.

1 Introduction

A recent survey [2] reveals that most of the Software Product Lines (SPLs) are built following an extractive approach, where a set of existing products is reengineered into a SPL [12]. The resulting SPL is capable of generating the products used as input (among others) with the benefit of having the variability among the products formalized, enabling a systematic reuse.

Several reverse engineering approaches can be used to identify and locate the features [4–6,14,16,18] from the existing product models and formalize them in the form of a model-based SPL (where the features are realized in the form of model fragments). In our previous work [5] we show that Conceptualized Model Patterns to Feature Location (CMP-FL) provides features more recognizable by the engineers that must use them thanks to the inclusion of information from the domain experts into the feature location process.

This work has been partially supported by the Ministry of Economy and Competitiveness (MINECO), through the Spanish National R+D+i Plan and ERDF funds under The project Model-Driven Variability Extraction for Software Product Lines Adoption (TIN2015-64397-R).

© Springer International Publishing Switzerland 2016
G.M. Kapitsaki and E. Santana de Almeida (Eds.): ICSR 2016, LNCS 9679, pp. 39–54, 2016.
DOI: 10.1007/978-3-319-35122-3_3

However, in CMP-FL the set of possible solutions is too big to be evaluated exhaustively, resulting in the need of very precise information from the domain engineers to accelerate the process. If the information provided is not accurate enough the feature location will fail, not being able to provide the expected solution. When the family of product models is built following clone-and-own techniques, the variability among the products is not always properly documented, resulting in a lack of precise information.

To cope with the above, we propose an approach based on a Genetic Algorithm to Feature Location (GA-FL) among a set of product models. Specifically, we propose new model-based genetic operations capable of working with model fragments: (1) the crossover operation, that combines information from two possible solutions into a single offspring; (2) the mutation operation, that randomly mutates one model fragment (while keeping the consistency with the product model where the fragment was extracted from); (3) a fitness function that evaluates the population of possible solutions and ranks them depending on how they solve the problem and (4) a parent selection operation to find candidates that feed the rest of genetic operations.

We have compared the CMP-FL with GA-FL through the use of an oracle extracted from our industrial partner (BSH), whose induction department produces the firmware for their induction hobs (sold under the brands of Bosch and Siemens) based on a model-based SPL. It turns out that our GA-FL is able to provide the solution expected in scenarios where the CMP-FL fails. When the information provided is accurate, the GA-FL algorithm is able to enrich the set of best solutions produced given that it explores a broader search space.

The rest of the paper is organized as follows: next section presents some background about the domain of our industrial partner and its SPL. In Sect. 3 we present our approach, the GA-FL. Section 4 compares the presented approach with the best alternative from literature. In Sect. 5 we discuss some related work. Finally, we conclude the paper.

2   Formalizing the Variability

This section presents the Domain Specific Language (DSL) used by our industrial partner to formalize their products, the IHDSL. It will be used through the rest of the paper to present a running example. Then, the Common Variability Language (CVL) is presented, CVL is the language used by our approach (GA-FL) to formalize the location of the features as reusable model fragments.

2.1   The Induction Hobs Domain Specific Language (IHDSL)

The newest Induction Hobs (IHs) feature full cooking surfaces, where dynamic heating areas are automatically generated and activated or deactivated depending on the shape, size, and position of the cookware placed on top. In addition, there has been an increase in the type of feedback provided to the user while cooking, such as the exact temperature of the cookware, the temperature of the food being cooked, or even real-time measurements of the actual consumption of the IH. All of these changes are made possible at the cost of increasing the software complexity.

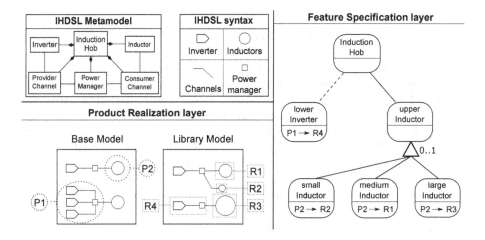

Fig. 1. CVL applied to IHDSL

The Domain Specific Language used by our industrial partner to specify the Induction Hobs (IHDSL) is composed of 46 meta-classes, 74 references among them and more than 180 properties. However, in order to gain legibility and due to intellectual property rights concerns, in this paper we use a simplified subset of the IHDSL (see Fig. 1).

Inverters are in charge of transforming the input electric supply to match the specific requirements of the IH. Then, the energy is transferred to the inductors through the channels. There can be several alternative channels, which enable different heating strategies depending on the cookware placed on top of the IH at runtime. The path followed by the energy through the channels is controlled by the power manager. Inductors are the elements where the energy is transformed into an electromagnetic field. Inductors can be organized into groups to heat larger cookware while sharing the user interface controllers.

2.2   The Common Variability Language Applied to IHs

To formalize the variability among the products of the SPL, we need a variability model that captures which model fragments are used by each of the products that can be built from the SPL. To build it, the presented approach uses the Common Variability Language (CVL) [8], given its expressiveness to properly formalize the feature realizations in terms of model fragments. CVL defines variants of a base model conforming to MOF (Meta-Object Facility, the Object Management Group metalanguage for defining modeling languages) by replacing variable parts of the base model by alternative model replacements found in a library.

The base model is a model described by a given DSL (here, IHDSL) that serves as the base for different variants defined over it. In CVL the elements of the base model that are subject to variations are the placement fragments (hereafter placements). A placement can be any element or set of elements that is subject to variation. To define alternatives for a placement we use a replacement library, which is a model that is described in the same DSL as the base model that will serve as a base to define alternatives for a placement. Each one of the alternatives for a placement is a replacement fragment (hereafter replacement). Similarly to placements, a replacement can be any element or set of elements that can be used as variation for a replacement.

Figure 1 shows an example of variability specification of IH through CVL. In the product realization layer, two placements are defined over an IH base model (P1 and P2). Then, four replacements are defined over an IH library model (R1, R2, R3, and R4). In the feature specification layer, a Feature Model is defined that formalizes the variability among the IH based on the placements and replacements. For instance, P1 can only be substituted by R4 (which is optional), but P2 can be replaced by R1, R2, or R3. Note that each fragment has a signature, which is a set of references (boundaries) going from and towards that replacement. A placement can only be replaced by replacements that match the signature. For instance, the P2 signature has a reference from a power manager (outside the placement) to an inductor (inside the placement), while the R4 signature is a reference from a power manager (inside the replacement) to an inductor (outside the replacement). P2 cannot be substituted by R4 since their signatures do not match.

Through the rest of the paper, we will use the term feature location in models formalized through CVL as "the process of obtaining the particular model fragments (or alternatives e.g. R1, R2 and R3) that are used in a particular placement (or variation point e.g. P1) among a set of products". Therefore, we will refer to the variation point as the feature being located and each of the alternative model fragments will be referred as different realizations for that feature (in fact, they are realizations of the alternatives of the feature).

3   Genetic Algorithm for Feature Location

This section present our approach, a Genetic Algorithm to Feature Location (GA-FL). Figure 2 shows an overview of the GA-FL process. The input of the process is a set of interrelated product models with implicit variability among them.

In the Genetic Algorithm process, the set of solutions that will be iterated need to be properly encoded (see **A - Encoding of the Population**), enabling the GA to work with them. The DE (domain expert or domain engineer) provides information about the set of product models to initialize the population of model fragments (see **B - Initialize Population**), the DE will select some product models to locate a particular feature and an initial model fragment for each of the selected product models. Next, each possible individual from the

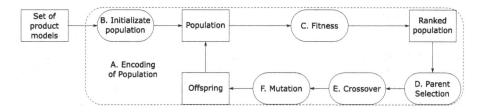

Fig. 2. Overview of the genetic algorithm to feature location

population is evaluated to determine how good is as a solution to the problem (see **C - Fitness**), as a result the population of solutions is ranked depending on their fitness value. Based on the ranked population, the parents for the new element are randomly selected (see **D - Parent Selection**), giving a higher probability to the solutions with higher fitness values. The first operation applied to the parents is the crossover, that joins two parents into a new solution (see **E - Crossover**). The resulting model fragment will be bound by a different product model and thus will evolve differently than the original one. The second operation applied to the solution resulting from the crossover is the mutation (see **F - Mutation**), the model fragment will evolve, growing or shrinking, resulting in a different model fragment that will be evaluated as possible solution in further generations. Finally, the set of solutions obtained will be presented to the DE, to select the solution that best represent their understanding of the feature being located.

3.1   Encoding of the Population

Traditionally, genetic algorithms encoded each possible solution of the problem (or chromosome) as a fixed-size string of binary values. Each position of the chromosome string (called locus) has two possible values (called alleles): 0 or 1.

However, to encode each model fragment as a string of binary values is not straightforward. As suggested by Davis [3], we decided to use an encoding natural for our problem and then devise a GA for that specific encoding. Therefore, we will encode our individuals as model fragments. To do so, we rely on MOF as the standard to define the models and CVL to specify fragments over those models and manipulate them.

Each individual of our Genetic Algorithm will be a model fragment defined over one of the product models. That is, each individual is a set of model elements and relationships among them that is present in one of the product models (see right part of Fig. 3 to see the representation of the individual). Therefore, to work with these individuals (model fragment defined over a product model), we will present genetic operations that can be applied directly to those model fragments. Through the rest of the paper we will refer to each individual as a model fragment that is always part of a product model.

3.2   Initialize Population

The first step of the process is to initialize the population of the GA. This is done by the DEs, preferably the same DE that created the products or work directly with them. The initialization is done based on DE's knowledge of the domain and the products themselves. This step is performed only one time for each feature that wants to be located.

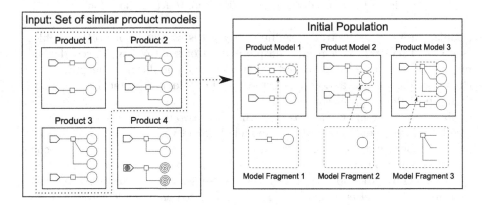

Fig. 3. Initialize population

Figure 3 shows an overview of this step. Top part shows the set of similar product models that where the feature will be located (Product Model 1 to 4). First, (1) the DE selects a subset of product models representative of the feature that will be used as input (in this example Product Model 1, 2 and 3), then, (2) for each product model from the subset the DE selects a model fragment that he believes will be part of the realization of that particular feature (Model Fragment 1, 2 and 3). As a result we get an initial population composed of pairs of model fragments and the product models where they were extracted from.

It is important to remark that we focus in the location of the features, leaving out of the scope of this work the features constraints discovery. That is, there could exists a cross-tree constraint among the feature 'upper heating spot' and the feature 'lower heating spot' (e.g. power consumption of combination of several inductors is higher than power consumption of single small inductors), but feature constraint discovery is not covered by this work.

3.3   Fitness Function

The fitness function is used as an heuristic to find the best solutions for the given problem. It is applied to each individual in the population and the function assigns a value that assesses how good is the solution. This information can be used in two ways: to determine that the algorithm should terminate as a desirable level of fitness has been reached and to determine the best candidates as parents for the next generation.

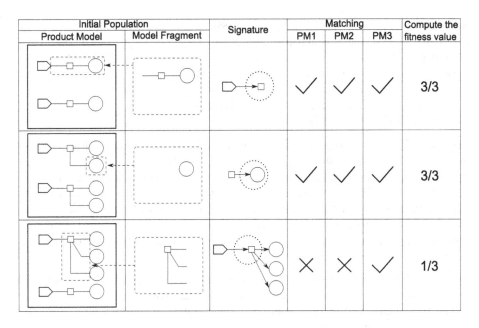

Fig. 4. Fitness function application

Our fitness function proceeds as follows: (1) the process abstracts from each model fragment to a placement signature in their referenced model fragment; (2) placement signatures are compared and grouped together if they are equal; (3) each placement signature is matched against all the product models from the initial subset of product models; (4) the fitness is computed for each placement signature and the fitness values are spread to the elements of the population.

Figure 4 depicts an overview of the model pattern extraction process [5] adapted to be used as a fitness function. The input of the process is the present population (the set of model fragments and their reference to a product model), see first and second column.

Step 1: The first step (see third column of Fig. 4) is to obtain a placement signature for each of the individuals (model fragment and the product model). The placement signature formalizes the set of elements that must be present in a model in order to connect the given model fragment. This is done comparing the model fragment with the product model from which it was originally extracted (when the initial population was created). The model fragment is present in the product model and connected to other model elements of the product model. The process looks for those boundary elements that link an element from the model fragment with the rest of the product model and extracts them as a placement signature. That is, the set of elements needed to connect the given model fragment. Therefore, the model fragment used as input match this placement signature. As a result, step 1 produces a placement signature for each model fragment used as input.

Step 2: The second step (not shown in Fig. 4, there are no duplicates) is to compare the placement signatures and group the ones that are equal. To do so, the process compares pairwise the placement signatures. If two placement signatures have the same elements in the boundaries, they are considered to be equal. Then, both placement signatures are grouped together. As a result, this step produces a set of unique placement signatures and each model fragment is associated to a single placement signature.

Step 3: The third step (see fourth, fifth and sixth columns of Fig. 4) is to match each placement signature with all the product models present in the initial subset of product models. That is, the process looks for spots where a given placement signature matches in each of the given product models. When a placement signature matches a particular spot of a product model, means that the model fragments associated to that placement signature could be inserted in the given spot. As a result, step 3 provides a set of spots (across all the product models) where the given placement signature matches.

Step 4: The fourth step (see seventh column of Fig. 4) is to compute the fitness value for each of the placement fragments and spread it to the associated model fragments. The process computes the number of product models where the placement matches (no matter how many times). This value indicates the number of product models where the resulting placement could be used. As the purpose of the genetic algorithm is to locate variation points and alternative realizations across the product models, the higher the number of product models that match the better. Finally, the value of each placement signature is spread to the associated model fragments. As a result, step 4 assigns a fitness value for each model fragment present in the population.

After applying these steps, each model fragment gets a fitness value. The higher the number of products where the placement signature is present the better, as this means that it will be able to formalize the variability of a higher number of product models.

Once the population fitness has been assessed, it is time to create the next generation of individuals. This new generation will be based on present generation and the fitness value will be used to ensure that best candidates are chosen as parents for the evolution process. To do so, the process makes use of three different genetic operations that will act over the individuals of the population to generate new ones. First, a selection operation will be used to select the elements that will be used as parents of the new individual. Then, a crossover operation will be used to broad the solution space that a particular solution can reach. Finally a mutation operation will be used to introduce variations in the individual hoping that the new individual performs better than its antecessor.

3.4   Selection of Parents

The selection of parents is performed following the roulette wheel selection method [1], one of the most common methods used in GA. In this method, each individual is assigned with a share of a wheel roulette proportional to their fitness. By doing so, fitter individuals will have higher chance to be selected and go forward with the rest of genetic operations while weaker individuals will have lower probability of being selected. Other selection strategies present in literature can be used with our model fragments, as the operation simply selects individuals, the encoding does not affect the selection.

This operation selects the individuals that will be parents of the new individual that is going to be generated. Traditionally, genetic algorithms select two elements as parents with the only restriction of avoiding the same element being 'father' and 'mother' (as this would nullify the effect of the crossover operation). However, when applying our genetic algorithm to model fragments a new restriction applies: both fragment selected must reference different product models. By doing so we ensure that the crossover operation can be properly applied.

First, we perform the selection of the first parent with no restrictions. Then, when selecting the second parent, we will only allow selections of elements referencing a product model different from the first parent. However, in order to allow the algorithm to browse into a broader search space, the product models not included into the input subset by the DE will be also eligible (with a low fitness value). That is, elements already present in the population will have the fitness value from the previous step while product models not present in the population will have a fitness value of 1.

As a result, the selection operation provides a parent model fragment (obtained from the present population) and another product model (that could not be present in the actual population) that will be used for the crossover operation.

3.5 Crossover

In genetic algorithms, crossover enables the creation of a new individual generated combining the genetic material of both parents. In our encoding there are two elements that can be mapped across the different individuals: the model fragment and the referenced product model. Therefore, our crossover operation will take the model fragment from the first parent and the product model from the second parent, generating a new individual that contains elements from both parents and thus preserving the basic mechanics of the crossover operation.

To achieve the latter, our crossover operation is based on model comparisons. Figure 5 shows an example of application of the crossover operation over model fragments. First we select the model fragment from the first parent. Then we select the product model from the second parent. Then the model fragment (from first parent) is compared with the product model (from the second parent). If the comparison finds the model fragment in the product model, the process creates a new individual with the model fragment taken from the first parent but referencing the product model from the second parent. In the case that the comparison does not find a similar element, the crossover will return the first parent unchanged.

This operation enables to broad the search space to a different product model. That is, both model fragments (the one from the first parent and the one from

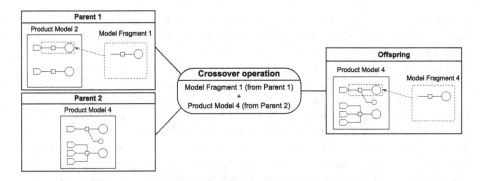

Fig. 5. Crossover operation

the new individual) will be the same. However, as each of them is referencing a different product model, they will mutate differently and provide different individuals in further generations. As the solution we are looking for should apply to all the models provided as input, it can be reached from any of them, but some product models can yield to the solution faster than others.

3.6   Mutation

In genetic algorithms, mutation operation introduces a random variation to the new individuals generated by the crossover operation. The mutation operation often results in a weaker individual, but occasionally the result might be a stronger individual.

Figure 6 shows an example of our mutation for model fragments. Each model fragment is associated to a product model and the model fragment mutates in the context of their associated product model. That is, the model fragment will gain or drop some elements, but the resulting model fragment will be still part of the referenced product model. The mutation possibilities of a given model fragment are driven by their associated product model.

To perform the mutation, the type of mutation that will occur (either addition or removal of elements) is decided randomly:

Removal of Elements: This kind of mutation randomly removes some elements from the model fragment. The only constraint is that elements are selected from the edges of the model fragment (they are connected with a single element), so the resulting model fragment is still connected (we can navigate from any element to any other element through the connections between the elements) and is not split in two isolated groups of elements. As the resulting model fragment is a subset of the original model fragment, and the original was present in the referenced product model, the resulting product model will be always present in the referenced product model.

Addition of Elements: This kind of mutation randomly adds some elements to the model fragment. The only constraint is that the resulting model fragment is present in the referenced product model. To achieve it, the boundaries of the model fragment with the rest of the product model are identified and then a random element from the boundary is added to the resulting model fragment. By doing so, the mutated model fragment will be part of the referenced product model.

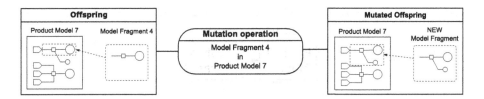

Fig. 6. Mutation operation

As a result, a new model fragment is created but it still references the same product model. That is, the individual represent other possible feature realization present in the product model for the particular feature being located. The next time the fitness is calculated, the placement signature described by this model fragment will be extracted and evaluated to assess how good it is as a solution.

4 Case Study

To evaluate the approach we are going to compare the presented GA-FL approach with CMP-FL, an approach to Feature Location in product models that makes use of the information provided by DEs. We are going to validate the results from both approaches against an oracle obtained from our industrial partner (BSH), the leading manufacturer of home appliances in Europe. Their induction division has been producing induction hobs (under the brands of Bosch and Siemens among others) for the last 15 years. The firmware of the different induction hobs is generated following a model-based SPL approach. First, a resolution for a product is created choosing from the set of features present in the variability model (each feature is formalized as model fragments). Then, a product model is generated by executing the product resolution (CVL execution capabilities produce a product model including the model fragments from the features selected). Finally, the firmware of the induction hob is obtained applying a model transformation to the resulting product model.

4.1 Case Study Setup

Figure 7 presents an overview of the process followed to evaluate the presented approach. Top part shows the oracle, a set of product models and their formalization of features. The product models from the oracle are used to construct three different scenarios regarding how good is the input fed to the approaches (left part of Fig. 7). Then each scenario is test against both approaches, (CMP-FL) and the presented approach (GA-FL). As a result each approach provides a set of placement signatures that realize the feature being located. Each set of solutions is compared with the placement signature present in the oracle for that particular feature being located (right part of Fig. 7). We want to determine if the solution used by our industrial partner (from the oracle) is present among the solutions provided by each approach in each scenario.

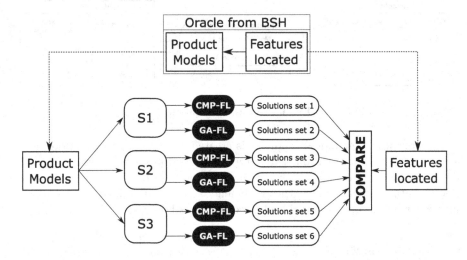

Fig. 7. Overview of the evaluation with the oracle

The oracle is composed of a set of product models and the set of features (used to define the products) properly located. That is, for each feature used by the products (around 100 features) has been previously located and validated by our industrial partner (the oracle is extracted from a set of product models that are currently under production). Therefore, we will consider the oracle as the ground truth for the evaluation process. The set of product models consist of 46 induction hob models, each of them model composed of around 100 elements (on average) that can be part or not of a model fragment. Therefore, the number of possible combinations can be calculated as the power set of the set S of elements $P(S)$, resulting in around 2^{100} ($|P(S)| = 2^n$ $where |S| = n$) different potential model fragments. We generate the product models attending to the oracle to distinguish three different scenarios regarding how accurate is the input fed to the approaches:

S1 High Accuracy: The first scenario corresponds to what we consider a high accuracy input from the user. More than a 75 % of the products used as input for the approaches corresponds to the subset of product models (46 available) that actually include a formalization of the feature that is being located (extracted from the oracle); and thus the placement signature will match with those product models.

S2 Medium Accuracy: The second scenario corresponds to a medium accuracy input from the user. Between 25 % and 75 % of the products used as input for the approaches include a formalization of the feature that is being located. Therefore, a similar percentage (25 % to 75 %) of the products do not contain a formalization of the feature being located.

S3 Low Accuracy: The third scenario corresponds to a low accuracy input from the user. Only less than a 25 % of the products used as input include a formalization of the feature that is being located. This results in some deliberately bad cases (e.g. select only products that do not include the feature being located).

In the three scenarios, the size of the input is randomly selected and ranges from 1 to 5 product models. The seed fragments have been obtained randomly. For each of the features present in the oracle we generate 100 different test cases for each of the three scenarios (S1, S2 and S3). Then, each test case is tested against both approaches (CMP-FL and GA-FL). Finally, the solutions sets (placement signatures) provided by the approaches are compared against the oracle. As a result, we can determine if the feature realizations that is actually being used by our industrial partner (the expected solution) is present among the solution sets returned by the approaches. We do this comparing the placement signature from the oracle with the set of placement signatures provided as solution and determining whether it is present or not.

4.2 Results

The CMP-FL was able to provide a set of solutions that included the expected solution in 86 % of the cases from S1 (high accuracy input). Nevertheless, the presented GA-FL was able to include the expected solution in 79 % of the cases. The CMP-FL was able to include the expected solution into the solutions set in 48 % of the cases from S2 (medium accuracy input). When the information provided by the user is not accurate enough, the approach fails to include the expected (oracle) option into the resulting set. By contrast, the GA-FL was able to include it in 73 % of the cases. Finally, the CMP-FL was able to include the expected solution into the solutions set in 16 % of the cases from S3 (low accuracy input). The approach only search in the product models provided by the user and is not able to look for the solution in other product models. By contrast, the GA-FL approach was able to include the expected solution in 63 % of the cases from S3. Given the stochastic nature of the Genetic Algorithm, the approach is able to find the solution even if the input provided is not accurate.

The justification of the different results provided by both approaches resides in how the search space is traversed. That is, the different elements evaluated as possible solutions by each of the approaches. The CMP-FL approach only explores the portion of the solution space delimited by the product models used as input. In contrast, the GA-FL approach is capable of traversing the entire solution space, independently of the input.

The GA-FL approach is capable of reaching any possible solution from the search space, as it can move across the search space in any direction. The mutation enables the exploration of solutions within the same product, while the crossover operation enables to switch to another product (an further explore it with subsequent random mutations). By contrast, the CMP-FL approach is bounded by the input of the user and only explores solutions within the product provided as input; thus, some areas of the search space cannot be reached.

As a result, the CMP-FL is not able to provide better results than the input provided; that is, upon a 75 % of accuracy will provide the expected result 75 % of the cases. In particular in all the cases where the accuracy was 0 % (from S3) the expected solution was not included. In contrast, the presented approach is able to explore solutions beyond the input provided by the user. This means that upon the scenarios where the input is not accurate enough, the crossover operation will (eventually) be able to switch to different product models that convey to the expected solution.

5   Related Work

Some works report their industrial experiences in a wide range of fields transforming legacy products into Product Line assets [10,11,13]. These approaches focus on capturing guidelines and techniques for manual transformations. In contrast, our approach introduces automation into the process while taking advantage from the knowledge of the domain experts.

Other works focus on the automation of the extraction process [6,9,14,16–18], obtaining the variability from legacy products by comparing the products with each other. In [17], the similarity between models is measured following an exchangeable metric, taking into account different attributes of the models. Then, the approach is further refined [9] to reduce the number of comparisons needed to mine the family model. Rubin et al. [16] propose a generic framework for mining legacy product lines and automating their refactoring. They compare the elements of the input with each other, matching those whose similarity is above a certain threshold and merging them together. The authors in [18], propose a generic approach to automatically compare products and extract the variability among them in terms of a CVL variability model. The authors in [14] propose an approach based on comparisons to extract the variability of any kind of asset. However, these approaches are based on mechanical comparisons, automatically turning identical elements into common parts of the SPL, similar elements as alternatives for a feature and unmatched elements into optional features. In contrast, our work enables the DE to decide which elements should be formalized as part of a feature based on the results of the comparisons.

Finally, there are some research efforts that apply genetic algorithms to the SPLs domain. For instance, the authors in [7] present GAFES, an artificial intelligence approach for optimized feature selection in SPLs. The authors in [15] present a genetic algorithm that finds optimal configurations of a Dynamic SPL at run-time. However, the solutions of those genetic algorithms are encoded as strings of binary values specifying the presence or absence of each feature. By contrast, our approach is applied directly to the product models and model fragments, resulting in a different encoding and set of genetic operations customized to work with model fragments.

6   Conclusion

In this paper we have presented a Genetic Algorithm to Feature Location (GA-FL) approach. To the best of our knowledge it is the first Genetic Algorithm applied to feature location over models. We have provided a custom encoding that enable the GA to work with model fragments and a set of genetic operations that can be applied to individuals following that encoding. We have presented a fitness function, a parent selection operation, a crossover operation (capable of bring together elements from two parents into a single offspring) and a mutation operation (that produces slight variations of the individual being mutated).

Finally we have compared the presented GA-FL with CMP-FL in terms on how both approaches traverse the search space. This comparison shows that CMP-FL does not traverse the whole space, failing to find a solution under some scenarios, while the GA-FL is capable of traversing the whole search space reaching the solutions. In addition, in scenarios where the CMP-FL approach is able to find the best solution, our GA-FL approach is also able to do so while traversing more elements from the search space, providing a more complete solution.

The ideas of the presented approach are generic and can be applied to any MOF-based models. Our next steps will involve the application of the presented GA-FL approach to CAF[1], an international company that builds and deploy railway solutions. They are currently shifting to a model-based SPL approach and there is a need of locating the features among their existing product models.

References

1. Affenzeller, M., Winkler, S., Wagner, S., Beham, A.: Genetic Algorithms and Genetic Programming: Modern Concepts and Practical Applications, 1st edn. Chapman & Hall/CRC, London (2009)
2. Berger, T., Rublack, R., Nair, D., Atlee, J.M., Becker, M., Czarnecki, K., Wasowski, A.: A survey of variability modeling in industrial practice. In: 7th International Workshop on Variability Modelling of Software-Intensive Systems (VaMoS) (2013)
3. Davis, L.: Handbook of Genetic Algorithms. Van Nostrand Reinhold, New York (1991)
4. Dit, B., Revelle, M., Gethers, M., Poshyvanyk, D.: Feature location in source code: a taxonomy and survey. J. Softw.: Evol. Process **25**(1), 53–95 (2013)
5. Font, J. , Arcega, L., Haugen, Ø., Cetina, C.: Building software product lines from conceptualized model patterns. In: Proceedings of the 19th International Conference on Software Product Line (SPLC), pp. 46–55 (2015)
6. Font, J., Ballarín, M., Haugen, Ø., Cetina, C.: Automating the variability formalization of a model family by means of common variability language. In: Proceedings of the 19th International Conference on Software Product Line (SPLC), pp. 411–418 (2015)
7. Guo, J., White, J., Wang, G., Li, J., Wang, Y.: A genetic algorithm for optimized feature selection with resource constraints in software product lines. J. Syst. Softw. **84**(12), 2208–2221 (2011)

---

[1] www.caf.es/en.

8. Haugen, Ø., Moller-Pedersen, B., Oldevik, J., Olsen, G., Svendsen, A.: Adding standardized variability to domain specific languages. In: 12th International Software Product Line Conference, SPLC 2008, pp. 139–148, September 2008

9. Holthusen, S., Wille, D., Legat, C., Beddig, S., Schaefer, I., Vogel-Heuser, B.: Family model mining for function block diagrams in automationsoftware. In: Proceedings of the 18th International Software Product Line Conference, vol. 2, pp. 36–43 (2014)

10. Kim, K., Kim, H., Kim, W.: Building software product line from the legacy systems "experience in the digital audio and video domain". In: 11th International Software Product Line Conference, SPLC 2007, pp. 171–180, September 2007

11. Kolb, R., Muthig, D., Patzke, T., Yamauchi, K.: Refactoring a legacy component for reuse in a software product line: a case study: practice articles. J. Softw. Maint. Evol. **18**(2), 109–132 (2006)

12. Krueger, C.W.: Easing the transition to software mass customization. In: van der Linden, F. (ed.) Software Product-Family Engineering. LNCS, vol. 2290, pp. 282–293. Springer, Heidelberg (2002)

13. Lee, H., Choi, H., Kang, K.C., Kim, D., Lee, Z.: Experience report on using a domain model-based extractive approach to software product line asset development. In: Edwards, S.H., Kulczycki, G. (eds.) ICSR 2009. LNCS, vol. 5791, pp. 137–149. Springer, Heidelberg (2009)

14. Martinez, J., Ziadi, T., Bisyandé, T.F., Klein, J., Traon, Y.L.: Bottom-up adoption of software product lines,: a generic and extensible approach. In: Proceedings of the 19th International Conference on Software Product Line (SPLC), pp. 101–110 (2015)

15. Pascual, G.G., Pinto, M., Fuentes, L.: Self-adaptation of mobile systems driven by the common variability language. Future Gener. Comput. Syst. **47**, 127–144 (2015). Special Section: Advanced Architectures for the Future Generation of Software-Intensive Systems

16. Rubin, J., Chechik, M.: Combining related products into product lines. In: de Lara, J., Zisman, A. (eds.) FASE 2012 and ETAPS 2012. LNCS, vol. 7212, pp. 285–300. Springer, Heidelberg (2012)

17. Wille, D., Holthusen, S., Schulze, S., Schaefer, I.: Interface variability in family model mining. In: Proceedings of the 17th International Software Product Line Conference: Co-located Workshops, pp. 44–51 (2013)

18. Zhang, X., Haugen, Ø, Moller-Pedersen, B.: Model comparison to synthesize a model-driven software product line. In: Proceedings of the 15th International Software Product Line Conference (SPLC), pp. 90–99 (2011)

Carrying Ideas from Knowledge-Based Configuration to Software Product Lines

Juha Tiihonen[1]([✉]), Mikko Raatikainen[2], Varvana Myllärniemi[2],
and Tomi Männistö[1]

[1] University of Helsinki, Helsinki, Finland
{Juha.Tiihonen,Tomi.Mannisto}@cs.helsinki.fi
[2] Aalto University, Espoo, Finland
{Mikko.Raatikainen,Varvana.Myllarniemi}@aalto.fi

Abstract. Software variability modelling (SVM) has become a central concern in software product lines – especially configurable software product lines (CSPL) require rigorous SVM. Dynamic SPLs, service oriented SPLs, and autonomous or pervasive systems are examples where CSPLs are applied. Knowledge-based configuration (KBC) is an established way to address variability modelling aiming for the automatic product configuration of physical products. Our aim was to study what major ideas from KBC can be applied to SVM, particularly in the context of CSPLs. Our main contribution is the identification of major ideas from KBC that could be applied to SVM. First, we call for the separation of types and instances. Second, conceptual clarity of modelling concepts, e.g., having both taxonomical and compositional relations would be useful. Third, we argue for the importance of a conceptual basis that provides a foundation for multiple representations, e.g., graphical and textual. Applying the insights and experiences embedded in these ideas may help in the development of modelling support for software product lines, particularly in terms of conceptual clarity and as a basis for tool support with a high level of automation.

Keywords: Variability modelling · Feature modelling · Knowledge-based configuration · Conceptualization · Variability management

1 Introduction

Software product lines (*SPL*) have emerged as an important means for reuse in the context of a set of products that share a common *SPL architecture* and other assets (e.g. [5]). For SPLs, variability management has become a central concern. *Variability* is the ability of a system to be efficiently extended, changed, customised or configured for use [19]. *Domain engineering* develops assets for reuse while exploiting reusable commonalities and catering for differentiating variability. *Application engineering* realises the products of a SPL by reusing the assets, by resolving the variability, and by developing product specific extensions. *Software variability modelling (SVM)* represents the variability of the assets.

© Springer International Publishing Switzerland 2016
G.M. Kapitsaki and E. Santana de Almeida (Eds.): ICSR 2016, LNCS 9679, pp. 55–62, 2016.
DOI: 10.1007/978-3-319-35122-3_4

A special class of SPLs is a *configurable software product line* (CSPL), in which all differences between the product variants have been pre-defined and implemented in domain engineering. Product derivation involves merely making decisions on the predefined and implemented assets and variability therein [3]. This specification of an individual product is also called a *configuration* for short (cf., [7]). Recently, CSPLs have received increasing attention in different forms: Dynamic SPLs, the application of SPL to autonomous or pervasive systems, and service oriented SPLs are examples where the idea of CSPL can be applied.

In the field of physical, such as mechanical products, *knowledge-based configuration (KBC)* (e.g., [10]) is a related domain to SPL in general, and CSPL in particular. KBC aims to model and manage variability in a way that enables automated product derivation. Besides similarity, the long history since 1980's and relative maturity makes KBC an interesting field to compare with CSPLs.

Compared to previous work [1,12,14], we aim to investigate synergies between KBC and SVM in more depth and from the variability modelling point of view. The research problem of this paper is: *What ideas from knowledge-based configuration can be applied to software variability modelling and configuration?* We highlight three ideas of KBC and discuss their potential implications for SVM in general and especially in the context of CSPLs.

In terms of the methodology, our analysis and comparison of the literature focuses on core KBC modelling literature and feature models that are the most common modelling method of SVM. A search based on title and abstract through all special issues on configuration and the proceedings of configuration workshops since 2000 was performed to augment already known relevant KBC literature on modelling conceptualisations. We focus on aspects of variability modelling that are relevant to supporting product derivation and configurability.

The rest of this paper is organised as follows. Section 2 identifies previous work. Section 3 presents the three identified potentially useful ideas from KBC. Section 4 provides discussion and concludes.

2   Previous Work

Knowledge Based Configuration emerged from various domains of physical products such as computers and elevators. It is a relatively general, widely deployed and domain-independent approach with quite a long history [10]. The core of knowledge representation in KBC forms two widely cited and fundamentally similar conceptualisations of Soininen et al. [18] and Felfernig et al. [9]. In the conceptualisation of Soininen et al. *configuration model knowledge* specifies the entities that can appear in a *configuration* specifying an individual product, their properties, and the rules on how the entities and their properties can be combined. *Individuals* (instances) of configuration model concepts describe individual configurations and thus represent configuration solution knowledge. Finally, *requirements knowledge* specifies the systematised requirements on the configuration to be constructed. Besides being widely cited by researchers, these types of configuration knowledge representations are "typically provided in today's commercial configuration environments" [11].

Software Variability Modelling has been elevated as a central concern for SPLs in addition to reuse [4]. Feature modelling (*FM*) is probably the first and the most widely known means to represent SPL variability. A *feature* represents a characteristic of a system that is visible to the end-user [13], or in general, a system property that is relevant to some stakeholder and is used to capture commonalities or discriminate among product variants [6]. Other variability modelling approaches include the orthogonal variability modelling approaches such as OVM [15] that define a separate model that is associated with the base model such as an UML model; and decision-oriented [16] approaches model variability as questions and possible answers to be presented in the style of wizards.

3   Ideas from Knowledge Based Configuration

3.1   I1: Separating Types and Instances

In KBC, domain and application models are clearly separated: domain models are expressed as types (that are instances of a meta-model) and application models as instances of the types.

SPL engineering makes a clear distinction between domain and application engineering activities [5]. However, most of the research on variability modelling seems to focus on domain engineering and variability representation; and application engineering has often remained more implicit [7].

Conceptual separation of domain and application models. In feature modelling, there is no clear difference between a domain model and an application model, but the same modelling concepts are used for both purposes. This is illustrated in Fig. 1. Instantiating a product feature model takes place by *specializing* the product line feature model. Each operation in resolving variability results in another feature model containing less variability. When all variability has been resolved, the remaining features represent the valid, fully resolved (*specific*) configuration [6]; for an example see the lower part of Fig. 1. The only way to recognize that a feature model describes a product variant is to investigate whether all variability has been resolved. Additionally, it can become challenging to differentiate the product line feature model from a series of specialized models or to distinguish evolution of the variability models from their specialization.

In KBC, a clear separation between domain and application models is made. Figure 2 illustrates how a product line feature model and a product feature model could be represented. In the product line feature model, modelling concepts are called *feature types*, whereas modelling concepts in the product feature model are called *feature instances*. Instead of specializing, the model of the product is *instantiated* from the model of the product line. In KBC terminology, a generic description of a product family (*configuration model*) is instantiated into an unambiguous specification of a concrete product individual (*configuration*). Consequently, feature types in the configuration model are instantiated as feature instances in the configuration (Fig. 3). When following the distinction between types and instances, the different levels of feature modelling can be seen

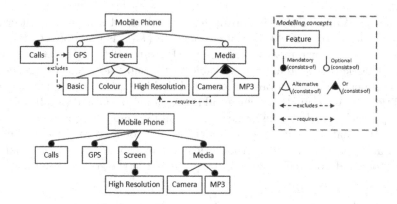

Fig. 1. A sample feature model [2]. Same modelling concepts are used to represent both the product line feature model (top) and product feature model (bottom); the latter is specialized from the former.

as instantiations: modelling concepts are instantiated as concrete feature types in the domain models, which are then instantiated as concrete feature instances in the application models (Fig. 3).

Types modularize models and facilitate reuse. Besides conceptual differentiation, there are other advantages to apply types and instances. A type declaration provides a convenient means for modularizing a reusable asset so that each logical entity can be defined and managed independently. A type is a natural place to collect specifications of compositional structure, attributes, constraints, and other modelling constructs. The set of type declarations forms a repository of reusable assets. The types can then be reused in the context of larger entities and eventually to model an entire SPL. Another advantage of types and instances is the reuse of a type within a product of a product line via instantiation. This seems conceptually cleaner than *referencing* and *cloning* suggested for feature models [6].

3.2   I2: Conceptual Clarity

In KBC, there are two main relations: classification (*is-a*) and composition (*haspart*) with *cardinality* to expresses compositional rules such as mandatory or optional. With these, two respective major hierarchies emerge. Composition can pick e.g. alternatives from various branches of the classification hierarchy.

Initially, FODA [13] defined *features* and *mandatory*, *optional* and *alternative* relations between features, along with *mutually exclusive with* and *requires* constraints (Fig. 1). Over time, the need for representing more complex variability has emerged. For example, there is a need to represent *or* (Fig. 1), which indicate that one or more features from the child features must be included [2]. The exact nature of the modelling concepts should be explicit and unambiguous.

Distinct relationships such as *has-part* and *is-a*. In the context of FM, particularly, the *alternative* relation has proved to be difficult to interpret

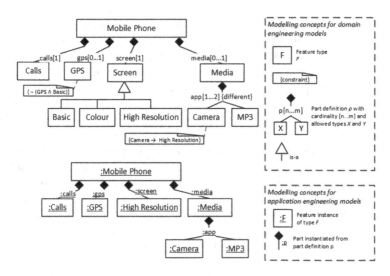

Fig. 2. The sample feature model in Fig. 1 represented to follow the KBC conceptualizations: a distinction between domain and application models is made. The features in the product model are instantiated from the feature types in the product line model.

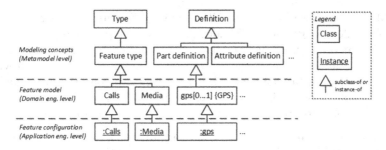

Fig. 3. Following the KBC conceptualizations, feature modelling involves three instantiation levels: modelling concepts, product line feature models with feature types, and product feature models with feature instances. Adapted from [18].

(Fig. 4(a) and (b)). Originally, this relation denoted *specialisation*: "[a]lternative features can be thought of as specializations of a more general category" [13]. This is concretely manifested by the *alternative* relation in Fig. 4(a): the domain engineer does not read the model as *"the mobile phone consists of one screen, and the screen consists of basic, colour or high resolution screen"*. Instead, the obvious intention is that *"the mobile phone consists of one screen, and the screen can be a basic, colour or high resolution screen."* (fig. 4(b)).

To organise and specialise types, KBC adopts classification (*is-a*) and inheritance of features in the usual object-oriented manner. For example, *Screen* can be specialised into *Basic*, *Colour* and *High Resolution* screens (Fig. 2).

Cardinality as a basis for compositional relationships. In the context of FM, composition is the fundamental relationship and the need to represent different kinds of cardinalities [6] has been identified. However, instead of replacing *mandatory, optional, alternative* and *or* with cardinalities, cardinalities are feature model extensions Fig. 4(c) and (d). That is, instead of *refining* previous modelling conceptualisations, the existing conceptualisations are *extended* by adding new concepts on top of the old ones.

In KBC, a means to model varying compositional structure is via *part definitions* [18] that include cardinalities. In the example of Fig. 2, type *Mobile phone* has a part definition *calls[1]* of allowed type *Calls*: one feature *Calls* must be present in a valid configuration. As another example, type *Media* has a part definition *apps[1...2]* of allowed types *MP3* and *Camera*. The semantics of a part definition is that in a configuration, a valid instance of the whole type has the number of part instances specified by the *cardinality* as parts with the specified *part name*; each instance as a part must be of one of the *allowed types*. Note that allowed types do not have to be subtypes of the same type. Naturally, it is possible to reuse a type as an allowed type in several contexts.

3.3   I3: Separate Domain Phenomena, Concepts and Representations

The modelling concepts in KBC are defined and provided with semantics independently of the representations of concepts.

SVM in terms of FM started with graphical feature diagrams (cf., [17]). Numerous dialects of graphical FM notations have been proposed [2,17] and even textual FM languages have emerged (cf., [8]) — some of these also introduce new concepts. The full semantics of the concepts or notations has also been provided, although often as an afterthought [17]. However, two concerns are combined: what are usable or otherwise appropriate representations and what phenomena a model needs to capture.

Domain *phenomena* as *concepts* with semantics. Well-defined concepts are the fundamental basis for capturing the phenomena of the domain. They are an asset on which representation formats for various (but similar) purposes can be developed. In KBC, modelling conceptualisations have been defined independent

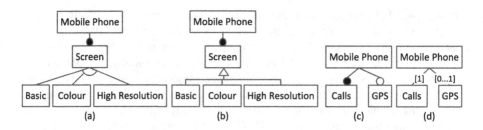

(a)   (b)   (c)   (d)

Fig. 4. (a) Alternative originally implied specialisation. (b) Idea to model specialisation as is-a, not consists-of. (c, d) Extending but not refining FM concepts: consists-of with cardinality could have replaced mandatory, optional and other consists-of relations.

of direct representations [9, 18]. The idea is that concepts can be defined independently of representations so that appropriate concepts capture the domain phenomena aptly.

Multiple equivalent representations of concepts. When concepts capture domain phenomena, it is more straightforward to support multiple representations than when attempting to directly capture the domain phenomena or to perform model transformations between representations. First, it is easier to have simultaneous representations when the representations are based on the same concepts. Second, changes or adaptations such as shorthand notations or semantic sugar are easier to add to representations without affecting other representations. Consequently, completely new representations are easier to add. An example from KBC is described in [20] where a model is kept in internal data structures and it can be edited in textual representation, as called for also in SVM (cf. [8]), and via a graphical editor.

4   Discussion and Conclusions

We explored the research in Knowledge-Based Configuration (KBC) to identify major ideas that could be applied to Software Variability Modelling (SVM), particularly in Configurable Software Product Lines. We reflected the ideas to the existing research in SVM with the hope that the ideas could provide fresh insight and novel ideas for advancing the state of the art and practice in SVM. This analysis was performed assuming that automation is desired – the ideas might not fit less rigorous SVM, e.g., when exploring the variability of a domain. Fully exploiting some of the benefits requires tool support, e.g., to benefit from multiple representations of the concepts or modelling with types and instances.

We argue for having separate models for domain and application engineering, i.e., separate models for the product line and for product variants. Further, we see room for re-factoring the feature modelling concepts and relationships for better conceptual clarity. This could apply types and instances as a mechanism to simplify the reuse of assets within and between the products of a product line. The separation of well-defined concepts from representations makes the management of variability models more straightforward. If a model has a well-defined conceptualisation with declarative semantics, a straightforward translation can be carried out to produce an equivalent model that can be reasoned upon.

Some of the ideas are already reflected in some SVM approaches, but not in mainstream SVM. However, the ideas address interrelated concerns – full benefits stem from being applied simultaneously.

Future work can identify additional ideas that can be applied to SVM from KBC and vice versa. Concretising, refining and extending the ideas into conceptualisations, representations and supporting tools would enable practical utilisation. Both theoretical and empirical research is needed, e.g., conceptual re-factoring would benefit from empirical investigation on what concepts are needed to form a clear conceptual foundation that is neither too minimal nor bloated.

References

1. Benavides, D., Felfernig, A., Galindo, J.A., Reinfrank, F.: Automated analysis in feature modelling and product configuration. In: Favaro, J., Morisio, M. (eds.) ICSR 2013. LNCS, vol. 7925, pp. 160–175. Springer, Heidelberg (2013)
2. Benavides, D., Segura, S., Ruiz-Cortés, A.: Automated analysis of feature models 20 years later: a literature review. Inf. Syst. **35**(6), 615–636 (2010)
3. Bosch, J.: Maturity and evolution in software product lines: approaches, artefacts and organization. In: Chastek, G.J. (ed.) SPLC 2002. LNCS, vol. 2379, pp. 257–271. Springer, Heidelberg (2002)
4. Chen, L., Ali Babar, M.: A systematic review of evaluation of variability management approaches in software product lines. IST **53**(4), 344–362 (2011)
5. Clements, P., Northrop, L.: Software Product Lines Practices and Patterns. Addison-Wesley Longman Publishing Co., Inc., Boston (2001)
6. Czarnecki, K., Helsen, S., Eisenecker, U.: Formalizing cardinality-based feature models and their specialization. Softw. Process Improv. Pract. **10**(1), 7–29 (2005)
7. Deelstra, S., Sinnema, M., Bosch, J.: Product derivation in software product families: a case study. J. Syst. Softw. **74**(2), 173–194 (2005)
8. Eichelberger, H., Schmid, K.: Mapping the design-space of textual variability modeling languages: a refined analysis. Int. J. Softw. Tools Technol. Transf. (2014)
9. Felfernig, A., Friedrich, G.E., Jannach, D.: UML as domain specific language for the construction of knowledge-based configuration systems. Int. J. Softw. Eng. Knowl. Eng. **10**(4), 449–469 (2000)
10. Felfernig, A., Hotz, L., Bagley, C., Tiihonen, J. (eds.): Knowledge-Based Configuration: From Research to Business Cases. Morgan Kaufmann, San Francisco (2014)
11. Hotz, L., Felfernig, A., Stumptner, M., Ryabokon, A., Bagley, C., Wolter, K.: Configuration knowledge representation and reasoning. In: Felfernig, A., Hotz, L., Bagley, C., Tiihonen, J. (eds.) Knowledge-Based Configuration: From Research to Business Cases, pp. 41–72. Morgan Kaufmann, San Francisco (2014)
12. Hubaux, A., Jannach, D., Drescher, C., Murta, L., Männistö, T., Czarnecki, K., Heymans, P., Nguyen, T., Zanker, M.: Unifying software and product configuration: a research roadmap. In: ECAI 2012 Workshop on Configuration, pp. 31–35 (2012)
13. Kang, K., Cohen, S., Hess, J., Novak, W., Peterson, S.: Feature-oriented domain analysis feasibility study (FODA). Technical report CMU/SEI-90-TR-021, Carnegie Mellon U., Software Engineering Institute, Pittsburgh, PA, USA (1990)
14. Männistö, T., Soininen, T., Sulonen, R.: Product configuration view to software product families. In: ICSE Software Configuration Management Workshop (2001)
15. Pohl, K., Böckle, G., van der Linden, F.: Software Product Line Engineering: Foundations, Principles, and Techniques. Springer, New York (2005)
16. Schmid, K., Rabiser, R., Grünbacher, P.: A comparison of decision modeling approaches in product lines. In: 5th Workshop on Variability Modeling of Software-Intensive Systems, pp. 119–126. ACM, New York (2011)
17. Schobbens, P.-Y., Heymans, P., Trigaux, J.-C., Bontemps, Y.: Generic semantics of feature diagrams. Comput. Netw. **51**(2), 456–479 (2007)
18. Soininen, T., Tiihonen, J., Männistö, T., Sulonen, R.: Towards a general ontology of configuration. AI EDAM **12**(04), 357–372 (1998)
19. Svahnberg, M., van Gurp, J., Bosch, J.: A taxononomy of variability realization techniques. Softw. Pract. Experience **35**(8), 705–754 (2005)
20. Tiihonen, J., Heiskala, M., Anderson, A., Soininen, T.: WeCoTin–A practical logic-based sales configurator. AI Commun. **26**(1), 99–131 (2013)

Tax-PLEASE—Towards Taxonomy-Based Software Product Line Engineering

Ina Schaefer[1]([⊠]), Christoph Seidl[1], Loek Cleophas[2,3], and Bruce W. Watson[2,4]

[1] Institute for Software Engineering, Technische Universität Braunschweig,
Braunschweig, Germany
{i.schaefer,c.seidl}@tu-bs.de

[2] Department of Information Science, Stellenbosch University,
Stellenbosch, South Africa
{loek,bruce}@fastar.org

[3] Software Engineering and Technology, Technische Universiteit Eindhoven,
Eindhoven, The Netherlands

[4] Centre for Artificial Intelligence Research, CSIR Meraka Institute,
Stellenbosch, South Africa

Abstract. Modern software systems, in particular in mobile and cloud-based applications, exist in many different variants in order to adapt to changing user requirements or application contexts. Software product line engineering allows developing these software systems by managed large-scale reuse in order to achieve shorter time to market. Traditional software product line engineering approaches use a domain variability model which only captures the configuration options of the product variants, but does not provide any guideline for designing and implementing reusable artifacts. In contrast, software taxonomies structure software domains from an abstract specification of the functionality to concrete implementable variants by successive correctness-preserving refinements. In this paper, we propose a novel software product line engineering process based on a taxonomy-based domain analysis. The taxonomy's hierarchy provides guidelines for designing and implementing the product line's reusable artifacts while at the same time specifying possible configuration options. By deriving reusable product line artifacts from a software taxonomy, the well-defined structuring of the reusable artifacts yields improved maintainability and evolvability of the product line.

Keywords: Taxonomy-Based Software Construction (TABASCO) · Software Product Line (SPL)

1 Introduction

Modern software—in particular data-intensive, mobile or cloud-based applications—exists in many different variants in order to adapt to changing user requirements or environment contexts. Software Product Line (SPL) engineering [10] is a software development approach aiming at systematic reuse for a family

© Springer International Publishing Switzerland 2016
G.M. Kapitsaki and E. Santana de Almeida (Eds.): ICSR 2016, LNCS 9679, pp. 63–70, 2016.
DOI: 10.1007/978-3-319-35122-3_5

of related software variants from a common domain. An SPL comprises a set of software variants, which are software products with well-defined commonalities and variabilities. The SPL engineering process is split into a domain engineering and an application engineering stage (see Sect. 2). During domain engineering, the product variants that should be incorporated into the SPL are identified in a domain analysis phase. In the subsequent domain design and implementation phases, reusable core assets are developed from which the variants can be derived during application engineering. Existing approaches to domain analysis [10] in SPL engineering rely on a conceptual variability model—such as a feature model [9] or a decision model [12]—which only focuses on the different configuration options for the individual product variants. However, this model does not provide guidelines on how to structure the reusable core assets for the variants, such as source code.

Taxonomy-Based Software Construction (TABASCO) [3] is a method for systematic domain analysis aiming at providing a software taxonomy of a given domain. A taxonomy hierarchically structures the domain of a particular family of variants, usually data structures and/or algorithms. It forms a tree or directed-acyclic graph where nodes correspond to variants in the family. Edges connecting two variant nodes correspond to correctness-preserving refinements between variants and express the differences between those variants from a realization perspective. Intermediate nodes, especially those closer to the taxonomy root, tend to correspond to abstract algorithms, while nodes closer to the leaves correspond to concrete implementations. Nodes that are closer together are more similar than nodes that are further away from each other. A taxonomy provides guidelines on how to structure the implementations of different variants in the taxonomy. In TABASCO, taxonomies are used to structure the implementation of a toolkit, i.e., a library implementing the domain's algorithms and data structures as included in the taxonomy. Principally, TABASCO can bridge the gap between SPL variability models and the realization of variability in reusable artifacts, such as source code, because taxonomies can capture the set of reusable variants both from a conceptual and a realization perspective. However, taxonomies have not been used for domain analysis in SPL engineering yet.

We propose a Taxonomy-based Software Product Line Engineering Process (Tax-PLEASE) with the taxonomy as the first and central artifact resulting from domain analysis. The taxonomy-based domain analysis follows TABASCO [3], which provides a systematic approach to obtain taxonomies. From such a taxonomy, we derive a conceptual variability model in the form of a feature model [9] as part of domain analysis. For domain design and implementation, we derive the structure of the reusable realization artifacts from the taxonomy. This leads to clear engineering principles for obtaining reusable artifacts. Furthermore, these artifacts follow a more stringent structure, which leads to improved maintainability and evolvability of the resulting SPL. We illustrate our approach using the Forest FIRE taxonomy [4], which provides data structures and algorithms for analyzing tree structured data, including XML. The different algorithmic variants can be used in applications aiming at big data analysis of XML data.

The next two sections provide foundations on SPL engineering and on software taxonomies. Section 4 presents the conceptual ideas of the Tax-PLEASE process for SPL engineering. In Sect. 5, we review related work; Sect. 6 concludes the paper.

2   SPL Engineering

Software Product Line (SPLs) [10] are a large-scale reuse mechanism for closely related software systems. These systems are modeled as SPL consisting of common and variable parts. The configuration options for individual products are captured on a conceptual level within a *variability model*, e.g., in the form of a *feature model*, which arranges *features* (increments in program functionality) along a decomposition hierarchy [8].

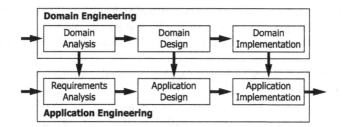

Fig. 1. SPL engineering process according to [10].

The development process of SPLs can be divided into two principal phases as illustrated in Fig. 1 [10]. The *domain engineering* phase builds and maintains the software family: The *domain analysis* identifies all sensible common and variable parts to capture them conceptually, e.g., in a feature model. The *domain design* creates a software architecture suitable for the SPL. The *domain implementation* realizes it by providing realization artifacts (e.g., source code) for all possible products of the SPL. Moreover, these two steps implement a *variability realization mechanism* for the SPL that can create realization artifacts for individual products of the SPL, e.g., by removing parts from source code that are not needed for the specified variant. The *application engineering* phase is concerned with creating individual products of the SPL: *Requirements analysis* collects user demands for individual software systems, *application design* determines the architecture of the system and *application implementation* realizes the system.

Domain engineering guides the design of the SPL in its entirety as well as the creation of individual products in application engineering, so that this phase is of utmost importance for the success of SPL. However, the standard development process provides little guidance on how to perform the tasks within the domain engineering phase, which may result in fundamentally different realizations of SPL with little regard to best practices in design. In this paper, we address this problem by using software taxonomies to guide the domain engineering phase of SPL development.

3   Software Taxonomies

Software taxonomies form a means of classifying software. Such algorithm taxonomies, in various shapes, have been used for decades [1,4,6,13]. In this paper, we consider algorithm taxonomies as they have been used in Taxonomy-Based Software Construction (TABASCO) [3].

A taxonomy hierarchically structures the domain of a particular family of variants, usually data structures and/or algorithms. It forms a tree (or more generally a single-rooted directed-acyclic graph) where nodes correspond to variants in the family. Such an algorithm taxonomy has a starting point, i.e., a root algorithm corresponding to a highly abstract solution to the algorithm problem at hand. Edges connecting two variant nodes correspond to *refinements* between variants and express the differences between those variants from a realization perspective. Intermediate nodes in the taxonomy, especially those closer to the taxonomy's root, tend to correspond to abstract algorithms, while nodes closer to the leaves correspond to concrete implementations. Nodes that are closer together in the taxonomy are more similar than nodes that are further away from each other.

To illustrate such algorithm taxonomies, we consider a relatively small example. Figure 2 depicts this taxonomy of *tree acceptance algorithms*, one of the Forest FIRE taxonomies [4]. Such algorithms allow determining whether a particular subject tree is part of a set of trees, called a *tree language*; in essence a type of *pattern matching* on trees. The taxonomy contains three main branches. The first one introduces the use of a tree acceptor—a finite state device for processing trees, similar to a finite state machine for string processing—, and then has variants that process trees from the leaves to the root (refinement FR) or vice-versa (RF). Such tree acceptors in principle are nondeterministic, but deterministic variants can be obtained (refinement Det). The middle root branch considers another view on deterministic leaves-to-root tree acceptors, based on the computation of so-called *match sets* per node of the subject tree. Here, various refinements can be applied to obtain different match-set based algorithms. The branch labelled S-Path contains algorithms that are based on decomposing a tree into strings uniquely encoding the tree, and then using string pattern matching techniques. The taxonomy and its corresponding toolkit (library) provide a family of data structures and algorithms for analyzing tree structured data, such as parse trees for natural languages, XML documents, or programming languages. These different algorithmic variants can be used in applications aiming at big data analysis of such tree structured data.

4   A Taxonomy-Based SPLE Process

The central idea of the taxonomy-based SPL engineering process, Tax-PLEASE (Taxonomy-based Product Line Engineering and Architecture of SoftwarE), which we propose in this paper, is to base the SPL engineering process on a taxonomy of the considered domain of product variants. This process is depicted in

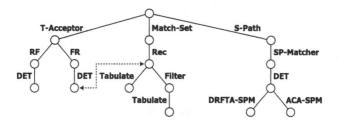

Fig. 2. Algorithm taxonomy graph of tree acceptance algorithms [4]. Branches are labeled by algorithm detail identifiers (i.e., refinements).

Fig. 3. The taxonomy is developed as the first and central artifact during domain engineering. It is used to derive a conceptual variability model (in the context of this work, a feature model) as part of domain analysis. Furthermore, the structure of the reusable artifacts that are developed in domain design and realized in domain implementation is derived from the taxonomy. The application engineering phase of the traditional SPL engineering process remains unchanged and relies on the artifacts that are produced during the taxonomy-based domain engineering phase. The following subsections provide details on how variability models and reusable realization artifacts are derived from the taxonomy.

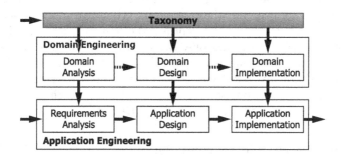

Fig. 3. Tax-PLEASE Engineering Process.

4.1   Domain Analysis

For domain analysis in Tax-PLEASE, we assume that a TABASCO-based taxonomy for the given domain exists. The derivation of a feature model from a taxonomy requires domain-knowledge and, hence, cannot be automated fully. In [11], we provided general guidelines on how to obtain a feature model from a taxonomy for transforming an existing taxonomy and toolkit into SPL. The same guidelines can now be used for developing a feature model from a taxonomy.

Candidates for features in the feature model are the refinements in the taxonomy as well as its core concepts. Core concepts might be different from the refinement operations, form separate clusters in the taxonomy, and need to be

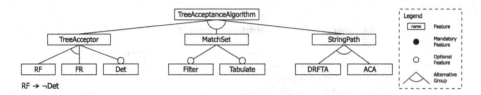

Fig. 4. Feature model for the Forest FIRE toolkit (cf. Fig. 2) [11].

identified by domain knowledge. The clusters are represented as alternative features on the first level of the feature model. The variability inside the clusters is captured as a sub feature-model of these features. The same process can be repeated recursively. For transforming refinements into features, refinements which are alternatives are also alternative features. Refinements in the taxonomy after a taxonomy node representing a concrete variant are transformed to optional features as there may be variants with and without this feature. Sequences of taxonomy nodes which do not correspond to concrete variants can be combined into one feature whose variability is determined from the starting point of the path. Constraints can be added to the feature model if certain feature combinations are not valid.

Figure 4 shows the feature model derived from the taxonomy shown in Fig. 2. In this example, the feature model structure mimics the taxonomy structure which, however, is not generally the case (cmp. [11]) as features represent configuration options while the taxonomy captures the structure of the family of variants. The refinements of the taxonomy can be transformed into features where alternative and optional refinements become alternative and optional features, respectively. Additionally, taxonomy nodes that do not correspond to concrete variants are combined into one feature, e.g., refinements Match-Set and Rec into feature MatchSet; and S-Path, SP-Matcher and Det into StringPath.

4.2 Domain Design and Implementation

In Tax-PLEASE, the design of the reusable realization artifacts does not follow immediately from the TABASCO-based taxonomy. Some choices still have to be made whose outcome may depend on the designer's experience and creativity. However, the TABASCO method [3] and the derived feature model make the task of domain design and implementation more straightforward. Different implementation language constructs [5] or design patterns [7] can be used to structure and realize the design of the reusable artifacts, depending on the type of commonality and variability of the variants present in the taxonomy.

For example, the different tree acceptor kinds in Forest FIRE are naturally presented by classes, with all such classes sharing an operation for computing acceptance (i.e. for executing the pattern matching), yet differing in algorithm, data structure etc. In Java, this is naturally represented by an interface defining the acceptance operation, with classes implementing this interface: classes

DFRAcceptor, NRFAcceptor etc. in Forest FIRE therefore implement an interface *IAcceptor*. (In C++, this would naturally be represented by using inheritance with virtual functions [5, p. 151].) As another example, in the match set branch of the taxonomy, the particular match set computation function used can encapsulate the use or absence of so-called *filtering* techniques; this corresponds to the use of the *Strategy* design pattern [5, p. 250], [7, p. 315].

By capturing the set of reusable variants from both a conceptual and a realization perspective, taxonomies and their derived feature models bridge the gap between the two perspectives and hence provide clear engineering principles for obtaining reusable artifacts. As evidenced by the examples given above, standard design techniques can be used to map the different types of commonality and variability to the implementation language level [5]. The resulting, stringently structured domain design ensures that the resulting SPL has improved maintainability and evolvability compared to those of a less principled, less stringent realization as typically used in SPL engineering.

5 Related Work

In SPL engineering, domain engineering aims to develop reusable core assets and application engineering applies them to build specific product variants [10]. Domain engineering requires domain analysis in order to determine which characteristics, i.e., commonalities and variabilities, the variants within the SPL have and which products should be included in the SPL [10]. The most prominent domain analysis approach in SPL engineering is Feature Oriented Domain Analysis (FODA) [9] where the commonalities and variabilities of the product variants are expressed by means of product features and their valid combinations, commonly expressed in feature models. Alternative approaches express the commonality and variability of the product variants in decision models [12] or orthogonal variability models [10]. However, these variability models focus on configuration options of variants, but do not provide a structuring of the artifacts developed in domain design and implementation. In this paper, we replace traditional configuration-only variability models as output of domain analysis with taxonomies which also guide the structuring of the reusable realization artifacts.

TABASCO [3] is an approach to domain engineering. Algorithm taxonomies have been around since at least Darlington's [6] and Broy's [1] work. Dijkstra's correctness-by-construction algorithm development style was applied in taxonomies of algorithms for garbage collection, attribute evaluation, and finite automata algorithms [2]. In [11], we considered an extractive SPL engineering approach for transforming a TABASCO taxonomy and toolkit into an SPL.

6 Conclusion

We presented the conceptual ideas for a taxonomy-based SPL engineering process, Tax-PLEASE. The central artifact of domain analysis in this process is a taxonomy of the variants included in the SPL to be developed. This taxonomy drives the development of a conceptual variability model, in this work a feature model, and guides the structuring of the reusable realization artifacts in domain analysis and implementation. In order to support large-scale software development and achieve industrial adoption, architectural concepts such as component-based modularization will have to be integrated with Tax-PLEASE, and appropriate tool support is needed. In order to evaluate applicability and scalability, we are planning on conducting real world case studies. Another topic of interest is whether agile development and Tax-PLEASE can be combined, using the reactive taxonomy-based SPLE techniques as mentioned in [11].

Acknowledgments. This work was partially supported by the DFG (German Research Foundation) under grant SCHA1635/2-2, by the NRF (South African National Research Foundation) under grants 81606 and 93063, and by the European Commission within the project HyVar (grant agreement H2020-644298).

References

1. Broy, M.: Program construction by transformations: a family tree of sorting programs. In: Biermann, A.W., Guiho, G. (eds.) Computer Program Synthesis Methodologies. NATO Advanced Study Institutes Series, vol. 95, pp. 1–49. Springer, Netherlands (1981)
2. Cleophas, L., Watson, B.W.: Applying and spicing up TABASCO: taxonomy-based software and how to increase its usability. In: Formal Aspects of Computing— Essays dedicated to Derrick Kourie, pp. 173–183, Shaker Verlag (2013)
3. Cleophas, L., Watson, B.W., Kourie, D.G., Boake, A., Obiedkov, S.A.: TABASCO: using concept-based taxonomies in domain engineering. S. Afr. Comput. J. **37**, 30–40 (2006)
4. Cleophas, L., Algorithms, T.: Two Taxonomies and a Toolkit. Ph.D. thesis, TU Eindhoven, April 2008
5. Coplien, J.O.: Multi-Paradigm DESIGN for C++. Addison-Wesley, Boston (1998)
6. Darlington, J.: A synthesis of several sorting algorithms. Acta Inf. **11**, 1–30 (1978)
7. Gamma, E., Helm, R., Johnson, R., Vlissides, J., Patterns, D.: Elements of Reusable Object-Oriented Software. Addison-Wesley, Boston (1995)
8. Kang, K., Cohen, S., Hess, J., Novak, W., Peterson, A.: Feature-Oriented Domain Analysis (FODA) Feasibility Study. Technical report, DTIC Document (1990)
9. Kang, K.C., Kim, S., Lee, J., Kim, K., Shin, E., Huh, M.: FORM: a feature-oriented reuse method with domain-specific reference architectures. Ann. Softw. Eng. **5**, 143–168 (1998)
10. Pohl, K., Böckle, G., van der Linden, F.J.: Software Product Line Engineering - Foundations. Principles and Techniques, 1st edn. Springer, Heidelberg (2005)
11. Schaefer, I., Seidl, C., Cleophas, L., Watson, B.W.: SPLicing TABASCO: Custom-Tailored Software Product Line Variants from Taxonomy-Based Toolkits. In: SAIC-SIT 2015, pp. 34:1–34:10. ACM (2015)
12. Schmid, K., Rabiser, R., Grünbacher, P.: A comparison of decision modeling approaches in product lines. In: VaMoS 2011. ACM (2011)
13. Watson, B.W.: Taxonomies and Toolkits of Regular Language Algorithms. Ph.D. thesis, TU Eindhoven (1995)

Business Aspects of Software Reuse

A Method to Support the Adoption of Reuse Technology in Large Software Organizations

Luiz Amorim[1(✉)] and Manoel Mendonça[2]

[1] Department of Computer Science, Federal University of Bahia, Salvador, Brazil
luizamamorim@hotmail.com
[2] Fraunhofer Project Center at UFBA, Salvador, BA, Brazil
manoel.mendonca@ufba.br

Abstract. The process of adopting a software technology in a large organization is significantly influenced by organizational culture and behavioral aspects of the practitioners involved in the process. The adoption of software reuse technology in particular significantly alters the software process of the organization as well as the modus operandi of the practitioners involved. The identification of factors that will facilitate or hinder this process is strongly correlated with the existing system of beliefs and represents a key element to the planning of this process. Our aim is to propose an action model based on classes of beliefs that will support the process of adoption of software reuse technology. An industrial case study was conducted in a large organization to validate and refine the proposed method. As a result, we propose a method based on the identification of classes of beliefs and re-signification of those that hinders the adoption of software reuse technologies.

Keywords: Adoption of software reuse technology · Software reuse beliefs · Reasoned action model · Beliefs system and knowledge · Re-signification of beliefs · Industrial case study

1   Introduction

The adoption of a new technology is an innovation process for the organization and is strongly related to organizational learning and directly interferes with its human resources. Organizational learning that integrates individual learning is a vital factor to increase the practice of innovation in organizations.

Technology adoption within software organizations involves cognitive and social aspects that permeate the engineers, team leaders, practitioners and users involved in the software engineering activities.

Beliefs are propositions or premises - or even a formed opinion or conviction - that an individual holds as true [51]. The basis of models referring to mental processes that affect people's behavior is their belief system. This beliefs system also significantly influences their position facing a change in an organizational process [42, 59]. Understanding belief system can significantly help to influence technology acceptance.

© Springer International Publishing Switzerland 2016
G.M. Kapitsaki and E. Santana de Almeida (Eds.): ICSR 2016, LNCS 9679, pp. 73–88, 2016.
DOI: 10.1007/978-3-319-35122-3_6

The adoption of reuse technology in a large organization significantly changes the software process of the organization as well as the modus operandi of the technicians involved. Thus, human and organizational obstacles often outweigh the technical obstacles in this context [4, 25]. Knowing and treating these obstacles is, therefore, an important step during the adoption of reuse technology, in order to minimize the risks of failure.

The goals of this research are expressed by answering the following research questions:

RQ1: What factors facilitate or hinder the adoption, acceptance, deployment and use practices of software reuse in a large organization?

RQ2: How do you to treat these factors to facilitate the process of technology adoption?

In this work, we developed a systematic way to identify and treat factors that facilitate or hinder the adoption of reuse practices in large software organizations. Our approach is based on the study of the underlining belief systems, from the practitioners involved in the process.

All our research is being developed through qualitative studies in an industrial setting, a software division of a very large organization. The acquisition and organization of knowledge through the use of empirical methods have become increasingly present in the field of software engineering enabling the understanding of various factors involved in the area, trying to make it more predictable and manageable [9, 55]. The use of an industrial organization setting is a key factor to improve external validity of empirical studies in software engineering [60]. This type of environment provides real processes, significant scale and realistic settings for studies. The use of qualitative methods is more suitable to this type of study and setting. The real world environment is more difficult to control and demands a more constructivist approach where data is collected by reviews and interviews, as opposed as, quantitative measures. In particular, we used an ethnographic approach where one of the researches was inserted in the studied environment during a major effort of reuse technology adoption.

The main contribution of this work is to present a method based on the identification of classes of beliefs to support the process of adoption of reuse technology in a large organization and a catalog of beliefs referring to the reuse technology. We use an approach of re-signification of beliefs that may represent a risk to the technology adoption process. The work is focused on the adoption of software reuse technology, but we also suggest how to extend the use of this method to help the adoption of others software technologies.

The rest of this paper is organized as follows. Section 2 presents an overview of the software reuse technology adoption problem and discusses the major cognitive models that represent the way people act. Section 3 presents the framework for our method and a Catalog of Software Reuse Beliefs'. Section 4 presents our ethnographic industrial case study, developed over two years, regarding the adoption of reuse technology in a large organization. Section 5 presents our conclusions and recommendations for future works.

2   Background

Society currently has knowledge as a rather significant value and the various technologies represent an important means to make this knowledge more and more useful and available, stimulating constant evolution and innovation in organizations [36]. Understanding the factors that interfere in the process of adoption of new technologies in organizations helps us to predict and manage this adoption process [41].

Straub [56] suggests three conclusions about technology adoption an diffusion: "(a) technology adoption is a complex, inherently social, developmental process; (b) individuals construct unique (but malleable) perceptions of technology that influence the adoption process; and (c) successfully facilitating a technology adoption needs to address cognitive, emotional, and contextual concerns".

New technology finds barriers in the organization such as incompatibilities with other technologies used, technical skills, resistance of people to change [28]. In general we see the great importance of the people, their beliefs and organizational culture in a process of technology adoption.

2.1   The Adoption of a Software Technology

The diversity and the growing need of organizations in adopting new technologies for the development and evolution of software, has led to a concern in better understanding the factors involved in the process of introducing these technologies.

Adopting a software technology in an organization requires different levels of learning, because it changes the skill of the practitioners and the organizational structure and procedures of the company. This requires the definition of strategies most appropriate to the organization's culture.

Technological changes in software processes should consider the human factor involved as a critical element to their success as well as some important aspects that affect the adoption of software engineering technologies as described by Punter et al. [47].

In this way we can obtain better support to understand, predict and modify human behavior to better plan and manage the process of adoption of technologies to facilitate its acceptance.

2.2   The Adoption of Software Reuse Technology

The introduction of software reuse technology in organizations has a very positive impact on issues of cost, productivity and quality of software [8, 20, 44].

The adoption of software reuse technology in an organization is costly in terms of time and resources. Failure in this process causes significant damage to the organization, including, with respect to its market share [23]. The transition from a traditional software development process to a process using the technology of reuse requires a great deal of change in the way the organization works and the behavior of practitioners involved [39].

Pietro-Diaz [45] proposed a model of incremental reuse of adoption to reduce the risk involved in the adoption process, emphasizing the importance of the organizational structure for successful adoption. We also found in the literature other significant work on the adoption of reuse among them we can mention [12, 14, 33, 34, 38, 48, 54].

As Griss [27] said, "Reuse is a business issue that involves technology transition and organizational change. Instituting a reuse culture, providing training, adhering to standards and securing management commitment, are the key success factors". Empirical studies by Morisio [38] in industrial organizations show that non-technical factors, such as organization, processes, business drivers, and human involvement, appear to be the most important factors for a successful reuse adoption process.

The human aspects are presented, [53] emphasizing the importance of empirical evidence to demonstrate their degree of influence as a factor to help or hinder the process. Human, organizational, managerial and economic obstacles often outweigh the technical and should be considered in each organization to ensure that the risks associated with them are properly handled.

2.3 Organizational Culture, Belief System and Knowledge

The organizational culture comprises the context in which software development takes place [32] and consists of beliefs, attitudes, values, norms, standards of behavior, customs, practices, symbols and organizational knowledge.

The adoption of new technologies adds new knowledge to the organization's culture which will iterate directly with the organization's belief system and with the belief system of its members. The learning of new thing requires a review and generally changes stable portions of the cognitive structure of people in organizations [6]. This is a very significant aspect of the process of adoption of new technologies.

To understand the process of change in the culture of organizations it is necessary to deal with the concepts of beliefs, belief systems and knowledge and their relationships. Beliefs are the elements that primarily determine the way people act and are the main barriers to the learning process and changes in organizations.

We found in scientific studies, the importance of beliefs as a determinant of the behavior of individuals and groups in different fields and in software engineering as we see in [32, 42, 59] among many others.

Belief is a proposition or premise or even an opinion formed or conviction that an individual holds as true [57]. This refers to the subjective probability of judging people on some aspect of their environment, focusing on the understanding of the person about oneself and the environment.

A belief system is a set of beliefs which guide and govern a person's attitude. Attitudes and beliefs in these systems are closely associated with one another and retained in memory [46]. Our belief system is the set of precepts which govern our thoughts, words, and actions.

Beliefs are formed from several different sources as our own experiences, observations, reads, hear things, reflections, generalizations, learning, advertising, acceptance of what is said by people who are references, influences of the environment. People often examine the captured information against evidence and facts and produce their inferences with a greater or lesser degree of analysis. Once are beliefs formed, changes in them are usually not made easily.

Knowledge has a philosophical definition that says it is the justified true belief in the "standard analysis" [18]. The adoption of a new technology in an organization implies a process of knowledge transfer changing the organization's belief system and the individuals who compose it. Learning is a process of growth of knowledge and takes place on a large scale during the adoption process.

2.4   Cognitive Models that Represent the Way People Act

Cognitive psychology is the study of mental processes such as "attention, language use, memory, perception, problem solving, creativity and thinking" [5]. Its focus is the mental processes that affect people's behavior. We selected some models that will be the basis for the model that we propose to support the adoption of new technologies.

In social psychology, we find three theories developed by Fishbein & Ajzen. The first, called the Theory of Reasoned Action - TRA [21] presents a model to represent the way people act. According to TRA, people construct beliefs about various personal, technological and environmental aspects, which may facilitate or complicate their attempts to adopt certain behaviors. The TRA suggests that beliefs, attitudes and intentions are the main determinants of human behavior, and there are additional elements such as knowledge, skills, and environmental factors.

The TRA has been extended, aimed to predict and explain human behavior in specific context, having been baptized as Theory of Planned Behavior-TPB [3]. The TPB beliefs can be of three types: behavioral, normative and control.

The two theories were consolidated [22] and called theory of behavioral prediction-TBP, where "human social behavior follows reasonably and often spontaneously from the beliefs people possess about the behavior under consideration". The authors present cases of use in various experimental studies and its uses were cited in over 1000 experiments.

In social cognitive perspective Bandura [7] proposes that the theory of self-efficacy has a central role in this context [7]. The concept of perceived self-efficacy is defined as people's beliefs about their capabilities to achieve certain levels of performance.

The growing diversity of software technology and the need to explain the acceptance or rejection of these technologies led to Davis's proposition Technology Acceptance Model -TAM [17] which determined three motivating behavioral factors: Perceived Ease of Use, Perceived Usefulness and Attitude Toward Using. TAM is an adaptation of the TRA version to emphasize characteristics of the behavior of users of computer technology. It was extended later to incorporate new features proposed for the evolution of the TRA and generated the TAM2 [57]. The third version of the TAM model called TAM3 was proposed by Venkatesh and Bala [58] by adding determinants of perceived ease of use (self-efficacy computer, perceptions of external control, computer anxiety, computer playfulness, perceived enjoyment and usability objective) which aims at making the process of adopting a new technology more precise.

The importance of the software teams´ beliefs system for the decision-making process in regards to new technologies is emphasized by Passos et al. [43].

3   A Method Based on an Action Model Reasoned on Classes of Beliefs to Support the Adoption of Software Reuse Technology

The model that we propose has a basic model, the theory of TBP-behavioral prediction [22]. This choice is a consequence of their conceptual scope and its wide range of use in experiments in various fields of knowledge.

The reasoned action approach of TBP provides theoretical support to understand, predict, and modify human behavior and plan how to implement interventions to change behavior.

We adapt this model to support the planning process of adopting a software technology in an organizational environment and use the models previously cited as support for the creation of classes of beliefs.

A belief generates an attitude (latent disposition or tendency to respond in a favorable or unfavorable degree to an object) which in turn produces an intention (promptness of a person to perform the behavior) which in turn determines behavior (observable acts that are performed by the person in question).

For the process of adoption of reuse technology, we can cite an example of chaining these elements by a practitioner of an organization. The belief "Technology reuse is complex and expensive", generates an intention "Resist the deployment of reuse technology" produces the behavior "Do not engage/hinder the execution of the tasks of adoption."

While investigating the beliefs system of software practitioners we can identify their latent intentions and consequently predict possible behaviors against the process of technology adoption (Fig. 1).

The model to support the adoption of software technologies proposed here is based on the four basic types of beliefs. The first three types of beliefs: behavioral, normative and of control were previously described in the theory of behavioral prediction-TBP. The fourth type is the beliefs of self-efficacy proposed by Bandura [7].

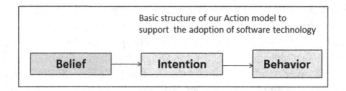

Fig. 1. Basic structure of our Action model

To structure the process of identifying the beliefs in the software technology area, we stratify each basic type of belief in a set of significant classes of beliefs to be mapped to support the adoption of new software technology. These classes of beliefs are identified from the literature review, relative to others models of acceptance of technologies presented in the next section.

3.1   Classes of Beliefs

Classes of beliefs are significant aspects related to software technology that guide the identification of beliefs of the software practitioners'. From an analysis of the various existing models in the literature mentioned above, we construct classes of beliefs by grouping the main aspects identified for each basic type of belief. In Fig. 2 we show our action model reasoned on beliefs classes.

The **Behavioral beliefs** are defined as "people hold beliefs about the positive or negative consequences they might experience if they performed the behavior" [22].

The **Normative beliefs** are defined "as people form beliefs that important individuals or groups in their lives would approve or disapprove of their performing the behavior as well as beliefs that these referents themselves perform or don't perform the behavior in question" [22].

The **Perceived Control Beliefs** are defined as "people form beliefs about personal and environmental factors that can help or hinder their attempts to perform the behavior" [22].

The **Self-efficacy beliefs** are defined as "people's ability to produce well-defined performance levels" [7]. Experience and abilities (lack or presence) are important to prevent/encourage people to take action.

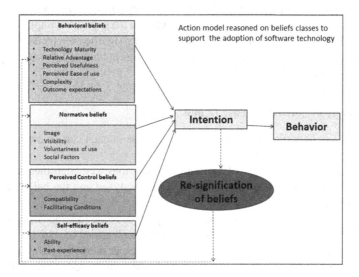

Fig. 2.   Action model reasoned on beliefs classes

3.2   The Re-Signification of Beliefs

The re-signification of beliefs, also cited in the literature as "change beliefs" or "beliefs revision" [16, 18], is defined as the process that leads the individual to assign new meaning to objects or events through a change of vision. Through it, the individuals learn to think differently about things, seeing new points of view or considering other factors as stated by Gardner [26]: "The key to change the mind is to shift the way a person perceives, codes, retains and accesses information".

Cognition involves the act or process of belief formation, acquisition of knowledge and reasoning. This process can be conscious or unconscious [18] being related to perception, memory and emotion. Techniques that encourage individuals to adapt or change their beliefs from the identification and awareness regarding false beliefs and elicitation of conflicting true beliefs are developed. The formation of new true beliefs and alignment of other beliefs with reality are stimulated, thus creating a process for enabling the acquisition of knowledge. Emotions, fear, anxiety and wrong perceptions often lead the individual to have defensive thoughts and false beliefs which make the process of re-signification a difficult task that requires the use of appropriate techniques for each type of situation.

The model identifies false, true and conflicting group of beliefs with the practitioners involved. Re-signification activities have to act mostly upon false individual beliefs.

The beliefs that cause difficulties in the adoption process or false beliefs related to new technology are the most frequent cause of misconceived knowledge [13] such as missing or incomplete knowledge or wrong knowledge. Other significant causes are past experiences in conflict with the new conception [16] and distorted perceptions of environmental factors.

For missing or incomplete beliefs, we seek to develop new beliefs through the provision of new knowledge. From false beliefs, we will use the explicit or implicit refutation to support belief revision. In our method, we can use re-signification techniques such as readings process, reflective process, discussion and presentation of cases and experience with alternative models [16].

3.3   A Catalog of Software Reuse Beliefs'

To identify the beliefs regarding the adoption of reuse in each class we use a research process that consists of three steps.

In step-1 review and analysis of literature, publications were identified and selected on the topic under study. These publications were analyzed and the beliefs presented were identified for each class of beliefs.

In step-2 were conducted interviews with experts in reuse in large companies, with the objective of validate and expand the list of beliefs identified in step-1.

In step-3, an ethnographic study was done in the process of adoption of reuse technology in a large company where the researcher sought to observe among the practitioners involved throughout the adoption process, existing beliefs and how those beliefs evolved.

A review and analysis of the literature was performed with the use of search engines with search strings defined to select articles, books and conferences on the subject. The selected publications were analyzed and marked the identified beliefs [1, 2, 10, 11, 15, 23–25, 29–31, 34, 35, 37, 38, 40, 48, 49, 52, 53].

These beliefs were consolidated and fairly categorized in their classes. A preliminary list of beliefs grouped in classes was produced, which was submitted to analysis and complementation by practitioner with reuse experience in the organization.

As a result of these steps, we present the Catalog of Software Reuse Beliefs with 68 beliefs, classified according to the model defined, presented below:

Behavioral beliefs
Technology Maturity
1. The reuse technology is mature.
2. The reuse technology has a well-defined development methodology of assets.

Relative Advantage
3. Reuse promises a quick time to market and a reduction in cost.
4. The cost of adoption of reuse technology is described as very high without significant short-term returns.
5. Managerial levels think the investment with reuse is accounted for indirect costs not directly related to application development.

Perceived Usefulness
6. Developers believe that reuse reduces the cost and time for the development of a new application.
7. Reuse would require a structured process for quality release of the assets which would slow down the development process.
8. The benefits of reuse will depend on the range of products the asset is planned to assist and the stability of the domains.
9. The lack of metrics for reuse makes it difficult to identify costs and benefits.
10. Managers react to implementation reuse due to lack of quantitative measures to assess the benefits and costs of their utilization.

Perceived Ease of Use
11. Reuse is difficult to implement in one organization.
12. The use of object orientation facilitates the creation of reusable assets.
13. The communication between creators and users of assets facilitates the adoption process.
14. The cost of developing a reusable asset depends on the technical competence of the staff in the methodology used.
15. The cost of developing a reusable asset depends on the quality of the development methodology used.
16. Developers believe that reuse increases the quality of a new application.
17. A systematic reuse process increases the developer's productivity.

Complexity
18. Building reusable assets and assembling them to build future systems is a complex activity.
19. Reuse technology is complex because it involves the identification, construction, and maintenance of assets availability.
20. Developers believe that reuse is an opportunistic "hunter/gatherer" process that depends on the cognitive abilities of developers to locate the right domains and components.
21. The use of assets of limited scope or wide scope requires excessive effort to adapt to the new context.
22. The excess of parameterization of assets requires a high investment in the testing process.

Outcome expectations
23. Developers are wary of the quality and performance of the assets to be reused.
24. The lack of reusable components to meet the future needs of a domain limits the success of technology adoption.
25. The lack of adequate assets documentation hinders and limits its use in the development process.
26. Software developer's belief that reuse will inhibit creativity: the "Not Invented Here" syndrome.
27. The evolution of the assets may create problems with older applications that use them.
28. Architecture of many levels that can be used in different applications is a critical factor for success of reuse implantation.
29. A Quality Management assets approach has a significant impact on the development process.
30. The quality of the assets is important to obtain the desired benefits such as defect/time reduction.

B. Normative beliefs
Image
31. To develop software with reuse is a positive differential for my company and for me as a professional.
Visibility
32. Participate in a project with reuse is a positive factor for my work in the company.
Voluntariness of use
33. I use the reuse technology voluntarily in my work.
Social Factors
34. The use of the technology reuse will facilitate my interaction with other technicians within and outside of my company.

C. Control Beliefs
Compatibility
35. The reuse activities have incompatibility with the methodology of software development organization.
36. The use of asset repository when it is not considered a critical factor of success breeds dissatisfaction with the use of technology reuse.
37. Elements such as the organizational structure of the reuse group and their way to work hinder the deployment of technology reuse.
38. The lack of an educational and training program/mentoring program is a complicating factor for reuse.
39. The organization is resistant to a structure required to support the reuse technology which makes the adoption process very hard.

(*) For reason of space we not show the others beliefs of the catalog.

4   A Industrial Case Study with Ethnography

The proposed method was applied in the process of reuse technology adoption in a large organization as a form of experimentation, refinement and validation of the results. To accomplish this task we used a qualitative multi-method procedure [19] with a main method, a long-term case study [50] conducted during a project of technology adoption in a large organization. We apply an ethnographic approach in this case study so as to be immersed in the everyday life of the project group.

4.1   Case Study Description

We conducted a case study on a project of adoption of reuse technology in a large company during 24 months where we investigated the beliefs related to reuse of existing technology among those involved in the project, its effects (strength and impact) in the process of adoption and means of re-signification to them to make the process more effective. To do this we used an ethnographic approach where we were involved throughout the project following and observing all the activities performed.

The organization has areas of software development in various locations in the country and this project of adoption was carried out in one of those areas that have around 250 practitioners involved in the process of development/evolution of software. The area of software development organization is certified ISO 9001:2008 and has an established and mature software's development and evolution process and a project management process based on PMBOK and SCRUM.

The focus of the project to adopt the reuse technology was one of the main business areas of the organization and was conducted with a description of the main business processes, evaluation of the organization's software development/evolution process, proposed modifications in this process and training of practitioner involved (22 technicians). Analysis of process software environment support to the business process was also performed to identify opportunities for reuse, business component identification, specification and implementation of some of these components.

The project was carried out through a consulting contract with a research/consultancy institution, having as the first phase (one year duration), the project definition, the domain analysis of the business area involved and the survey of the main software that provide support for the business processes and the mapping of software features, identifying potential features for reuse.

Eight existing software to support the business process were analyzed and their complexity was measured in function points (fp), where one fp is equivalent on average to 10 h of development effort. The software are presented below:

The organization's software development methodology was altered to incorporate the domain analysis practices (Table 1).

A quantity of 136 features were identified and used to create the application map at this stage. Upon completion of this phase, adjustments were made in the organization's software development process, previously adapted.

Table 1. - Software involved in project

Software	Complexity (in fp)	Technology Platform
P	2757	Java Open Source Tools
C	1719	MS.NET
G	1011	Java Open Source Tools
S	650	Java Open Source Tools
I	382	Java Open Source Tools
J	618	Java Open Source Tools
K	377	MS.NET
L	335	MS.ASP

The second phase of the project (one year duration) focused on defining the application architecture to support reuse, in accordance with the development frameworks Java and MS.NET which are used as standards for software development in the organization. The construction of reusable components adhering to this defined architecture was held. As in the previous phase, this phase was also started by a team training process, followed by adjustment of the organization's software development methodology to incorporate reuse practices.

A pilot was conducted with refactoring of software adequacy for the proposed architecture and use of components developed.

At the end of the phase, adjustments were made to previously adapted software development processes, as occurred in the previous phase.

The data collection involves semi-structured interviews, observation of meetings and project tracking, observation of the practitioners' behavior, observation of the work processes, and analysis of existing documents produced during the process.

Using the Catalog of Software Reuse Beliefs, the qualified beliefs of the practitioners were classified into four groups that should be treated according to the model.

We can summarize these results as:

(a) False Beliefs that can hinder the adoption process: 5
(b) True Beliefs with high impact that can facilitate the adoption process: 11
(c) True Beliefs with high impact that can hinder the adoption process: 7
(d) Conflicting beliefs of high impact: 4

The false and conflicting beliefs identified were separated to be worked first through the process of re-signification of beliefs. The true beliefs with high impact that can hinder the adoption process were managed/treated during the adoption process so that the negative effects on the process were neutralized.

4.2   Re-Signification of Beliefs Identified

The process of re-signification of beliefs was conducted through the use of various techniques. Two workshops, involving 40 technicians, one at the beginning of the project and the other half way through, presented practical cases employing reuse technology. In developing the work, those involved were encouraged to use the techniques, practices and conduct such as domain analysis activities as a means of supplementing the knowledge and encouraging reformulation of beliefs.

The work of revision and adaptation of the software process of the organization led the participants through a detailed reflective process of the technology operationalization approach. We observe how existing beliefs were discussed and adjusted/modified during the execution of the work. This led to a change of view that was confirmed in several follow-up meetings.

The re-signification process has as its first focus the false beliefs as we can see:

The belief 1 "The reuse technology isn't mature" and the belief 9 "The lack of metrics for reuse makes it difficult to identify costs and benefits" and the belief 4 "The cost of adoption of reuse technology is described as very high, without significant short-term returns" were re-signified through examples that showed the use of technology in various large organizations, associated with reading articles with reported practical experiences.

The belief 2 "The reuse technology has a well-defined development methodology of assets" was re-signified through the presentation of the methodology and its use in a pilot of analysis and domain implementation and validation of key components.

The belief 37 "Elements such as the organizational structure of the reuse group and their way to work hinder the deployment of technology reuse" was re-signified through the experience during the group work process in which it was to take responsibility for the parts certification process. This process was experimented in the pilot phase.

For reason of space we not show how other beliefs were re-signified.

Some specific cases of individual beliefs (false and conflicting) were objects of special treatment through conversation and discussion of practical situations that stimulated the technician to perform a critical analysis and review of their positions.

In some cases, declared true beliefs were abandoned during the execution of activities. This was verified through behaviors that skipped meaningful activities which leads us to believe that many beliefs do not always generate consistent behavior (matching) during execution of activities.

In the observation process we found some cases where the beliefs presented by a practitioner were conflicting with their behavior when performing actions. We can cite the case of a practitioner who believes in the modeling process and to implement decides to abandon the model and merge two different components to simplify the process. Another significant observation was the surprise of the technicians with the effectiveness of the technique of domain analysis for identification of components. This represents a practical case of practitioner's beliefs re-signification.

In this way we triangulated data from different qualitative sources: interviews and observations, document analysis and group meetings, project meetings which was important to corroborate findings from the case study and provide more reliable results.

The process of re-signification of beliefs occurred effectively during the whole process of adoption of reuse technology. Through observation and recording of conversations with the practitioner involved in the adoption process, we can validate the positive results of re-signification of the beliefs throughout the process.

The adoption process of reuse technology in the organization was successful and received many compliments from the practitioners involved. Practitioner particularly praised the way activities were developed and the form in which the project was conducted.

5   Conclusions and Further Works

In this paper, we presented a systematic way to identify and treat factors that facilitate or hinder the adoption of reuse practices in large software organizations. Our approach is based on the study of the underlying belief systems of the practitioners involved in the process.

The main contribution of this work is **an action model reasoned on classes of beliefs to support the adoption of software technology** where we present a structured method to guide the process of mapping the belief' systems of the practitioners involved in the process of technology adoption. Another contribution is a **catalog of the beliefs regarding the adoption of reuse** where we use the class of beliefs of the model, preceded by a literature review and an analysis of the publications identified, to map a set of beliefs for each class. This list was refined by interviews conducted with experts in reuse in large companies, with the objective of validating and expanding the list of identified beliefs. The set of beliefs was applied, refined and validated with a **long-term ethnographic case study done during the process of adoption of reuse technology in a large company**. The third significant contribution is a **method to capture, weigh and re-signify the beliefs of practitioners** involved in the process of adoption of reuse technology, where criteria have been proposed to prioritize beliefs to be submitted to a re-signification process. The method of treatment of the selected beliefs was described.

The answer to research question **RQ1** is presented through the **action model reasoned on classes of beliefs to support the adoption of software technology** and through the **catalog of the beliefs regarding the adoption of reuse** that complements the model to support the adoption of reuse in large organizations. The answer to research question **RQ2** is presented through the **method to capture, weigh and re-signify the beliefs of practitioners** where these beliefs are processed and properly classified so that all beliefs that cause difficulties to the adoption process are treated through specific re-signification techniques, involving specific groups and technicians.

A case study with ethnography was undertaken and through its description we show the application of the process and improvements to the method is proposed. Application of this method produced positive results in the adoption process of reuse technology in the large organization.

From the results presented in this work, we can identify several future research opportunities that complement this work or explore other aspects that have not been investigated here and have relevance for the field of software engineering. Thus, the points that can be investigated in the future are a catalog of the beliefs regarding the adoption of reuse based on expert opinion that is currently in the elaboration phase, the application of the method to support the adoption of software reuse technology in other large organization and the application of the action model reasoned on classes of beliefs to map the beliefs regarding the adoption of other mature software technology.

The results of this work show the growing importance of considering and treating human and organizational factors involved in developing and adopting new software technologies. This is because software technologies are always embedded in processes that significantly require the participation of the human element.

References

1. Ahmed, F., Capretz, L., Sheikh, S.: Institutionalization of software product line: An empirical investigation of key organizational factors. JSS **80**, 836–849 (2007)
2. Ahmed, F., Campbell, P., Lagharid, M.: Cognitive factors in software product line engineering. In: Proceedings of the UK Sim 2009, pp. 352–355. IEEE, USA (2009)
3. Ajzen, I.: The theory of planned behavior. Organ. Behav. Hum. Decis. Process. **50**(2), 179–211 (1991)
4. Almeida, E.: RiDE: The RiSE Process for Domain Engineering. Ph.d Thesis, Universidade Federal de Pernambuco, Brazil (2007)
5. American Psychological Association, Glossary of psychological terms, Apa.org. (2013). http://www.apa.org/research/action/glossary.aspx
6. Argyris, C., Putnam, R., McLain Smith, D.: Action Science: Concepts, Methods, and Skills for Research and Intervention. Jossey-Bass, San Francisco (1985)
7. Bandura, A.: On the functional properties of perceived self-efficacy revisited. J. Manage. **38**(1), 9–44 (2012)
8. Basili, V., Briand, L., Melo, W.: How reuse influences productivity in object-oriented systems. Commun. ACM **39**(10), 104–116 (1996)
9. Basili, V., Rombach, D., Selby, R. (eds.): Experimental Software Engineering Issues: Critical Assessment and Future Directions. LNCS, vol. 706. Springer, Heidelberg (1993)
10. Bastos, J., Neto, P., Almeida, E., Meira, S.: Adopting software product lines: a systematic mapping study. In: 15th EASE, Durham City (2011)
11. Bosch, J.: Software product lines: organizational alternatives. In: Proceedings of the 23rd ICSE, pp. 91–100. IEEE Computer Society, Washington, DC (2001)
12. Bongard, B., Gronquist, B., Ribot, D.: Impact of reuse on organizations. In: Proceedings of the Reuse 1993. IEEE Computer Society Press, Los Alamitos (1993)
13. Broughton, S., Sinatra, G., Reynolds, R.: The refutation text effect: Influence on learning and attention. American Educational Researchers, Chicago (2007)
14. Caldiera, G.: Domain factory and software reusability. In: Proceedings of the Software Engineering Symposium: New Frontiers for Software Maintenance (1991)
15. Catal, C.: Barriers to the adoption of software product line engineering. SIGSOFT Softw. Eng. Notes **34**, 1–4 (2009)
16. Chi, M.: Three types of conceptual change: Belief revision, mental model transformation, and categorical shift. In: Vosniadou, S. (ed.) International Handbook of Research on Conceptual Change. Erlbaum, Hillsdale (2008)
17. Davis, F., Bagozzi, R., Warshaw, P.: User acceptance of computer technology: A comparison of two theoretical models. Manage. Sci. **35**, 982–1003 (1989)
18. Douglas, N., Wykowski, T.: From Belief to Knowledge Achieving and Sustaining an Adaptive Culture in Organizations. CRC Press, USA (2011)
19. Easterbrook, S., Singer J., Storey, M., Damian, D.: Selecting empirical methods for software engineering research. In: Shull, F., Singer, J., Sjøberg, D.I.K. (eds.) Guide to AESE, Section III, pp. 285–311. Springer, London (2008)
20. Ezran, M., Morisio, M., Tully, C.: Practical Software Reuse. Springer, London (2002)
21. Fishbein, M., Ajzen, I.: Belief, Attitude, Intention, and Behavior: An Introduction to Theory and Research. Addison-Wesley, Reading (1975)
22. Fishbein, M., Ajzen, I.: Predicting and Changing Behavior: The Reasoned Action Approach. Psychology Press, New York (2010)
23. Frakes, W., Kang, K.: Software Reuse Research, Status and Future. IEEE Trans. Software Eng. **31**(7), 529–536 (2006)

24. Gacek, C., Knauber, P., Schmid, K., Clements, P.: Successful software product line development in a small organization. In: SPL: Practices and Patterns. Addison Wesley (2001)
25. Garcia, V., Lisboa, L., Meira, S., Almeida, E., Lucrécio, D., Fortes, R.: Towards a maturity model for a reuse incremental adoption. In: SBCARS (2007)
26. Gardner, H.: Changing Minds. Harvard Business School Publishing, Boston (2006)
27. Griss, M.: Software Reuse: Objects and Frameworks are not Enough. Object Mag. **5**(2), 77–87 (1995)
28. Hoffman, N., Keppler, R.: Assimilating New Technologies: The Role of Organizational Culture. Inf. Syst. Manage. **17**(3), 36–42 (2000)
29. Joanes, L., Northrop, L.: Clearing the way for software product line success. IEEE Softw. **27**, 22–28 (2010)
30. Knauber, P., Muthig, D., Schmid, K., Widen, T.: Applying product line concepts in small and medium-sized companies. IEEE Softw. **17**, 88–95 (2000)
31. Li, D., Chang, C.: Initiating and institutionalizing software product line engineering: from bottom-up approach to top-down practice. In: Proceedings of the 2009 33rd Annual IEEE ICSAC, vol. 01, pp. 53–60. IEEE Computer Society, USA (2009)
32. Livari, J., Livari, N.: The relationship between organizational culture and the deployment of agile methods. IST **53**(5), 509–520 (2011)
33. Lloréns, J., Fuentes, J.M., Prieto-Diaz, R., Astudillo, H.: Incremental Software Reuse. In: Morisio, M. (ed.) ICSR 2006. LNCS, vol. 4039, pp. 386–389. Springer, Heidelberg (2006)
34. Lucredio, D., Brito, K., Alvaro, A., Garcia, V., Almeida, E., Fortes, R., Meira, S., Software reuse: The brazilian industry scenario. JSS **81**, 996–1013 (2008)
35. Lynex, A., Layzell, P.: Organizational considerations for software reuse. Ann. Softw. Eng. **5**, 105–124 (1998)
36. Lytras, M., Pablos, P.: Software Technologies in Knowledge Society. J. UCS **17**(9), 1219–1221 (2011)
37. Mannion, M., Organizing for software product line engineering. In: Proceedings of the 10th International Workshop on STEP. IEEE Computer Society, USA (2002)
38. Morisio, M., Ezran, M., Tully, C.: Success and failure factors in software reuse. IEEE Trans. Softw. Eng. **28**(04), 340–357 (2002)
39. Muthig, D.: A Light-weight Approach Facilitating an Evolutionary Transition Towards Software product Lines. Ph.d. thesis, Universitär Kaiserlautern (2002)
40. Northrop, L.: Software product line adoption roadmap. Technical Note CMU/SEI-2004-TR-022, SEI (2004)
41. Partala, T., Saari, T.: Understanding the most influential user experiences in successful and unsuccessful technology adoptions. CHB **53**, 381–395 (2015)
42. Passos, C., Braun, A., Cruzes, D., Mendonça, M.: Analyzing the impact of beliefs in software project practices. In: ESEM (2011)
43. Passos, C., Mendonça M., Cruzes, D.: The role of organizational culture in software development practices: a cross-case analysis of four software companies. In: Proceedings of SBES 2014, Maceio, Brazil (2014)
44. Poulin, J.S.: The Business Case for Software Reuse: Reuse Metrics, Economic Models, Organizational Issues, and Case Studies. In: Morisio, M. (ed.) ICSR 2006. LNCS, vol. 4039, p. 439. Springer, Heidelberg (2006)
45. Prieto-Díaz, R.: Making software reuse work: An implementation model. ACM SIGSOFT Softw. Eng. Notes **16**, 61–68 (1991)
46. Psychology Dictionary (2015). http://psychologydictionary.org/
47. Punter, T., Krikhaar, R., Bril, R.: Software engineering technology innovation: turning research results into industrial success. JSS **82**(1), 993–1003 (2009)

48. Rine, D.: Success factors for software reuse that are applicable across domains and businesses. In: ACM Symposium on Applied Computing, USA, pp. 182–186 (1997)
49. Rine, D., Sonnemann, R.: Investment in reusable software. A study on software reuse investment success factors. J. Syst. Softw. **41**, 17–32 (1998)
50. Runeson, P., Host, M.: Guidelines for conducting and reporting case study research in software engineering. Empirical Softw. Eng. **14**(2), 131–164 (2008)
51. Schwitzgebel, E.: Belief. In: Zalta, E. (ed.) The Stanford Encyclopedia of Philosophy, Stanford. http://plato.stanford.edu/entries/belief/
52. Sharp, H.: Software reuse: Survey and Research Directions. J. Manage. Inf. Syst. **14**(4), 113–147 (1998)
53. Sherif, K., Vinze, A.: Barriers to adoption of software reuse A qualitative study. Inf. Manage. **419**, 159–175 (2003)
54. Sherif, K., Appan, R., Lin, Z.: Resources and incentives for the adoption of systematic software reuse. Int. J. Inf. Manage. **26**, 70–80 (2006)
55. Sjoberg, D., Hannay, J., Hansen, O., Kampenes, V., Karahasanović, A., Liborg, N.: A survey of controlled experiments in software engineering. IEEE TSE **31**(9), 733–753 (2005)
56. Straub, E.: Understanding technology adoption: Theory and future directions for informal learning. Rev. Educ. Res. **79**(2), 625–649 (2009)
57. Venkatesh, V., Davis, F.: A theoretical extension of the technology acceptance model: four longitudinal field studies. Manage. Sci. **45**(2), 186–204 (2000)
58. Venkatesh, V., Bala, H.: Technology acceptance model 3 and a research agenda on interventions. Decis. Sci. **39**(2), 273–315 (2008)
59. Wernick, P., Hall, T.: Can Thomas Kuhn's paradigms help us understand software engineering. Eur. J. Inf. Syst. **13**(3), 235–243 (2004)
60. Wohlinf, C., Runeson, P., Höst, M., Ohlsson, M., Regnell, B., Wesslén, A.: Experimentation in Software Engineering. Springer, Heidelberg (2012)

A Practical Use Case Modeling Approach to Specify Crosscutting Concerns

Tao Yue[1,2(✉)], Huihui Zhang[3], Shaukat Ali[1], and Chao Liu[3]

[1] Simula Research Laboratory, Oslo, Norway
{Tao,Shuakt}@simula.no
[2] University of Oslo, Oslo, Norway
[3] Beihang University, Beijing, China
{zhhui,liuchao}@buaa.edu.cn

Abstract. Use case diagrams together with use case specifications are commonly used to specify system requirements. To reduce imprecision, ambiguity, and incompleteness in use case specifications, an approach with template and restriction rules is often recommended to achieve better understandability of use cases and improves the quality of derived analysis models. However, when crosscutting concerns are modeled together with non-crosscutting concerns as use case models, resulting use case models often result in cluttered diagrams and redundant information in use case specifications. Therefore, the overall reusability of the use case models is usually low. To tackle this, we extend a general use case approach, named as RUCM, for modeling crosscutting concerns, along with a weaver to automatically weave aspect use case models into their corresponding base model to facilitate, e.g., automated requirements analysis. The extended approach has been evaluated with three real-world applications from communication, maritime and energy domains and aviation. We compared the modeling effort required to model three sets of crosscutting concerns from the real-world applications, when using and not using the extended RUCM approach. Results show that more than 80 % of modeling effort can be saved.

Keywords: Use case modeling · Reuse · Crosscutting concern · Aspect

1 Introduction

Use case models (UCMods) are widely used for specifying functional requirements of systems, which are generally text-based and contain ambiguity. To decrease such ambiguity, previously we proposed the Restricted Use Case Modeling (RUCM) methodology [19]. RUCM contains standard UML use case diagram notations, a use case template and a set of restriction rules for textual Use Case Specifications (UCSs).

Use case modeling of communication and control systems poses special requirements such as specifying the communication medium and its various properties (e.g., packet loss). Behaviors related to such properties are often redundant across use cases and if modeled directly with them can result in cluttered use case diagrams and redundant UCS fragments, thus making them difficult to comprehend and reuse. However, such behaviors are essential for specifying use cases, e.g., for robustness

© Springer International Publishing Switzerland 2016
G.M. Kapitsaki and E. Santana de Almeida (Eds.): ICSR 2016, LNCS 9679, pp. 89–105, 2016.
DOI: 10.1007/978-3-319-35122-3_7

testing [5]. Therefore, it is required to capture sufficient information in the UCMod such that this kind of analysis/testing can be facilitated. One possible way of facilitating such analysis/testing is to transform UCMods specified using our approach into other software artifacts (e.g., standard UML state machines or even aspect state machines [5]).

Inspired by Aspect-Oriented Requirements Engineering (AORE) [12] and also driven by needs of industry to deal with specifying crosscutting concerns, we extend our RUCM approach to support modeling crosscutting concerns, named as AspectRUCM. The AspectRUCM methodology comprises of the AspectRUCM profile (extending UML use case diagram notations) and a set of guidelines (formalized as a UML activity diagram) for applying the profile for specifying crosscutting behaviors.

Eliciting and identifying crosscutting behaviors or applying the AspectRUCM methodology to support other requirements engineering activities (e.g., requirements verification and validation) is not the focus of the paper. However, as the first step towards supporting automated analysis or generation (e.g., test cases), we need a formalization mechanism to model textual UCMods. We have already developed such a formalization mechanism: a use case metamodel referred to as UCMeta, in our previous work [20]. Based on it, we present a weaver to automatically weave aspect UCMods specified using AspectRUCM to their corresponding base UCMod.

Our work is evaluated with three real world applications and results demonstrate that AspectRUCM is applicable for real world applications. We also evaluated modeling effort required when using AspectRUCM and not using AspectRUCM to model three sets of crosscutting concerns of the three real-world applications. Results show that more than 80 % of modeling effort can be saved when using AspectRUCM.

The rest of the paper is organized as follows. In Sect. 2, we briefly discuss RUCM, UCMeta, and the running example used to illustrate our approach. The AspectRUCM methodology is discussed in Sect. 3. Section 4 presents the evaluation. Related work is presented in Sect. 5. The paper is concluded in Sect. 6.

2   Background

We present the running example in Sect. 2.1. In Sect. 2.2, we introduce RUCM. The metamodel of formalizing RUCM and AspectRUCM is presented in Sect. 2.3.

2.1   Running Example

We used a subsystem of a Video Conferencing System (VCS) as the running example, which has been used in our previous works [5]. Figure 1 shows that the VCS is responsible for sending/receiving multimedia streams, i.e., audio and video to a number of other Endpoints. The core functionality of such a VCS includes establishing/disconnecting audio/videoconferences and starting/stopping presentations in addition to audio/videoconferences. The other Endpoints have the similar functionality.

We group use cases into two packages corresponding to VCS or EndPoint. Both have the same set of use cases as they are equivalent communication end points. However, their implementations might be different, forming different products with the

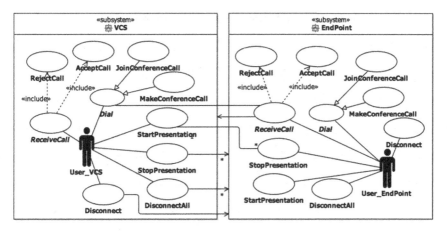

Fig. 1. Use case diagram of VCS

same functionalities. In Fig. 1, we have defined associations between use cases, e.g., *StartPresentation* of VCS with *StopPresentation* of Endpoint with cardinality 0 to many (*) on the *StopPresentation* side. This means when presentation is started on VCS, it stops the presentation of any other endpoint, which is currently presenting.

2.2   RUCM

There exist many requirements specification techniques, which are either fully formal or fully informal [16]. Use case modeling is widely applied in practice for specifying requirements specifications in a structured manner, which combines diagrammatic (use case diagrams) and textual descriptions (in a use case template) and offers an easy-to-apply and precise foundation for requirements specification.

We have previously devised a methodology named as Restricted Use Case Modeling (RUCM) [19] to reduce ambiguity and improve understanding of requirements, and facilitate automated analysis. Table 1 is an example of UCS documented with an editor implemented the RUCM methodology. Use case *Disconnect* contains one basic flow and two specific alternative flows. The two specific alternative flows are used to branch from the basic flow under specific conditions. RUCM specifies three different types of alternative flows. Specific and bounded flows indicate from which step in which flow of reference they branch whereas a global flow can branch from any step. For instance, the specific alternative flow in Table 1 branches from Reference Flow Step (RFS) 2 in the basic flow, and the condition for branching is the negation of step 2 of the basic flow. Restrictions to natural language take the form of keywords, such as VALIDATES THAT [19].

RUCM has been defined as the foundation of the Zen-RUCM framework [21], which is built on RUCM, and extends it for specifying test case specifications (RTCM) and transforming RUCM models to test case specifications [23], and generating

Table 1. Use case disconnect (specified in the RUCM editor)

Use Case Name	Disconnect
Brief Description	User disconnects an Endpoint participating in a conference call.
Precondition	The system is in a conference call.
Primary Actor	User_VCS
Secondary Actors	None
Dependency	None
Generalization	None

Basic Flow	Steps	
(Untitled) ▼	1	User_VCS sends a message to the system to disconnect an Endpoint.
	2	The system VALIDATES THAT Endpoint to be disconnected is in the conference call.
	3	The system sends a disconnection notification to Endpoint via Ethernet network.
	4	Endpoint sends an acknowledgement message back to the system via Ethernet network.	
	5	The system VALIDATES THAT The conference call has only one EndPoint.
	6	The system disconnects Endpoint.
	Postcondition	The system is idle.

Specific Alternative Flow	RFS 2	
"alt1" ▼	1	The system sends a failure message to User_VCS.
	2	ABORT
	Postcondition	The system is in a conference all.

Specific Alternative Flow	RFS 5	
"alt2" ▼	1	The system disconnects Endpoint.
	2	ABORT
	Postcondition	The system is in a conference call.

executable test cases from RTCM models [17]. In this paper, we report another extension of RUCM for specifying crosscutting behaviors (i.e., AspectRUCM).

2.3 UCMeta

UCMeta is the intermediate model in aToucan [20], used to bridge the gap between a textual UCMod and a UML analysis model (e.g., class and sequence diagrams). As a result, we have two transformations: from the textual UCMod to the intermediate model, and from the intermediate model to the analysis model. UCMeta can also be considered as a way to formalize textual UCMods and therefore the formalized UCMods can be used for automated analysis or test generation. Metamodel UCMeta also complies with the restrictions and use case template of RUCM.

UCMeta is hierarchical and contains five packages: *UML::UseCases*, *UCSTemplate*, *SentencePatterns*, *SentenceSemantics*, and *SentenceStructure*. *UML::UseCases* is a package of UML 2 superstructure [2], which defines the key concepts used for modeling use cases such as actors and use cases. Package *UCSTemplate* not only models the concepts of the use case template but also specifies three kinds of sentences: *SimpleSentence*, *ComplexSentence*, and *SpecialSentence*. In linguistics, a *SimpleSentence* has one independent clause and no dependent clauses [8]: one *Subject* and one *Predicate*. UCMeta has four types of *ComplexSentences*: *ConditionCheckSentence*, *ConditionalSentence*, *IterativeSentence*, and *ParallelSentence*, which correspond to four keywords (i.e., VALIDATES THAT, IF-THEN-ELSE-ELSEIF-ENDIF, DO-UNTIL, and MEANWHILE) that are specified in RUCM to model conditions, iterations, concurrency, and validations in UCS sentences. UCMeta also has four types of special sentences to specify how flows in a use case or between use cases relate to each other. They correspond to keywords RESUME STEP, ABORT, INCLUDE USE CASE, and EXTENDED BY USE CASE.

3 The AspectRUCM Approach

This section presents our AspectRUCM approach. Section 3.1 presents the domain model capturing main aspect concepts, Sect. 3.2 discusses the profile, Sect. 3.3 defines weaving directive interaction overview diagram, and modelling guidelines are presented in Sect. 3.4.

Table 2. Use *Case AdaptCallRate* (specified in the RUCM editor)

Use Case Name	AdaptCallRate
Brief Description	The system adjusts the call rate based on the quality of services of the network.
Precondition	Network connection is established.
Primary Actor	Timer
Secondary Actors	None
Dependency	EXTENDED BY USE CASE SelectedUseCases
Generalization	None

Basic Flow	Steps	
(Untitled) ▼	1	The system VALIDATES THAT the network is experiencing packet loss.
	2	The system gradually decreases conference call rate.
	Postcondition	The system is in a degraded mode.

Specific Alternative Flow	RFS 1	
(Untitled) ▼	1	ABORT
	Postcondition	The system is in a normal operation mode.

Our weaver is presented in Sect. 3.5. We used example of *AdaptCallRate* (Table 2) to explain the concepts.

3.1 Domain Model

A domain model for AspectRUCM is shown in Fig. 2. An aspect describes a cross-cutting concern, which in our context is a set of system requirements, which crosscuts another set of system requirements describing the main functionalities of the system. A joinpoint is a model element, which corresponds to a pointcut where an advice (e.g.,

use cases and actors in a use case diagram, and additional steps of flows of events, preconditions and postconditions in UCSs) might be applied. Theoretically, all model elements in UML use case diagrams and constructs of UCSs are possible joinpoints. However, we only define five types of joinpoints in

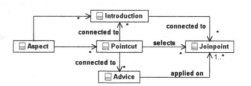

Fig. 2. Domain model

AspectRUCM: actors, use cases, preconditions, postconditions, and steps of flows of events, which are sufficient based on our experience of evaluating AspectRUCM with three real world case studies (Sect. 4.1). A pointcut selects one or more joinpoints with similar properties. A model element (e.g., actor) can be introduced in two different ways. It can be introduced to an aspect UCMod without being connected to any pointcut and it can also be connected to a pointcut through another model element.

3.2 AspectRUCM Profile

The profile diagram of AspectRUCM is provided in Fig. 3. An aspect describes a crosscutting concern and we specify stereotype «Aspect», which extends UML *Package*. «Aspect» has two attributes: *baseUCM* specifying the comma separated name(s) of the base UCMod(s), on which an aspect UCMod will be weaved, and the name of the aspect itself. We use a package to group model elements including use cases and actors to specify a crosscutting concern. For example, as shown in Fig. 4, package *NetworkDegradation* stereotyped with «Aspect» contains use case *Adapt-CallRate*, actor *Timer*, etc. Another example is provided in Fig. 5, where the cross-cutting concern *Standby* is modeled as an aspect UCMod. The *Standby* behavior of the VCS becomes active when it is idle for 5 min (a property of *Timer*). When any activity is performed by any actor of the system while it is in *Standby*, the system becomes active. One benefit of using a package to group model elements of an aspect UCMod, is that the model elements contained in the package and without stereotypes (from the AspectRUCM profile) applied are by default considered as elements newly introduced to the base UCMod. By not explicitly stereotyping model elements in an aspect UCMod reduces modeling effort (in terms of the reduced number of elements that could have stereotypes applied instead) and therefore results in less cluttered use case diagrams.

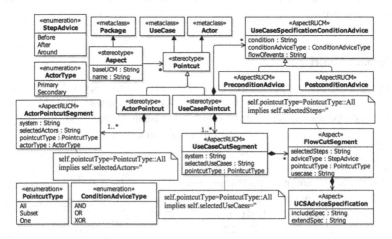

Fig. 3. Profile diagram of AspectRUCM

As shown in Fig. 3 an aspect UCMod might have one or more pointcuts. We specify two types of pointcuts in our profile: «UseCasePointcut» and «Actor Pointcut» specializing «Pointcut».

Use Case Pointcut. A use case pointcut selects one or more use cases of a system and the flows of events of the UCSs of the selected use cases. This is realized via the composition association between stereotype «UseCasePointcut» and class *UseCaseCutSegment*, which is further associated to class *FlowCutSegment* (Fig. 3). Class *UseCaseCutSegment* specifies the system where a selected use case belongs to (attribute system: String), a set of selected use cases (*selectedUseCases: String*), and the type of the pointcut (enumeration *PointcutType* and attribute *poincutType: PointcutType*), which can be selecting*All*, *Subset*, or *One* use case(s) of the system.

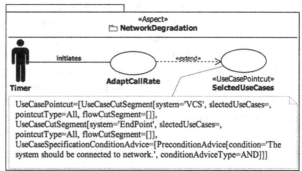

Fig. 4. Aspect use case diagram of *network degradation*

As shown in Fig. 4, we apply «UseCasePointcut» to use case *SelectedUseCases*. The values of the attributes of the stereotype show that we select all the use cases of the VCS and EndPoint systems. *AdaptCallRate* extends all the selected use cases and is triggered by *Timer* periodically. The example in Fig. 5 shows that this aspect introduces two new use cases (i.e., *Standby* and *ExitStandby*) by extending all the use cases of the two systems as indicated by the values of the attributes of «UseCasePointcut». Use case *Standby* is triggered by *Timer* and any actor of the two systems can trigger use case *ExitStandby* (via actor pointcut *SelectedActors*).

As shown in Fig. 3, *UseCasePointcut* should have at least one *UseCaseCutSegment*. A *UseCaseCutSegment* is composed of zero to many *FlowCutSegments*, which specify the selected steps of the flows of events of a selected use case (*selectedSteps: String*), where *Before, After,* or *Around* advice (*adviceType: StepAdvice*) should be applied. This part of the pointcut should also indicate the type of the pointcut: selecting *All, Subset,* or *One* step of a UCS, and the step sentence to be introduced through advice (*adviceSpec: UCSAdviceSpecification*). Note that it is possible that a *UseCaseCutSegment* does not contain any *FlowCutSegment* when there is no need to get into the UCS level. When the pointcut type of a *UseCaseCutSegment* or *FlowCutSegment* is *PointcutType::All*, then there is no need to specify attribute *selectedUseCases* of metaclass *UseCaseCutSegment* or attribute *selectedSteps* of class *FlowCutSegment*. This constraint is formalized as the OCL expression attached to metaclass *UseCaseCutSegment* (Fig. 3). For example, as shown in Fig. 5, the use case pointcut *SelectedUseCases* consists of two *UseCaseCutSegment*s: one is to select all the use cases of the VCS system and the other is to select all the use cases of the EndPoint system. In these two *UseCaseCutSegments*, no *FlowCutSegment* is specified.

If there is no UCS specified for a newly introduced use case in the aspect UCMod or if the aspect UCMod does not need to get into the level of UCSs, the use case is weaved into the base use case diagram through three different types of relationships of use case diagrams: *Extend*, *Include*, *Generalization*, which are explicitly captured in the use case diagram of the aspect UCMod. However, the use case pointcut should also specify the steps of the selected use cases (via use case pointcut) where the newly introduced use case should extend or be included. This is realized by *FlowCutSegment* and *UCSAdviceSpecification* of *UseCasePointcut*. Attributes *includeSpec* and *extendSpec* of class *UCSAdviceSpecification* specify two sentences: *INCLUDE USE CASE <name of the newly introduced use case>* and *EXTENDED BY USE CASE <name of the newly introduced use case>*. During weaving, these two sentences should be added before, after the selected steps of *FlowCutSegment*, or replace existing ones, through *Before*, *After* or *Around* advice. For the cases when the selected use cases extend or are included by a newly introduced use case in the aspect UCMod, the inclusion and extension points are however specified in the newly introduced use case and therefore no extra information is required in the point cut specification.

We specify a special type of advice *UseCaseSpecificationConditionAdvice*, with two sub-types: *PreconditonAdvice* and *PostconditionAdvice*, to introduce precondition and postcondition sentences to the selected UCSs. The introduced sentences can be weaved with the ones of the base UCSs in three different ways: *AND*, *OR* and *XOR*, which are defined as the enumeration *ConditionAdviceType* as shown in Fig. 3. As shown in Fig. 4, the use case pointcut has one *PreconditionAdvice* with condition "The system should be connected to network". This precondition sentence should be weaved to the preconditions of the UCSs of the use cases selected by the use case pointcut, via a conjunction, which is indicated by assigning "AND" to attribute *conditionAdviceType: ConditionAdviceType* of *UseCaseSpecificationConditionAdvice*.

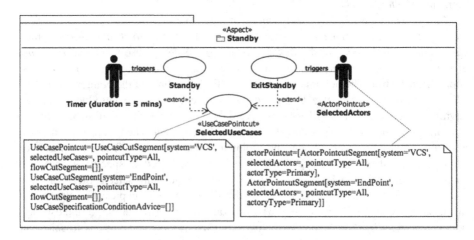

Fig. 5. Aspect use case diagram of *Standby*

Actor Pointcut. An actor pointcut selects one or more actors and consists of one or more *ActorPointcutSegment*s, which specify the system that the actor belongs to, the selected actors, and the pointcut type. In Fig. 5, actor *SelectedActor*s is stereotyped with «ActorPointcut». The values of its attributes show that all the actors of the two systems are selected. Same as for *UseCaseSegment*, if an *ActorPointcutSegment* has *poincutType* as *PointcutType::All*, there is no need to specify *selectedActors*. Note that, there are two types of actors: *Primary* and *Secondary*, as shown in enumeration *ActorType*, which makes it easier to specify actor pointcut expressions. For instance, the actor pointcut selects all the primary actors of the base UCMod (Fig. 5).

3.3 Definition of Weaving Directive Specification

Each crosscutting concern is specified as a separate aspect UCMod. Aspect UCMods of multiple crosscutting concerns should be weaved into their corresponding base UCMod in a specific order to ensure that the woven UCMod is correct. To achieve this, an ordering must be defined and provided to the weaver as an input. However, UML use case diagram does not provide such a capability. We therefore choose to use the UML interaction overview diagram notations to specify such orderings, denoted as weaving-directive interaction overview diagrams.

UML interaction overview diagrams define interactions through a variant of Activity Diagrams, in a way that promotes overview of the control flow [2]. Weaving-directive interaction overview diagrams contain interaction uses representing and referencing to all aspect UCMods, ordered using UML activity diagram's flow control features such as decision, join, and fork. Of course, UML activity diagrams can equally perform the same functionality. Choosing UML interaction overview diagram notations instead of activity diagram notations is simply because the former is simpler than the later since interaction overview diagrams abstract away *Messages* and *Lifelines* and therefore the approach would be easier to be accepted in practice.

A weaving-directive interaction overview diagram contains the following model elements: (1) An initial activity node; (2) A set of interaction uses, each of which refers to an aspect UCMod; and (3) A set of control flow edges that can be of any of the following two types: a control flow edge from the initial activity to an interaction use representing the first aspect UCMod to weave, and a set of control flow edges connecting interaction uses (e.g., decision, join and fork) to show the order in which the interaction uses (aspect UCMods) will be weaved into the base UCMod.

3.4 Modeling Guidelines

The AspectRUCM profile (Sect. 3.2) provides a notation to specify crosscutting concerns as aspect UCMods (Sect. 2.3). Before applying AspectRUCM, crosscutting concerns have to be first identified at the requirements level (activity *A1*), as shown in Fig. 6. Different approaches (e.g., [15]) can be used for this purpose. Our AspectRUCM approach can be used in conjunction with these existing works. However, we do not discuss this further in this paper as it is out of the scope of this paper.

Core concerns of the system are specified using RUCM (activity *A2*), leading to the creation of *Base UCMod*. Followed by *A2*, *A3* specifies crosscutting concerns using the AspectRUCM profile, which includes sub-activities of creating a UML package stereotyped with «Aspect», then specifying pointcut(s) and creating other model elements of the use case diagram (e.g., actors, use cases), and finally specifying UCSs of the introduced use cases in the aspect UCMod using the RUCM template. The output of this activity is a set of *Aspect UCMods* created for each identified crosscutting concern. Activity *A4* specifies the weaving ordering and outputs the weaving directive interaction overview diagram.

Aspect UCMods (from *A3*) are weaved into their corresponding *Base UCMod* (from *A2*), based on the weaving ordering specified in the interaction overview diagram (from *A4*), to automatically generate a woven UCMod (A5), which can be used to facilitate automated analyses (*A6*) such as requirements analyses, automated creation of analysis and design models, and automated derivation of test cases. It is sometimes more effective to perform various requirements analyses (e.g., identifying and managing conflicts and tradeoffs among concerns [9]) based on the same woven UCMod, instead of separate aspect UCMods and the base

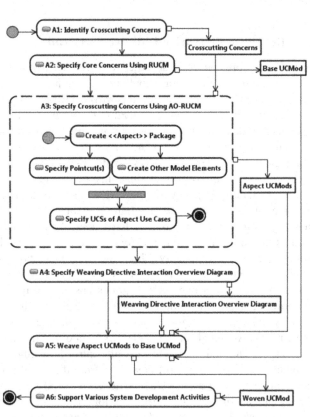

Fig. 6. Guidelines for applying AspectRUCM

UCMod. Based on [20], automated transition from the woven UCMod to different UML diagrams can be supported. If the derivation or generation of downstream artifacts (e.g., test cases) relies on the transformation from an AOM approach at the requirements level (e.g., AspectRUCM) to another AOM approach at the design or testing level (e.g., AspectSM [5]), there is no point to perform weaving at the requirements level and hence activities *A4*, *A5* and *A6* are unnecessary.

3.5 Weaver

Aspect UCMods are weaved into their base UCMod by a weaver, which reads the base and aspect UCMods and the weaving-directive interaction overview diagram, and produces a woven UCMod. We developed a weaver for AspectRUCM using Java to weave one or more aspect UCMods into a base UCMod. Aspect UCMods are specified in AspectRUCM (Sect. 3.2). A base UCMod is modeled using RUCM.

Due to the reason that UCSs of both the base and the aspect UCMods are textual, all of them have to be formalized such that weaving can be performed. Therefore, the weaver has a formalization engine, which contains a set of transformation rules transforming textual UCMods into instances of UCMeta (Sect. 2.3). The aspect UCMods are formalized into instances of extended UCMeta with AspectRUCM while the base UCMod is transformed into an instance of UCMeta. UCMeta and its extension are implemented as an Ecore model, using Eclipse EMF [1]. We also use the Stanford Parser [3] as a NL parser for the transformation of textual sentences in UCSs to instances of UCMeta. The parser is written in Java and generates a syntactic parse tree for a sentence and the sentence's grammatical dependencies (e.g., subject, direct object). It is important to notice that it is not necessary to have the transformation from UML use case diagrams (either with or without the AspectRUCM profile applied) to instances of the *UML::UseCases* package of UCMeta (Sect. 2.3), as UCMeta directly imports the *UML::UseCases* package and the AspectRUCM profile.

The weaver takes the formalized aspect and base UCMods and the weaving-directive interaction overview diagram as inputs and generates a woven UCMod, which is an instance of UCMeta. The automatically generated woven UCMod can be used as an input for further analysis (e.g., automated requirements verification and validation) or generation (e.g., generating UML analysis models). Currently our approach and its weaver do not support modeling and weaving interactions that may occur between different aspects and will be investigated in the future.

4 Evaluation

Section 4.1 presents the three case studies, Sect. 4.2 discusses how AspectRUCM reduces modeling effort, and Sect. 4.3 summarizes evaluation results.

4.1 Case Studies

We used three case studies from the telecommunication domain, the maritime and energy sector and the aviation domain: VCS, Subsea Oil Production System (SOPS) and Navigation System (NAS). Table 3 presents the characteristics of their UCMods.

VCS. VCS contains four systems/endpoints with same functionality (e.g., call, presentation) modeled as the same set of use cases. Each endpoint has 10 use cases and in total 40 use cases per system. A timer periodically initiates the adaption of the call rate. The following eight crosscutting concerns are specified using AspectRUCM: *Network Degradation, Standby, Media Quality Recovery, Do Not Disturb, Synchronization*

Table 3. Characteristics of Base and Aspect UCMods

System	# of Base Use Case	Total # of UCSs	# of Aspect UCMods	# of Actors
VCS	40	10	8	5
SOPS	65	12	6	9
NAS	46	11	7	9

Mismatch, Intelligent Packet Loss Recovery, Echo Reduction, and *Noise Cancellation* based on our previous work [5].

SOPS. SOPSs are systems of systems for managing the exploitation of oil and gas production fields. SOPS has four different types of systems, three of which are located above the sea level and the other is located in subsea. These systems have distinct functionalities and are connected through different types of communication media. We modelled 12 out of 65 representative use cases were specified for our evaluation. We modeled six crosscutting concerns using AspectRUCM: *Operation Mode Exchange, Backup Communication, Communication Timeout, Runtime Configuration, Communication Bandwidth Limiting*, and *Data Update Mechanism Switch*.

NAS. NAS [22] controls and guides an aircraft, based on control law computation that takes data sampled from sensors as input and sends commands to actuators. NAS has two operating modes: Auto mode and Manual mode and a pilot can switch the modes during flight. To ensure safe operation, NAS is fault tolerant with a redundant design. At the end of each clock cycle, redundant inputs from sensors are given to the autopilot system and multiple computation methods produce redundant outputs to be voted. There are many periodical tasks in the system and the system period is set as 20 ms—the minimal one among the periods of all the tasks (with periods as 20 ms, 40 ms or 60 ms). We specified the following seven crosscutting concerns using AspectRUCM: *System Synchronization, Flight Mode Exchange, Periodical Action, Data Monitoring, Data Voting, Fault Handling*, and *Communication Timeout*.

Notice that both VCS and SOPS have eight common network abnormal use cases since both of these systems employ the same type of Ethernet communication medium. VCS has two extra abnormal use cases, which are specific to video conferencing protocols, i.e., H323 and SIP.

4.2 AspectRUCM Evaluation

One way of evaluating if AspectRUCM reduces modeling effort is to estimate modeling effort through a surrogate measure, e.g., as the number of modeling elements required to be modeled. This number can then be compared in aspect UCMods and RUCM UCMods when modeling crosscutting concerns. Table 4 summarizes the modeling tasks involved when using and not using AspectRUCM for modeling three sets of crosscutting concerns from the three case studies. We do not count modeling effort required to specify UCSs and only focus at the level of use case diagrams.

For the VCS case study, we have eight crosscutting concerns, which are described in Sect. 4.1. When we used AspectRUCM to model these eight crosscutting concerns, we significantly reduced modeling effort for modeling relationships between use cases

(95 % (= 420/440) on average, see Table 4). In other words, for all the eight cross-cutting concerns together, we modeled 20 relationships when using AspectRUCM, whereas we need to model 440 relationships without using AspectRUCM. In terms of actors, using AspectRUCM we modeled 10 actors in all eight crosscutting concerns, whereas we modeled 8 actors without using AspectRUCM. For use cases, we modeled 19 use cases using AspectRUCM for all eight crosscutting concerns together, whereas we modeled 11 use cases when not using AspectRUCM. Considering that modeling effort for an actor, use case, and a relationship is roughly equal, for all eight cross-cutting concerns together, we modeled 459 modeling elements without using Aspec-tRUCM, whereas with AspectRUCM we modeled only 49 modeling elements. This means on average we saved 89 % of modeling effort in our case studies.

Table 4. Evaluation results of the three case studies

Case Study	Crosscutting concerns	Using AspectRUCM					Without AspectRUCM				Effort saved (%)
		UCs	Actors	Rels	Pointcut	Total	UCs	Actors	Rels	Total	
VCS	1	2	1	2	1	6	1	1	40	42	86 %
	2	3	2	4	2	11	2	1	80	83	87 %
	3	3	1	2	1	7	2	1	80	83	92 %
	4	3	2	4	1	10	2	1	80	83	88 %
	5	2	1	2	1	6	1	1	40	42	86 %
	6	2	1	2	1	6	1	1	40	42	86 %
	7	2	1	2	1	6	1	1	40	42	86 %
	8	2	1	2	1	6	1	1	40	42	86 %
	Total	19	10	20	9	58	11	8	440	459	87 %
SOPS	1	3	1	4	1	9	2	1	78	81	89 %
	2	3	2	6	2	13	2	1	56	59	78 %
	3	2	1	2	1	6	1	1	48	50	88 %
	4	2	1	2	1	6	1	1	12	14	57 %
	5	3	2	6	2	13	2	1	47	50	74 %
	6	3	1	4	1	9	2	0	25	27	67 %
	Total	16	8	24	8	56	10	5	266	281	80 %
NAS	1	2	2	4	1	9	1	2	42	45	80 %
	2	2	1	2	1	6	1	1	14	16	62 %
	3	5	3	6	2	16	3	3	74	80	80 %
	4	2	3	2	1	8	1	2	48	51	84 %
	5	2	3	2	1	8	1	2	50	53	85 %
	6	3	1	2	1	7	2	1	46	49	86 %
	7	3	3	4	2	12	2	3	62	67	82 %
	Total	19	16	22	9	66	11	14	336	361	82 %

With AspectRUCM, we needed to model pointcuts for all crosscutting concerns. In total, we modeled 10 pointcuts (Table 4) for VCS and modeling these pointcuts is the additional modeling effort required in AspectRUCM. In conclusion, modeling 10 pointcuts can save us modeling 410 modeling elements. We assume that the modeling effort of 10 pointcuts is less than modeling 410 modeling elements and thus modeling effort using AspectRUCM can be reduced. For SOPS/NAS, we modeled 6/7 cross-cutting concerns. Similar to VCS, as one can observe from Table 4, using Aspec-tRUCM significantly reduced the modeling effort equivalent to 80 %/82 %.

Overall, results on the three case studies seem to suggest that the modeling effort can be significantly reduced when using AspectRUCM for modeling crosscutting concerns. Since using AspectRUCM requires the modeling of use case pointcuts and actor pointcuts with the «UseCasePointcut» and «ActorUseCasePoint» stereotypes, there will only be a benefit if modeling, more than 80 % additional relationships on a UCMod is more time-consuming than modeling few pointcuts. Though this seems to be likely, it would need to be confirmed via controlled experiments involving human designers to determine the actual percentage of modeling effort saved when using AspectRUCM. In addition, modeling crosscutting concerns as aspect UCMods keeps the base UCMod less cluttered; hence, they are easier to read and maintain, and support reuse, as crosscutting concerns are modeled separately from the base ones.

4.3 Empirical Evaluation of RUCM

AspectRUCM extends use case diagrams, but has no extensions to the RUCM template and no new restrictions introduced. Hence, in terms of describing UCSs, AspectRUCM should be exactly the same as RUCM. In our previous work [19], we have conducted two controlled experiments to evaluate RUCM in terms of its applicability and impact on the quality of manually derived UML analysis models. Experiment results [19] show that RUCM is easy to apply and RUCM results into significant improvements over traditional approaches in terms of the quality of derived class and sequence diagrams. These two controlled experiments particularly focus on the evaluation of the RUCM template and the restriction rules; therefore we can conclude that the evaluation results for RUCM are also applicable to AspectRUCM.

However, as discussed in Sect. 3.2, the AspectRUCM profile is introduced to extend the use case diagram notations and it should be evaluated to test its applicability and other benefits similar to other aspect-oriented modeling approaches such as enhanced separation of concerns, improved maintainability, reusability and under-standability. In the future, we plan to conduct empirical studies for further evaluation.

5 Related Work

It is a common practice to follow a template to structure UCSs, thereby helping their reading and reviewing. Various templates (e.g., [6]) have been suggested to satisfy different application contexts and purposes. These templates share common fields such as: use case name, brief overall description, precondition, postcondition, basic flow, and alternative flows. The systematic review [18] we conducted to examine literature that transform textual requirements into analysis models revealed that six approaches require use cases (e.g., [14]). RUCM was built on the state of art.

An aspect-oriented use case modeling approach was proposed in [7] to connect advice use cases to base ones through a relationship stereotyped with a newly proposed stereotype «Aspect». A grammar is proposed to specify pointcut expressions based on wildcards in steps of flows of events of use cases. Four types of advices are specified: before, after, around, and concurrent. The approach does not directly introduce aspect to use case diagrams and therefore there is no graphical notation reused from use case diagrams or newly introduced. Aspect use cases are weaved with their corresponding base use cases into a petri net model, which is used as an input for further analysis. We however extend UML use case diagrams by reusing their inherent graphical notations with limited extensions via UML stereotypes.

Jacboson and Ng proposed an aspect-oriented use case modeling approach [10], by extending the meaning of extension points as joint points. With it, the base model has to be modified by inserting textual sentences of extension points directly to the UCSs of the Pointcut use cases of the base UCMod. If there are more than one Pointcut use cases (most probably the case in the context of AOM), more than one places of the UCSs of these Pointcut use cases have to be modified. This implies that this approach does not really separate aspects from their base. The approach has only one type of Advice: the extension behavior specified in an aspect use case as the whole.

Sillito et al. [13] proposed a textual aspect language called AspectU, to support modularization of crosscutting concerns in UCMods. AspectU aspects are then transformed into AspectJ implementation. AspectU is purely textual and very similar to programming languages. AspectRUCM relies on the inherent graphical notations of UML use case diagrams. Therefore, in terms of usability, AspectRUCM should be easier to understand and apply for engineers, especially requirements engineers.

Mussbacher et al. [11] proposed an aspect-oriented requirements modeling approach with use case maps. In this approach, advice and pointcut are both captured using the use case map inherit graphical notations. Several works on adding aspect concepts to goal models (e.g., [4]) have been also proposed. Other aspect oriented modeling approaches (e.g., [5]) have been proposed at different levels of abstraction of a software development lifecycle than UCMods.

6   Conclusion

Use case modeling is commonly used for capturing functional requirements. However, use case specifications (UCSs) are text-based having ambiguity. This paper proposed an extension of RUCM (a generic use case approach), named as AspectRUCM, to model crosscutting concerns at the level of use case models to alleviate its complexity. AspectRUCM is a UML profile to support the modeling of crosscutting concerns as aspects in use case diagrams and UCSs. We performed and reported on three real world case studies, which suggest that using AspectRUCM results in reducing on average more than 80 % modeling effort.

Acknowledgement. This work was supported by the MBT4CPS project (No. 240013) funded by the Research Council of Norway under the category of Young Research Talents of the FRIPO funding scheme. Tao Yue and Shaukat Ali are also supported by the Zen-Configurator project (No. 240024), the EU Horizon 2020 project U-Test (http://www.u-test.eu/), the MBE-CR (No. 239063) and the Certus SFI.

References

1. Eclipse EMF. https://eclipse.org/modeling/emf/
2. OMG. UML2.2. http://www.omg.org/spec/UML/2.2/Infrastructure/PDF/
3. The Stanford Parser version 1.6. http://nlp.stanford.edu/software/lex-parser.shtml
4. Alencar, F., Moreira, A., Castro, J., Silva, C., Mylopoulos, J.: Using aspects to simplify iModels. In: 14th IEEE International Conference on Requirements Engineering, pp. 335–336. IEEE, Minneapolis/St. Paul, MN (2006)
5. Ali, S., Briand, L.C., Hemmati, H.: Modeling robustness behavior using aspect-oriented modeling to support robustness testing of industrial systems. Softw. Syst. Model. **11**(4), 633–670 (2012)
6. Alistair, C.: Writing Effective Use Cases. Addison-Wesley, Boston (2001)
7. Anthonysamy, P., Somé, S.S.: Aspect-oriented use case modeling for software product lines. In: EA-AOSD 2008, p. 5. ACM (2008)
8. Brown, E.K., Brown, K., Miller, J.: Syntax: A Linguistic Introduction to Sentence Structure. Psychology Press, Abingdon (1991)
9. Chitchyan, R., Rashid, A., Rayson, P., Waters, R.: Semantics-based composition for aspect-oriented requirements engineering. In: Proceedings of the 6th International Conference on Aspect-Oriented Software Development, pp. 36–48. ACM (2007)
10. Jacobson, I., Ng, P.-W.: Aspect-Oriented Software Development with Use Cases Reading. Addison-Wesley Professional, Reading (2004)
11. Mussbacher, G., Amyot, D., Weiss, M.: Visualizing aspect-oriented requirements scenarios with use case maps. In: REV 2006. IEEE (2006)
12. Sampaio, A., Rashid, A., Chitchyan, R., Rayson, P.: EA-Miner: towards automation in aspect-oriented requirements engineering. In: Rashid, A., Akşit, M. (eds.) Transactions on AOSD III. LNCS, vol. 4620, pp. 4–39. Springer, Heidelberg (2007)
13. Sillito, J., Dutchyn, C., Eisenberg, A.D., de Volder, K.: Use case level pointcuts. In: Odersky, M. (ed.) ECOOP 2004. LNCS, vol. 3086, pp. 246–268. Springer, Heidelberg (2004)
14. Somé, S.S.: Supporting use case based requirements engineering. Inf. Softw. Technol. **48**(1), 43–58 (2006)
15. Sousa, G., Soares, S., Borba, P., Castro, J.: Separation of crosscutting concerns from requirements to design: adapting the use case driven approach. In: Early Aspects, pp. 93–102 (2004)
16. van Lamsweerde, A.: Requirements Engineering: from System Goals to UML Models to Software Specifications. Wiley, New York (2009)
17. Yue, T., Ali, S., Zhang, M.: RTCM: a natural language based, automated, and practical test case generation framework. In: Proceedings of the 2015 International Symposium on Software Testing and Analysis, pp. 397–408. ACM (2015)
18. Yue, T., Briand, L.C., Labiche, Y.: A systematic review of transformation approaches between user requirements and analysis models. Requirements Eng. **16**(2), 75–99 (2011)

19. Yue, T., Briand, L.C., Labiche, Y.: Facilitating the transition from use case models to analysis models: Approach and experiments. TOSEM. **22**(1), No. 5 (2013)
20. Yue, T., Briand, L.C., Labiche, Y.: aToucan: An Automated Framework to Derive UML Analysis Models from Use Case Models. TOSEM. **24**(3), No. 13 (2015)
21. Zhang, G., Yue, T., Wu, J., Ali, S.: Zen-RUCM: A Tool for Supporting a Comprehensive and Extensible Use Case Modeling Framework. In: Demos/Posters/StudentResearch@ MoDELS, pp. 41–45. Springer (2013)
22. Zhang, H., Yue, T., Ali, S., Liu, C.: Facilitating requirements inspection with search-based selection of diverse use case scenarios. In: BICT (2015, in press)
23. Zhang, M., Yue, T., Ali, S., Zhang, H., Wu, J.: A systematic approach to automatically derive test cases from use cases specified in restricted natural languages. In: Amyot, D., Fonseca i Casas, P., Mussbacher, G. (eds.) SAM 2014. LNCS, vol. 8769, pp. 142–157. Springer, Heidelberg (2014)

An Approach for Prioritizing Software Features Based on Node Centrality in Probability Network

Zhenlian Peng[1,2], Jian Wang[1(✉)], Keqing He[1], and Hongtao Li[1]

[1] State Key Laboratory of Software Engineering, Computer School,
Wuhan University, Wuhan, China
{zlpeng,jianwang,hekeqing,htli}@whu.edu.cn
[2] Computer School, Hunan University of Science and Technology, Xiangtan, China

Abstract. Due to the increasing complexity of software products as well as the restriction of the development budget and time, requirements prioritization, i.e., selecting more crucial requirements to be designed and developed firstly, has become increasingly important in the software development lifetime. Considering the fact that a feature in a feature model can be viewed as a set of closely related requirements, feature prioritization will contribute to requirements prioritization to a large extent. Therefore, how to measure the priority of features within a feature model becomes an important issue in requirements analysis. In this paper, a software feature prioritization approach is proposed, which utilizes the dependencies between features to build a feature probability network and measures feature prioritization through the nodes centrality in the network. Experiments conducted on real world feature models show that the proposed approach can accurately prioritize features in feature models.

Keywords: Feature prioritization · Feature model · Feature probability network · Centrality

1 Introduction

Due to the increasing complexity of software products as well as the restriction of the budget and time, how to select more crucial software requirements to be further developed becomes increasingly important, because it can save development costs, plan reasonable products releases and improve the market competition of software products.

The lack of practical efficient requirements prioritization technologies in the software requirements phase has been viewed as one of the most important reasons that lead to project failures [1,2]. Requirements prioritization is a complex multi-criteria decision-making process. Most existing requirements prioritization approaches [3–9] take the following steps: Firstly, the target criterion is determined; secondly, the specification of requirement attributes related to the chosen

© Springer International Publishing Switzerland 2016
G.M. Kapitsaki and E. Santana de Almeida (Eds.): ICSR 2016, LNCS 9679, pp. 106–121, 2016.
DOI: 10.1007/978-3-319-35122-3_8

criterion is encoded; thirdly, the concrete values for the attributes of all requirements is set, and finally, the ranking of each requirement will be calculated based on the attributes associated to the target criterion. These approaches take each requirement as the object to be prioritized and most of them neglect the dependencies between requirements [1,3,10].

Since Kang et al. [11] proposed feature-oriented domain analysis (FODA) that utilizes feature models to organize the reusable software requirements, feature-oriented software development and software reuse have been widely used by software practitioners. Radatz et al. [12] defined the feature as "a software characteristic specified or implied by requirements documentation" in IEEE standard glossary of software engineering terminology. Zhang et al. [13] defined the feature as "a collection which is comprised of a group of closely related individual requirements in terms of intension and feature is a software characteristic which has user values in terms of extension". Due to the close relationship between requirements and features according to the above definitions, we argue that feature prioritization will contribute to requirements prioritization to a large extent. Existing related researches on feature models mainly focus on features selection in the derivation of feature model configurations (specific software products) [14–16]. The concept of feature prioritization is firstly proposed in [17] and a method named stratified analytic hierarchy process (S-AHP) is presented to help rank and select the most relevant features from the feature model. The ultimate goal of these approaches is to achieve automated derivation of specific software products by associating stakeholders' business requirements with features. However, the structures of feature models are not considered in these work.

We use an example to illustrate the feature prioritization. Assume that a software to be developed contains a text editor, and we need to prioritize the two features "Text Editing" and "File Operations" shown in Fig. 1 such that the one with a higher priority will be firstly developed or reused in the next release of the software product. A general approach usually takes the following steps: Firstly, the specific requirements associated with the two features are identified. Next, these requirements are prioritized using existing software requirements prioritization technologies. And finally, the prioritization of the two features is completed by some weighted measurements. Clearly, this approach should consider all the possible factors such as value, cost and risk of each requirement. However, it is not an easy task to accurately collect these factors at the early stage of requirements engineering. In our opinion, a possible solution is that given a feature model created from a software family, the structure of the feature model can be leveraged to prioritize the features. The basic assumption we made is that a feature will have a higher priority if it is required by more features in the feature model. To this end, a feature prioritization approach is proposed in this paper. In our approach, we build a feature probability network (FPN) through dependencies between features and measures the feature priorities by computing centrality values of nodes in the network.

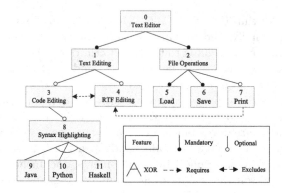

Fig. 1. Feature model of text editor

The main contributions of our work consist of:

– A software feature prioritization approach is proposed in this paper. Specifically, an approach of generating FPNs is presented and a measurement method of node centrality in the probability network is adopted. The proposed approach provides a complementary and reference indicator for multi-criterion decision in the process of requirements prioritization.
– Case studies on real world feature models are conducted to evaluate the effectiveness of the proposed approach.

The remainder of the paper is organized as follows. Section 2 introduces the preliminary knowledge of feature models. The feature prioritization approach is presented in Sect. 3. The evaluation of the proposed approach is discussed in Sect. 4. Section 5 discusses related work. We conclude the paper in Sect. 6.

2   Feature Model

The concept of feature model comes from software engineering disciplines, aiming to discover and express commonalities and variabilities among the members in software product line (SPL). A feature diagram is a graphical representation of the feature model, which is generally represented as a tree structure. The root node of the tree is called root feature, which represents the concept of the domain. Branches of the tree are defined as refinement relations, including *mandatory*, *optional, OR* and *XOR*. Furthermore, there exist cross-tree constraints between features, including *requires* and *excludes* [18–20]. Figure 1 depicts a text editor feature model, which comes from SPLOT[1], a feature model repository. Each node in Fig. 1 denotes a feature, which is represented by its name and record number.

Referring to the literature [18,19], feature model and feature model configuration are defined as follows:

---

[1] http://www.splot-research.org/.

Definition 1 (feature model, FM). A feature model is defined as a tuple $FM =$ $(G, E_{MAND}, E_{OPT}, G_{OR}, G_{XOR}, RE, EX)$. $G = (F, E, r)$ is a rooted tree where $F=(F_{fun}, F_{att})$ is a finite set of features, F_{fun} is a set of functional features, F_{att} is a set of non-functional features, $E \subseteq (F \times F)$ is a finite set of edges and $r \in F$ is the root feature; $E_{MAND} \subseteq E$ is a set of edges that define *mandatory* features with their parents; $E_{OPT} \subseteq E$ is a set of edges that define *optional* features with their parents; $G_{XOR} \subseteq P(F) \times F$ defines feature groups where exactly one child feature exists when their common parent feature exists; $G_{OR} \subseteq P(F) \times F$ defines feature groups where at least one child feature exists when their common parent feature exists; $P(F)$ represents a set of parent feature of feature F; RE is a set of implies *requires* constraints with the form of $A \Rightarrow B$; EX is a set of *excludes* constraints with the form of $A \Rightarrow \neg B$ ($A \in F$ and $B \in F$).

Definition 2 (feature model configuration). A feature model configuration is defined as a set of selected features. It is an optional decision result in the software product configuration process and it only represents a software product design which satisfies the semantic constraints in the FM.

For example, as shown in Fig. 1, {Text Editor, Text Editing, File Operations, Load, Save} is a valid configuration of the FM. However, {Text Editor, Text Editing, File Operations, Load, Save, Print} is not a valid configuration because it violates the *requires* constraint.

A feature model is viewed as consistent if it contains neither dead feature nor false optional feature, where a dead feature refers to the feature that does not appear in any software products, and a false optional feature refers to the feature that is declared to optional feature but appears in all software products. Many approaches, e.g., [21], have been proposed to detect and eliminate the inconsistencies in feature models.

3   Software Feature Prioritization

3.1   Overall Framework

The proposed approach is based on the hypothesis that feature models have already been created before requirements analysts customize applications. FM extraction is not the focus of this paper and many approaches have been reported in this field. For example, Acher et al. [18] presented a semi-automated procedure to support the transition from tabular format product descriptions to a FM. Davril descriptions to a feature model. Davril et al. [20] proposed an automated approach to construct FMs from available product descriptions published in online product repositories such SoftPedia[2].

As shown in Fig. 2, the process of computing feature prioritization consists of two steps:

---

[2] http://www.softpedia.com/.

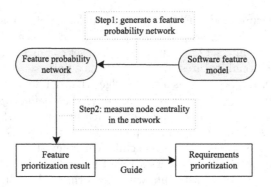

Fig. 2. Framework of feature prioritization approach

Step 1: A FPN is generated from a FM according to the dependencies between features. The FPN is represented as a directed acyclic weighted graph.

Step 2: The centrality values of all nodes in the generated FPN are calculated and regarded as metrics for feature prioritization.

3.2 Generating a Feature Probability Network

According to the definition of the feature model, the relations between features can be classified into refinement relations and cross-tree constraints. We aim to quantify these relations between features, which are characterized by the probabilities of the emergence between features in the FPN in our approach. A FPN is a directed acyclic weighted graph, where its nodes represent features in the FM, its edges represent the direct and indirect relationships between features in the FM, and weights on edges represent the dependency degree of the relationships. Next, we discuss how to convert a FM to a FPN.

In particular, we need to define generating rules of nodes, edges between the nodes and weights on the edges for the FPN.

Generating nodes in the FPN: The nodes in the FPN correspond to the features in the FM and they do not change in the transformation process.

$$ND_{N}(i) = ND_{F}(i), i \in [0, n-1], \tag{1}$$

where $ND_{N}(i)$ denotes node i in the FPN, $ND_{F}(i)$ denotes feature i in the FM, and n denotes the number of nodes or features.

Generating edges in the FPN: Given two features i and j in the FM, four cases need to be considered about their connection in the FPN:

(1) If feature i is a parent feature of feature j in the FM, there will be bidirectional edges between node i and j in the FPN. The generation rule is depicted using Eq. (2).

$$E_{F}(i,j) \in E_{RF} \Rightarrow E_{N}(i,j) = 1 \wedge E_{N}(j,i) = 1, \tag{2}$$

where $E_F(i,j)$ denotes the edge from feature i to feature j in the FM; $E_{RF}=$ $E_{MAND} \cup E_{OPT} \cup G_{OR} \cup G_{XOR}$ denotes a set of edges that satisfy any one of relations including mandatory, optional, OR and XOR; $E_N(i,j)$ denotes an edge from node i to j in the FPN and $E_N(i,j) = 1$ indicates that there is a directed edge from i to j in the FPN.

(2) If feature i is an ancestor feature of feature j in the FM, there will be bidirectional edges between node i and j in the FPN. The corresponding generation rule is depicted using Eq. (3).

$$\exists k_1, k_2, ..., k_{m-1}(\{E_F(i, k_1), E_F(k_1, k_2), ..., E_F(k_{m-1}, j)\}$$
$$\subseteq E_{RF}) \Rightarrow E_N(i, j) = 1 \wedge E_N(j, i) = 1, \tag{3}$$

where d_i and d_j denote the depths of features i and j in the FM, respectively; $m = d_j - d_i$; $k_t (t \in [1, m-1])$ are features between features i and j in the FM, and the collection of edges constructed by them is a subset of E_{RF}.

(3) If feature i requires feature j in the FM, there will be a directed edge from node i to j in the FPN,

$$E_F(i, j) \in E_{RE} \Rightarrow E_N(i, j) = 1, \tag{4}$$

where E_{RE} is a set of edges that satisfy the *"requires"* relation.

(4) In other cases, nodes i and j in the FPN do not connect with each other, i.e., $E_N(i, j) = 0$ and $E_N(j, i) = 0$. Please note that $E_N(i, i) = 0$, because the FPN is a directed acyclic weighted graph.

Figure 3(a) shows the connectivity of nodes in the FPN converted from the text editor feature model shown in Fig. 1.

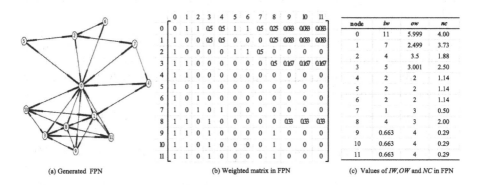

(a) Generated FPN

(b) Weighted matrix in FPN

	0	1	2	3	4	5	6	7	8	9	10	11
0	0	1	1	0.5	0.5	1	1	0.5	0.25	0.083	0.083	0.083
1	1	0	0	0.5	0.5	0	0	0	0.25	0.083	0.083	0.083
2	1	0	0	0	0	1	1	0.5	0	0	0	0
3	1	1	0	0	0	0	0	0	0.5	0.167	0.167	0.167
4	1	1	0	0	0	0	0	0	0	0	0	0
5	1	0	1	0	0	0	0	0	0	0	0	0
6	1	0	1	0	0	0	0	0	0	0	0	0
7	1	0	1	0	1	0	0	0	0	0	0	0
8	1	1	0	1	0	0	0	0	0	0.33	0.33	0.33
9	1	1	0	1	0	0	0	0	1	0	0	0
10	1	1	0	1	0	0	0	0	1	0	0	0
11	1	1	0	1	0	0	0	0	1	0	0	0

(c) Values of *IW,OW* and *NC* in FPN

node	*iw*	*ow*	*nc*
0	11	5.999	4.00
1	7	2.499	3.73
2	4	3.5	1.88
3	5	3.001	2.50
4	2	2	1.14
5	2	2	1.14
6	2	2	1.14
7	1	3	0.50
8	4	3	2.00
9	0.663	4	0.29
10	0.663	4	0.29
11	0.663	4	0.29

Fig. 3. A generated feature probability network from Fig. 1

Weights on edges in the FPN: Given two nodes i and j in the FPN, $E_N(i,j)$ is quantified with the emergence probability of node j on the condition that node i exists. To compute weights of edges between nodes i and j, four cases also need to be considered:

(1) If there is no edge from node i to node j in the FPN, the weight of edge from node i to j (denoted as $W(i,j)$) is set to 0.

$$E_N(i,j) = 0 \Rightarrow W(i,j) = 0, \tag{5}$$

where $W(i,j)$ is the weight of the directed edge from node i to j in the FPN.

(2) If i is the parent feature of j in the FM, according to the edge generation rules mentioned above, bidirectional edges will be created between nodes i and j in the FPN. $W(j,i)$, the weight on the edge from j to i, equals to 1, which means that the parent feature must exist if its child feature exists in the FM. $W(i,j)$ is calculated according to the following situations:

① If $E_F(i,j)$ in the FM is a "mandatory" relation, $W(i,j)$ is computed using Eq. (6).

$$E_F(i,j) \in E_{MAND} \Rightarrow W(i,j) = 1. \tag{6}$$

② If $E_F(i,j)$ in the FM is an "optional" relation, $W(i,j)$ is computed using Eq. (7).

$$E_F(i,j) \in E_{OPT} \Rightarrow W(i,j) = 0.5. \tag{7}$$

③ If $E_F(i,j)$ in the FM is a "XOR" relation, assume that the number of features that share the same parent feature of j by "XOR" relations is g, $W(i,j)$ is computed using Eq. (8).

$$E_F(i,j) \in G_{XOR} \Rightarrow W(i,j) = 1/g. \tag{8}$$

④ If $E_F(i,j)$ in the FM is an "OR" relation, assume that the number of features that share the same parent feature of j by "OR" relations is g, $W(i,j)$ is computed using Eq. (9).

$$E_F(i,j) \in G_{OR} \Rightarrow W(i,j) = rand(1/g,1), \tag{9}$$

where $rand(1/g,1)$ is a uniformly random number between $1/g$ and 1, in other words, the appearance probability of i is between $1/g$ and 1 when j exists.

(3) If feature i is an ancestor feature of feature j in the FM, according to the edge generation rules mentioned above, bidirectional edges will be created between nodes i and j in the FPN. $W(j,i)$ equals to 1 because the ancestor feature must exist if its descendant feature exists in the FM. $W(i,j)$ is computed according to Eq. (10).

$$\exists k_1, k_2, ..., k_{m-1}(\{E_F(i,k_1), E_F(k_1,k_2), ..., E_F(k_{m-1},j)\} \subseteq E_{RF})$$

$$\Rightarrow W(i,j) = W(i,k_1) \times \prod_{t=1}^{m-2} W(k_t, k_{t+1}) \times W(k_{m-1},j). \tag{10}$$

(4) If feature i requires feature j in the FM, $W(i,j)$ equals to 1 in the FPN, as depicted in Eq. (11).

$$E_F(i,j) \in E_{RE} \Rightarrow W(i,j) = 1. \tag{11}$$

Figure 3(b) shows the weighted matrix of the FPN, which is generated from the text editor feature model. Note that the value in cell $\{i,j\}$ of the matrix represents the weight value $W(i,j)$.

3.3   Computation of Node Centrality in Network

Many metrics on how to measure the node centrality have been investigated in complex networks and social networks. Typical metrics consists of betweenness centrality, degree centrality, indegree centrality, outdegree centrality and their hybrid metrics [22]. In this paper, the summation of input weights of the node (*abbr. IW*, similar to in-degree) and the summation of output weights of the node (*abbr. OW*, similar to out-degree) are adopted to measure the centrality of the node. For a specific feature in a feature model, the larger IW means that more features rely on this feature, and on the contrary, the larger OW means that this feature relies on more features. $IW(i)$ and $OW(i)$ are computed using Eqs. (12) and (13), respectively.

$$IW(i) = \sum_{t=0}^{i-1} W(t,i) + \sum_{t=i+1}^{n-1} W(t,i). \tag{12}$$

$$OW(i) = \sum_{t=0}^{i-1} W(i,t) + \sum_{t=i+1}^{n-1} W(i,t). \tag{13}$$

where n denotes the number of features in the feature model.

The node centrality (*abbr. NC*) is computed using Eq. (14). As shown in Eq. (14), the centrality of a node will increase with the increase of its IW and the decrease of its OW.

$$NC(i) = \alpha \times IW(i)/(1 + (1 - \alpha) \times OW(i)). \tag{14}$$

Where α is a weighted factor, which indicates the importance of IW in the node centrality measurement.

Figure 3(c) shows the values of IW, OW and NC in the FPN converted from the text editor feature model in Fig. 1. Here α is set to 0.8.

3.4   Feature Prioritization Algorithm

Algorithm 1 shows the pseudo-code of feature prioritization based on the node centrality in the feature probability network.

The input of the algorithm is a software feature model and the output is a priority ranking list of features. Firstly, each node in the FPN is generated based on the FM (Line 1). Then $E_N(i,j)$ and $W(i,j)$ are initialized (Lines 2~3). When the FM is traversed using the breadth-first search (BFS), the edges in the FPN are generated according to relations between features in the FM and the weights on edges are computed (Lines 4~5). Then the values of IW, OW and NC in the FPN are computed (Line 6). If feature i requires feature j in the FM and $NC(i)$ is larger than $NC(j)$ in the FPN, $NC(i)$ and $NC(j)$ are exchanged (Lines 7~8). If feature i excludes feature j in the FM, the smaller one of $NC(i)$ and $NC(j)$ and its descendant features are added to a set denoted as REAR (Lines 9~10). If there are multiple *excludes* relations, the nodes in REAR are sorted in

---

Algorithm 1. Feature Prioritization Algorithm.

Input: a software feature model;
Output: a priority ranking list of features;
  1: Copy the nodes in the FM to the FPN according to Equation(1);
  2: For each node pair i and j in the FPN
  3:      $E_N(i,j)=0$, $W(i,j)=0$;
  4: Traverse the FM using the breadth-first search until each node and edge is traversed
  5:      Generate edges in the FPN according to Equations(2)$\sim$(4)
          and compute weights on edges in the FPN according to
          Equations(5)$\sim$(11);
  6: Compute IW,OW,NC for each node according to Equations(12)$\sim$(14), respectively;
  7: If feature i requires feature j in the FM and $NC(i)>NC(j)$
  8:      Exchange $NC(i)$ with $NC(j)$;
  9: If feature i excludes feature j in the FM and $NC(i)>NC(j)$
 10:      Add feature j and its descendant features in REAR;
 11: If REAR.length>1
 12:      Sort the features in REAR according to their NC values;
 13: Sort the order of features outside REAR according to their NC value;
 14: Merge the sorted results where results in REAR are placed after the ones outside
      REAR;
 15: **return** the ranking list.

---

descending order with NC values (Lines 11$\sim$12); The nodes outside REAR are also sorted in descending order with NC values (Line 13). Two groups of results are merged and returned (Lines 14$\sim$15).

Finally, we estimate the time complexity of the algorithm. Among the steps in the algorithm, Lines 2$\sim$5 spend the most time and the time complexity of these steps is $O(n^2)$, where n represents the number of features in the FM. Line 12 is a sorting process, and its time complexity in the worst case is also no more than $O(n^2)$. For other steps, the time complexity is no more than $O(n)$. Therefore, the time complexity of the whole algorithm is $O(n^2)$.

4   Evaluation

4.1   Setup

We conducted several groups of case studies to evaluate the effectiveness of the proposed approach. The algorithm proposed in this paper was developed in Java and conducted on a PC with 3.19 GHz Intel Core i3 CPU and 4 GB RAM, running Windows 7 Operating System.

Three feature models selected from SPLOT, including text editor (*abbr.* TE), help system (*abbr.* HS) and software stack (*abbr.* SS), are used in our case studies. SPLOT maintains a publicly available feature model repository, and the feature models registered in SPLOT are created by experts in the SPL field, which have certain credibility. Although feature models are selected, there is no available information about the priorities of features. We have to manually create such a ground truth. In order to decrease the efforts in creating the ground truth, the three selected feature models are small or medium sizes. Details of the three feature models are shown in Table 1.

Table 1. Details of the three selected feature models

Name	Number of features	Root	Mandatory	Optional	OR	XOR	Requires	Excludes
TE	12	1	4	4	0	3	1	1
HS	25	1	6	0	3	15	5	0
SS	37	1	1	2	9	24	7	0

4.2 Ground Truth Building

In order to evaluate the effectiveness of the proposed approach, the ground truth needs to be built as a reference of priorities between features in the FM. According to the idea of the analytic hierarchy process (AHP) [5] that has been widely used in requirements prioritization, the process of building the ground truth is implemented as follows:

(1) For each of the three selected feature models, we created a $n \times n$ table, where n represents the number of features, and cell(i,j) in the table will record the priority comparison result of feature i (row i) with feature j (column j), $i, j \in [0, n-1]$. All the initial values of the cells are set to null. Two PhD students and three master students in our research group were invited to participate in a small group meeting. They were emailed to introduce the goal of the group meeting and give examples about how to fill in the three tables.

(2) A small group meeting was held after a day. In the meeting, the objective of the group meeting was explained again and the related domain knowledge about the FM was also introduced by the first author of the paper for about 20 min. Then the idea of the AHP method was explained for about 10 min. Participants of the meeting were requested to fill in cells of the tables with 1 (denoted as "greater than"), 0 (denoted as "equal to") and -1 (denoted as "less than") to represent the comparison result of feature i (i.e., row i) with feature j (i.e., column j) following the examples provided in the email after the group meeting. Because the priority comparison value in cell(i,j) is opposite with the value of cell(j,i) in a table, participants only need to fill in the upper (or lower) triangular tables.

(3) The first author of the paper collected all the results of the tables filled in by participants and conducted statistical analysis on the results of inconsistencies. The group meeting was held again a day later. Participants discussed and negotiated with the inconsistent results until agreement could be recognized. Furthermore, The ranked scores (the larger is prioritized) of all features in each FM were also discussed and negotiated.

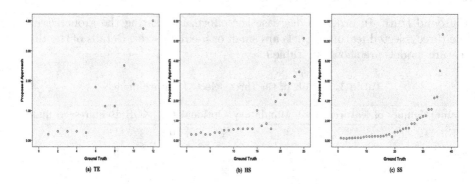

Fig. 4. Scatter diagrams of evaluation results on three feature models

4.3 Evaluation Indicator

Spearman's rank correlation coefficient [23], accuracy and execution time are selected as the evaluation indicators to evaluate the proposed approach.

Spearman's rank correlation coefficient (denoted as r_s) is a widely used non-parametric measure of statistical dependence between two variables [23]. In this paper, we used Spearman's rank correlation coefficient to measure the statistical dependence between the proposed approach (described as the values of node centrality and the ground truth (described as the ranked values). That is, it evaluates how well the relationship between the proposed approach and the ground truth can be described using a monotonic function.

For each feature model whose feature number is n, the node centrality values X_i of n features are firstly converted to rank rgX, rgY denotes the ranked values in the ground truth, and r_s is computed using Eq. (15):

$$r_s = cov(rgX, rgY)/(\sigma_{rgX} \times \sigma_{rgY}), \tag{15}$$

where, $cov(rgX, rgY)$ is the covariance of the ranked variables of the proposed approach and the ground truth, and σ_{rgX} and σ_{rgY} are the standard deviations of the rank variables (the proposed approach and the ground truth).

Accuracy is measured by the value of disagreements. Disagreements refer to the total number of inconsistent priority comparison value for each feature pairwise between the proposed approach and the ground truth. Both the priority comparison values have the range of $\{-1, 0, 1\}$. If the corresponding value of the proposed approach and the ground truth is not the same, then the count of disagreements will be added. Accuracy is calculated using Eq. (16).

$$accuracy = 1 - 2 \times disagreements/(n \times (n - 1)). \tag{16}$$

4.4 Results and Analysis

The first experiment is conducted to verify whether the proposed approach can accurately predict the priority between features in the feature models. By the

analysis of comparing the results with the ground truth, the statistical information of the scatter diagram of each feature model is depicted in Fig. 4.

As can be seen from the scatter diagrams shown in Fig. 4, the two rank
variables of the proposed approach (described as the values of NC) and the
ground truth (described as the ranked values) in the three feature models always
form monotonic functions on the whole. Therefore, they have the same positive
sign, which implies that they have a perfect monotone increasing relationship.
Moreover, according to the Spearman's rank correlation coefficient (r_s) shown
in Table 2, r_s in feature models TE, HS and SS are 0.921, 0.976 and 0.988 (the
maximum value is 1), respectively. All the r_s values are above 90 %, which implies
once again that the two rank variables in the three feature models are closely
related. In other words, the ranking of features in the proposed approach is close
to that of the ground truth.

Table 2. Disagreements, accuracy and r_s of each feature model

FM	Number of feature pairwise	Disagreements	Accuracy/%	r_s
TE	66	8	87.9	0.921
HS	300	25	91.7	0.976
SS	666	49	92.6	0.988

In addition, the disagreements and accuracy in the three feature models are
shown in Table 2. The values of disagreements in feature models TE, HS and SS
are 8, 25 and 49, respectively. The accuracy values in TE, HS and SS feature
models are 87.9 %, 91.7 % and 92.6 %, respectively. With the increase of the
number of features, both the number of feature pairwise and disagreements are
increasing. Moreover, when the number of features increase, the increasing speed
of disagreements is slower than that of the number of feature pairwise, which is
the reason why the accuracy is gradually increasing. In conclusion, the results
of this group of experiments show that the proposed approach can accurately
predict the priority of the features in the FM.

The second experiment is conducted to verify whether the execution time of
the proposed approach is acceptable. The feature numbers of the three selected
feature models are 12, 25, and 37, respectively. In order to observe the trend of
the execution time with the number of features in our proposed approach, we
generate a series of feature models with larger feature number according to the
generating rules described as the feature model editor in SPLOT[3]. The number
of features in these generated feature models is 50, 75, 100, 125, 150, 175, and
200, respectively. Figure 5 shows the trend of the execution time of the proposed
approach with the increase of the number of features.

As can be seen from Fig. 5, the execution time of TE, HS and SS feature
models is 9, 23 and 32 ms, respectively. The execution time of the proposed approach increases with the increase of the number of features in the FM, because

---

[3] Feature Model Editor, http://www.splot-research.org/.

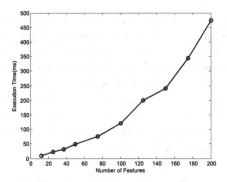

Fig. 5. Change trend of execution time

the nodes and edges to be considered in the FPN will also increase. In addition, Fig. 5 shows that the execution time grows nearly in a trend no more than $O(n^2)$ with the increase of the number of features. Therefore, it can be concluded that the execution time of the proposed approach is acceptable, which means that the proposed approach can be capable of supporting feature prioritization for a software feature model that contains a large number of features. Therefore, it is possible to help requirements analysts focus their attentions on the important features to be developed or reused in the initial phase of requirements engineering. Please note that besides the feature number in a feature model, the number of different relations between features including *XOR*, *OR* and *excludes* is another important factor that may affect the execution time of the proposed approach, albeit it has minor influence than the feature number. More analysis on this point will be one of our future work.

4.5   Threats to Validity

With respect to the internal validity, the main threat is that the proposed approach only considers the priority between features from the structure complexity in the FM. In fact, there are many other factors involved in the feature prioritization, such as stakeholders preferences, semantic constraints of the feature model configurations and values, as well as costs and risks. In our opinion, the feature prioritization approach based on structure complexity provides an important and complementary factor to prioritize requirements.

Threats to the external validity concern the scale of feature models and the authority of determining the ground truth. For simplicity, only feature models in small or medium scale are selected in this paper. We are not quite sure that the proposed approach is also effective in precision and execution time when the scale of the FM is very large. In addition, in the process of building the ground truth, due to the difference of expertise and experience of the participants, it is difficult to ensure that the ground truth is absolutely accurate in practice. To decrease such kind of uncertainty as more as possible, we recruited five students to construct the ground truth.

5   Related Work

We focus the related work discussion on two fields: requirements prioritization as well as feature selection.

Currently, most prioritization related studies focus on software requirements prioritization. Researchers and practitioners have proposed a number of software prioritization techniques. Perini et al. [3] presented a method for requirements prioritization called case-based ranking (CBRank), which combines stakeholders preferences with requirements ordering approximations computed through machine learning techniques. A case study by comparing with analytic hierarchy process (AHP) [5] showed the effectiveness of CBRank. They claimed that requirements dependencies should be handled in the future work. Tonella et al. [6] proposed an interactive genetic algorithm (IGA) that includes incremental knowledge acquisition and combines it with the dependencies and priorities from requirements documents. A real case study by comparing with incomplete analytic hierarchy process (IAHP) [7] showed the effectiveness and robustness of IGA. Easmin et al. [8] proposed a scheme for requirements prioritization addressing the feedback issue along with a highly significant ranking function that has decisive impact on true ranking. Khari and Kumar [9] compared six techniques of numerical assignment technique (NAT), AHP, value oriented prioritization (VOP), cumulative voting (CV), binary search tree (BST) and planning game (PG) in a controlled experiment. Tong et al. [1] conducted systematic reviews for current software requirements prioritization techniques from technical perspective. Achimugu et al. [10] conducted systematic reviews for current software requirements prioritization techniques from literature perspective. They pointed out that most of the current techniques neglect requirements dependencies. To summarize, most of existing techniques treat each specific requirement as the unit of priority comparison and focus on factors such as value, cost and risk of specific requirement. Also they usually neglect dependencies between requirements [1, 3, 10].

Related studies of the FM mainly focus on feature selection problem for the feature model configuration. Czainecki et al. [14] introduced the concept of staged configuration which can be achieved by the stepwise specialization of the FM. This multi-stage selection considered cases in which the selection of features in a previous stage impacts the validity of later stage features selections. White et al. [15] provided the study of multi-step configuration for SPL. They presented a formal model of multi-step SPL configuration and mapped the model to constraint satisfaction problems (CSPs). Stoiber and Glinz [16] presented an approach to support stepwise, incremental derivation of a product requirements specification from a product line specification. The starting point of these methods is automated reasoning on the FM and feature prioritization is not considered. Bagheri et al. [17] introduced the concept of feature prioritization. They proposed an extension of the FM with capabilities for capturing business oriented requirements and a method named stratified analytic hierarchy process (S-AHP) was presented on top of this extension to help rank and select the most relevant features from the FM. However, automated derivation of specific product was the goal of the method and they did not prioritize features as well. To the best of our knowledge, there are no more researches on the feature prioritization.

6 Conclusion

In this paper, an approach for software feature prioritization based on the node centrality in the probability network is proposed. The approach can be applied in the early stage of software requirements engineering. Through feature prioritization in the FM, requirements analysts and software practitioners can focus more on the important features to be further developed or reused in the specific software product development. In order to prioritize features, a method of generating the FPN from the FM is presented and a measurement method for network node centrality is adopted to calculate the priority of features to guide software requirements prioritization. The proposed approach is validated by using three real feature models.

In the future, we plan to extend our work from the following directions. Firstly, we plan to further evaluate the performance of the proposed approach when the feature number grows to a large scale (for example, greater than 1000). Secondly, we will investigate how to combine the proposed approach with automated reasoning methods to support staged feature model configuration problem.

Acknowledgments. The work is supported by the National Basic Research Program of China under grant No. 2014CB340404, and the National Natural Science Foundation of China under Nos. 61373037, 61272111, 61572186 and 61562073. The authors would like to thank anonymous reviewers for their valuable suggestions. Jian Wang is the corresponding author.

References

1. Tong, Z., Zhuang, Q., Guo, Q., Ma, P.: Research on technologies of software requirements prioritization. In: Yuan, Y., Wu, X., Lu, Y. (eds.) ISCTCS 2013. CCIS, vol. 426, pp. 9–21. Springer, Heidelberg (2014)
2. Hofmann, H.F., Lehner, F.: Requirements engineering as a success factor in software projects. IEEE Softw. **4**, 58–66 (2001)
3. Perini, A., Susi, A., Avesani, P.: A machine learning approach to software requirements prioritization. IEEE Trans. Softw. Eng. **39**(4), 445–461 (2013)
4. Peter, H., Olson, D., Rodgers, T.: Multi-criteria preference analysis for systematic requirements negotiation. In: 26th Annual International Conference on Computer Software and Applications, pp. 887–892. IEEE Press, New York (2002)
5. Saaty, R.W.: The analytic hierarchy process: what it is and how it is used. Math. Model. **9**(3), 161–176 (1987)
6. Tonella, P., Susi, A., Palma, F.: Interactive requirements prioritization using a genetic algorithm. Inf. Softw. Technol. **55**(1), 173–187 (2013)

7. Harker, P.T.: Incomplete pairwise comparisons in the analytic hierarchy process. Math. Model. **9**(11), 837–848 (1987)
8. Easmin, R., Gias, A.U., Khaled, S.M.: A partial order assimilation approach for software requirements prioritization. In: 3rd International Conference on Informatics, Electronics and Vision (ICIEV), pp. 1–5. IEEE Press, New York (2014)
9. Khari, M., Kumar, N.: Comparison of six prioritization techniques for software requirements. J. Glob. Res. Comput. Sci. **4**(1), 38–43 (2013)
10. Achimugu, P., Selamat, A., Ibrahim, R., Mahrin, M.N.: A systematic literature review of software requirements prioritization research. Inf. Softw. Technol. **56**(6), 568–585 (2014)
11. Kang, K.C., Cohen, S.G., Hess, J.A., Novak, W.E., Peterson, A.S.: Feature-oriented domain analysis (FODA) feasibility study. Technical report, Carnegie Mellon University (1990)
12. Radatz, J., Geraci, A., Katki, F.: IEEE standard glossary of software engineering terminology. IEEE Stand. **610121990**(121990), 3 (1990)
13. Zhang, W., Yan, H., Zhao, H., Jin, Z.: A BDD-based approach to verifying clone-enabled feature models' constraints and customization. In: Mei, H. (ed.) ICSR 2008. LNCS, vol. 5030, pp. 186–199. Springer, Heidelberg (2008)
14. Czarnecki, K., Helsen, S., Eisenecker, U.: Staged configuration using feature models. In: Nord, R.L. (ed.) SPLC 2004. LNCS, vol. 3154, pp. 266–283. Springer, Heidelberg (2004)
15. White, J., Dougherty, B., Schmidt, D.C., Benavides, D.: Automated reasoning for multi-step feature model configuration problems. In: 13th International Conference on Software Product Line, pp. 11–20. Carnegie Mellon University (2009)
16. Stoiber, R., Glinz, M.: Supporting stepwise, incremental product derivation in product line requirements engineering. In: 4th International Workshop on Variability Modelling of Software-Intensive Systems. ICB-Research report, pp. 77–84. University Duisburg-Essen (2010)
17. Bagheri, E., Asadi, M., Gasevic, D., Soltani, S.: Stratified analytic hierarchy process: prioritization and selection of software features. In: Bosch, J., Lee, J. (eds.) SPLC 2010. LNCS, vol. 6287, pp. 300–315. Springer, Heidelberg (2010)
18. Acher, M., Cleve, A., Perrouin, G., Heymans, P., Vanbeneden, C., Collet, P., Lahire, P.: On extracting feature models from product descriptions. In: 6th International Workshop on Variability Modeling of Software-Intensive Systems, pp. 45–54. ACM, New York (2012)
19. Benavides, D., Segura, S., Ruiz-Corts, A.: Automated analysis of feature models 20 years later: a literature review. Inf. Syst. **35**(6), 615–636 (2010)
20. Davril, J.M., Delfosse, E., Hariri, N., Acher, M., Cleland-Huang, J., Heymans, P.: Feature model extraction from large collections of informal product descriptions. In: 9th Joint Meeting on Foundations of Software Engineering, pp. 290–300. ACM, New York (2013)
21. Rincn, L.F., Giraldo, G.L., Mazo, R., Salinesi, C.: An ontological rule-based approach for analyzing dead and false optional features in feature models. Electron. Notes Theoret. Comput. Sci. **302**, 111–132 (2014)
22. Opsahl, T., Agneessens, F., Skvoretz, J.: Node centrality in weighted networks: generalizing degree and shortest paths. Soc. Netw. **32**(3), 245–251 (2010)
23. Zar, J.H.: Significance testing of the Spearman rank correlation coefficient. J. Am. Stat. Assoc. **67**(339), 578–580 (1972)

VCU: The Three Dimensions of Reuse

Jörg Kienzle[1], Gunter Mussbacher[1(✉)], Omar Alam[2], Matthias Schöttle[1], Nicolas Belloir[3], Philippe Collet[4], Benoit Combemale[5], Julien DeAntoni[4], Jacques Klein[6], and Bernhard Rumpe[7]

[1] SOCS/ECE, McGill University, Montréal, QC, Canada
{joerg.kienzle,gunter.mussbacher}@mcgill.ca,
matthias.schoettle@mail.mcgill.ca
[2] Trent University, Peterborough, Canada
oalam@acm.org
[3] Université de Pau, Pau, France
nicolas.belloir@univ-pau.fr
[4] Université Nice Sophia Antipolis, Nice, France
philippe.collet@unice.fr, julien.deantoni@polytech.unice.fr
[5] Université de Rennes 1, Rennes, France
benoit.combemale@irisa.fr
[6] Université du Luxembourg, Luxembourg, Luxembourg
jacques.klein@uni.lu
[7] RWTH Aachen, Aachen, Germany
rumpe@se-rwth.de

Abstract. Reuse, enabled by modularity and interfaces, is one of the most important concepts in software engineering. This is evidenced by an increasingly large number of reusable artifacts, ranging from small units such as classes to larger, more sophisticated units such as components, services, frameworks, software product lines, and concerns. This paper presents evidence that a canonical set of reuse interfaces has emerged over time: the variation, customization, and usage interfaces (VCU). A reusable artifact that provides all three interfaces reaches the highest potential of reuse, as it explicitly exposes how the artifact can be manipulated during the reuse process along these three dimensions. We demonstrate the wide applicability of the VCU interfaces along two axes: across abstraction layers of a system specification and across existing reuse techniques. The former is shown with the help of a comprehensive case study including reusable requirements, software, and hardware models for the authorization domain. The latter is shown with a discussion on how the VCU interfaces relate to existing reuse techniques.

Keywords: Reuse · Interfaces · Variability · Customization · Configuration · Extension · Usage · Concern-oriented reuse

1 Introduction

Complex systems are rarely built from scratch, but rather rely on the existence of reusable artifacts for improved productivity and higher quality. Reuse of artifacts

© Springer International Publishing Switzerland 2016
G.M. Kapitsaki and E. Santana de Almeida (Eds.): ICSR 2016, LNCS 9679, pp. 122–137, 2016.
DOI: 10.1007/978-3-319-35122-3_9

comes in very different flavors, and can be investigated by looking at how the reusable artifact is manipulated during the reuse process, and by looking at various reuse techniques.

A long list of reuse techniques exist, each with its own unit of reuse [15]. Many of them are considered success stories, starting from isolated classes managed in libraries to sophisticated components and services [6] and finally to large reusable entities such as frameworks and Software Product Lines [20]. Recently, concerns have been proposed as variable and generic units of reuse [3]. Successful reuse also includes development artifacts, such as analysis and design models describing interaction, function, data, or architecture. In recent years, it has been shown that even crosscutting elements can be reused with aspect-based merging and weaving techniques. Instead of concrete artifacts, it is also possible to reuse conceptual knowledge, such as design patterns [8], or to encode reuse knowledge in model transformations or code generators.

Dimensions of reuse may be considered by categorizing the manipulations performed on the reusable artifact during the reuse process. These manipulations range from the simple act of *using* an existing artifact to the more mature, coordinated *customization* (also called adaptation or extension) of reusable artifacts to a new reuse context, and thus also include white-box and black-box forms of reuse. As a prerequisite to all previously mentioned activities, a specific reusable artifact must first be *identified* (i.e., *selected* from a set of possibly applicable reusable artifacts). The following paragraph gives some examples of these common activities.

A simple example of repeated *use* of an artifact is the common case of a software application started several times. Often, however, a reusable artifact needs to be adapted to its reuse context. Source code may be reused through *copy/paste* and free adaptation (a common, but bad form of reuse as it is error-prone and difficult to maintain). On the other side of the reuse spectrum, there is the common reuse scenario, where, e.g., an operating system is installed on different computers with different, predefined features required for different forms of use and preferences. This is a case of reuse of an artifact through the *selection from a planned set of variations*, which also is the case for the popular Software Product Lines (SPL) paradigm. Modern applications more and more often have the ability to adapt themselves to their environment, i.e., to automatically *select* the most appropriate variation depending on their context. This requires the consequences of a *selection* on the system to be made explicit, so that it can be reasoned about. Last but not least, a piece of software can also be reused by embedding it in different applications (e.g., generic reusable class libraries, components, and frameworks). However, genericity is hard to achieve. While class libraries provide crisp interfaces describing an intended form of reuse, they may easily be too narrow to be usable. Frameworks often add customization ability through subclassing of their concepts to cover a wider range of supported reuse contexts.

Nowadays, it is generally agreed that reuse of artifacts with explicitly defined, clear boundaries through their interfaces is the most appropriate to reach high levels of reuse maturity. In this way, internal complexity and properties are encapsulated, and thus do not affect the (re-)users. While interfaces have traditionally been mostly employed to formalize the usage of an artifact, we stipulate that all forms of manipulating a reusable artifact should be supported by interfaces in today's complex development processes, starting with *identification*, followed by *customization*, and finally the *usage* of a reusable artifact. Consequently, we have identified the need for three interfaces that every reusable artifact should consider providing:

- a Variation (V) Interface,
- a Customization (C) Interface, and
- a Usage (U) Interface.

We call them interfaces, because people with different roles interact with the artifact during different activities of the development process through the appropriate interface to achieve a desired result. Each interface targets a different dimension of reuse, and together they streamline the reuse process. However, depending on the reusable artifact, these interfaces may be broader or smaller and explicit or implicit.

The long-term aim of this work is to define fundamental concepts for the reuse of (modeling) languages that can then be made available to any (modeling) language, e.g., through metamodeling or other software language engineering techniques.

In the remainder of this paper, we first introduce the VCU interfaces in more detail in Sect. 2. The following two sections intend to provide convincing evidence that these three interfaces capture all dimensions required to achieve effective reuse. Section 3 presents several example models from the *Authorization* domain expressed in different modeling notations that were made reusable by adding VCU interfaces. In Sect. 4, we discuss how the explicit and implicit interfaces of existing units of reuse can be categorized with the VCU approach. Section 5 presents our conclusions and discusses future work.

2   The VCU Approach – Definitions

VCU stands for the three interfaces: *variation*, *customization*, and *usage*. We start with the last and most known.

2.1   Usage Interface

The *Usage Interface* (UI) describes what functionality can be requested by the developer of the application who wants to reuse the artifact, i.e., which structural and behavioral elements within the artifact are accessible. For example, the UI of a software design artifact is typically comprised of the *public* classes and methods made available by the artifact. For a reusable security artifact this might include an *authentication* operation that an administrator can invoke in order to gain access to restricted behavior. Sometimes usage interfaces are explicitly published, which includes the promise of developers that those are stable over evolution steps.

2.2   Customization Interface

The *Customization Interface* (CI) describes how the developer of an application tailors a generic artifact to a specific application. The term customization here has an extended meaning compared to the SPL paradigm. A reusable artifact is described as generically as possible to increase reusability. Therefore, some elements in the artifact are only *partially* specified and need to be complemented with concrete modeling elements of the application that intends to reuse the artifact. Sometimes, parameters have to be filled in a template. Sometimes, complete new classes have to be provided and injected into the reused artifact, e.g., as hot spots in frameworks or as plug-ins in pluggable applications. The CI is hence used when a reusable artifact is *composed* with the application. For example, a security artifact may define generic *Users* and *Administrators* as partial classes that need to be merged with the concrete application classes that describe the actual users of the system, e.g., *Customer* or *CrisisCoordinator*, respectively. At the implementation/source code level, Java generics, for example, exist, which require the provision of a concrete type when they are reused. Databases are customized with schema definitions. The Eclipse IDE framework became so popular, because it is strongly decoupled and structured as a plug-in system, allowing the IDE to be customized.

2.3   Variation Interface

The *Variation Interface* (VI) exposes the available variants that the artifact encapsulates and from which the developer has to choose. It helps organize possible variations and their impact on goals and system qualities. From this VI the application developer selects one concrete variant of the artifact that fits the stakeholders needs best. Variations are typically described by a *feature model* [11] that specifies the individual features of the artifact, as well as their mandatory, optional, alternative, requires, and excludes relationships. The impact of choosing a feature can be specified with goal models [10] when relationships among goals are more complex or otherwise with attributed feature models [4]. For example, a reusable authentication artifact may offer various alternatives for authentication, from *key-based* to *biometrics-based solutions*, each with differing impacts on the *level of security* as well as *cost* and *end-user convenience*.

2.4   VCU Approach to Reuse

Variant selection and customization typically happen during development time. Use of an artifact in terms of connecting it to the rest of the application also

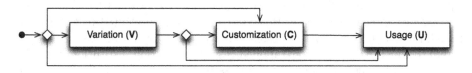

Fig. 1. The VCU reuse approach

happens at development time, while actually using its functionality happens at runtime when the application is executed. Some kinds of artifacts allow deferring the variant selection and customization at least partially to installation or runtime. Modern operating systems allow users to customize or at least adapt customization during installation, prior to or even while executing it. Plug-in systems allow extending an application and thus building new variants partially even at runtime. Recently, adaptive systems have started to automate the selection process, switching among variations at runtime. Still, the three interfaces should be methodically distinguished to simplify understanding of reusability techniques.

Existing techniques (see Sect. 4) may only use some of the three interfaces from the least mature to the most mature levels of reuse: only U, V&U, C&U, and all three interfaces as indicated in Fig. 1. Actually, a developer that wants to reuse an artifact is typically exposed to the VCU interfaces of the artifact in the opposite order (V, then C, then U), roughly following these *methodical guidelines*:

1. The developer determines the variant of the artifact that best suits her needs. This is done by *selecting* the feature(s) with the best impact on relevant stakeholder goals and system qualities from the VI of the artifact based on provided impact analysis.
2. The developer *customizes* the resulting artifact by filling all parameterizations (generics, partial elements), connecting the resulting artifact to the application under development with the help of the CI.
3. The developer actually *uses* the UI of the artifact in the rest of the application under development, such that the artifacts structural and behavioral properties are integrated at the desired locations.

In practice, however, this is an evolutionary process, e.g., changing the chosen variant due to adapted goals and therefore switching between variant selection, customization, and usage.

3   VCU Interfaces Across Levels of Abstraction

This section illustrates the applicability of the VCU approach by building a unit that encapsulates reusable requirements, design, and hardware models that describe general structural and behavioral properties of *Authorization*. The approach that was followed to create these models is called concern-orientated reuse (CORE), and described in more detail in [3].

Among authorization models, the most used ones are based on access control policy. The main idea is that access to a resource is controlled by some rules, such as, e.g., in the widely used Role-Based Access Control (RBAC) [7,21]. In RBAC, the access of a user to a resource is based on the role of the user in the system to which RBAC rules are applied (e.g., in a banking institution, the role of a user can be customer or teller). Access to a resource is usually defined as a set of actions that the user can perform on the resource (e.g., a customer can withdraw or deposit money from or in an account).

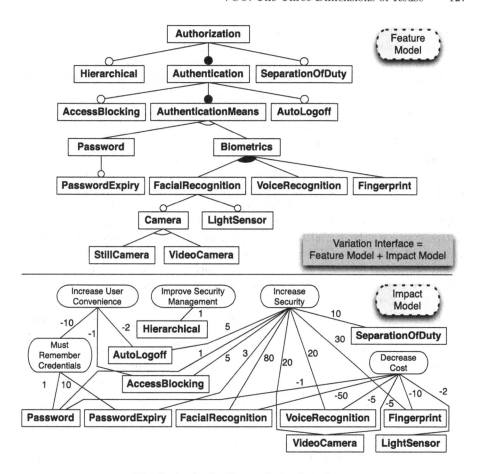

Fig. 2. Authorization variation interface

We first model the VI of *Authorization*, i.e., the different RBAC and Authentication features and their impacts using feature diagrams and impact models (Sect. 3.1). We then present the interaction workflow of *Authorization* using Aspect-oriented Use Case Maps (Sect. 3.2), the structural and behavioral design models using class and sequence diagrams with Reusable Aspect Models (RAM) (Sect. 3.3), as well as the hardware configurations using enhanced SysML block diagrams (Sect. 3.4). For space reasons, the descriptions focus mostly on the CI and UI of each model. Then, we show how to reuse the *Authorization* concern in a simple bank application (Sect. 3.5).

3.1 Variation Interface Models

Inspired by the RBAC specification in the NIST standard [7] and an RBAC feature model [14], we created a feature model [11] for the *Authorization* concern as shown at the top of Fig. 2.

The base functionality that any RBAC system must provide is encapsulated in the root feature *Authorization* and the mandatory *Authentication* child feature. The optional feature *Hierarchical* adds the ability for role inheritance, whereas *SeparationOfDuty* (SoD) adds the ability to restrict permissions based on constraints. Furthermore, the child features of *Authentication* provide different means for performing authentication (*Password* and *Biometrics* with its three sub-options), as well as the optional features *Access Blocking*, *Auto Logoff*, and *Password Expiry*. Hardware variability is also depicted by different *Camera* configurations and an optional *LightSensor* for *FacialRecognition*.

The impact model of the *Authorization* concern is shown at the bottom of Fig. 2. Four high-level goals are defined: *Increase Security*, *Decrease Cost*, *Increase User Convenience*, and *Improve Security Management*. The impact of variable features on these goals are indicated with weighted contributions in a relative way, e.g., the *Facial Recognition* feature impacts security sixteen times more than the *Auto Logoff* feature (80 vs. 5).

The Variation Interface (VI) for the *Authorization* concern is comprised of the feature and impact models. The feature model presents all encapsulated variants of the concern to the developer, and the impact model helps the developer to determine the best solution for a specific reuse context by enabling impact analysis on high-level system qualities. It is the VI that all other requirements, design, and hardware models presented in the remainder of this section have in common, i.e., the other models are realizations of the features defined in the feature model and the impact model relates the impact of these realization models to system qualities.

3.2 Requirements Models

The workflow model describes the two main user-system interactions of the *Authorization* concern in Fig. 3. First, the |*Administrator* may choose to define roles at any time (define start point), possibly using hierarchies (Hierarchical) and constraints (*SeparationOfDuty*). Second, the |*User* may have to authenticate herself (*authenticate* start point), but the authentication behavior must be combined with application-specific behavior of the system reusing *Authorization*. Therefore, a pointcut stub (dashed diamond shape with *P*) represents all those locations in the application that require authentication. Those locations are identified with a pattern, stating that authentication is needed when the |*User* interacts with a |*ProtectedResource* by attempting a |*protectedAction*.

The vertical bar | in the model highlights generic model elements that need to be customized to the actual application under development, i.e., these model elements constitute the Customization Interface (CI) of the workflow model. In Fig. 3 the CI elements are highlighted in orange. For example, |*ProtectedResource* may have to be matched against *Account* and |*protectedAction* against *withdraw* and *transfer*. Given these customizations, the *authenticate* behavior would be composed with the *withdraw* and *transfer* actions, resulting in an authentication check before performing these actions (because the authenticate behavior occurs before the *requiresAuthentication* pointcut stub).

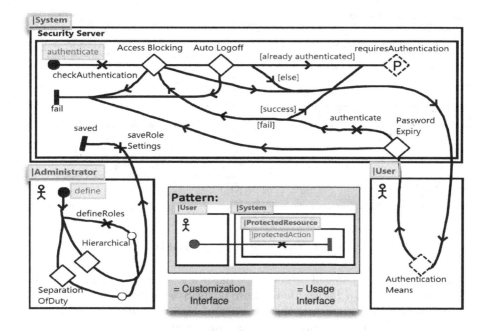

Fig. 3. Authorization requirements models (Color figure online)

The UI is defined by the start points (i.e., *define*, *authenticate*, and all start points of lower-level workflow models of the variable features depicted by stubs (diamonds)). In Fig. 3 the UI elements are highlighted in yellow.

We used Aspect-oriented Use Case Maps (AoUCM) to represent the workflow of *Authorization*. However, the approach is not AoUCM-specific and could have considered other languages like activity diagrams or BPMN models and their aspect-oriented extensions.

3.3 Design Models

To illustrate reusable software design models, we design realization models for each feature of *Authorization* using RAM [13]. For space reasons, only the RAM model realizing the root feature of *Authorization* is shown in Fig. 4. The RAM model comprises two compartments, the structural view showing the class diagram and the message view defined using sequence diagrams. The partial structural entities such as the class |*User* and the operation |*execute* again designate the CI. The UI is comprised of all public classes and operations.

3.4 Hardware Models

Often, software is connected to specific hardware elements with which it tightly interacts. In the context of *Authorization*, this is the case for specific *Authentication Means* like *Fingerprint* or *Facial Recognition*. To illustrate that our

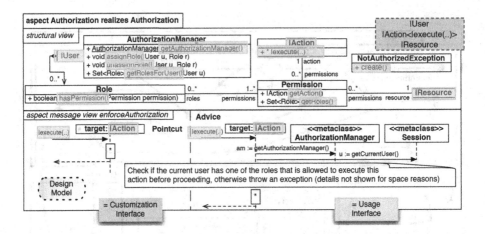

Fig. 4. Authorization design models

interfaces are also capable of dealing with hardware, we present hardware models realizing the *Facial Recognition* feature in the System Model in Fig. 5.

We used SysML to represent the execution platform of *Authorization* because a *Block* in SysML can be realized by hardware or physical elements. However, the approach is not SysML-specific and could have considered other suitable modeling languages like MARTE or AADL. Features are therefore realized not only by workflow models and UML design models, but also by a SysML block diagram specifying the hardware and by a SysML allocation model specifying how the software is linked to the hardware.

Our facial recognition artifact could contain lots of hardware variability (such as different quality cameras, optional light sensors) as shown in the feature model, but for space reasons we are only illustrating one hardware model using a video camera and a luminosity sensor.

The SysML internal block diagram describes the hardware elements that *FacialRecognition* provides to measure physical data: a *VideoCamera* and a *LightSensor*. It also depicts required hardware elements, such as a *PowerSource*, a *LightSource*, a *USB plug*, and at least one *CPU*, and specifies how they are connected to the provided hardware. These elements constitute the CI of our hardware model, highlighted again with the vertical bar. Allocations of drivers to ≪part≫ model elements show how the software relates to the hardware.

The remainder of this subsection summarizes the VCU interfaces for a reusable artifact for system modeling, i.e., when software and hardware are to be made reusable. In this case, the VI also includes the hardware variability offered by the unit of reuse, and the resulting impacts on high-level goals such as cost, power consumption, impact on environment, and noise. The CI also includes hardware elements or physical elements in addition to software elements (e.g., the temperature in the environment), and constraints on their properties (e.g., greater than 100 Watt). The UI includes the functionality needed by the user of the hardware artefact during execution/simulation of the model, i.e., interfaces

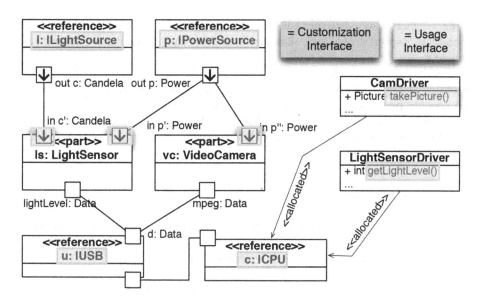

Fig. 5. Authorization system models

offered by the drivers (e.g., takePicture()) but it also includes the physical data flow ports needed to make the system operational (e.g., a specific amount of electricity through a power connection, a minimum and maximum quantity of lumens into a lens). This hardware model highlights that even if the nature of the UI is different from the one in a software model (i.e., it is not based only on method declarations), the notion of UI is still valid and correctly encompasses these different notions.

3.5   Reusing Authorization

This section illustrates how the *Authorization* concern is reused in a simple ATM machine. The ATM developer selects from the *Authorization* VI the desired features with the best impact (step 1 in 2.4). Based on this selection, the workflow, design, and system models linked to the selected features are composed by the reuse tool to create workflow, design, and system models for *Authorization* that only contain the selected features.

The next step (step 2 in 2.4) is to customize each kind of model by establishing mappings from the *Authorization* CI to the ATM models. To customize *Authorization* to the ATM context at the workflow and design level, |*User* of *Authorization* is mapped to the *Customer* component in the ATM workflow model and the *Customer* class in the ATM design model. Similarly, |*ProtectedResource* in the workflow as well as |*Action* and |*Resource* in the design are mapped to *Account*. Finally, the |*protectedAction* responsibility in the workflow and the |*execute* operation of *Action* are mapped to the *withdraw* and *deposit* responsibilities and operations of *Account*, respectively:

|User → Customer; |ProtectedResource → Account; |protectedAction →
withdraw, deposit; |Action, |Resource → Account; |execute → withdraw,
deposit.

The internal block diagram model of the ATM machine contains parts representing the specific CPU that was chosen, the memory used, the USB ports, the specific power source chosen, etc. To customize the *Authentication* hardware model, mappings must be established that link the CI model elements to model elements in the ATM machine that satisfy the property constraints, e.g.: |PowerSource → SeaSonicSS; |USB → MediasonicHP1-U34F; ...

4   VCU Interfaces Across Reuse Techniques

While the last section demonstrated the use of the VCU interfaces in requirements, design, and hardware models across various levels of abstraction, this section focuses on VCU interfaces in existing reuse techniques.

Usage Interface: The prototypical example of a UI is the API of a class in an object-oriented programming language. Standard classes do not have a customization interface, as all of their public operations and attributes are fully specified and defined (as opposed to generic classes described in the next paragraph). UIs can also be of considerable size, such as the API of an entire library. Libraries, even if comprised by several classes that offer alternative functionality, typically do not have an explicit VI. Information about variants encapsulated in the library, and impacts of the different variants on non-functional requirements and qualities are informally described in textual documentation, if at all.

Customization and Usage Interfaces: Generic classes are a popular reuse mechanism in programming languages, such as Ada, Java, and C++ (where they are called template classes). In essence, a generic class provides a crisp set of functionalities, and for that purpose encapsulates some structure and behavior that is generically applicable for all parameter types. The CI is defined by the parameters, which are classes, types, and often also operations that define what the generic class needs from the reuse context. The programmer must provide the correct parameters at development time, when instantiating the generic class, to customize the class to a particular reuse context and to access its tailored UI.

In modeling, the CI is defined in similar form. The UML template parameters provide the mechanism to tailor models to different reuse contexts. They can be applied to a class as in programming languages. However, template parameters can also be applied to UML packages, thus effectively parameterizing the entire model contained in the package. Many aspect-oriented modeling techniques offer UML template parameters or similar CIs to adapt aspect models that encapsulate reusable structure and behavior to specific reuse contexts (e.g., [3]).

Application frameworks are also composed of classes, but usually focus on providing reusable structure and behavior related to a specific domain (e.g., Graphical User Interfaces, Persistence, Banking). By definition, frameworks impose an application architecture, drive the execution control flow, and require the programmer to tailor the framework to their needs and integrate the application's behavior by implementing interfaces or extending classes provided by the framework. The CI of a framework is defined by the interfaces and abstract classes that need to be subclassed by the programmer to reuse the framework. The UI of the framework consists of the public (or published) operations defined in its API.

Components are broad units of reuse that encapsulate a set of classes whose instances collaborate to provide a reusable service. The required interface of a component is a form of CI, since it allows the component to list the services it needs from the reuse context in order to be operational. The provided interface describes the service(s) that the component offers, and hence is equivalent to the UI.

All four discussed mechanisms have clearly defined CIs and UIs. Customization is in all forms applied by binding open holes, namely generic parameters or super classes, with concrete types or subclasses. Usage in all forms is defined by the public (published) interfaces. None of them however explicitly provide mechanisms for expressing the variation they encapsulate, if any. It would be very interesting to add such explicit variation mechanisms into the respective programming or modeling techniques, in order to allow documenting and understanding possible variation and selecting variants at design time. Currently variation can only implicitly be achieved by using the UI, i.e., calling mode-setting functions to adapt behavior, or using the CI by defining several subclasses for hot spots in frameworks. In the latter case, creational design patterns such as *Factory* [8] can be used to select variations encapsulated by the framework at initialization time or at run time.

Variation and Usage Interfaces: A common approach to handle variability at the domain level is to follow a Software Product Lines (SPL) approach [20]. SPL engineering focuses on how to organize similar software products as a family within a closed domain, exploiting commonalities, and managing variabilities among them. Many implementation techniques have been proposed for SPLs, but when the variability is explicitly represented, feature models [11] are then widely used. In this context, feature models are a perfect mechanism for the VI, as they express the (closed) variability of an SPL.

The UI is usually obtained by a derivation process on the SPL assets. Assets can be code, models, or other software artifacts. Two main groups can be distinguished by their way to derive a product, i.e., annotative and compositional. At the model level, annotative approaches [5] normally use annotations on model elements and prune them during derivation. On the other hand, compositional approaches rely on several models or fragments corresponding to the selected features that then need to be well integrated. For structural models, such as class diagrams composition, techniques can notably rely on aspect-oriented modeling [17], model merging [19] or delta modeling techniques [9]. Related to our authorization case study, a recently proposed compositional approach [14] captures the variability of RBAC models in a feature model to configure an associated UML model.

In the SPL field, researchers have also proposed extensions to feature models so that the VI is enriched with properties on features. This can be done with attributes on features [4], typically representing non-functional properties within the SPL that can be reasoned about. By the scoped and closed nature of a SPL, the CI is not explicitly present, but it is of course possible that the selected and composed assets provide individual customization mechanisms (as already discussed in the *"Customization and Usage Interfaces"* subsection).

The Service-Oriented Architecture (SOA) is a software architecture style that views the system as set of services that are self-contained, loosely coupled, and can be easily composed. SOA provides guidelines that govern how services are represented and used. Services are designed to address business-related behaviour and logic, and are meant to be assembled to build enterprise solutions [16]. Connections between services are flexible, as services are dynamically invoked at run time through a UI that is described, for instance, by means of the Web Service Description Language (WSDL).

There exist SOA approaches that provide a sort of variability interface, which is helpful in choosing the most appropriate service during run-time. Service Level Agreements (SLAs) specify non-functional properties of services, which is a way of specifying the impacts of services that allows for a limited form of trade-off analysis when multiple services providing similar functionality are available.

Table 1. Summary of common units of reuse

Units of reuse	Usage interface	Customization interface	VI variation	VI impact
Classes	Yes	No	No	No
Generic classes	Yes	Yes	No	No
Components	Yes	Yes	No	No
Frameworks	Yes	Yes	Informal	Informal
Feature models	Yes	No	Yes	No
Feature models with attributes	Yes	No	Yes	Yes
Services	Yes	No	Limited	Limited

Variation, Customization, and Usage Interfaces: A summary of the analysis of the most common units of reuse and their support for usage, customization and variation interfaces is shown in Table 1. Although none of the units provides out-of-the-box support for all three interfaces, there has been lots of research extending their reuse potential.

Perrouin et al. [19] have proposed an approach to provide some flexibility by broadening the scope of the captured variability. In a first reuse step, variability is resolved from a feature model selection and a product is generated by automatically merging model elements associated to the selected features. A second reuse step involves a customization process implemented by a model transformation and validated by OCL constraints defined on the model elements. This can be seen as a first, but not very explicit, form of the CI.

Handling variability while being able to consider unplanned contexts is a problem that has already been tackled in other works, mainly by introducing variability management in reusable units such as components [18, 22] or modules [12]. van der Storm defines variable components [22] and uses solving techniques for checking compatibility among them. In a similar way, Plastic Partial Components [18] are components equipped with several variable interfaces and implemented internally with aspect-oriented techniques in model-driven software architectures. These approaches are more flexible than common SPL techniques, as they are handling variability at the component level, providing VIs (although with limited support for specifying impacts) and UIs. Nevertheless, the customization part is not as fine-grained as in our definition, as it is obtained by the different compositions of components, and not at the level of each component.

Recently, Kästner et al. [12] proposed a core calculus for variability-aware modules, complemented by a C-based implementation. Variability is handled on module interfaces and inside modules, providing a solution that covers all three VCU interfaces. Modular type checking of internal variability is supported and the composition of two compatible modules yields a well-typed module with combined variabilities. However, the notion of impact model in the VI is not covered.

Finally, there have also been efforts to provide CI for services through parameterization and personalization [1] and using templates [23]. [2] proposes an approach that allows customized use of web services in XML documents. The approach uses an XML schema that allows to specify elements/subelements of the XML document that can be specified/replaced dynamically. They provide an example of a schema for news exchange, where the element <item> can be given by a service call that matches the news service call pattern, which allows to use any service call that returns an element (news <item>) of the correct type.

5   Conclusion

Reuse is one of the most important concepts in software engineering to improve system quality, product reliability and in particular developer efficiency, thus reducing development costs. This paper argues that while there is a huge variety in the kinds of reusable artifacts, almost all forms of reuse have in common the need to provide some or all of three key interfaces, i.e., the variation, customization, and usage interface, summarized as VCU interfaces. We have discussed the commonalities and potential consequences of different kinds of reuse dimensions: (a) selecting a variant based on information about impacts, (b) adapting the generic artifact to a specific context, and (c) using the functionality. Furthermore, we discussed how the three interfaces explicitly pinpoint down "where" this reuse happens. The variation interface is needed to select from a set of choices offered by a reusable artifact while being informed about the impact of the selection. The customization interface is required to adapt a generic reusable artifact to a specific reuse context. The usage interface is needed to define how the services of a reusable artifact may be accessed.

For a better understanding of these interfaces, we have examined their concrete appearance across levels of abstraction (i.e., from requirements to software design and hardware design model) and across reuse techniques (from classes and components to software product lines and services). Based on these findings, we have found that all examined reusable artifacts indeed make use of and only of the VCU interfaces. Today we do not know of situations, where the VCU modeling approach will not hold, but these are preliminary findings. We invite the software reuse community to challenge the sufficiency of the VCU interfaces in the context of reuse. In the future, we plan to make generic support for the VCU interfaces available to several mainstream modeling notations.

References

1. Amazon: Amazon web services
2. Abiteboul, S., Amann, B., Baumgarten, J., Benjelloun, O., Ngoc, F.D., Milo, T.: Schema-driven customization of web services. In: Proceedings of the 29th International Conference on Very Large Data Bases, VLDB 2003, vol. 29, pp. 1093–1096. VLDB Endowment (2003)
3. Alam, O., Kienzle, J., Mussbacher, G.: Concern-oriented software design. In: Moreira, A., Schätz, B., Gray, J., Vallecillo, A., Clarke, P. (eds.) MODELS 2013. LNCS, vol. 8107, pp. 604–621. Springer, Heidelberg (2013)
4. Benavides, D., Trinidad, P., Ruiz-Cortés, A.: Automated reasoning on feature models. In: Pastor, Ó., Falcão e Cunha, J. (eds.) CAiSE 2005. LNCS, vol. 3520, pp. 491–503. Springer, Heidelberg (2005)
5. Czarnecki, K., Antkiewicz, M.: Mapping features to models: a template approach based on superimposed variants. In: Glück, R., Lowry, M. (eds.) GPCE 2005. LNCS, vol. 3676, pp. 422–437. Springer, Heidelberg (2005)
6. Erl, T.: Service-Oriented Architecture: Concepts, Technology, and Design. Prentice Hall PTR, Upper Saddle River (2005)
7. Ferraiolo, D.F., Sandhu, R.S., Gavrila, S.I., Kuhn, D.R., Chandramouli, R.: Proposed NIST standard for role-based access control. ACM Trans. Inf. Syst. Secur. 4(3), 224–274 (2001). doi:10.1145/501978.501980
8. Gamma, E., Helm, R., Johnson, R., Vlissides, J.: Design Patterns. Addison Wesley, Reading (1995)
9. Haber, A., Kutz, T., Rendel, H., Rumpe, B., Schaefer, I.: Delta-oriented architectural variability using monticore. CoRR abs/1409.2317 (2014)
10. International Telecommunication Union (ITU-T): Recommendation Z.151 (10/12): User Requirements Notation (URN) - Language Definition. Accessed Oct 2012
11. Kang, K., Cohen, S., Hess, J., Novak, W., Peterson, S.: Feature-oriented domain analysis (FODA) feasibility study. Technical report, CMU/SEI-90-TR-21, SEI, CMU, Nov 1990
12. Kästner, C., Ostermann, K., Erdweg, S.: A variability-aware module system. In: Leavens, G.T., Dwyer, M.B. (eds.) Proceedings of the 27th Annual ACM SIGPLAN Conference on Object-Oriented Programming, Systems, Languages, and Applications, OOPSLA 2012, Part of SPLASH 2012, pp. 773–792, Tucson, AZ, USA, 21–25 Oct 2012. ACM (2012)

13. Kienzle, J., Al Abed, W., Klein, J.: Aspect-oriented multi-view modeling. In: Proceedings of the 8th International Conference on Aspect-Oriented Software Development - AOSD, pp. 87–98, 1–6 Mar 2009. ACM Press (2009)
14. Kim, S., Kim, D.K., Lu, L., Kim, S., Park, S.: A feature-based approach for modeling role-based access control systems. J. Syst. Softw. **84**(12), 2035–2052 (2011). doi:10.1016/j.jss.2011.03.084
15. Krueger, C.W.: Software reuse. CSURV: Comput. Surv. **24**, 131–183 (1992)
16. Krut, R., Cohen, S.: Service-oriented architectures and software product lines - putting both together. In: 12th International Software Product Line Conference - SPLC 2008, p. 383, Sept 2008
17. Morin, B., Vanwormhoudt, G., Lahire, P., Gaignard, A., Barais, O., Jézéquel, J.-M.: Managing variability complexity in aspect-oriented modeling. In: Czarnecki, K., Ober, I., Bruel, J.-M., Uhl, A., Völter, M. (eds.) MODELS 2008. LNCS, vol. 5301, pp. 797–812. Springer, Heidelberg (2008)
18. Pérez, J., Díaz, J., Soria, C.C., Garbajosa, J.: Plastic partial components: a solution to support variability in architectural components. In: WICSA/ECSA, pp. 221–230. IEEE (2009)
19. Perrouin, G., Klein, J., Guelfi, N., Jézéquel, J.M.: Reconciling automation and flexibility in product derivation. In: SPLC, pp. 339–348. IEEE Computer Society (2008)
20. Pohl, K., Böckle, G., van der Linden, F.J.: Software Product Line Engineering: Foundations, Principles and Techniques. Springer-Verlag New York, Inc., Secaucus (2005)
21. Sandhu, R.S., Coyne, E.J., Feinstein, H.L., Youman, C.E.: Role-based access control models. IEEE Comput. **29**(2), 38–47 (1996)
22. van der Storm, T.: Variability and component composition. In: Dannenberg, R.B., Krueger, C. (eds.) ICOIN 2004 and ICSR 2004. LNCS, vol. 3107, pp. 157–166. Springer, Heidelberg (2004)
23. ten Teije, A., van Harmelen, F., Wielinga, B.J.: Configuration of web services as parametric design. In: Motta, E., Shadbolt, N.R., Stutt, A., Gibbins, N. (eds.) EKAW 2004. LNCS (LNAI), vol. 3257, pp. 321–336. Springer, Heidelberg (2004)

Reuse vs. Reusability of Software Supporting Business Processes

Hermann Kaindl[1(✉)], Roman Popp[1], Ralph Hoch[1], and Christian Zeidler[2]

[1] Institute of Computer Technology, TU Wien, Vienna, Austria
{kaindl,popp,hoch}@ict.tuwien.ac.at
[2] Adaptive GmbH, Vienna, Austria
zeidler@adaptive.at

Abstract. Reusing software is desirable, and so is reusing business processes. For reusing both in the course of developing software supporting business processes, an integration of related reuse approaches is necessary. Of course, such reuse is not for free and requires reusability of related artefacts, i.e., business process models and software parts supporting them. For successful reuse, of course, trade-offs with making artefacts reusable (or acquiring them) have to be beneficial.

In this paper, we present an integration of business process and software reuse and reusability (R&R). Based on it, we compare trade-offs between making reusable and reusing in the context of developing software supporting business processes. As a consequence, it should become easier to make rational judgments on whether and how to engage in R&R of such software.

Keywords: Reuse and reusability · Business process · Business software

1 Introduction

The context of this work is *reuse* in the course of creating and adapting software (SW) supporting *business processes*, where *reusability* depends on the explicit availability (and use) of a business process model (BPM). Reuse of software and of related BPMs together has the potential to increase efficiency and thus to reduce costs and time-to-market. However, the trade-offs with related investments into reusability need to be better understood.

More specifically, we focus on reuse based on repositories, as illustrated in Fig. 1. This approach integrates reuse of (similar) business processes and their adaptation for the case at hand (possibly also involving their composition) with reuse of related software parts (such as components or Web-services) and their adaptation. It requires repositories filled with reusable artefacts of both kinds, which can be efficiently looked-up for retrieval of (similar) artefacts as needed. This, in turn, requires some effort for making artefacts reusable. So, we discuss trade-offs between investments into reusability and related benefits for efficient software and process reuse.

© Springer International Publishing Switzerland 2016
G.M. Kapitsaki and E. Santana de Almeida (Eds.): ICSR 2016, LNCS 9679, pp. 138–145, 2016.
DOI: 10.1007/978-3-319-35122-3_10

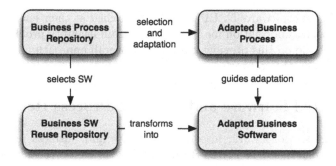

Fig. 1. Business software development with reuse from repositories

The remainder of this paper is organized in the following manner. First, we provide an overview of related work both on software and business process reuse and reusability. Then we explain an integration of software and business process reuse. For such a reuse approach, we compare trade-offs between making reusable and reusing in the context of developing software supporting business processes.

2   Related Work

Software reuse and reusability have a long tradition in general, see, e.g., [4], where Frakes and Terry reviewed, among other things, metrics and cost-benefit models. Rotaru and Dobre [14] studied the adaptability and composability of software components, both qualitatively and quantitatively (through metrics). Recently, Mohr [10] presented metrics for functional reusability of services based on their relevance. So, for software parts even quantitative measures related to their reusability are available. These could be used in the context of our approach for software reuse.

Reuse of business process models is the act of designing business processes by using existing process models. To this end, typically BPM repositories are employed. Requirements for such repositories from a stakeholders' perspective were defined in [16]. Elias and Johannesson [3] provided a survey on repositories for process models. A similar survey was carried out by Yan et al. [17]. Such repositories may serves as building blocks in the context of our approach for BPM reuse.

For retrieving relevant BPMs from such a repository, Dijkman et al. [2] described graph matching on business processes to search and find similar processes. Business process fragments may be reused during business process modeling by integration [9]. According to [1], business processes are compositions of sub-processes or process fragments. Both composability and variability are necessary for deploying a business process in an adapted way. This work may be used in the context of our approach for BPM retrieval and adaptation.

When both a BPM and related software parts are available, software supporting the modeled process may be directly driven by the BPM [11]. Based on this idea, we recently proposed a software architecture including a BPMN 2.0 engine and a model of business artefacts for aligning the architectures of the business and its supporting software [5]. BPMs can be enriched at their enactment with additional artefact information for addressing certain usability problems of such software. We build on this previous work in our overall approach for integrating a BPM directly in the software.

3   Integrated Software and Business Process Reuse

Based on this previous work, integrated software and business process reuse is possible as illustrated in Fig. 2. Business Software Reuse as sketched at the bottom of the figure may happen with virtually any software reuse approach. The figure shows a simple case-based approach, where software cases are stored in a repository, selected using some similarity measure, and adapted for the case at hand. Even a single scenario was sufficient for finding useful software cases in [7]. Such an approach is also part of a feature-similarity model for product line engineering recently co-proposed by one of these authors [8].

Business Software Reuse is integrated in our approach with Business Process Reuse as sketched at the top of the figure. Also for such a reuse, different approaches are possible. Analogously to software reuse, the figure sketches the selection of a business process (more precisely a BPM) from a repository and its adaptation. According to [13], such a process adaptation can be an *adjustment* or a *refinement*. Both may be performed even automatically through model transformations specifying business rules (see also [12]). Model transformations have also been used for automated tailoring of a software process [6], but we consider this outside the scope of our approach as presented here.

Ideally, every BPM in the repository could be executed using the software artefacts in the repository. After a process adaptation, however, some part of the adapted BPM, e.g., a Task (as illustrated in green in Fig. 2), may *not* be executable by any piece of software in the repository. Then a related software adaptation will be necessary. It may have to be done manually, but model transformations could be employed as well.

4   Comparison of R&R Trade-offs

The R&R trade-offs in the context of software supporting business processes are between an initial investment to create *reusable* software or BPM artefacts, and the benefits from having either or both of them available for later *reuse*. We compare such trade-offs in three different scenarios that primarily differ in what is given for a development or change effort:

- *Software development from scratch*
  This is the extreme case where nothing would exist yet for being reused, not even software built for prior (similar) projects.
- *Software available, but neither BPMs nor repositories for reuse*
  This is a case where software exists, which has to be changed or may be informally used somehow for creating similar software. However, no investment

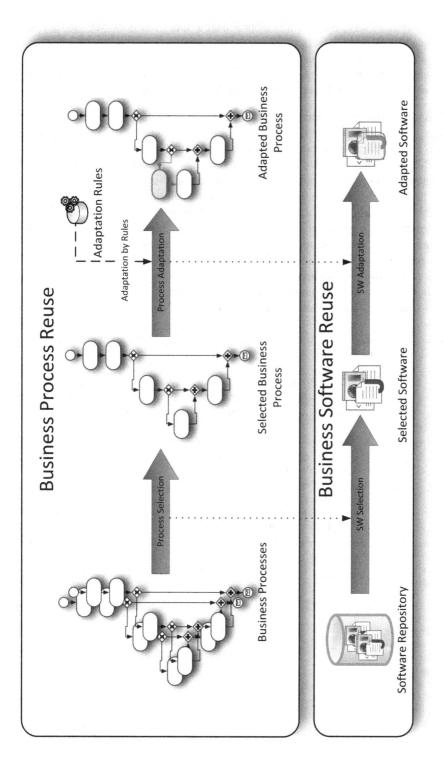

Fig. 2. Integrated business process and software reuse

into (systematically) making artefacts reusable has been done yet, neither for software nor BPM artefacts.

– *Repositories filled with reusable artefacts*
This is the other extreme case where investments have been made for creating both software and BPM repositories with reusable artefacts.

These scenarios are obviously on different levels of R&R maturity for software (see, e.g., [4]). However, they do not involve software artefacts and processes only but also related business process artefacts or processes dealing with them.

In Table 1, these scenarios are given in its rows. The columns contrast software development without any systematic reuse or reusability with the R&R approaches illustrated above in Fig. 2. In the third column, a software repository filled with reusable software artefacts is assumed to be available and used. In the fourth column, in addition, a related BPM repository filled with reusable BPMs is assumed to be available and used. "**MR**" indicates an investment through *making reusable*, while "**R**" stands for *reusing*.

Such a trade-off can obviously be in terms of some *cost* measure. As discussed below, however, investing some cost for MR may have a positive return by R in terms of *time*, e.g., time-to-market, i.e., in a different 'currency'. We also discuss

Table 1. A comparison of approaches to software development and change based on reuse and reusability

	Software development without R&R	Reuse with software repository	Reuse with BPM repository
Software development from scratch	Software development only	**MR**: repository has to be available (or created)	**MR**: repository has to be available (or created)
	Developers directly encode BP in source code	**MR**: enrich software parts with meta-data	**MR**: enrich BPMs with meta-data
	Alternative: executable BPM available or created	**MR**: organize software parts in repository	**MR**: organize BPMs in repository
Software available, but neither BPMs nor repositories for reuse	Source code has to be changed	*Same as in cell above*	*Same as in cell above*
	Depending on the architecture, more or less complicated	Possibly some reverse engineering	Possibly some reverse engineering
Repositories filled with reusable software artefacts and BPMs	—	**R**: possibility to retrieve software artefacts from repository for reuse	**R**: possibility to retrieve BPMs from repository for reuse
			R: possibility to retrieve related software artefacts from repository for reuse

positive and negative results in terms of *quality*. So, we discuss trade-offs with a triple (cost, time, quality), which was also inspired by [15].

Let us start with the scenario of software development from scratch. If it focuses on development only, then there is no investment into explicit reuse later. If there is no BPM available, developers directly encode the business process in the source code. However, if an executable PBM is explicitly given or created for the software supposed to support this process, this BPM may be directly included into a specific software architecture and drive the software at runtime (see, e.g., [5]). While this approach can be efficient, it reduces the flexibility of the software and may even entail usability problems. In terms of making such software reusable, investments should be made here to enter pieces of software such as components or Web services into a software repository. This requires that a repository is technically available or has to be created, and the artefact to be stored has to be enriched with meta-data and organized into the repository. In addition, the BPM should be made reusable as well by entering it into a repository, analogously to entering pieces of software. These investments are usually in terms of cost. While they will also take extra time, it can be spent in parallel to development projects.

When software is already available from previous projects, but neither BPMs nor repositories for reuse, then source code has to be added or changed directly. The difficulty of doing this will depend, e.g., on the software architecture. If an executable BPM drives the software, primarily adaptations of such a model will have to be made. Investments for making such software or BPMs reusable in repositories are basically the same as indicated above. When this is done only after several projects have already created software and models without making them reusable, then even some reverse engineering may have to be done additionally now.

For the scenario with repositories already filled with reusable artefacts, development will try to reuse as many as possible to make best use of them. Let us first have a brief look at the well-known case where software artefacts (only) are available for reuse in a repository. In general, it will be more efficient than software development from scratch, i.e., there will be a return of invest from MR for R in terms of cost. Actually, there should also be an improvement in time-to-market, where the investment by MR in terms of cost is paid back in terms of time. When software artefacts are often reused, it is well-known that they may become more mature, i.e., there may be a return of invest in terms of quality.

If an executable BPM drives the software, primarily adaptations of such a model will have to be made and, if they can be implemented completely by software parts from the repository, ideally no software developer will have to make any change to the source code. This requires a given framework for automatic execution of BPMs, however, with the possible downside of reduced flexibility and quality, e.g., of the user interface.

If, in addition, a repository full of BPMs is available, then they can be reused as well. In particular, BPMs may be found in the repository as needed, and two or more of these BPMs may be merged. If these BPMs are supported well by stored software parts, then ideally not much new software will have to be created anew, in stark contrast to pure software development in such a case without reuse. The return of invest from MR on this level may also be in terms of cost, time and quality through R of BPMs, much as through indirect R of related software artefacts.

5   Conclusion

In this paper, we discuss trade-offs between reuse and reusability of software supporting business processes, depending on different development approaches with and without explicit business process models and corresponding repositories. This discussion is based on the literature and on previous work of these authors.

This work aims to contribute an improved understanding of these trade-offs for different development approaches for software supporting business processes. In particular, such trade-offs may arise with different currencies, e.g., cost vs. time-to-market, with effects on quality as well. We found an argument why efforts into making artefacts should be invested early, since otherwise even additional effort in some reverse engineering may arise. Overall, a reuse approach integrating both business processes and software artefacts appears to have a high potential.

Still, our comparison is based on qualitative assessments only. Based on already existing work on metrics especially in the context of software reuse and reusability, future work should investigate such trade-offs quantitatively as well.

Acknowledgment. Part of this research has been carried out in the ProREUSE project (No. 834167), funded by the Austrian FFG.

References

1. Angles, R., Ramadour, P., Cauvet, C., Rodier, S.: V-BPMI: A variability-oriented framework for web-based business processes modeling and implementation. In: 2013 IEEE Seventh International Conference on Research Challenges in Information Science (RCIS), pp. 1–11, May 2013
2. Dijkman, R., Dumas, M., García-Bañuelos, L.: Graph matching algorithms for business process model similarity search. In: Dayal, U., Eder, J., Koehler, J., Reijers, H.A. (eds.) BPM 2009. LNCS, vol. 5701, pp. 48–63. Springer, Heidelberg (2009). doi:10.1007/978-3-642-03848-8_5
3. Elias, M., Johannesson, P.: A survey of process model reuse repositories. In: Dua, S., Gangopadhyay, A., Thulasiraman, P., Straccia, U., Shepherd, M., Stein, B. (eds.) ICISTM 2012. CCIS, vol. 285, pp. 64–76. Springer, Heidelberg (2012). doi:10.1007/978-3-642-29166-1_6
4. Frakes, W., Terry, C.: Software reuse: metrics and models. ACM Comput. Surv. **28**(2), 415–435 (1996). doi:10.1145/234528.234531

5. Hoch, R., Kaindl, H., Popp, R., Zeidler, C.: Aligning architectures of business and software: software driven by business process models and its user interface. In: Proceedings of the 2016 49th Hawaii International Conference on System Sciences, HICSS 2016. IEEE Computer Society (2016)

6. Hurtado Alegría, J.A., Bastarrica, M.C., Quispe, A., Ochoa, S.F.: An MDE approach to software process tailoring. In: Proceedings of the 2011 International Conference on Software and Systems Process, ICSSP 2011, pp. 43–52, ACM, New York, NY, USA (2011). http://doi.acm.org/10.1145/1987875.1987885

7. Kaindl, H., Śmiałek, M., Nowakowski, W.: Case-based reuse with partial requirements specifications. In: 18th IEEE International Requirements Engineering Conference (RE 2010), pp. 399–400, IEEE, New York, NY, USA (2010)

8. Kaindl, H., Mannion, M.: A feature-similarity model for product line engineering. In: Schaefer, I., Stamelos, I. (eds.) ICSR 2015. LNCS, vol. 8919, pp. 34–41. Springer, Heidelberg (2014). doi:10.1007/978-3-319-14130-5_3

9. Markovic, I., Pereira, A.C.: Towards a formal framework for reuse in business process modeling. In: ter Hofstede, A., Benatallah, B., Paik, H.-Y. (eds.) BPM Workshops 2007. LNCS, vol. 4928, pp. 484–495. Springer, Heidelberg (2008). http://dl.acm.org/citation.cfm?id=1793714.1793769

10. Mohr, F.: A metric for functional reusability of services. In: Schaefer, I., Stamelos, I. (eds.) ICSR 2015. LNCS, vol. 8919, pp. 298–313. Springer, Heidelberg (2014). doi:10.1007/978-3-319-14130-5_21

11. Ouyang, C., Dumas, M., Van Der Aalst, W.M., Ter Hofstede, A.H., Mendling, J.: From business process models to process-oriented software systems. ACM Trans. Softw. Eng. Methodol. 19(1), 2:1–2:37 (2009). doi:10.1145/1555392.1555395

12. Popp, R., Kaindl, H.: Automated adaptation of business process models through model transformations specifying business rules. In: Nurcan, S., Pimenidis, E., Pastor, O., Vassiliou, Y. (eds.) Joint Proceedings of the CAiSE 2014 Forum and CAiSE 2014 Doctoral Consortium Co-located with the 26th International Conference on Advanced Information Systems Engineering (CAiSE 2014), Thessaloniki, Greece, CEUR Workshop Proceedings, vol. 1164, pp. 65–72. CEUR-WS.org, 18–20 June 2014. http://ceur-ws.org/Vol-1164/PaperVision09.pdf

13. Popp, R., Kaindl, H.: Automated refinement of business processes through model transformations specifying business rules. In: 9th IEEE International Conference on Research Challenges in Information Science, RCIS 2015, Athens, Greece, pp. 327–333. IEEE, 13–15 May 2015. http://dx.doi.org/10.1109/RCIS.2015.7128893

14. Rotaru, O., Dobre, M.: Reusability metrics for software components. In: The 3rd ACS/IEEE International Conference on Computer Systems and Applications, p. 24 (2005)

15. Sametinger, J.: Software Engineering with Reusable Components. Springer, New York (1997)

16. Shahzad, K., Elias, M., Johannesson, P.: Requirements for a business process model repository: a stakeholders' perspective. In: Abramowicz, W., Tolksdorf, R. (eds.) BIS 2010. LNBIP, vol. 47, pp. 158–170. Springer, Heidelberg (2010). doi:10.1007/978-3-642-12814-1_14

17. Yan, Z., Dijkman, R., Grefen, P.: Business process model repositories - framework and survey. Inf. Softw. Technol. 54(4), 380–395 (2012). http://www.sciencedirect.com/science/article/pii/S0950584911002291

Component-Based Reuse

A Case Study on the Availability of Open-Source Components for Game Development

Maria-Eleni Paschali[1(✉)], Apostolos Ampatzoglou[2], Stamatia Bibi[3], Alexander Chatzigeorgiou[4], and Ioannis Stamelos[1]

[1] Department of Computer Science,
Aristotle University of Thessaloniki, Thessaloniki, Greece
{mpaschali,stamelos}@csd.auth.gr
[2] Institute of Mathematics and Computer Science,
University of Groningen, Groningen, The Netherlands
a.ampatzoglou@rug.nl
[3] Department of Informatics and Telecommunications,
University of Western Macedonia, Kozani, Greece
sbibi@uowm.gr
[4] Department of Applied Informatics,
University of Macedonia, Thessaloniki, Greece
achat@uom.gr

Abstract. Nowadays the amount of source code that is freely available inside open-source software repositories offers great reuse opportunities to software developers. Therefore, it is expected that the implementation of several requirements can be facilitated by reusing open source software components. In this paper, we focus on the reuse opportunities that can be offered in one specific application domain, i.e., game development. In particular, we performed an embedded multiple case study on approximately 110 open-source games, exploiting a large-scale repository of OSS components, and investigated: (a) which game genres can benefit from open source reuse, and (b) what types of requirements can the available open-source components map to. The results of the case study suggest that: (a) game genres with complex game logic, e.g., First Person Shooter, Strategy, Role-Playing, and Sport games offer the most reuse opportunities, and (b) the most common requirement types that can be developed by reusing OSS components are related to scenarios and characters.

1 Introduction

The last two decades video games have become one of the most important forms of entertainment in modern societies, with respect to their social and economic impact. Specifically, in recent years, and especially among the youth, playing games has outperformed many other types of entertainment, like listening to music or watching movies. Additionally, it is reported that the worldwide revenue of the game industry increased from nearly $11 billion in 2003 to $50 billion in 2007 [13] and is still rising until now. One of the most important business requirements of successful game series,

© Springer International Publishing Switzerland 2016
G.M. Kapitsaki and E. Santana de Almeida (Eds.): ICSR 2016, LNCS 9679, pp. 149–164, 2016.
DOI: 10.1007/978-3-319-35122-3_11

which is a prerequisite for surviving demanding competition, is the need for continuous release of newer game versions or patches. Therefore, game development is an intense process, which requires techniques that will shorten the product time to market and simultaneously minimize the effort spent for debugging and testing activities [3, 30].

Reuse is a software engineering technique that offers such benefits, since it increases development productivity [8, 32] and product quality [16, 21]. In addition, despite the fact that games are usually large and complex software projects with high individuality, one can identify a variety of common concepts (e.g., maps, weapons, terrains, etc.), which can enable reuse among games of the same genre. To introduce reuse into the game development process, several studies have proposed software architectures that improve the reusability of games (e.g., [15, 18, 28]). The aim of such architectures is to deliver more stable and extensible software, with enhanced interoperability, robustness and scalability.

In most of the cases, solutions that facilitate reuse discuss the utilization of componentized opportunities (e.g., [12, 34]). In software engineering, components are typically equivalent to software packages or groups of classes that encapsulate a set of related and well defined functions [40]. By taking into account the enormous amount of source code that is available in Open Source Software (OSS) repositories (e.g., Sourceforge, Github, etc.), in this paper we perform an exploratory case study to investigate the opportunity to reuse OSS components in game development. To achieve this goal, we exploit a large-scale repository of OSS components (namely Percerons[1]) that at this point offers approximately 3,000 components retrieved from open source games. The case study aims at investigating the available open source components, which can be supplied for reuse in the game development community, based on:

(p1) *Game genre specificity*: By taking into account that software reuse is more efficient when performed within the same application domain [24], we investigate how many components have been identified for each game genre (e.g., *sports* games, *strategy* games, *RPGs*, etc.). It is expected that game genres with high availability of components, can more easily benefit from OSS reuse. The game genres that we investigate are extracted from sourceforge.net, i.e., the source code repository, on which the games have been originally published. The studied genres are: *arcade, board, card, first person shooter, puzzle, role-playing, sports* and *strategy* games.

(p2) *Requirements specificity*: Even within a specific game genre, components can be further classified, based on the requirement that they implement. Such a classification would provide an even more fine-grained level of specificity, based on which we can further quantify the supply of components. For instance, a component that is related to the scenario of a game, e.g., an inventory of a player in an RPG, is only reusable in scenarios that involve the management of objects collected by game characters. To this end, we have manually classified a subset of the components of the *Percerons* database in seven categories: *scenario, controls, community, speed, characters, sound,* and *graphics*. The categories have been retrieved from the work of Ham et al. [22], on gamers' satisfaction

---

[1] http://www.percerons.com.

factors. The connection between game satisfaction factors and requirements is discussed in Sect. 2.3.

(p3) **Reusability**: However, the identification of a software component is only the first step towards its reuse. The next step is its adaptation to the target system. The ease of adapting a software component in a new system is quantified through the *reusability* quality attribute [1]. Therefore, we investigate if there are statistically significant differences in the reusability of components, identified in games of different genres.

The rest of the paper is organized as follows: In Sect. 2 we introduce the concepts of *software reuse* and *component-based software engineering*. Additionally, we provide background information that is used in this study, i.e., aspects of *game engineering* and *the component extraction algorithm* of Percerons. In Sect. 3 we present the study design in the form of a case study protocol. In Sect. 4 we provide the results, organized by research question, and discuss them in Sect. 5. In Sect. 6 we discuss the threats to validity of our study, and in Sect. 6, we conclude the paper.

2 Background Information

2.1 Software Reuse

Software reuse is the process of implementing or updating software systems using existing software assets [26]. Software reuse according to Baldassaire [8] is a software engineering technique that, when adopted systematically, can improve and even guarantee software quality. Additionally, it is suggested that reuse **has a positive effect on productivity and quality** [8]. The results of the previous study are verified in [32] where traditional and reuse-based software productions are compared in an industrial context. Furthermore, a failure mode model for part-based software reuse was proposed to improve the reuse processes [16].

Source code **reuse** is considered to be more **intense** in OSS development compared to commercial/closed source software [31]. Heinemann et al. performed an empirical multiple-case study in 20 popular OSS Java projects and concluded that third party reuse is common in OSS [23], while Raemaekers et al. [36] pointed out that logging frameworks (e.g., log4j) are the most frequently reused libraries. Sojer and Henkel [39] investigated, through a survey among 686 open-source developers, the usage of existing open-source code for the development of new open-source software. Their results showed that on average 30% of the offered functionality is based on reuse.

Another type of studies aims at **diversifying between white-box and black-box reuse**. According to Heinemann et al. [23] black-box reuse is the predominant form of reuse. These findings are in accordance with those of Haefliger et al. [21], who concluded that black-box reuse is the dominant form of reuse by analyzing six open source projects and interviewing their developers. Schwittek and Eicker [38] examined black-box reuse in OSS web applications resulting that on average this type of applications reuse 70 libraries, 50% of which come from the Apache Foundation. White-box reuse has been studied by Frakes et al. and Mockus et al. on 38.7 thousand OSS projects, by measuring filename overlapping. The results showed that more than

50% of the components are reused in more than one projects [16] and [31]. In general it seems that identifying application domains [38], requirements specificity [36] and type of reuse [16, 23, 31] is of great importance in guiding practitioners on where to find appropriate components of reuse.

2.2   Component-Based Software Engineering

Component-Based Software Engineering (CBSE) is an approach that relies on software reuse. CBSE purpose is twofold: (a) to facilitate the development of reusable components that can be used in various independent systems, apart from the one initially implemented for (i.e. development *for* reuse), and (b) to exploit reusable components for the development of new systems (i.e. development *with* reuse).

In the literature a variety of terms regarding software components can be found, as the term "component" is considered so generic that is used to denote any software part: architectural, design, source code, or requirements unit [17], patterns or even methods and lines of code [14, 40]. In JavaBeans the component is considered to be a class, in Component Object Model (COM) and CORBA Component Model (CCM) a component is an object, whereas in SOFA, PECOS and Pin it is an architectural unit [27]. However, Szyperski [40] distinguishes between classes and components: components are more abstract than classes and can be considered to be stand-alone service providers consisting of one or more classes. Components are "fired" during execution and therefore considered as deployment units, while classes are considered as development artifacts. Unlike classes, components can be synthesized with different technologies and can contain elements such as global variables, images, html files, etc.

Component adoption in software reuse may occur in many levels of granularity from a few lines of code to even a whole system [2]. Franch et al. point out the importance of the component selection process in software engineering, a fact that indicates the growing need for establishing software reuse patterns and guidelines [17]. The separation of the components' interface from the components' functionality is an important aspect of a component that may increase its reuse. For this reason according to [14] the use of design patterns in components analysis and design can be useful in increasing component cohesion and minimizing component internal coupling.

2.3   Game Engineering

The main requirement of every game is to be entertaining (see [11, 25, 41]) and therefore gamers' satisfaction factors are of paramount importance in the game analysis phase. The first study that investigated the factors from which gamers gain satisfaction was performed by Ham et al. [22]. The results of the study suggested that game satisfaction factors are game genre specific. Ham et al. investigated seven satisfaction factors (Scenario, Graphics, Sound, Game Speed, Game Control, Character and Community) and several game genres (Role Playing Games - RPG, First Person Shooter - FPS, Sport Video Games and Computer-Mediated Board Games). The average importance of each factor, calculated over all game genres, is depicted in Table 1.

Table 1. User satisfaction factors [22]

Id	Factor	Importance	Id	Factor	Importance
1	Character	20,0 %	5	Scenario	11,1 %
2	Graphics	17,6 %	6	Sound	10,8 %
3	Game Control	16,7 %	7	Community	10,1 %
4	Game Speed	13,7 %			

While discussing the results of this paper, we have to note that this study has been published a decade ago, when the state of practice in game industry was substantially different. A replication of the aforementioned study has been published in 2014, by Paschali et al. [33]. In the recent study, the results have been updated: Character Solidness, Scenario and Sound are highlighted as the most important factors for gamers' satisfaction, followed by Game Speed, Game Community, Controls and Graphics. The fact that the results of the two studies are contradicting is considered rather intuitive, in the sense that such factors are highly related to the most popular game genre, and the state of practice in the industry. In this study, we reuse the *game satisfaction factors* as *types of requirements*.

2.4 An Algorithm for Component Identification

In this section we shortly describe the methodology that is used in the study to identify components from open source games, as proposed by Ampatzoglou et al. [4]. The used algorithm is based on the identification of reusable sets of classes, by applying a path-based strong component algorithm [19]. To apply this algorithm a directed graph is created that depicts the dependencies among the classes of the system and then depth-first search is performed to identify strongly connected components, in our case: sets of classes. The algorithm successively provides sets of classes that are as independent as possible, grouped together according to the functionality that they offer. In particular the steps of the applied methodology are the following:

step 1. Create a dynamic two dimensional array where *Candidate Components* will be stored in. Each row will store groups of classes that depend on each other. In row 1 only one class will be stored depending solely on itself. In row two, couples of classes will be stored that depend on each other, in row three triplets of classes will be stored presenting dependencies, etc. Each row number defines the maximum number of classes that can be included in a *Candidate Component*. The columns represent the number of possible *Candidate Components* that can be used for each component size. At this step only the first *Component Candidate*, of size 1, is created for one class of the system.

step 2. Identify the classes that the participants in the *Candidate Components* identified in the previous step are connected to.

step 3. Sort the dependencies according to their number of external dependencies in a descending order.

step 4. For every dependency create an updated *Component Candidate* and place it in the corresponding position in the array according to the number of classes in the dependency group.

step 5. Return to step 2, for every Component Candidate created in the previous step, according to the order that they have been added in the array. The process stops if the maximum number of components is reached or if there are no external dependencies.

step 6. For every dependency in the list create an updated *Component Candidate* and place it in the corresponding position in the data structures.

step 7. For every Component Candidate created in the previous step, following the order that each candidate was identified, return to step 2. Stop if maximum number of components is reached or if there are no external dependencies.

For example, by applying the algorithm on the dependency graph of Fig. 1, we obtain the candidate components presented in Table 2. The intermediate steps on the application of the algorithm are presented in detail in the original study [4]. We note that from the candidate components identified by this algorithm, we only investigate those that are independent of other system classes (i.e., have zero efferent coupling [29]).

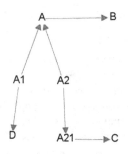

Fig. 1. Dependency graph (Example)

Table 2. Extracted components (Example)

	A	A1	A2	A21	B	C	D
Size 1	A	A1	A2	A21	B	C	D
Size 2	A,B	A1,D	A,A1	A,A2	A2,A21	A21,C	A,C
Size 3	A,A1,D	A,A1,B	A,A2,B	A,A2,A21	A,A21,C	A2,A21,C	A,B,C
Size 4	A,A1,B,D	A,A2, A21,B	A,A2,A21,C				
Size 5	A,A2,A21, B,C						

3   Case Study Design

In this section, we present the protocol that has been used for guiding the execution of this case study. The case study has been designed and is reported based on the guidelines of Runeson et al. [37]. Therefore, in Sect. 3.1 we present the aim of the study and the research questions in which we decompose it, in Sects. 3.2 and 3.3 we describe the case selection and the data collection processes, and in Sect. 3.4, we provide an overview of the data analysis process.

3.1   Research Question

The goal of this case study, based on GQM [10], is to **characterize** OSS components **with respect to** their domain-specificity and reusability **from the point of view of** software engineers *in the context of* game development. To ease the design and reporting of the case study, we split the aforementioned goal into three research questions, based on the analysis perspectives (i.e., game genre specificity, requirements type specificity, and reusability) that we introduced in Sect. 1, as follows:

[RQ₁]: *Which game genres offer the most open source components?*
This research question aims at identifying game genres that offer the larger pool of components. The game genres that are used in this study have been extracted from sourceforge.net, i.e., the repository from which the OSS projects have been retrieved. The categorization on sourceforge.net is performed by the game developers, and therefore is considered accurate. The analysis will provide an overall view of how many components are found on average in each game genre.

[RQ₂]: *Which are the game requirements to which most open source components are related?*
This question explores the types of requirements for which the most components are implemented. Requirements are mapped to game satisfaction factors, as presented in Sect. 2.3 (see [33]). The analysis will provide insight on the game requirements for which components are more easily accessible, based on the quantitative analysis.

[RQ₃]: *What is the reusability of open source components for each game genre?*
The two quality attributes related to software reuse are functionality and reusability. These attributes will be analyzed for the components retrieved across different game genres.

[RQ₃.₁]: *Is there a difference in the average functionality offered by open source components for various game genres?*

[RQ₃.₂]: *Is there a difference in the average reusability of open source components for various game genres?*

The results of this research question are expected to provide insights on how easy it is to reuse one component, upon its identification.

3.2 Case Selection

The case study of this paper is a holistic multiple-case study [37] for RQ_1 and an embedded-multiple case study for RQ_2 and RQ_3. The context of the study is OSS game development, the cases are open source games (for RQ_1 games are also the units of analysis), and units of analysis (for RQ_2 and RQ_3) are open source components.

In order to select as many cases as possible for our case study, we exploited a repository of open source components, namely Percerons (see http://www.percerons. com). Percerons is a software engineering platform [5] created by one of the authors with the aim of facilitating empirical research in software engineering, by providing: (a) indications of componentizable parts of source code, (b) quality assessment, and (c) design pattern instances. The platform is consistently used for empirical research in the last three empirical software engineering conferences (ESEM' 13 [6], ESEM'14 [20], and ESEM' 15 [7, 35]). The identification of units of analysis is performed automatically, by dumping the complete database of the repository.

In its current state *Percerons* provides 6.4 million candidate components that concern 8 application domains. From these candidate components, 1.1 million have been retrieved from OSS computer games. However, we need to note that the majority of these components are not completely independent, since the algorithm described in Sect. 2.4 stores components with efferent coupling less than 10. In our case study as units of analysis, we consider approximately 3,000 components that are completely independent and compileable (i.e., efferent coupling equals zero). The average size of the components that are used as units of analysis is 6.52 classes (standard deviation: 8.92), ranging from single class components to components up to 40 classes.

3.3   Data Collection

In order to answer our research questions for every open source game that we analyzed we recorded the following variables:

- *Game Name*: The name of the open source game that we analyzed.
- *Game Genre*: The genre of the game—*Arcade, Board, Card, FPS, Puzzle, RPG, Sports* and *Strategy*. We note that some categories that are obtained from Percerons have been excluded or merged, due to the low number of games that they involved. For example, *Educational* games have been removed, *Turn-Based* and *Real-Time* Strategy games have been merged in a common category, named *Strategy*.
- *Number of Components*: The number of independent and compileable components that have been identified for the current game.

Additionally, for each component the following variables have been recorded:

- *Component ID*: A unique identifier for the component.
- *Game Genre*: Derived from the case variables.
- *Requirement Type:* The type of requirement that the component implements. The possible classes for this variable are: *Scenario, Controls, Community, Speed, Characters, Sound,* and *Graphics*. We note that since this was a manual process, it was performed on only a limited number of components. In particular, we explored 100 random components, of various sizes, extracted from different games, belonging to various game genres.
- *Reusability:* The reusability, as provided by the Percerons database, is calculated based on the Quality Model for Object-Oriented Design (QMOOD) [9]. QMOOD suggests that reusability is calculated as a function of component size in classes, cohesion, coupling, and public interface. By taking into account: (a) the rigorous empirical validation of QMOOD by experienced software engineers, and (b) its popularity in the software engineering literature, we assume that it is a valid model for quantifying reusability. In any case, we note that at this stage we are not interested in the actual value of reusability, but only on components ranking.

- *Functionality:* As a measure of functionality we use Afferent Coupling (AffC), as proposed by Martin [29]. Afferent coupling counts the number of system classes that actually invoke any method of the public interface of the component. In that sense, it is a proxy of the functionality that this component offers to the rest of the system. Thus, a component that provides high functionality to other system classes is more probable to be reused than another that only provides limited services, even in its original system.

3.4 Data Analysis

The data analysis step of this case study includes the calculation of descriptive statistics, and the application of independent sample t-tests and Analysis of Variance (ANOVA). Table 3 summarizes the data analysis process that we have applied in this case study.

In particular for RQ_1 the number of components retrieved per game genre is presented along with basic descriptive statistics (i.e., minimum, maximum, and average number of components per game). Also the standard deviation which is calculated to quantify the amount of variation in the number of components per game is presented. Additionally Analysis of Variance is performed to identify whether there are certain game genres that offer significantly more components. One limitation of ANOVA is the fact that it identifies differences in the mean value of the testing variable, among groups, but it does not specify which groups are different. Therefore, the results of ANOVA are further explored with independent sample t-tests, in order to identify which game genres (i.e., the grouping variable) are different in terms of the number of components they offered (i.e., independent variable).

Concerning RQ_2, we discuss the frequency with which components implement various requirement types. The results are presented in the form of a pie chart. The same descriptive statistics as RQ_1 are presented for reusability and functionality metrics with respect to the various game genres, addressing **RQ3**. In that case ANOVA and independent samples t-test are performed to identify whether different game genres offer components that present *significant* differences in reusability and functionality.

Table 3. Data analysis and presentation overview

RQ	Variable	Analysis
Components / Genre	Number of Components *Grouping Variable*: Game Genre	• Descriptive statistics (mean, min, max, std. dev.) • Frequencies • ANOVA
Components / Requirements	Number of Components *Grouping Variable*: Requirement Type	• Frequencies (pie chart)
Reusability / Genre	Reusability Functionality *Grouping Variable*: Game Genre	• Descriptive statistics (mean, min, max, std. dev.) • Frequencies • ANOVA

4   Results

In this section we present the results of our case study, organized by research question, and based on the data analysis plan, as presented in Sect. 3.4. Therefore, first we present the results as obtained by the statistical analysis and then interpret them.

RQ1 (Availability of Components for Game Genres). Table 4 presents the results that have been obtained by splitting the dataset by game genre and then calculating basic descriptive statistics. The results of Table 4 are ranked by the mean value of components offered by one game (see column 4). It can be observed that the game genre that has the highest number of components (see Frequency—column 3) is *Board* games, followed by *Puzzles*. However, we need to underline that these game genres are the ones with the most games in the dataset (see N—column 2). In terms of average components per game, we observe that the maximum value exists for *FPS* and *Strategy* games, whereas the least components per game are found in *Board, Card* and *Puzzle* games. Thus, based on this ranking we can claim that the amount of components that are available for Board and Puzzle games are only due to the number of explored games, and not due to game-specific characteristics.

To investigate if the aforementioned differences are statistically significant, we first perform an Analysis of Variance (ANOVA), which suggested that some of the game genres offers significantly more components per game (F: 3.62, sig: 0.00). Next, in order to identify which game genres are those that stand out, either positively or negatively, we performed independent sample t-tests. The results revealed that the top-2 genres (i.e., *FPS* and *Strategy* games) are indeed having more available components than the rest game genres. The second group of game genres (i.e., *RPG* and *Sport* games), although offer on average approximately 10 additional components compared to the other genres, this result is not statistically significant.

A possible explanation of the aforementioned ranking is the level of game logic complexity of every game genre. For example, *Arcade, Puzzle, Card* and *Board* games have a rather limited game logic (at least compared to the other genres), less impressive graphics, etc. Therefore, the amount of possible components is limited. On the other hand, the various characters, scenario objects, etc. offered in FPS, Strategy, Sports games and RPGs, offer many reuse opportunities.

Table 4. Component per game genre

Genre	N	Frequency	Mean	Std. Dev	Min	Max
First Person Shooter (FPS)	8	400	50.00	36.02	3	99
Strategy	9	438	48.67	23.71	17	83
Sports	6	212	35.33	27.48	7	72
RPG	10	348	34.80	26.34	9	76
Arcade	17	407	23.94	12.19	8	45
Puzzle	21	464	22.10	18.39	1	64
Card	7	153	21.86	18.89	5	59
Board	31	647	20.87	18.49	4	80

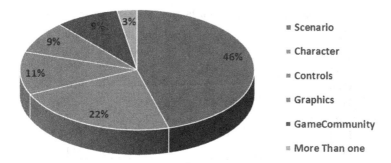

Fig. 2. Pie Chart (Frequency of Requirement types)

RQ2 (Availability of Components for Requirement Types). Concerning RQ_2, we discuss the frequency with which components implement the various requirement types (see Fig. 2). The results of the pie chart suggest that most of the identified components are implementing requirements that concern the game *Scenarios*, followed by *Characters*. Another interesting finding is that we were not able to identify any component that is related to game *Speed*[2].

The fact that game speed has not been associated with any component is intuitive in the sense that speed is a run-time characteristic that cannot be identified with static source code analysis. In addition, the extensive linkage of components to scenarios and characters is in accordance to our discussion for RQ_1 suggesting that most of the components are found in games with complex game logic.

RQ3 (Reusability of Components for Game Genres). In order to investigate the reusability of components that are extracted from different game genres, we performed descriptive statistics, ANOVA, and independent sample t-tests for two testing variables: component functionality (afferent coupling) and component reusability. In Table 5, we present descriptive statistics concerning the afferent coupling of components extracted from different game genres. The results suggest that *RPGs*, *FPSs*, and *Sport* games offer components that are more intensively used inside their games. This fact can be explained by the average size of these games, in the sense that games with more classes are expected to have more method invocations to the extracted components. Another interesting finding is that all differences that are presented in Table 5 are statistically significant and therefore generalizable to the population, according to the individual independent sample t-tests. As expected, ANOVA has also revealed a difference between the groups (F: 46.18, sig: 0.00).

Similarly in Table 6, we present the results on the reusability of components extracted from different game genres. The descriptive statistics imply that differences between games genres are rather small in absolute numbers with the only exception of

---

[2] A very small number of classes has been related to sound requirements, but due to its negligible number has not been included in the pie chart.

Table 5. Component functionality per game genre

Genre	N	Mean	Std. Dev.	Min	Max
Arcade	407	11.76	13.00	0	61
Board	647	19.70	24.48	0	109
Card	153	28.83	41.70	0	207
First Person Shooter (FPS)	400	38.72	49.84	0	234
Puzzle	464	15.54	19.33	0	70
RPG	348	43.69	86.97	0	337
Sports	212	33.62	39.14	0	148
Strategy	438	24.12	35.97	0	152

Table 6. Reusability per game genre

Genre	N	Mean	Std. Dev.	Min	Max
Arcade	407	3.313	2.433	0.375	15.633
Board	647	3.576	2.525	0.250	22.516
Card	153	3.623	2.741	0.333	24.025
First Person Shooter (FPS)	400	4.328	4.039	-0.385	69.250
Puzzle	464	3.685	2.868	0.119	18.517
RPG	348	3.768	2.603	0.500	17.034
Sports	212	3.681	4.081	0.308	66.552
Strategy	438	3.550	2.727	0.500	20.026

FPS games. Additionally, although the results of ANOVA (F: 10.11, sig: 0.00) suggest the existence of significant differences, the independent sample t-tests revealed that these are limited to the difference of FPSs with all other game genres. The outcome of the statistical analysis suggests that differences in the reusability of open source games are rather small, regardless of game genre.

5 Discussion

The results of this paper revealed that the top-2 genres *FPS and Strategy* games *offer significantly more components* than the rest game genres. In terms of *requirements specificity*, most of the identified components are implementing requirements that concern the game *Scenarios*, followed by *Characters*. Concerning *component functionality RPGs*, *FPSs*, and *Sport* games offer components that are more intensively used inside their games, while in terms of *component reusability* no significant differences between games genres are found with the only exception of *FPS* games. The results of this study provide useful information both to researchers and practitioners:

- *Guidance on the existence of reuse opportunities for practitioners.* Based on the results of this study, game developers can have indications on the feasibility of reuse in different game genres.

- *FPS game developers can exploit the great reuse opportunities offered by OSS components.* This application domain offers the most components per game that offer substantial functionality inside games, and are of optimum design-time reusability.
- *Strategy, Sport and Role-Playing game developers can also exploit the large number of components offered by OSS games,* although they have some limitations. For example, *RPGs* offer the most functional components, of high structural reusability. However, their availability is lower than that of FPS games. On the other hand, despite the fact that *Sport* games that offer a high number of components, these components are not of optimal reusability or functionality.
- Game developers of any game genre should *consider reuse* of OSS components *when implementing requirements related to scenarios and character management.*

- *Guidance on case selection for researchers.* Nowadays, more and more researchers perform empirical studies on OSS projects. The results of the study can guide researchers in selecting appropriate game genres to identify as many cases/units of analysis as possible.
- *Future work opportunities for researchers.* Some interesting future work directions are derived from this study: (a) the actual reuse rates of these components in OSS games can be calculated, (b) the reusability of these components can be tested by software engineers through experiments, and (c) a process for systematically reusing these components can be introduced.

6   Threats to Validity

In this section we discuss threats to the validity of our case study, with regard to construct, reliability and external aspects [37]. Threats to internal validity are not discussed in this paper, since identifying causal relations was out of the scope of this study. A possible threat to **construct validity** is related to the metrics that are used to answer our research questions and the extracted components. In particular, we have used QMOOD to measure reusability and Afferent Coupling (AffC) to measure functionality. Although we acknowledge that if different measures are used, the results might be slightly altered, we believe that both choices provide adequat assessments of the corresponding quality attributes. QMOOD, is an established quality model that has been rigorously validated [9], whereas AffC offers a well-known proxy of functionality, as explained in Sect. 3.3. Finally, another threat to construct validity is whether the candidate components are indeed reusable artifacts that can be ported to settings beyond their own game. We believe that the component selection algorithm, which is based on an exhaustive search process, provides adequate recall rates, and therefore is fitting for the purposes of this study. In any case to the best of our knowledge there is no algorithm that 100% accurately captures all intended components of the original developers.

With regard to *reliability*, we consider any possible researchers' bias, during the data collection and data analysis process. In particular in the data collection phase, the only possible bias can be identified in RQ_2. To gather data on the types of requirements that components implement we employed a manual process performed by the first author. In order to increase the reliability of this process the second and the third author validated the results. Finally, concerning *external validity*, a potential threat to generalization is that if the component extraction algorithm was performed on additional, or different games, the results might be altered. However we believe that the selected cases (open source games), offer a large and representative sample of the population. Additionally, we need to clarify that although, the small amount of cases for RQ_3 is a threat to generalization, the manual inspection of additional games was not possible due to the time consuming nature of the manual inspection.

7 Conclusion

In this paper, we empirically explore an important topic in game development, i.e., the opportunity to reuse components from existing games. As parameters in this empirical study we selected two aspects that can affect reusability: the application sub-domain of the game, namely the *game genre*, and the *requirement specificity* that a certain component may fulfill. To evaluate the relation of the game genre and the requirement types in games components, approximately 3,000 components were retrieved from over 100 open source games. The results of the study suggested that specific game genres offer more reuse opportunities than others, and that most components are related to scenario and characters. Based on these results, we have been able to provide useful implications for researchers and practitioners. As future work, we plan to replicate the study with more refined metrics/algorithms and feedback from game developers. Additionally, we plan to perform an in-depth study of a small number of games where the actual components that were envisioned for reuse are actually used for this purpose.

References

1. 9126-2001: ISO/IEC, Software engineering - Product quality (Part 1: Quality model), Geneva, Switzerland (2001)
2. Ajila, S.A., Wu, D.: Empirical study of the effects of open source adoption on software development economics. J. Syst. Softw. Elsevier **80**(9), 1517–1529 (2007)
3. Ampatzoglou, A., Stamelos, I.: Software engineering research for computer games: A systematic review. Inf. Softw. Technol. Elsevier **52**(9), 888–901 (2010)
4. Ampatzoglou, A., Stamelos, I., Gkortzis, A., Deligiannis, I.: Methodology on extracting reusable software candidate components from open source games. In: Proceeding of the 16th International Academic MindTrek Conference, pp. 93–100. ACM, Finland (2012)
5. Ampatzoglou, A., Michou, O., Stamelos, I.: Building and mining a repository of design pattern instances: Practical and research benefits. Entertainment Comput. Elsevier **4**(2), 131–142 (2013)

6. Ampatzoglou, A., Gkortzis, A., Charalampidou, S., Avgeriou, P.: An embedded multiple-case study on oss design quality assessment across domains. In: 7th International Symposium on Empirical Software Engineering and Measurement (ESEM 2013), pp. 255–258. ACM/IEEE Computer Society, Baltimore, USA, 10–11 October 2013

7. Arvanitou, E.M., Ampatzoglou, A., Chatzigeorgiou, A., Avgeriou, P.: Introducing a ripple effect measure: a theoretical and empirical validation. In: 9th International Symposium on Empirical Software Engineering and Measurement (ESEM 2015), ACM/IEEE Computer Society, Beijing, China

8. Baldassarre, M.T., Bianchi, A., Caivano, D., Visaggio, G.: An industrial case study on reuse oriented development. In: 21st International Conference on Software Maintenance (ICSM 2005), IEEE Computer Society, 283–292, September 2005

9. Bansiya, J., Davies, C.G.: A hierarchical model for object-oriented design quality assessment. Trans. Softw. Eng. IEEE Comput. Soc. **28**(1), 4–17 (2002)

10. Basili, V.R., Caldiera, G., Rombach, H.D.: Goal question metric paradigm, Encyclopedia of Software Engineering, pp. 528–532. John Wiley & Sons, New York (1994)

11. Callele, D., Neufeld, E., Schneider, K.: Emotional requirements in video games. In: 14th International Conference on Requirements Engineering, IEEE Computer Society, Minneapolis, USA, 11 – 15 September 2006

12. Cho, H., Yang, J.S.: Architecture patterns for mobile games product lines. In: Proceedings of the 2008 International Conference on Advanced Communication Technology (ICACT 2008), pp. 118–122. IEEE Computer Society Korea, 17 – 20 February 2008

13. Consumer Electronics Association, "Digital America", published electronically at. http://www.ce.org

14. Crnkovic, I., Hnich, B., Johnson, T., Kiziltan, Z.: Specification, implementation, and deployment of components. Commun. Assoc. Comput. Mach. **45**(10), 35–40 (2002)

15. Folmer, E.: Component based game development – a solution to escalating costs and expanding deadlines? In: Schmidt, H.W., Crnković, I., Heineman, G.T., Stafford, J.A. (eds.) CBSE 2007. LNCS, vol. 4608, pp. 66–73. Springer, Heidelberg (2007)

16. Frakes, W.B., Fox, C.J.: Quality improvement using a software reuse failure modes model. Trans. Softw. Eng. IEEE Comput. Soc. **22**(4), 274–279 (1996)

17. Franch, X., Carvallo, J.P.: Using quality models in software package selection. Softw. IEEE Comput. Soc. **20**(1), 34–41 (2003)

18. Furini, M.: An architecture to easily produce adventure and movie games for the mobile scenario. Comput. Entertainment Assoc. Comput. Mach. **6**(2), 1–16 (2008)

19. Gabow, H.N.: Path-based depth-first search for strong and bi-connected components. Inf. Process. Lett. Elsevier **74**(3–4), 107–114 (2000)

20. Griffith, I., Izurieta, C.: Design pattern decay: the case for class grime. In: 8th International Symposium on Empirical Software Engineering and Measurement (ESEM 2014), ACM/IEEE Computer Society, Torino, Italy, 18–19 September 2014

21. Haefliger, S., von Krogh, G., Spaeth, S.: Code reuse in open source software. Manage. Sci. PubsOnline **54**(1), 180–193 (2007)

22. Ham, H., Lee, Y.: An empirical study for quantitative evaluation of game satisfaction. In: 2006 International Conference on Hybrid Information Technology, pp. 724–729. ACM, November 2006

23. Heinemann, L., Deissenboeck, F., Gleirscher, M., Hummel, B., Irlbeck, M.: On the extent and nature of software reuse in open source java projects. In: Schmid, K. (ed.) ICSR 2011. LNCS, vol. 6727, pp. 207–222. Springer, Heidelberg (2011)

24. Johnson, I., Snook, C., Edmunds, A., Butler, M.: Rigorous development of reusable, domain-specific components, for complex applications. In: 3rd International Workshop on Critical Systems Development with UML (CSDUML 2004), Springer (2004)

25. Kasurinen, J., Maglyas, A., Smolander, K.: Is requirements engineering useless in game development? In: Salinesi, C., Weerd, I. (eds.) REFSQ 2014. LNCS, vol. 8396, pp. 1–16. Springer, Heidelberg (2014)
26. Krueger, C.W.: Software reuse. Comput. Surv. ACM **24**(2), 131–184 (1992)
27. Lau, K.K., Wang, Z.: A taxonomy of software component models. In: 31st EUROMICRO Conference on Software Engineering and Advanced Applications (EUROMICRO-SEAA), pp. 88–95. IEEE (2005)
28. Lee, W.P., Liu, L.J., Chiou, J.A.: A component-based framework to rapidly prototype online chess games for home entertainment. In: Proceedings of the International Conference on Systems, Man and Cybermetrics (SMC 2006), IEEE Computer Society, Taipei, Taiwan, pp. 4011–4016, 8–11 October 2006
29. Martin, R.C.: Agile software development: principles, patterns and practices. Prentice Hall, New Jersey (2003)
30. McShaffry, M.: Game Coding Complete. Paraglyph Press, Arizona, USA (2003)
31. Mockus, A.: Large-scale code reuse in open source software. In: 1st International Workshop on Emerging Trends in FLOSS Research and Development (FLOSS 2007), IEEE Computer Society (2007)
32. Morisio, M., Romano, D., Stamelos, I.: Quality, productivity, and learning in framework-based development: an exploratory case study. Trans. Softw. Eng. IEEE Comput. Soc. **28**(9), 876–888 (2002)
33. Paschali, M.E., Ampatzoglou, A., Chatzigeorgiou, A., Stamelos, I.: Non-functional requirements that influence gaming experience: A survey on gamers satisfaction factors. In: 18th Academic MindTREK Conference (MindTREK 2015), ACM, 4–6 November 2014, Tampere, Finland
34. Passos, E.B., Weslley, J., Walter, E., Clua, G., Montenegro, A., Murta, L.: Smart composition of game objects using dependency injection. Comput. Entertainment, Assoc. Comput. Mach. **7**(4), 408–423 (2009)
35. Reimanis, D.: A research plan to characterize, evaluate, and predict the impacts of behavioral decay in design patterns. In: 13th International Doctoral Symposium on Empirical Software Engineering (IDOSE 2015), Beijing, China
36. Raemaekers, S., van Deursen, A., Visser, J.: An analysis of dependence on third-party libraries in open source and proprietary systems. In: 6th International Workshop on Software Quality and Maintainability (SQM 2012), March 2012
37. Runeson, P., Host, M., Rainer, A., Regnell, B.: Case Study Research in Software Engineering: Guidelines and Examples. John Wiley & Sons, Hoboken (2012)
38. Schwittek, W., Eicker, S.: A study on third party component reuse in java enterprise open source software. In: 16th International Symposium on Component-based Software Engineering (CBSE 2013), pp. 75–80. ACM (2013)
39. Sojer, M., Henkel, J.: Code Reuse in Open Source Software Development: Quantitative Evidence, Drivers, and Impediments. J. Assoc. Inf. Syst. **11**(12), 868–901 (2010)
40. Szyperski, C.: Component Software: Beyond Object-Oriented Programming. Addison-Wesley International, Massachusetts, USA (1997)
41. van Lent, M., Swartout, W.: Games: Once more, with Feeling. Comput. IEEE Comput. Soc. **40**(8), 98–100 (2007)

RAGE Reusable Game Software Components and Their Integration into Serious Game Engines

Wim van der Vegt, Enkhbold Nyamsuren, and Wim Westera[✉]

Open University of the Netherlands, Heerlen, Netherlands
{wim.vandervegt,enkhbold.nyamsuren,wim.westera}@ou.nl

Abstract. This paper presents and validates a methodology for integrating reusable software components in diverse game engines. While conforming to the RAGE component-based architecture described elsewhere, the paper explains how the interactions and data exchange processes between a reusable software component and a game engine should be implemented for procuring seamless integration. To this end, a RAGE-compliant C# software component providing a difficulty adaptation routine was integrated with an exemplary strategic tile-based game "TileZero". Implementations in MonoGame, Unity and Xamarin, respectively, have demonstrated successful portability of the adaptation component. Also, portability across various delivery platforms (Windows desktop, iOS, Android, Windows Phone) was established. Thereby this study has established the validity of the RAGE architecture and its underlying interaction processes for the cross-platform and cross-game engine reuse of software components. The RAGE architecture thereby accommodates the large scale development and application of reusable software components for serious gaming.

Keywords: Serious game · Reuse · Software component · Integration · Game engine · Interoperability · RAGE

1 Introduction

Although games for learning have received attention from researchers and educators for several decades, the uptake of these "serious games" in schools and corporate training has been quite limited. Unlike the leisure game industry, which is an established industry dominated by major non-European hardware vendors (e.g. Sony, Microsoft and Nintendo) as well as major publishers and a fine-grained network of development studios, distributors and retailers, the serious game industry is scattered over a large number of small independent studios. This fragmentation goes with limited interconnectedness, limited knowledge exchange, limited specialisations, limited division of labour and an overall lack of critical mass [1, 2]. Moreover, driven by the successes of leisure games, quality standards of serious games as well as their production costs tend to increase substantially, which raises barriers to serious game adoption [3].

In 2014, the European Commission has designated serious games as a priority area in its Horizon 2020 Programme for Research and Innovation. It envisions a flourishing serious games industry that helps to address a variety of societal challenges in education,

© Springer International Publishing Switzerland 2016
G.M. Kapitsaki and E. Santana de Almeida (Eds.): ICSR 2016, LNCS 9679, pp. 165–180, 2016.
DOI: 10.1007/978-3-319-35122-3_12

health, social cohesion and citizenship, and at the same time stimulates the creation of jobs in the creative industry sector. Funded by the Horizon 2020 Programme, the RAGE project is a technology-driven research and innovation project that will make available serious game-oriented software modules (software assets) that game studios can easily integrate in their game development projects. Serious games studios would then benefit from reusing state-of-the-art technologies, while their development would become easier and faster, and upfront investments during development would be reduced.

In the RAGE project up to 40 advanced software assets are anticipated. These assets cover a wide range of functionalities particularly tuned to the pedagogy of serious gaming, e.g. player data analytics, emotion recognition, stealth assessment, personalisation, game balancing, procedural animations, language analysis and generation, interactive storytelling, social gamification and many other functions. One of the major challenges of RAGE is to ensure portability of the software assets across the wide diversity of game engines, game platforms and programming languages that game studios have in use. In the game industry game engines are the focal point of reuse [4]. They provide core libraries providing functionalities common to most games (e.g., rendering, scripting, networking). To support reusability within specific genres of games, game engines are supplemented with stores of plug-in "assets" [4]. These stores mostly concentrate on reuse of 2D/3D models and animation scripts. In rare occasions, software libraries with auxiliary functionalities are also available. For example, the store for the Unity game engine offers assets for game data analytics (https://www.assetstore.unity3d.com/). However, such libraries are bound to the architecture of the target engine. Furthermore, there is a lack of assets with explicitly pedagogical purposes.

RAGE has addressed these issues by devising a component-based architecture [5, 6] that preserves the portability of assets and that supports data interoperability between the assets [7]. In [7] the principles and constituents of the RAGE asset architecture have been described in detail and proofs of concept were presented that demonstrate its compliance with the following basic requirements: (1) minimal dependencies on external software frameworks and (2) interoperability between assets, and (3) portability of assets across different programming languages. This paper focuses on an additional requirement: the portability across different platforms, hardware and game engines. For the validation an existing RAGE Asset is used, the Heterogeneous Adaptation Asset (HAT).

We will first summarise the main features of the RAGE architecture and the set of communication modes it supports. Next, we will introduce the HAT asset and an exemplary game that were used for investigating the asset integration. Thereafter we will discuss the integration of the asset and the game and describe the principal asset classes and the main interaction processes that are required for system integration. Finally, we will discuss the portability of the HAT-asset to other game engines and verify the portability to diverse delivery platforms.

2   The RAGE Architecture

The RAGE asset architecture defines a component model (Fig. 1) for creating a reusable plug-and-play asset. The component model conforms to common norms of Component-Based Development [5–7]: (1) a component is an independent and replaceable part of a system that fulfils a distinct function; (2) a component provides information hiding and used as black box; (3) a component communicates strictly through a predefined set of interfaces that guard its implementation details.

The RAGE architecture [7] distinguishes between server-side assets and client-side assets. Remote communications of server-side assets with either the game engine (client) or a game server are readily based on a service-oriented architecture (SOA) using the HTTP-protocol (e.g. REST), which offers platform-independence and interoperability among heterogeneous technologies. In contrast, client-side RAGE assets are to be integrated with the game engine and are likely to suffer from incompatibilities. Therefore, the RAGE (client) asset architecture relies on a limited set of well-established software patterns and coding practices aimed at decoupling abstraction from its implementation. This decoupling facilitates reusability of an asset across different game engines with minimal integration effort. Figure 1 displays the UML class diagram of the RAGE asset architecture [7].

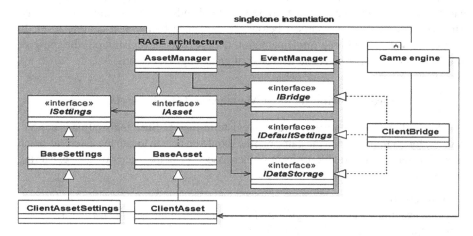

Fig. 1.   Class diagram reflecting the internal structure of a client-side software asset.

First, the asset does not provide any functionality related to the game user interface as to avoid platform-dependent code. The asset just provides processing functionality by returning processed data to the game engine (e.g. calculating user performance metrics based on logged behaviours). Second, since various assets may be linked together to express aggregates, a coordinating agent is needed: the Asset Manager, which is implemented as a Singleton, is needed for registration of the assets. It exposes methods to query these registrations. Also, the Asset Manager centralises shared code that is commonly used by multiple assets, such as the name and the type of the game engine, or user login/logout info for assets that would need a user model. For such data, the Asset Manager is the single interaction point with the outside game engine, and thus avoids duplicating code. Third, for allowing an asset to call a game engine method, the Bridge software pattern [8] is used, which is platform-dependent code implementing an interface. Alternatively, the communications could use the Publish/Subscribe pattern [9, 10] through the Event Manager, which is initialised by the Asset Manager during its Singleton instantiation. Fourth, the asset offers basic capabilities of storing configuration data (settings), be it delegated through the Bridge to the game engine. Storage also includes localisation data (string translation tables), version information and dependency information (dependency on other assets' versions). Fifth, assets largely rely on the programming language's standard features and libraries to maximise the compatibility across game engines. Therefore, assets could thus delegate the implementation of required features to the actual game engine, for example the actual storage of runtime data.

3   Communications Between Assets and the Game Engine

For allowing an asset or its sub-components to communicate with the outside world (e.g. with other assets, the game engine or a remote service), well-defined interfaces are needed. The RAGE architecture support 4 different communication modes, which are connected with asset registration and the use of RAGE architecture methods, the use of game methods, using web services and using Publish/Subscribe events, respectively. These modes will be summarised below are explained below at a generic level. In Sect. 6 we will provide the implementation details of asset registration, the reuse of RAGE architecture methods and the reuse of game engine methods.

3.1   Communications with the Asset Manager and Other Assets

The Asset Manager has the central role in registering assets. Such registration is needed, because for communication the game engine should be able to locate the assets, as much as each asset should be able to locate other assets. Principal steps of the registering process are:

- Asset creation
  Upon execution the game engine creates the asset by calling its constructor.
- Locating or creating the Asset Manager
  After its creation the asset tries to locate the Asset Manager. If no Asset Manager instance can be found, it creates the instance as a Singleton.
- Asset self-registration
  The asset registers itself at the Asset Manager by the name of its class. In return, it receives a unique identifier, so that multiple instances of the same class can be kept apart.
- Asset ID exchange
  The unique identifier is then returned to the game engine for later use.

The Asset Manager provides an interface for querying this registration of assets. An asset can also query the Asset Manager for other assets by their class names when inter-asset communication becomes necessary.

3.2   Communications Through a Game Method Call

For allowing an asset to call a game engine method a Bridge [8] is used. The Bridge includes platform-dependent code that implements one or more interfaces. The following actions are required:

- Bridge creation
  The game engine creates a Bridge and registers it with either a specific asset or with the Asset Manager. The asset can access its own Bridge or the Asset Manager´s Bridge to further communicate with the game engine.
- Calling the game engine
  Upon calling a game engine method, the asset would look for a suitable interface from the Bridge, which then forwards the method call to the game engine.
- Receiving the response of game engine method
  The game engine returns the method's response to the Bridge, which forwards it to the asset.

Overall, the Bridge pattern allows assets to call game engine methods while hiding the game engine's implementation details from the asset. Additionally, polymorphism is supported by allowing a Bridge to implement multiple interfaces, or allowing an asset to access multiple Bridges that implement different interfaces. The asset may identify and select a suitable Bridge and use its methods or properties to get the pursued game data.

3.3   Communications Through a Web-Service Call

The Bridge can also be used for the communications of client-side assets with remote services through web services. Obviously, this also applies for client-side assets calling server-side assets. The communication includes the following elements:

- Bridge creation
  If the Bridge was not instantiated yet, the game engine should create it and make it available to the asset.
- Using an adapter
  The Bridge uses an Adapter [11] provided by the game engine, which thus removes the dependency of the asset on specific communication protocols used by remote services, thereby allowing a greater versatility of the asset.
- Sending a request
  In turn the asset could send a request (e.g. load or save data) to the Adapter, which is then to be translated to a suitable format (e.g. REST) and sent to the web service.
- Receiving a response
  Eventually, the web service would return its response, which is then received and processed by the asset.

Obviously, the communication with remote services assumes an online connection. When a service is unavailable, e.g. when the game system is offline, the interface should be able to receive a call without processing it or acting on it.

3.4 Communications Through a Publish/Subscribe Event

Communications can also be arranged using the Publish/Subscribe pattern, which supports a 1-N type of communication (broadcasting). An example would be the game engine frequently broadcasting player performance data, which could be received by multiple assets.

- Creation of an Event Manager
  An Event Manager is needed, which is a centralised class that handles topics and events. It is initialised by the Asset Manager during its Singleton instantiation.
- Registration of an event
  The game engine registers a publication event at the Event Manager, for instance the broadcast of player performance data, or any other required state data from the game.
- Subscription to the event
  An asset that wants to use such data for further processing would subscribe to the registered event.
- Receiving updates
  Any publication or update of the event by the game engine will then be broadcast by the Event Manager. The assets that have subscribed to the particular event will receive the data and act upon it.

According to the Publish/Subscribe design pattern, subscribers do not have knowledge of publishers and vice versa. This allows an asset to ignore implementation details of a game engine or other assets. The communication can go both ways: asset and the game engine can be either publishers or subscribers. The Publish/Subscribe pattern of communication is more suitable for (asynchronous) broadcasting to multiple receivers than the Bridge-based communication, which realises bilateral communications only.

4 The Heterogeneous Adaptive Gaming Asset (HAT)

The Heterogeneous Adaptive Gaming asset (HAT) can be used for real-time adaptation of game features to player skills. The current version of the HAT asset supports adapting game difficulty to player's expertise using the CAP algorithm [12]. The CAP algorithm is based on the Elo rating system [13] that was originally developed to dynamically calculate and match expertise levels of two chess players. Similar to the Elo algorithm, CAP does not require pre-testing to estimate difficulty of items. Instead, CAP is capable of on the fly estimation of item difficulty and player's expertise parameters. The CAP algorithm is successfully being used in a wide array of games ranging from simple arithmetic games [14] to complex problem solving games such as Mastermind [15].

The HAT asset assumes that a player plays through a sequence of one or more game scenarios. The game delegates the choice of the scenarios to be played to the

HAT asset, which after each scenario adapts game difficulty to the player's expertise level. Quantitative ratings need to be assigned to both a player's expertise or skills level, and to the game scenarios' difficulties. After each played scenario, the HAT asset updates the player's expertise rating by taking into account a Boolean value indicating whether the player failed or succeeded in a scenario and the time needed by the player to finish the scenario. If the player performed better than expected then the expertise rating is increased, otherwise it is decreased. Based on the updated player's expertise rating, the HAT asset returns the most suitable difficulty level for the next scenario to the game. For this decision, the HAT asset uses a prefixed probability value indicating the probability that the player finishes the scenario successfully. Based on previous research this probability threshold was set to 0.75, as to balance the challenge provided by the game and player's motivation to continue to play [12, 16]. The player is initially assigned a low expertise rating and, therefore, will be provided with easier scenarios. However, as the player improves by gaining expertise, the expertise rating increases, and more difficult scenarios will be presented. Through this iterative process, the HAT asset ensures that the player is always given a reasonable amount of challenge even if the player gradually improves.

5   The TileZero Game

The TileZero game (Fig. 2) is a derivative of the popular turn-based board game Qwirkle (released by MindWare, http://www.mindware.com). In recent years, Qwirkle has captured interests of educational researchers for its potential use in developing children's spatial, mathematical, and fluid reasoning skills [17]. The game contributes to capacities to think logically and solve problems from different perspectives. It requires from a player a strategic reasoning ability to form, compare and choose from alternative combinations of moves. Finer grained skills include spatial manipulation of tiles in mind, mental arithmetic of in-game scores, and tactical consideration of other players' possible moves. The same considerations apply to the TileZero game. As the game has simple mechanics and rules that are easy to implement and control, it is a good candidate for testing the asset integration.

The mechanics of TileZero revolves around combining tiles into a sequence. Each tile has a picture of a coloured shape. There are six distinct colours and six distinct shapes resulting in 36 unique tiles. With three copies of each unique tile the total number of playable tiles is 108. Tiles that have not been used yet, are kept in a bag, and players cannot see them.

TileZero can be played with two to four players. A match starts with three random tiles put in a sequence on a board. Next, each player receives a set of six random tiles. Once tiles are distributed, players start taking turns. During their turn, the players can place one or more tiles on the board and replenish their set from the bag. The player has to follow several rules for tile placement. First, a tile should be placed next to another tile already on the board. Second, any sequence of tiles on the board should have either the same colour and different shapes or vice versa. Third, a player can only place tiles of either the same colour or same shape during a turn. A player receives a score for each

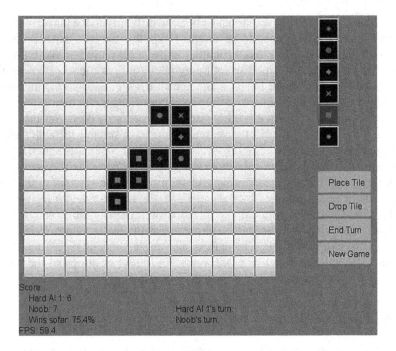

Fig. 2. A screenshot of the TileZero game against Hard AI Player.

tile placed on a board. The score is based on the length of the sequence that the tile forms on the board. The game ends if the bag of tiles is empty and the player put his last tile on the board. The player with the highest score is the winner.

In our implementation of TileZero, a human player plays against one of six available AI opponents. An AI opponent is considered as a scenario. AI opponents have different strategies and thus provide different degrees of challenge to the human player. The six AI opponents in an increasing order of difficulty are Very Easy AI, Easy AI, two versions of Medium AI, Hard AI and Very Hard AI. The TileZero was extended with the HAT asset to match difficulty of an AI opponent to the player's demonstrated expertise level. A beginner player is assigned a low initial rating and therefore, the first few matches will involve Very Easy or Easy AIs. However, as player gains expertise, the HAT asset starts gradually introducing more challenging AIs.

6   Integrating Assets with Game Engines

The TileZero game was implemented on MonoGame v3.0, which is a portable open-source Mono-based and OpenGL-based game engine (monogame.net) [18]. Both Tile-Zero and the HAT asset were written in C# using Visual Studio 2013. The integration of the HAT asset and the TileZero game was based on usage of the Asset Manager and the Bridge pattern for calling game engine methods. The implementation of Web Services and Publish/Subscribe patterns were not needed. In the next sections we will first explain game how to setup game code in MonoGame to be compliant with the RAGE architecture. Secondly, the principal classes required for this integration will be explained. Third, the main interaction processes that are required for system integration and the reuse of libraries are described. Finally, we will discuss the portability of the HAT-asset to other game engines and verify the portability to diverse delivery platforms.

6.1 MonoGame Implementation of TileZero

MonoGame uses a simple architecture of 5 methods being called.

- Initialize
- LoadContent
- Update
- Draw
- UnloadContent

When the game starts, the Initialize method is called and the main classes are created and configured. Then the LoadContent method is called which covers the loading of the tile bitmaps. Next MonoGame enters a loop of repetitively calling the Update and Draw methods around 60 times/s. In the Update method the keyboard and mouse states are examined and processed and forwarded to the game logic. In the Draw method the game model is rendered onto the screen. Finally, when the loop has ended (the end of the game), an UnloadContent method is called to free up previously loaded content.

Instead of directly implementing the HAT adaptation algorithm in the MonoGame code, reuse of the HAT asset requires to declare a separate class (*HATAsset*) wrapping all HAT functionality and thus exposing a minimum number of methods needed. Importantly, the HAT asset itself can already be tested without being embedded in the game. Because the HAT asset does not directly link with the game's user interface, the TileZero game code was separated in two distinct classes, covering the game logic (*TileZeroGame* class) and the display model (*VirtualTileZeroBoard* class), respectively. The *TileZeroGame* class uses the HAT asset to select the appropriate AI for the computer player when a new match is started. It is called by the MonoGame Update method, to process keyboard and mouse input into updates of the *VirtualTileZeroBoard* class. The *VirtualTileZeroBoard* class is used by the Draw method to visualise the user interface of the game.

6.2 HAT Asset Integration

Figure 3 shows a (simplified) UML class diagram depicting the main classes required for the integration of the HAT asset and the TileZero game.

In Fig. 3, the *TileZero* class represents the game. The *HATAsset* class represents the core functionality of the HAT asset, which is the adaptation algorithm. To gain access to the standardised functionality of the RAGE architecture, the *HATAsset* class extends the *BaseAsset* class from the architecture. This enables the *HATAsset* class to communicate with the game engine (the *TileZero* class) using the *Bridge* class that implements the Bridge pattern. The Bridge pattern enables the asset to call methods from the game engine without knowing the game's implementation details. Apart from the *IBridge* interface, the *Bridge*

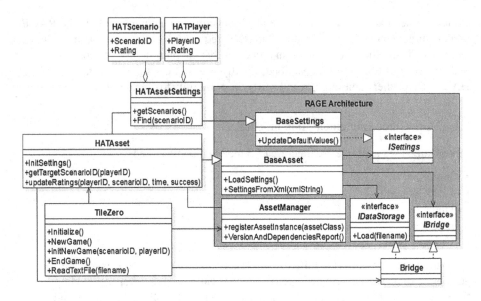

Fig. 3. Class diagram describing the integration of the HAT asset with the TileZero game.

class can realise additional interfaces that allow an asset to delegate common functionalities to a standard library provided by a game engine. For example, the *IDataStorage* interface allows an asset to request the game engine to load or save files.

6.3 The Reuse of Libraries by Using the RAGE Architecture

Figure 4 shows the UML sequence diagram reflecting interactions between the HAT asset and the game engine.

This figure shows five different communication processes, which are labelled at the right hand side. These processes will be briefly explained below, with occasional reference to Figs. 3 and 4.

Instantiation of system components. During its initialisation (step 1 in Fig. 4), the *Tile-Zero* class instantiates all other components of the system. First, a Singleton of the Asset Manager is created (step 2). Next, an instance of the *Bridge* class is created (step 3) and referred to a newly created instance of the *HATAsset* class (step 4). During initialisation, the *HATAsset* class performs two main operations. First, it registers itself with the Asset Manager and receives a unique id (step 5). Next, it instantiates *HATAssetSetting* class (steps 6 and 7) to load and manage player and scenario settings.

An asset reusing game engine libraries. The HAT asset uses the *IDataStorage* interface to load the asset's settings stored on a local XML file. This process is shown by steps 8 – 12 in the sequence diagram in Fig. 4. The *HATAsset* requests the *Bridge* object to load the file by its name. Contacting the *Bridge* object is a matter of calling the LoadSettings method inherited from the *BaseAsset* class. This method handles details

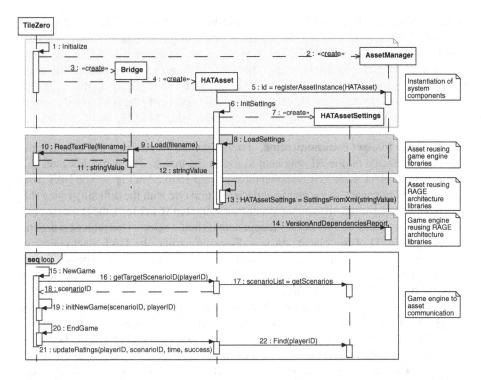

Fig. 4. UML sequence diagram depicting communication processes between the HAT asset and the game engine.

of the call such as ensuring that the *Bridge* object has realised the *IDataStorage* interface. In turn, the *Bridge* object uses libraries from the MonoGame engine to read textual files and it returns to the *HATAsset* the content as a string value. Such delegation of generic functions to game engines has main advantages of avoiding redundancy in code functionality and unnecessarily bloated implementation of an asset software component.

An asset reusing RAGE architecture libraries. One standardised functionality in the *BaseAsset* class is to deserialise XML specified data into instances of a RAGE compliant class for managing settings. In the HAT asset, settings include lists of available scenarios and players together with relevant adaptation parameters such as ratings. These settings are managed by the *HATAssetSettings* class shown before in Fig. 3. Within this class, settings for individual scenarios and players are managed as instances of the *HATScenario* and the *HATPlayer* classes respectively. For example, each scenario available in a game is identified in the HAT asset by its ID and assigned a difficulty rating. Because *HATAssetSettings* extends the *BaseSettings* class from the architecture, the HAT asset is able to use the SettingsFromXML method predefined in the *BaseAsset* class (step 13 in Fig. 4). This method automatically deserialises the asset's settings from an XML format into an instance of the *HATAssetSettings*.

A game engine reusing RAGE architecture libraries. Functionalities predefined in the RAGE architecture may also be reused by different game engines. One of the core components that offer reusable methods is the Asset Manager that assists the game engine in coordinating multiple assets. The Asset Manager can keep track of all assets by ID or class name and provide basic services relevant to all assets. In this particular example, the Asset Manager is used by the game engine to verify the HAT asset's version and check if it is dependent on any additional library (step 14 in Fig. 4).

Game engine to asset communication. Every time the player starts a new match, the game has to decide on the AI opponent to use in the match. The game delegates this decision to the HAT asset as it is shown through step 15 to 22 in Fig. 4. The HAT asset treats each AI opponent as a scenario and tries to find one with the difficulty rating that matches the player's expertise rating. As indicated by step 16 in Fig. 4, the game requests the HAT asset to return an ID of the AI opponent it should select. This request is accompanied with an ID of the player. As was discussed earlier, the HAT asset maintains players' and scenarios' ratings and IDs in the *HATAssetSettings* class. The HAT asset uses the player's ID to fetch the player's expertise rating from the *HATAssetSettings* class. Next, it also retrieves the list of all available AI opponents (step 17). Given this information, the asset can find an ID of the AI opponent best suitable for the indicated player. This ID is returned to the game, and a new match starts (step 19). Upon completion of the match, the game requests the HAT asset to update player's rating (step 21). This request includes player and AI IDs, duration of time the match lasted, and Boolean indication whether player succeeded over the AI opponent. The HAT asset uses these four parameters to recalculate player's expertise rating after each match.

Results of test gameplays. The TileZero and HAT asset were tested by a human player who played multiple consecutive matches against an AI opponent. The HAT asset was used to adapt the game difficulty. Initially, the player was assigned a low initial expertise level and matched against easier AIs. Figure 4 shows how the player's ratings changed during first 29 matches. The figure also depicts the type of AI opponent used in each match. Two main trends can be observed. First, the player's rating shows steady increase

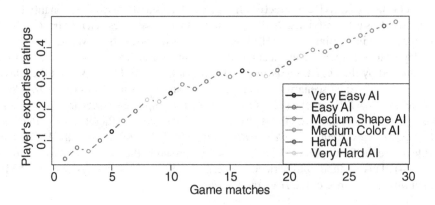

Fig. 5. Player's increasing expertise ratings during 29 matches.

indicating a positive overall performance growth of the player. Second, the frequencies of AI types change during 29 matches. The first half of matches shows overall prevalence of Very Easy and Easy AIs, while the second half shows prevalence of Medium and Hard AIs. These two trends together confirm that the HAT asset worked as expected and matched game difficulty to player's expertise (Fig. 5).

6.4 Portability Across Game Engines and Platforms

The principal reason for devising the RAGE asset architecture has been to make available software components that can be reused across different game engines and different platforms. For verifying this, the TileZero project was ported from the MonoGame engine (monogame.net) to both the Unity engine (unity3d.com) and the Xamarin mobile app platform (xamarin.com), which both support the C# implementation. The HAT asset was then added and integrated with each of these new game versions. No extensive user interfaces were implemented in the Unity and Xamarin game versions, as for testing the games' functioning simple buttons for mimicking player's decisions were sufficient. Exactly, because of the decoupling of RAGE assets and the game's user interface, testing of the system integration is completely independent of the user interface. Likewise the portability of RAGE assets across diverse delivery platforms is easily delegated to the game engines' rendering utilities, which in many cases include cross-platform delivery. Both MonoGame, Unity and Xamarin support a large number of leading platforms, covering different operating systems and hardware configurations. Successful system integration was established for all three game engines, and proper delivery was verified for Windows desktop, iOS, Android and Windows Phone, be it not in all possible combinations. Some issues were encountered, but these could be easily solved.

First, during the coding of a mock-up game in Unity for Android, XPath could not be used for performing some basic calculations. This was caused by the Mono version that Unity uses. The issue could be solved by replacing XPath by code using the .NET *XmlSerializer* class. It should be noted that this issue is not related to the RAGE asset architecture, but to differences between the Mono and .Net frameworks used.

A second issue was located in the Bridge and occurred when trying to create and access a platform-independent directory in Unity for storing the player's performance data. It turned out the Unity does not allow for this. The Application.dataPath method only provides a read-only directory on iOS. Likewise, the Environment class cannot be used as its main target is desktop. The issue could be solved by using Application.persistentDataPath, which is read-write on all tested platforms. Thereby the *Bridge* class became portable across Unity's target platforms.

Third, in our tests we used a Xamarin Forms project, which allows for referencing to assemblies for using their projects, but it also supports direct referencing to compiled assemblies. Assemblies can be compiled either against a common .Net framework or as a portable assembly. Although Android and iOS allow for both portable (mobile) and non-portable solutions, Windows Phone only allows portable assemblies. The implies that if a Windows Phone project is present, the HAT Asset and the Asset Manager assembly need to be compiled as portable assemblies and used on all respective platform projects.

Fourth, as Unity is using an older .NET version (v3.5) it cannot handle portable libraries. Indeed, .NET version 4.5, as used in Xamarin, is required for portable libraries. Obviously the issue is not an issue of the RAGE architecture.

Fifth, as the format of Visual Studio project files is different for common .Net projects and portable projects, respectively, separate project files are needed for each type of assembly. With some small adjustments the RAGE asset sources can still be shared for both types of assemblies. Two minor coding issues surfaced and were removed. The system libraries used by portable assemblies lack support for some property attributes used in RAGE assets (Category and Description). This was solved by removing these two attributes as they are only used by an experimental configuration editor based on a PropertyGrid and not of vital importance for the game. In the portable projects the affected lines where omitted using C# compiler directives. Also, the two projects have different methods for retrieving properties by reflection. This was addressed by adding some conditional code using C# compiler directives and refactoring the code in such way (using the constructor) that it does not need reflection.

Sixth, the Bridge for multi-target Xamarin Forms projects is composed of a common part and a device specific part. For Android and iOS the Bridge implementation is straightforward. For Windows Phone, however, the preferred file I/O API is asynchronous. This requires that the code in the Windows Phone Bridge waits for the result of asynchronous calls, which could lead to a deadlock. This issue was solved by including async helper methods that wait for their result in the synchronous interface in a correct way.

Seventh, if an asset's Bridge interfaces such as *IDataStorage* are to be used for all platforms and engines, including Unity, they must be coded synchronously, because the async keyword was included only after the .Net 3.5 framework, and is thus not available in Unity.

Finally, some minor portability issues have been reported before, e.g. confusion of separator characters (e.g. "/" versus "\"), conversion of debug symbol files for Unity, and the compilation of embedded resources in Unity [7].

7   Conclusion

In this study, we have provided further evidence for the validity of the RAGE game asset architecture. We have demonstrated that client-side game technology components that are compliant with the RAGE architecture can be easily integrated with existing game engines and allow for reuse across different engines and platforms. The power of the RAGE architecture is not limited to the potential reuse of assets, but is also based on the efficient reuse of existing libraries, either from the RAGE architecture or from the game engine in use. To maximise the reusability of assets among different games, the assets do not directly link with the game´s user interface and exchange only the basic forms of information with the game engine. In the HAT asset, for example, the code of the asset responsible for difficulty adaptation requires only the exchange of string IDs and a few numerical values such as the duration of a task. The qualifies the integration of RAGE assets as "lightweight", which may promote its adoption.

It should be noted that we have tested the integration of C# coded assets only. In a previous study, we have tested and validated the RAGE architecture by implementing a dummy asset prototype also in C ++, Java and TypeScript (JavaScript). Establishing the ecological validity for those languages by integrating real assets in real games for various game engines and platforms needs further investigation. Moreover, in the current study for C# some issues surfaced, be it minors issues. Yet, it demonstrates that cautious and prolonged investigation is needed of the practical factors and conditions that might corrupt seamless asset integration, both for C# and other languages. So far, this study has established the validity of the RAGE architecture and its underlying interaction processes for the cross-platform and cross-game engine reuse of software components. The RAGE architecture thereby accommodates the large scale development and application of reusable software components for serious gaming.

Acknowledgement. This work has been partially funded by the EC H2020 project RAGE (Realising an Applied Gaming Eco-System); http://www.rageproject.eu/; Grant agreement No 644187.

References

1. Stewart, J., Bleumers, L., Van Looy, J., Mariën, I., All, A., Schurmans, D., Willaert, K., De Grove, F., Jacobs, A., Misuraca, G.: The potential of digital games for empowerment and social inclusion of groups at risk of social and economic exclusion: evidence and opportunity for policy. Joint Research Centre, European Commission, Brussels (2013)
2. García Sánchez, R., Baalsrud Hauge, J., Fiucci, G., Rudnianski, M., Oliveira, M., Kyvsgaard Hansen, P., Riedel, J., Brown, D., Padrón-Nápoles, C.L., Arambarri Basanez, J.: Business Modelling and Implementation Report 2. GALA Network of Excellence (2013). www.galanoe.eu
3. Warren, S.J., Jones, G.: Overcoming educational game development costs with lateral innovation: chalk house, the door, and broken window. J. Appl. Instr. Des. **4**(1), 51–63 (2014)
4. Bergeron, B.: Developing Serious Games. Charles River Media, Hingham MA (2006)
5. Bachmann, F., Bass, L., Buhman, C., Comella-Dorda, S., Long, F., Robert, J., Sea-cord, R., Wallnau, K.: Technical concepts of component-based software engineering, vol. II. Carnegie Mellon University, Software Engineering Institute, Pittsburgh (2000)
6. Mahmood, S., Lai, R., Kim, Y.S.: Survey of component-based software development. IET Software **1**(2), 57–66 (2007)
7. Van der Vegt, G.W., Westera, W., Nyamsuren, N., Georgiev, A., Martinez Ortiz, I.: RAGE architecture for reusable serious gaming technology components. Int. J. Comput. Games Technol. (2016, to appear)
8. Gamma, E., Helm, R., Johnson, R., Vlissides, J.: Design Patterns: Elements of Reusable Object-Oriented Software, pp. 171–183. Pearson Education, London (1994)
9. Birman, K., Joseph, T.: Exploiting virtual synchrony in distributed systems. In: Proceedings of the Eleventh ACM Symposium on Operating systems principles (SOSP 1887), pp. 123–138 (1987)
10. Eugster, P.T., Felber, P.A., Guerraoui, R., Kermarrec, A.M.: The many faces of publish/ subscribe. ACM Comput. Surv. (CSUR) **35**(2), 114–131 (2003)

11. Benatallah, B., Casati, F., Grigori, D., Nezhad, H.R.M., Toumani, F.: Developing adapters for web services integration. In: Pastor, Ó., Falcão e Cunha, J. (eds.) CAiSE 2005. LNCS, vol. 3520, pp. 415–429. Springer, Heidelberg (2005)
12. Klinkenberg, S., Straatemeier, M., Van der Maas, H.L.J.: Computer adaptive practice of maths ability using a new item response model for on the fly ability and difficulty estimation. Comput. Educ. 57(2), 1813–1824 (2011)
13. Elo, A.E.: The Rating of Chess Players, Past and Present (Vol. 3). Batsford, London (1978)
14. Van der Maas, H.J.J., Van der Ven, S., Van der Molen, V.: Oefenen op niveau: het cijferspel in de Rekentuin. Volgens Bartjens 3, 12–15 (2014)
15. Gierasimczuk, N., Van der Maas, H.L., Raijmakers, M.E.: An analytic tableaux model for Deductive Mastermind empirically tested with a massively used online learning system. J. Logic Lang. Inform. 22(3), 297–314 (2013)
16. Eggen, T.J., Verschoor, A.J.: Optimal testing with easy or difficult items in computerized adaptive testing. Appl. Psychol. Meas. 30(5), 379–393 (2006)
17. Mackey, A.P., Hill, S.S., Stone, S.I., Bunge, S.A.: Differential effects of reasoning and speed training in children. Dev. Sci. 14(3), 582–590 (2011)
18. Pavleas, J., Chang, J.K.W., Sung, K., Zhu, R.: Learn 2D Game Development with C#, pp. 11–40. Apress, New York (2013)

Reusable Secure Connectors for Secure Software Architecture

Michael Shin[1(✉)], Hassan Gomaa[2], and Don Pathirage[1]

[1] Department of Computer Science, Texas Tech University, Lubbock, TX, USA
{michael.shin,don.pathirage}@ttu.edu
[2] Department of Computer Science, George Mason University, Fairfax, VA, USA
hgomaa@gmu.edu

Abstract. This paper describes the design of reusable secure connectors that are used in the design of secure software architectures for distributed software applications. The secure connectors are designed separately from application components by reusing the appropriate communication pattern between components as well as the security services required by these components. Each secure connector is designed as a composite component that encapsulates both security service components and communication pattern components. Integration of security services and communication patterns within a secure connector is provided by a security coordinator. The main advantage is that secure connectors can be reused in different applications. In this paper, secure connectors are reused in electronic commerce and automated teller machine applications.

Keywords: Reusable secure connector · Secure software architecture · Component-based software architecture · Secure software design · Message communication patterns · Dynamic modeling

1 Introduction

Secure software architecture for distributed software applications can be composed of components and connectors in which connectors encapsulate the details of communication between components. Although connectors are typically used in software architecture to encapsulate communication mechanisms between components, this paper describes how security concerns can also be encapsulated in software connectors, which are referred to as secure connectors, separately from application components that contain application logic. However, integrating security concerns with communication concerns in secure connectors could make applications more complex. It is therefore necessary to design secure connectors that are both modular and reusable.

Each secure connector is designed as a composite component using component concepts by reusing security service components and communication pattern components, which are designed separately from each other. Each security service component encapsulates a security service, such as confidentiality or integrity. Each communication pattern component encapsulates the communication pattern between application components, such as synchronous or asynchronous message communication. A secure

© Springer International Publishing Switzerland 2016
G.M. Kapitsaki and E. Santana de Almeida (Eds.): ICSR 2016, LNCS 9679, pp. 181–196, 2016.
DOI: 10.1007/978-3-319-35122-3_13

connector is then constructed by composing security service components and communication pattern components. Integration of security services and communication patterns within a secure connector is provided by a security coordinator. Once a secure connector is constructed, it can then be reused in different applications.

This paper describes the design of reusable secure connectors to be used in secure software architectures for distributed software applications in which application components communicate with each other via different communication patterns. Reusable secure connectors make complex software applications more maintainable by separating security concerns from application concerns in the software architectures. Reusable secure connectors described in this paper are applied to the software architectures for electronic commerce applications, such as Business to Business (B2B) and Business to Customer (B2C) electronic commerce applications, and an Automated Teller Machine (ATM) application.

This paper is organized as follows. Section 2 describes existing approaches to implementing security concerns in software applications. Section 3 describes reusable secure connector concepts followed by the design of reusable secure connectors in Sect. 4. Section 5 describes a reusable secure synchronous message communication with reply connector. Section 6 describes the validation of reusable secure connectors.

2 Related Work

Related work focuses on approaches to designing software architectures for secure applications and patterns for distributed communication. Authors in [3] identified several security dimensions, and related them to the building blocks of software architecture. The components, connectors and their configurations are the architectural building blocks, which can be customized to enforce the security dimensions.

Authors in [5] proposed a methodology to model secure software architectures and verify whether required security constraints are assured by the composition of components of the system. An extension of UML called UMLsec had been proposed to express security-relevant information within design diagrams in an effort to aid in the development of security-critical systems [9].

Using connectors as the central construct, a distributed software architecture in [6] is composed of a set of components and a set of connectors that can be used to interconnect the components. The Unified Modeling Language (UML) is used to describe the component interconnection patterns for synchronous, asynchronous and brokered communications [6]. In [10], a connector centric approach is used to model, capture, and enforce security. The security characteristics of a software architecture are described and enforced using software connectors.

Security patterns in [6, 11] address the broad range of security issues that should be taken into account in the stages of software development lifecycle. The authors describe the problem, context, solution, and implementation of security patterns with a template so that the presentations are consistent.

Methods in [1] propose SecArch to evaluate architectures with significant security concerns. The SecArch is an incremental evaluation tool for secure architectures, which utilizes implied scenarios and race conditions analysis.

In earlier work by the authors [8], an approach is described to model complex applications by modeling application requirements and designs separately from security requirements and designs using the UML notation. In later work by the authors [12], an approach is described for modeling the evolution of a non-secure application to a secure application in terms of a requirements model and a software architecture. In recent work by the authors [13], secure asynchronous and synchronous connectors are described for modeling the software architectures for distributed applications. In very recent work by one of the authors [2], an aspect-oriented approach is described for mapping from the objects in secure connectors to separate security and communication aspects. In contrast, this paper focuses on designing secure connectors using a component-based approach to make them reusable.

3 Concepts of Reusable Secure Connectors

The software architecture [14] for concurrent and distributed applications can be designed by means of components and connectors. The components address the functionality of an application, whereas connectors deal with communication between components. Each component defines application logic that is relatively independent of those provided by other components. A component may request services from other components, or provide services to them through connectors. A connector acts on behalf of components in terms of communication between components, encapsulating the details of inter-component communication.

Separately from application components, security services can be encapsulated in connectors between components in the software architecture for concurrent and distributed applications [12, 13]. The original role of connectors in the software architecture is to provide the mechanism for message communication between components [14]. However, in this paper, the role of connectors is extended to security by adding security services to the connectors, which are referred to as secure connectors. This can be done by either:

(a) Encapsulating a security service inside a secure connector, or
(b) Providing access from the secure connector to an external security service.

In the latter case, if security services cannot themselves be encapsulated in connectors, secure connectors can be designed to request security services from security service components.

The security services provided by secure connectors for components are confidentiality, integrity, non-repudiation, access control, and authentication, as follows:

- Confidentiality security service, which prevents secret information from being disclosed to any unauthorized party, can be achieved by secure connectors encapsulating cryptosystems [6].

- Integrity security service, which protects against unauthorized changes to secret information, can be performed by secure connectors using message digest or message authentication code [6].
- Non-repudiation security service protects against one party to a transaction later falsely denying that the transaction occurred. Non-repudiation security services can be realized using digital signatures [6] or Trusted Third Parties.
- Access control security service protects against unauthorized access to valuable resources. Access control may be implemented using mandatory access control, discretionary access control or role-based access control [4, 6].
- Authentication security service allows an entity (a user or system) to identify itself positively to another entity. This can be achieved using a password, personal-identification number or challenge response [6].

Although there are other types of communications between distributed components, typical message communication patterns between the components are synchronous message communication with reply, synchronous message communication without reply, asynchronous message communication, and bidirectional asynchronous message communication [7].

- In synchronous message communication with reply, a sender component sends a message to a receiver component and waits for a response from the receiver. When a response arrives from the receiver, the sender can continue to work and send the next message to the receiver.
- In synchronous message communication without reply, a receiver component acknowledges a sender component when it receives a message from the sender. As the sender is acknowledged by the receiver, it can continue to work and send the next message to the receiver.
- In asynchronous message communication, an asynchronous message is sent from a sender component to a receiver component and is stored in a queue if the receiver is busy. The sender component can continue to send the next message to the receiver component as long as the queue is not full.
- Bidirectional asynchronous message communication uses asynchronous message communication in both directions between the sender and receiver components, with the receiver component sending responses to the sender component asynchronously. Responses are sent to a queue from which the sender component retrieves each response.

A secure connector is designed by separately considering the message communication pattern and the security services required by application components. A secure connector is a distributed connector, which consists of a secure sender connector and a secure receiver connector that communicate with each other. Each secure connector is labeled with the UML stereotype « secure connector » to clearly identify its role in the software architecture. A secure sender or receiver connector (Fig. 1) consists of:

- A security coordinator. The security coordinator receives messages from a sender component or delivers messages to a receiver component. The security coordinator also sequences the interactions with one or more security services and with a communication object that encapsulates a communication pattern.

- One or more security service objects. A security service object encapsulates the specific security service being applied to the application message, such as encryption or decryption for a confidentiality security service. For some security services, such as authentication, authorization or non-repudiation, a secure connector might not encapsulate the security service. Instead the secure connector interacts with the security service contained in security service components.
- A communication object. The communication object encapsulates the communication pattern used to transmit the message (and possibly the response) from the sender component to the receiver component. For all secure connectors, there is a sender communication object and a receiver communication object.

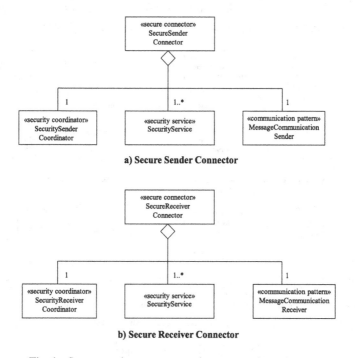

Fig. 1. Secure sender connector and secure receiver connector

It should be noted that most conventional connectors only consist of the communication object. A secure connector expands on this by providing the security service(s) and security coordinator. A secure connector separates the concerns of communication and security by encapsulating them in separate objects, which are unaware of each other's existence. This loose coupling is ensured by providing a security coordinator, which interacts with the application component (sender or receiver) and sequences the interactions with security service(s) and communication objects.

4   Design of Reusable Secure Connectors

The secure connectors are designed using component-based concepts in which a secure connector is designed as a composite component that contains simple components that encapsulate the security services and the message communication pattern. One or more security service components are encapsulated in a secure connector as application components could require several security services. Figure 2 depicts the security service components where each security service is designed with one or two security service components. The confidentiality security is designed with the encryption and decryption security service components, whereas the integrity security is designed with the integrity generation and integrity verification security components. The non-repudiation security is designed with the non-repudiation generation and non-repudiation verification security components. The authentication and access control securities are designed with the authentication and access control security service components respectively.

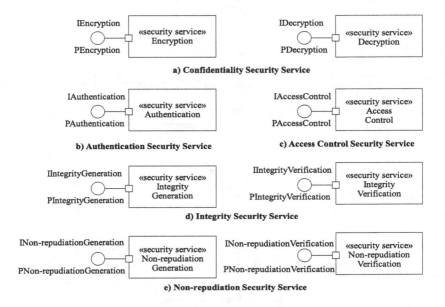

Fig. 2. Security service components

Each port of a component is defined in terms of provided and/or required interfaces [7]. Each security service component (Fig. 2) has a provided port through which the component provides security services to other components. The Encryption and Decryption security service components for confidential security have the provided PEncryption and PDecryption ports respectively. The Authentication security service component has the provided PAuthentication port, whereas the Access Control security service component has the provided PAccessControl port. The integrity security is provided by the Integrity Generation security service component via the provided PIntegrityGeneration port and by the Integrity Verification security service component via the provided PIntegrityVerification port. The Non-repudiation Generation and Verification security service components have the provided PNon-repudiationGeneration and PNon-repudiationVerification ports respectively for the non-repudiation security. Figure 3 depicts the interfaces provided by the ports of the security service components in Fig. 2.

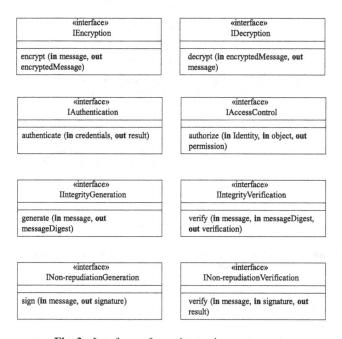

Fig. 3. Interfaces of security service components

Each communication pattern is designed with a sender communication pattern component (CPC) and a receiver communication pattern component (CPC), which are encapsulated in a secure sender connector and a secure receiver connector respectively. Figure 4a depicts the Synchronous Message Communication With Reply (SMCWR) Sender CPC and Synchronous Message Communication With Reply (SMCWR) Receiver CPC for the secure synchronous message communication with reply connector. The SMCWR Sender CPC ((a) in Fig. 4) has the provided PSyncMCWithReplySenderService port through which the Security Sender Coordinator component ((a) in Fig. 5) sends to the SMCWR Sender CPC a message being sent to the receiver application component, whereas it requests a service from the SMCWR Receiver CPC via the required RNetwork port. Similarly, the SMCWR Receiver CPC ((a) in Fig. 4) has the required RSecurityService port for sending to the Security Receiver Coordinator component a message received from the SMCWR Sender CPC ((a) in Fig. 6), whereas it receives a message from the SMCWR Sender CPC via the provided PNetwork port. (b) in Fig. 4 depicts the interfaces provided by each port of the SMCWR Sender and Receiver communication pattern components (CPCs).

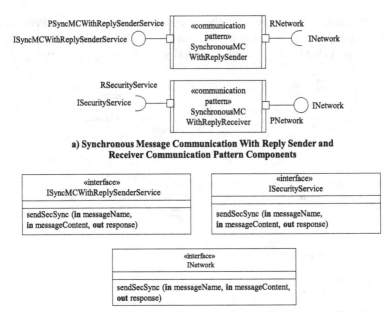

a) Synchronous Message Communication With Reply Sender and
Receiver Communication Pattern Components

b) Interfaces of Synchronous Message Communication With Reply Sender and Receiver
Communication Pattern Components

Fig. 4. Synchronous message communication with reply sender and receiver communication pattern components and their interfaces

The secure connectors are constructed by reusing security service components (Figs. 2 and 3) and CPCs (Fig. 4), with the security coordinator being a component that needs to be designed for each secure connector to integrate the selected security service components with the selected CPCs. Once one or more security services required by an application component are determined, the corresponding security service components are selected from the reusable security service components (Figs. 2 and 3). Similarly the required CPCs are selected from the reusable CPCs (Fig. 4) in accordance with the communication pattern between application components. The security coordinator component (Figs. 5 and 6) integrates the selected security service component(s) with the selected CPC by sequencing the interaction with those components. For the integration, the security coordinator component has required ports through which it requests security services from the security service components and communicates with the CPC. Also the security coordinator components (Figs. 5b and 6b) provides ports for receiving a service request message from or requesting a service from an application component.

5   Secure Synchronous Communication with Reply Connector

Secure synchronous message communication with reply between components is provided by means of a pair of reusable connectors, namely a secure synchronous message communication with reply sender connector and a secure synchronous message communication with reply receiver connector (shortened to secure sender connector and

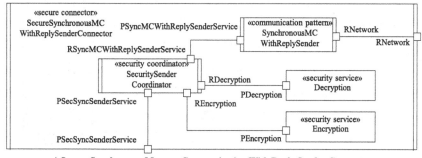

a) Secure Synchronous Message Communication With Reply Sender Connector

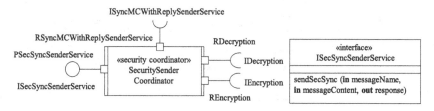

b) Security Sender Coordinator and its Interface

Fig. 5. Security sender coordinator and secure synchronous message communication with reply sender connector

secure receiver connector in this section). These secure connectors encapsulate the intricacy of sending and receiving messages for their respective components. When the secure sender connector receives a message from the sender component, it applies the security services to the message. The secured message is packed by the secure sender connector, which sends it to the secure receiver connector. With this message communication pattern, a sender component cannot process and send the next message until it receives a response from the receiver component. When the receiver connector receives a secured and packed message, it unpacks the message and checks the security of the message before sending it to the receiver component. Conversely, a response is sent from the receiver component to the sender component via secure receiver and sender connectors. If the response requires security services, the secure receiver and sender connectors apply the security services required by the components. When the sender component receives the response, it resumes processing and sends the next message to the receiver component. A reusable secure connector encapsulates security service components that implement security services, such as confidentiality, integrity, non-repudiation, access control, and authentication.

5.1   Design of Secure Synchronous Communication with Reply Connector

Figures 5 and 6 depict the design of a reusable secure SMCWR connector. This secure connector provides application components with the confidentiality security services

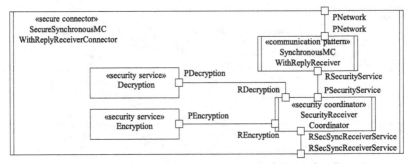

a) Secure Synchronous Message Communication With Reply Receiver Connector

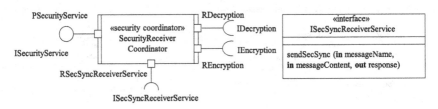

b) Security Receiver Coordinator and its Interface

Fig. 6. Security receiver coordinator and secure synchronous message communication with reply receiver connector

between the sender and receiver application components. This secure connector is composed of a secure SMCWR sender connector ((a) in Fig. 5) and a secure SMCWR receiver connector ((a) in Fig. 6). The secure SMCWR sender connector ((a) in Fig. 5) is designed as a composite component in which the Security Sender Coordinator component integrates the reusable Encryption and Decryption security service components (Fig. 2) for the confidentiality security with the reusable SMCWR Sender CPC (Fig. 4). For integrating the components, the Security Sender Coordinator component ((b) in Fig. 5) has a required REncryption port to communicate with a provided PEncryption port of the Encryption security service component, which encrypts messages being sent to the receiver component, and it also has a required RDecryption port to communicate with a provided PDecryption port of the Decryption security service component, which decrypts messages received from the receiver component. For synchronous message communication with reply, the Security Sender Coordinator component ((b) in Fig. 5) has a required RSyncMCWithReplySenderService port to communicate with a provided PSyncMCWithReplySenderService port of the SMCWR Sender CPC. Also the Security Sender Coordinator component has a provided PSecSyncSenderService port to communicate with an application component, and the interface of PSecSyncSenderService is depicted in (b) in Fig. 5. Similarly, the SMCWR Receiver Connector ((a) in Fig. 6) is designed as a composite component that encapsulates the Security Receiver Coordinator component, Encryption component, Decryption component, and SMCWR Receiver CPC. The Security Receiver Coordinator component communicates with the SMCWR

Receiver CPC, the Encryption and Decryption security service components, and an application component through ports.

5.2   Example of Secure Synchronous Communication with Reply Connector

This section describes how a reusable secure synchronous message communication with reply connector for confidentiality is applied to an E-Commerce application. A secure SMCWR connector (Figs. 5 and 6) for a confidentiality security service is applied for placing requisition in the business to business (B2B) electronic commerce application (Fig. 7). For requisition order confidentiality, the secure SMCWR sender connector contains a Security Sender Coordinator component, an Encryption security service component and a Decryption security service component, whereas the secure SMCWR receiver connector encapsulates a Security Receiver Coordinator component, a Decryption security service component and an Encryption security service component (Fig. 7). When a Customer Interface component places a requisition on a Requisition Server, the Requisition Order is encrypted by the Encryption security service component in the secure SMCWR sender connector (message Q2 in Fig. 7). The encrypted Requisition Order is sent by the SMCWR Sender CPC to the SMCWR Receiver CPC (messages Q4 and Q5 in Fig. 7). The encrypted Requisition Order is decrypted by the Decryption security component in the secure SMCWR receiver connector (message Q7 in Fig. 7). Similarly, the Requisition Status is encrypted by the Encryption security service component in the secure SMCWR receiver connector (message Q10 in Fig. 7) and the encrypted Requisition Status is sent by the SMCWR Receiver CPC to the SMCWR Sender CPC (messages Q12 and Q13 in Fig. 7). The encrypted Requisition Status is decrypted by the Decryption security service component in the secure SMCWR sender connector (message Q15 in Fig. 7).

The same secure SMCWR connector for a confidentiality security service that is used for placing requisition (Fig. 7) in the B2B electronic commerce application can be applied to different applications. Figure 8 depicts a secure SMCWR connector for a confidentiality security service, which is applied for validating a Personal Identification Number (PIN) in the Automated Teller Machine (ATM) application. When an ATM Client component requests validating a PIN, the Encryption security service component in the secure SMCWR sender connector encrypts a PIN and a card number (message P2 in Fig. 8), which are decrypted by the Decryption security service component in the secure SMCWR receiver connector (message P7 in Fig. 8) in order to check the confidentiality of a PIN and a card number. Similarly, the validation result is encrypted by the Encryption security service component (message P10 in Fig. 8) and it is decrypted by the Decryption security service component (message P15 in Fig. 8).

6   Validation of Reusable Secure Connectors

6.1   Implementation of Reusable Secure Connectors

The reusable secure connectors described in Sects. 4 and 5 have been implemented using object-oriented programming in Java. The implementation environment used is as

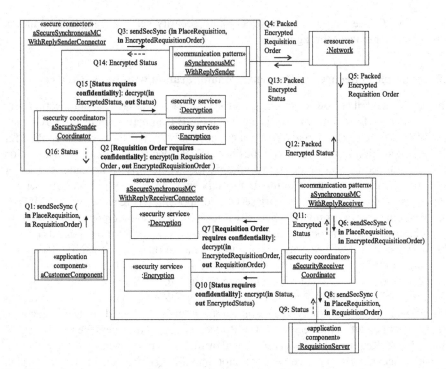

Fig. 7. Applying secure synchronous message communication with reply connector with confidentiality security service in the b2b electronic commerce application

follows: Eclipse 4.4.2 version on a Windows 7, 64 bit-based computer with 4 GB of memory and 2.20 GHz quad core i7 processor. All secure message communications between application components were implemented in a local machine.

The secure connector for a SMCWR CPC and confidentiality security service components (Fig. 5 through Fig. 8) has been implemented for the validation. The components handle the functionality of the application, while secure connectors address both security and communication between components. Encryption and decryption security service components for the confidentiality security service have been implemented using the Data Encryption Standard (DES) algorithm, which is a block cipher that operates on plain text blocks of a given size (64-bits) and returns cipher text blocks of the same size. It is based on a symmetric-key algorithm that uses a 56-bit key. DES works by using the same key to encrypt and decrypt a message, so both the sender and the receiver must know and use the same secret key. An encrypted message is passed to the receiver component, the receiver connector of which decrypts the message using the DES algorithm with the same secret key. Finally, the receiver component replies to the sender with an encrypted result using the same algorithms described above.

Another validation has been done by designing and implementing a secure asynchronous message communication connector with both confidentiality and non-repudiation security services. The secure asynchronous message communication connector has been designed by replacing the CPC with an asynchronous message CPC, and by modifying the

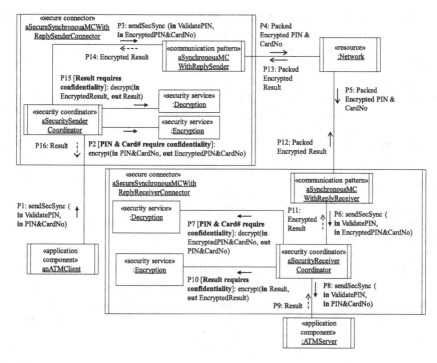

Fig. 8. Applying secure synchronous connector with confidentiality security service in the automated teller machine (ATM) application

security coordinator component in accordance with reusing both the confidentiality and non-repudiation security service components. The connector was implemented using two algorithms for security services, Digital Signature Algorithm (DSA) to sign/verify the message and DES to encrypt/decrypt the message. The non-repudiation security service was implemented using the DSA, which was running on a public key infrastructure. In the secure asynchronous message communication sender connector, the security service signs the message with the sender's private key using the DSA, which generates a digital signature so as to prove that the message is authentic and unforgeable. Then this message was packed and sent to the receiver by the asynchronous message communication sender CPC. Similarly, the secure asynchronous message communication receiver connector was implemented to unpack the signed message and check for the validity of the signature using DSA with the sender's public key.

6.2   Reusability of Secure Connectors

The implementation of the secure SMCWR connector (described in Sects. 4 and 5) was applied to different applications - Place Requisition (Fig. 7) in the B2B electronic commerce application and PIN Validation (Fig. 8) in the ATM application. The Place Requisition and the PIN Validation require both a confidentiality security service and SMCWR communication pattern. They were implemented using the reusable secure

SMCWR connector, which encapsulated the Encrypt and Decrypt security service components (Fig. 2) for a confidential security service. Test cases for a place requisition request and a PIN validation request were used to successfully validate the reusable secure connector.

The implementation of the secure asynchronous message communication connector was applied to different applications – Purchase Order in the B2C electronic commerce application and Confirm Shipment in the B2B electronic commerce application. The Purchase Order and the Confirm Shipment require both confidentiality and non-repudiation security services as well as asynchronous message communication pattern. Both were implemented using the reusable secure asynchronous message communication connector, which encapsulated the Encrypt and Decrypt security service components (Fig. 2) for a confidential security service, and the Non-repudiationGeneration and NonrepudiationVerification security service components (Fig. 2) for a non-repudiation security service. Test cases for a purchase order request and a confirm shipment request were used to successfully validate the reusable connector.

Table 1 shows reusable secure connectors that were implemented for different applications. The secure SMCWR connector was implemented and reused for the ATM, B2B, and B2C applications, in particular to implement use cases such as PIN validation (ATM), Browse Catalog and Place Requisition (B2B) and Pay Product (B2C). The secure asynchronous message communication connector was implemented and reused for Confirm Shipment (B2B) and Purchase Order (B2C) use cases.

Table 1. Reusable secure connectors for different applications

Reusable secure connector	Communication pattern	Security services	Applications
Secure synchronous message communication with reply connector	Synchronous Message Communication with Reply Communication Pattern	Confidentiality	PIN Validation (ATM, Fig. 8), Place Requisition (B2B, Fig. 7), Browse Catalog (B2B), Pay Product (B2C)
Secure asynchronous message communication Connector	Asynchronous Message Communication Pattern	Confidentiality, Non-repudiation	Confirm Shipment (B2B), Purchase Order (B2C)

7   Conclusions

A secure connector can be reused in different applications if it matches the security requirement and communication pattern required between application components. Reusable secure connectors have been designed as composite components using component concepts, which are designed by reusing the security service components providing security services required by application components as well as the CPCs for transmission of secure messages and responses between the components. Integration of security services and communication patterns within secure connectors is provided by security coordinators. To validate this approach, the secure connectors were implemented for an electronic commerce application and an ATM application.

The component-based approach described in this paper for designing reusable secure connectors is different from the aspect-oriented secure connectors described in [2]. The aspect-oriented approach [2] provides a mapping scheme from the objects constituting secure connectors to separate security and communication aspects so that the aspects can be implemented using aspect-oriented languages, such as AspectJ. In the aspect-oriented approach, the security aspects are separated from the communication aspects for the reusability of secure connectors. In contrast, the component-based approach focuses on designing reusable secure connectors that are internally structured into separately reusable security and communication components, which can themselves be assembled to form different reusable secure connectors. The component-based approach provides a basis of the implementation of reusable secure connectors using object-oriented programming languages, such as Java.

This paragraph describes future research for secure connectors. We will investigate how the component-based approach can be integrated with the aspect-oriented approach [2]. The component-based secure connectors might be mapped to the aspect-oriented secure connectors by considering the relationships between the ports/interfaces of components and the pointcuts/advices of aspects. In addition, security connectors can be specialized to realize specific algorithms. For example, a secure connector containing an access control security service can be implemented with role-based access control or mandatory access control. To realize these algorithms, a secure connector could be specialized to provide the appropriate security service.

Acknowledgement. Gomaa's research is supported by the Air Force Office of Scientific Research under grant number FA9550-16-1-0030.

References

1. Al-Azzani, S., Bahsoon, R.: SecArch: Architecture-level evaluation and testing for security. In: Joint Working IEEE/IFIP Conference on Software Architecture (WICSA) and European Conference on Software Architecture (ECSA), August 2012
2. Baker, C., Shin M.: Aspect-oriented secure connectors for implementation of secure software architecture. In: International Conference on Software Engineering and Knowledge Engineering (SEKE 2014), Vancouver, 1–3 July 2014
3. Banerjee, S., Mattmann, C.A., Medvidovic, N., Golubchik, L.: Leveraging architectural models to inject trust into software systems. In: Proceedings of the ICSE 2005 Workshop on Software Engineering for Secure Systems, St. Louis, Missouri, May 2005
4. Basin, D., Clavel, M., Egea, M.: A decade of model-driven security. In: 16th ACM Symposium on Access Control Models and Technologies (SACMAT 2011), Innsbruck, 15–17 June 2011
5. Deng, Y., Wang, J., Tsai, J.J.P., Beznosov, K.: An approach for modeling and analysis of security system architectures. IEEE Trans. Knowl. Data Eng. **15**(5), 1099–1119 (2003)
6. Fernandez, E.B.: Security Patterns in Practice. Wiley, New York (2013)

7. Gomaa, H.: Software Modeling and Design: UML, Use Cases, Patterns, and Software Architectures. Cambridge University Press, Cambridge (2011)
8. Gomaa, H., Shin, M.E.: Modeling complex systems by separating application and security concerns. In: 9th IEEE International Conference on Engineering of Complex Computer Systems (ICECCS 2004), Italy, April 2004
9. Jürjens, J.: UMLsec: extending UML for secure systems development. In: Jézéquel, J.-M., Hussmann, H., Cook, S. (eds.) UML 2002. LNCS, vol. 2460, pp. 412–425. Springer, Heidelberg (2002)
10. Ren, J., Taylor, R., Dourish, P., Redmiles, D.: Towards an architectural treatment of software security: A connector-centric approach. In: Proceedings of the Workshop on Software Engineering for Secure Systems, St. Louis, Missouri, 15–16 May 2005
11. Schumacher, M., Fernandez, E.B., Hybertson, D., Buschmann, F., Sommerlad, P.: Security Patterns. Wiley, New York (2006)
12. Shin, M.E., Gomaa, H.: Software modeling of evolution to a secure application: From requirements model to software architecture. Sci. Comput. Program. 66(1), 60–70 (2007)
13. Shin, M.E., Malhotra, B., Gomaa, H., Kang, T.: Connectors for secure software architectures. In: 24th International Conference on Software Engineering and Knowledge Engineering (SEKE 2012), San Francisco, 1–3 July 2012
14. Taylor, R.N., Medvidovic, N., Dashofy, E.M.: Software Architecture: Foundations, Theory, and Practice. Wiley, Chichester (2010)

Reuse-Based Software Engineering

Concept-Based Engineering of Situation-Specific Migration Methods

Marvin Grieger[1(✉)], Masud Fazal-Baqaie[1],
Gregor Engels[1], and Markus Klenke[2]

[1] s-lab – Software Quality Lab, Paderborn University,
Zukunftsmeile 1, 33102 Paderborn, Germany
{grieger,mfazal-baqaie,engels}@s-lab.uni-paderborn.de
[2] TEAM GmbH, Hermann-Löns-Straße 88, 33104 Paderborn, Germany
mke@team-pb.de

Abstract. Software migration methods enable to reuse legacy systems by transferring them into new environments. Thereby, the method used needs to fit to the project's situation by considering conceptual differences between the source and target environment and automating parts of the migration whenever suitable. Using an inappropriate migration method may lead to a decreased software quality or increased effort. Various method engineering approaches have been proposed to support the development of situation-specific migration methods. However, most do not provide a sufficient degree of flexibility when developing a method or fall short in guiding the endeavor. To address this problem, we introduce a situational method engineering framework to guide the development of model-driven migration methods by assembling predefined buildings blocks. The development is centered around the identification of concepts within a legacy system and the selection of suitable migration strategies. We evaluate the framework by an industrial project in which we migrated a legacy system from the domain of real estates to a new environment.

Keywords: Software migration · Model-driven · Concept modeling · Method engineering · Method base · Method fragments · Method patterns

1 Introduction

If an existing software system does not realize all of its requirements, but is still valuable to ongoing business, it has become legacy. This might be due to the fact that the underlying technology restricts the fulfillment of new requirements that arose over time. As redevelopment is risky and error-prone [19], a proven solution is to migrate the existing system into a new environment. The migration is performed by establishing a migration project during which a *migration method*

This work is supported by the Deutsche Forschungsgemeinschaft under grants EB 119/11-1 and EN 184/6-1.

G.M. Kapitsaki and E. Santana de Almeida (Eds.): ICSR 2016, LNCS 9679, pp. 199–214, 2016.
DOI: 10.1007/978-3-319-35122-3_14

is enacted. The method specifies the activities to perform, roles to involve, tools to apply, and artifacts to generate in order to systematically transfer the legacy system into the new environment.

Using a migration method that fits to the projects situation is essential, as the method determines the efficiency and effectiveness of the overall migration project. To demonstrate this relationship, consider the following two functionalities, i.e., *concepts* [13], realized by a legacy system. First, the system contains *Dialogs*, i.e., graphical user interfaces. Second, some of these dialogs contain buttons that enable to perform a navigation flow to another dialog, i.e., a *Dialog Flow*. The imperative source code shown on the left side of Fig. 1 realizes such a dialog flow concept. It gets executed whenever a user presses an associated button. The invocation of the platform-specific function `call_form` triggers the change to another dialog, i.e., the contract management dialog.

Fig. 1. Imperative realization of *Dialog Flow* in the source environment (left), declarative realization in the target environment (right)

Based on this example, we describe two situations in which the realization of the dialog flow in the target environment varies. In the first situation, we envision to realize dialog flows by imperative source code, too. This means, it is also required to call a platform specific function in the target environment. Then, using a migration method M_1 that specifies to perform an automatic transformation on a syntactical level can be efficient and effective. Following this *migration strategy* results in the desired realization and enables to migrate large parts of the system automatically, as it only required to develop parsers, code generators, and a mapping between the syntactic elements of the languages.

In the second situation, the realization in the target environment might be significantly different. Such a case can be seen on the right side of Fig. 1. In this situation, dialog flows should be realized by using the provided declarative language. The language enables to reference dialogs (`PropertyManagement`, `ContractManagement`) and to define flows between them (`manageContract`). Then, using the same method M_1 that prescribes to perform a transformation on a syntactical level would preserve the imperative realization in the target environment, possibly by emulating the platform specific function. As the functionality would be preserved, but its realization would not be adapted to the target environment, we consider the method to be ineffective [6].

Using a method M_2 that prescribes to perform a migration on a higher level of abstraction by extracting the underlying concept would increase the effectiveness of an automatic transformation. Following this migration strategy requires to extract contained dialogs and flows between them by interpreting the source code. But, this will influence the efficiency of the method as sophisticated program comprehension techniques are required.

If an automatic transformation is either inefficient or ineffective, a method M_3 that prescribes a guided manual migration can be a viable alternative. As illustrated by this example, developing a migration method for the situation at hand is a critical but cumbersome task.

To support the development of situation-specific methods, various method engineering approaches have been developed over time. However, we identified that existing approaches mainly suffer from two shortcomings [7]: First, they do not provide a sufficient degree of flexibility when developing a method. Therefore, a fine-grained adaptation of the method for the situation at hand is often not possible. Second, they fall short in providing sufficient guidance on how to develop a method, making the endeavor error-prone. During industrial projects, we observed situations in which no suitable migration method was available up front and no approach was available to guide the development of a new method. Eventually, this prevented the reuse of the legacy systems and led to a redevelopment instead.

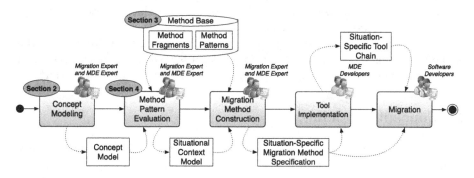

Fig. 2. Overview of the method engineering framework for the development and enactment of situation-specific migration methods

We address this problem by introducing a Situational Method Engineering (SME) [11] framework that guides the development and enactment of situation-specific migration methods. An overview of the method engineering process is shown in Fig. 2. The process begins with the activity called *Concept Modeling*. Thereby, the concepts that are present within the system to migrate are modeled, e.g., the *Dialog Flow* concept. The focus on the conceptual level enables to develop effective migration methods by choosing a suitable migration strategy for each concept, e.g., the migration on a syntactical level. Such strategies are encoded by *Method Patterns* stored in the *Method Base*. Intuitively, the patterns represent construction guidelines for methods that follow the associated strategy. Before choosing a pattern for a concept, we aim to assess their efficiency and effectiveness during the *Method Pattern Evaluation* activity. This allows to make informed decisions in the subsequent *Migration Method Construction* activity.

Thereby, a pattern is chosen for each concept and multiple patterns are integrated. If the resulting specification of the constructed method indicates that some parts of the migration are automated, then a corresponding tool chain is realized during the *Tool Implementation* activity. Thereby, we focus on model-driven tool chains. In the last activity called *Migration*, the developed method is enacted and the legacy system is transferred to the new environment. Thereby, developed tools get used and associated developers are included.

The contributions of this paper are threefold: We define a *method engineering framework* (C1) that enables a concept-based engineering of situation-specific, model-driven migration methods. We describe the content of the *method base*, i.e., the building blocks for migration methods, and the first two activities of the *method engineering framework* in detail (C2). In addition, we describe how we *evaluated* the framework (C3) by migrating a monolithic legacy system from the domain of real estates to a multilayered environment, in an industrial context.

The paper is structured as follows: In Sect. 2, we describe the first activity of the method engineering process named *Concept Modeling*. We introduce the content of the *Method Base* in Sect. 3. The second activity of the process named *Method Pattern Evaluation* is described in Sect. 4. Details of the project in which we evaluated the framework are described in Sect. 5. Related work is discussed in Sect. 6, before we draw conclusions in Sect. 7.

In the remainder, we use the *Dialog Flow* functionality introduced in the beginning of this section as a running example. It is an example of the industrial project in which we migrated a system from Oracle Forms[1] to Oracle ADF[2].

2   Concept Modeling

The purpose of this activity is to decompose the legacy system into distinct parts. We consider that this is essential for two reasons: First, it enables to choose a different strategy per part, e.g., to vary the abstraction level of the transformation as well as the degree of automation. Based on our observations in practice, we conclude that this is essential for situation-specific migration methods. Second, it enables to flexibly adapt the granularity of the method specification, which is dependent on the amount of parts identified. The more parts are used, the more coarse-granular the specification will become.

To decompose the legacy system, we use the established technique of *concept modeling*, described in [13]. A concept model describes a software system by a set of concepts, whereby different types of concepts on various levels of abstraction are differentiated. In terms of types, a distinction between *language concepts* and *abstract concepts* is made. Language concepts are syntactic entities defined by the programming language used, while abstract concepts "represent language-independent ideas of computation and problem solving methods" [13]. The abstract concepts can be further classified as *architectural* or *programming*

---

[1] http://www.oracle.com/technetwork/developer-tools/forms/overview.

[2] http://www.oracle.com/technetwork/developer-tools/jdev/overview/.

concepts, whereby the latter ones include "general coding strategies, data structures and algorithms" [13]. The concepts can be related to each other by *consists-of* relations, e.g., an abstract concept can consist of a language concept. In this case, the consists-of relation represents the technology-specific realization.

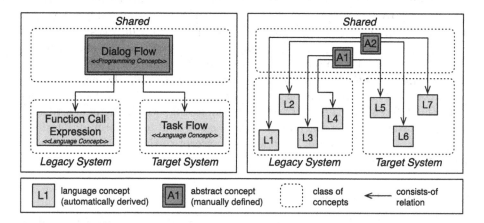

Fig. 3. Concepts for the running example (left), classes of concepts involved in a software migration scenario in general (right)

The concept model for the running example is shown on the left side of Fig. 3, while the general schema of concept models is shown on the right side. As illustrated, we classified the concepts into three classes. Abstract concepts belonging to the class of *Shared* concepts can be realized in both environments, like the *Dialog Flow* concept. The remaining two classes are associated with the *Legacy System* and the *Target System*, respectively. The legacy system already consists of a set of language concepts of the legacy environment, while the target system will consist of a set of target environment-specific language concepts after the migration. Related to the *Dialog Flow* concept, it can be seen that it currently consists of imperative *Function Call Expressions*. In the target environment, it will consist of the declarative language concept called *Task Flows*.

The purpose of the *Concept Modeling* activity is to define a concept model that conforms to the schema shown. Defining this model is the task of a migration expert who has expertise about both environments. In addition, he can perform interviews with experts of the legacy system or a coarse-grained analysis to derive the sets of concepts. In the subsequent activities of our framework, migration strategies for the concepts identified can be chosen. More specifically, we choose strategies for each concept that belongs to the set of shared, abstract concepts. This is due to the fact that choosing migration strategies for language concepts has several drawbacks: First, the method specification would get very fine-granular. As the method specification shall provide guidance for people, it needs to be more coarse-granular. Second, adapting the legacy system to the new environment requires to preserve the abstract concepts, but not necessarily their technical realization, i.e., the language concepts.

3   Method Base

So far, we identified the abstract concepts of the legacy system as well as their current and envisioned realization. The next activity of the method engineering process aims to assess migration strategies for each concept (cf. Sect. 4). To do this, we need to have knowledge of the migration strategies available. These are stored in the method base of the framework and described in this section.

In general, a method base is a repository that contains reusable building blocks of methods [11]. In our framework, we use two different types of building blocks, namely *method fragments* and *method patterns*. While methods fragments constitute atomic building blocks of migration methods, method patterns represent different migration strategies by indicating which fragments to use. Having knowledge of the different strategies is essential to perform an informed decision on which one to use. Therefore, an excerpt of the contained fragments and patterns is described subsequently.

3.1   Method Fragments

We defined method fragments based on principles hat have been developed in the context of the Architecture-Driven Modernization (ADM) initiative [20]. ADM was initiated by the Object Management Group (OMG) and aims to apply model-driven techniques on the domain of software migration. Thereby, a legacy system is represented by various models, while model transformations are used to realize conversions between them. Conceptually, ADM is related to the Model-Driven Architecture (MDA) by using the same levels of abstraction.

Figure 4 visualizes the proposed method fragments stored in the method base. In this figure, a fragment is either a single artifact or activity. For simplicity we do omit other constituents of a method, i.e., tools and roles. As illustrated, the fragments form an instance of the well-established *horseshoe-model* [12]. This is due to the fact that migration methods are used to perform a reengineering task. Therefore, each activity belongs to either one of the three reengineering processes, namely reverse engineering, restructuring or forward engineering [4].

The method fragments that constitute artifacts can be distinguished based on the abstraction layer they belong to, namely the *System-*, *Platform-Specific-*, or *Platform-Independent Layer*.

On the *System Layer*, textual artifacts are located that represent source code. This can either be the *Legacy Source Code* of the existing system, or the resulting *Migrated Source Code*. Besides textual artifacts, external systems like *Platforms* or *Databases* are also located there. If the legacy system uses their interfaces, it can be necessary to capture them as a model.

On the *Platform-Specific Layer*, Platform-Specific Models (PSMs) are located that represent the legacy system (*L-PSM*) and the migrated system (*M-PSM*) respectively. These models describe the source code of the legacy system and its environment by modeling the corresponding Abstract Syntax Graphs (ASGs). They are platform-specific since the systems are represented by the language concepts of the environments, e.g., by using a metamodel of a programming language

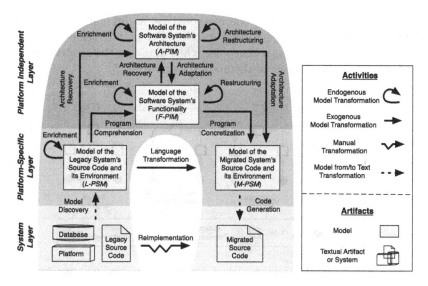

Fig. 4. Excerpt of method fragments (activities and artifacts) stored in the method base

like PL/SQL. From the ADM context, the Abstract Syntax Tree Metamodel (ASTM) [15] can be extended to derive such a platform-specific metamodel.

On the *Platform-Independent Layer*, Platform-Independent Models (PIMs) are located that act as an intermediate representation. We distinguish two kinds of them, based on the abstraction level of the contained information.

The model on the lower level of abstraction (*F-PIM*) represents the functionality of the system to transform, i.e., it explicitly models the abstract concepts. For example, using a metamodel of general programming language concepts, like loops, conditions or function calls, a platform-independent ASG can be modeled. However, the model is not limited to solely describing source code but any information that represents the functionality of the system. Such functionality can be implicitly described by the source code, examples being states of the system, structures of user interfaces or dialog flows.

On the highest level of abstraction, we consider a model that represents architectural structures of a software system (*A-PIM*), like existing components or layers. Architectural structures usually aggregate entities that are represented by a model on a lower level of abstraction, e.g., a component consists of classes in an object-oriented system. From the ADM context the Knowledge Discovery Metamodel (KDM) [16], which is separated into layers and packages, can be used to represent both platform-independent models.

3.2   Method Patterns

The method fragments introduced are atomic building blocks of migration methods. As solely using the fragments would not provide sufficient guidance on how to construct migration methods, the method base additionally contains a set of *method patterns* [5]. These patterns encode different migration strategies by indicating which method fragments to use when applying the strategy. In total, we observed 14 patterns. Four of them are shown in Fig. 5.

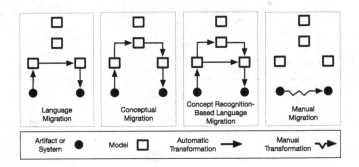

Fig. 5. Excerpt of observed method patterns to preserve functionality

Migration strategies to transform functionality, i.e., to preserve it, need to realize a consistent path from the *Legacy Source Code* to the *Migrated Source Code* in the horseshoe model. Note that the preservation of functionality is not ensured by realizing such a path, but it is an essential prerequisite. As shown in Fig. 5, each pattern indicates activities to execute, artifacts to create, roles to involve or tools to apply. Subsequently, we describe the strategies encoded by the patterns shown and go into detail on the first two.

Language Migration. This pattern prescribes to migrate the functionality by defining a mapping between language concepts of both environments. The mapping will be realized by a direct transformation between the L-PSM and M-PSM (cf. Fig. 4). While such a mapping can theoretically always be defined, we observed instances in practice in which the pattern has been perceived as not *suitable*. Based on our experience, this mainly depends on the complexity of the model transformation between both PSMs, as this transformation needs to address multiple concerns: First, it needs to *interpret* the L-PSM to identify the language concepts related to the abstract concept to transform. The complexity depends on the degree of program comprehension required. Second, it can be necessary to *restructure* the explicit representation of the abstract concept. Third, the language concepts of the legacy environment need to be *mapped* to the language concepts of the target environment. Therefore, we consider the pattern to be suitable if a concept is realized *comparably* in both environments, i.e., whenever the degree of interpretation and restructuring required is low. Also, the functionality needs to have a sufficient size. Only then, benefits gained by automating the transformation will outweigh the effort spend on developing required tools.

Related to the example, we consider that the pattern is not suitable for the migration of the *Dialog Flow* concept. The transformation from the imperative to the declarative realization at least requires a comprehensive interpretation of the source code. In addition, we aimed to restructure the application based on the navigation flows identified.

Conceptual Migration. This pattern prescribes to migrate the functionality by using an intermediate representation on a platform-independent layer. The functionality, i.e., the abstract concept, is explicitly represented by an F-PIM (cf. Fig. 4). Compared to the *Language Migration* pattern, the complexity of performing a transformation between both PSMs is reduced by following the separation of concerns principle: the *Model Understanding* activity specifically addresses the first concern of the transformation, i.e., the interpretation of the L-PSM. A *Restructuring* can be applied on the resulting model before it is mapped into the target environment by enacting the *Program Concretization* activity. Therefore, we consider the pattern to be suitable if a concept is realized *significantly different* in both environments, requiring to reduce the complexity of model transformations by separating different concerns. Also, the functionality needs to have a sufficient size.

Related to the running example, we consider the pattern to be particularly suitable for the *Dialog Flow*. Figure 6 shows an excerpt of the resulting L-PSM and F-PIM when enacting a method that conforms to the pattern.

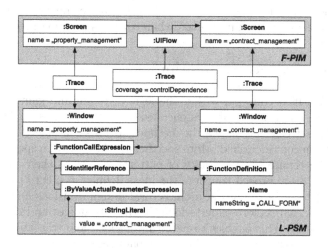

Fig. 6. Example of conceptual information represented in the F-PIM as a result of performing the *Model Understanding* activity

In the lower part of the figure, an excerpt of the L-PSM is shown which is a result of the *Model Discovery* activity. The instance of the model conforms to a Specific Abstract Syntax Tree Metamodel (SASTM) [15] for the programming language PL/SQL that we developed. This language provides syntactic elements to define certain functionalities declaratively, e.g., user interfaces are implemented by Window elements. The FunctionCallExpression corresponds to the one shown in Fig. 1. The control-flow relation is represented by an `IdentifierReference` object, while the platform-specific function is modeled by a `FunctionDeclaration`. The upper part of the figure shows an excerpt of the F-PIM, which is a result of performing the *Model Understanding* activity. The instance of the model conforms to the KDM specification of the OMG. It explicitly represents user interfaces as `Screen` objects as well as the flow between them. This is a result of interpreting the imperative source code to represent the underlying concept.

Concept Recognition-Based Language Migration. This pattern prescribes to migrate the functionality by using an intermediate representation on a platform-independent layer to improve a dependent transformation on the platform-specific layer. Parts of the functionality, i.e., the abstract concept, is explicitly represented by an F-PIM (cf. Fig. 4). We consider the pattern to be suitable if a concept is realized *differently* in both environments and when the complexity of a direct transformation becomes low if parts of the functionality are made explicit. Also, the functionality needs to have a sufficient size.

Manual Migration. This pattern prescribes to migrate the functionality by having it manually transformed by software developers. The developers explore the functionality of the legacy system and subsequently reimplement it in the new environment. We consider the pattern to be suitable whenever automatic transformations are not, e.g., if the size of the functionality is small or if the transformations are still complex even when concerns are separated.

4 Method Pattern Evaluation

So far, we identified concepts within the legacy system and gained knowledge about different migration strategies encoded as method patterns. The purpose of the current activity is to assess the method patterns contained in the method base for each concept identified. More specifically, the experts responsible for the activity shall estimate the suitability of patterns as well as their efficiency and effectiveness. This approach transfers the ideas defined in [21] to the domain of software migration. In this work, architectural design decisions and their alternatives are modeled, before experts identify the advantages and disadvantages of each alternative. This enables to perform informed and traceable decisions.

Indicators to estimate the suitability of a pattern have already been discussed in the previous section. To estimate the effectiveness, we estimate the outcome of the patterns, i.e., the resulting realizations in the target environment. In theory, each pattern can be effective, i.e., can be used to create the desired result. However, in practice we observed instances in which the application of the pattern led to a deviation from an initially desired realization, even though this negatively influenced the effectiveness. The main reason for a deviation is the interdependency between the effectiveness and efficiency, i.e., the fact that a decrease in the effectiveness can increase the efficiency.

Consider for example that we apply the *Language Migration Pattern* on the *Dialog Flow* concept. As the model transformation between the PSMs would be complex, we can decide to realize the concept imperatively in the target environment, too. This avoids an interpretation of the source code to identify dialog flows, making the transformation less complex and therefore the pattern more efficient. However, as it negatively influences the performance and maintainability of the resulting system, it decreases the effectiveness of the pattern.

To estimate the efficiency of a pattern, we systematically evaluate the method fragments indicated. We aim to identify influence factors on the efficiency that originate based on the use of a method fragment. For example, the availability of parsers, code generators and metamodels are critical influence factors for all patterns that encode an automated transformation. Whenever any of these artifacts are not available, effort needs to be spend to develop them.

The efficiency of the *Conceptual Migration Pattern* is particularly determined by the effort required to realize the *Model Understanding* activity. This effort depends on characteristics of the legacy system and the information that needs to be extracted. For example, the amount of different implementation variants of a concept influences the effort required to extract it, as each variant needs to be considered. Also, some implementation variants require more effort to extract than others, e.g., by requiring time-consuming analysis techniques. Related to the *Dialog Flow* concept of the running example, we used the coding convention that the same platform-specific function (`call_form`) was used throughout the system and a static value was bound as parameter to identify the target user interface. However, if the parameter of the function call would not have been bound statically but dynamically, e.g., by using a variable, then extracting the flows would have required time-consuming dynamic analysis techniques.

The gathered knowledge is preserved in a *situational context model*, based on which a decision for a pattern to use is performed. For the running example, the contents of this model are shown in Fig. 7. It contains the identified abstract concept, its realization in the legacy system as well as the envisioned realization in the target system. In addition, it contains the related assessment of the method patterns in terms of indicators for their suitability, efficiency and effectiveness.

The model forms the basis for the next activity, which is concerned with the construction of the migration method. During this activity a method pattern gets chosen for each concept and the resulting method parts get integrated into a coherent method. Thereafter, tools are implemented based on the resulting method specification, before the method gets enacted. Subsequently, we describe the evaluation of the framework by applying it within an industrial project.

5 Industrial Project

We evaluated the framework by developing and enacting a migration method to migrate a real-world legacy system from the domain of real estates in an industrial context. The system consisted of about 5 KLOC written in the programming language PL/SQL and 2 K declarative elements defined in the 4th generation language (4GL) of the source environment. While the amount of declarative elements does seem to be small, we want to point out that even one declarative element can contain a lot of information, e.g., up to 172 properties.

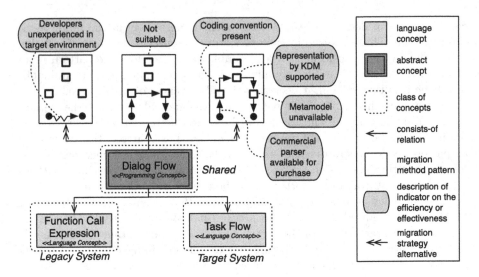

Fig. 7. Excerpt of the situational context model, showing the gathered knowledge related to the abstract concept *Dialog Flow* of the running example

In the legacy system, we determined 23 abstract concepts for which method patterns had been evaluated and selected. For each resulting activity that is a concretization of the *Model Understanding* activity, a pattern-based reverse engineering technique was applied [14]. Thereby, implementation patterns on the L-PSM were formalized by model transformations, using knowledge of the platform and of coding conventions. The constructed migration method also comprised an *Architectural Restructuring*. We realized an evolutionary algorithm to cluster the dialogs based on the extracted dialog flows [9]. Each cluster aggregates dialogs that are related in terms of the underlying business process.

A component-based tool chain had been implemented, according to the developed method specification. In terms of technologies used, models and metamodels had been implemented in the Eclipse Modeling Framework (EMF). This enabled to include several components that are based on EMF, like CDO[3] as model repository, Acceleo[4] for code generation or Henshin[5] for model transformations. In addition, we included metamodels defined by the ADM that had been implemented by MoDisco [3]. Automated transformations between the models as well as restructurings had been realized by 432 model transformations rules.

We aimed for an iterative migration of the legacy system, that is, an iterative enactment of the specified method. To systematically improve the method during each iteration, we defined the exchange of structured feedback between the participants involved [8]. Applying the tool chain on the legacy source code resulted in a model repository consisting of nearly 37 K entities. The L-PSM accounted

---

[3] http://www.eclipse.org/cdo/.

[4] http://www.eclipse.org/acceleo/.

[5] http://www.eclipse.org/henshin/.

for the largest part (70 %), followed by the M-PSM (13 %) and the PIMs (8 %). The remaining entities belonged to models that represented infrastructural information, consisting of traceability links (7 %) or language extensions like stereotypes (2 %). The discrepancy between the size of the L-PSM and the other models had two main reasons. On the one hand, the source code of the legacy system had not been optimized prior to the migration, in terms of dead code and software clones. These issues had been addressed during the migration. On the other hand, the use of languages that declaratively express concepts, often required less language constructs (cf. Fig. 6). This could be observed in the F-PIM as well as in the M-PSM.

Nearly one third of the overall effort for the migration was spent on constructing the migration method and implementing required tools, while the enactment of the method accounted for the rest. In total, 27 KLOC (about 50 % of the code) had been generated by the tool chain.

5.1   Discussion

The method engineering framework was developed in close cooperation with an industrial partner during a technology transfer project, supported by the German Federal Ministry of Economic Affairs and Energy (BMWi). The project had been motivated by a real-world problem, namely the platform migration from Oracle Forms to Oracle ADF. Although Forms has a large installation base and many companies consider migrating to ADF, the vendor does not provide guidance on how to perform the migration.

Together with our industrial partner, we investigated the reasons for the lack of a generic migration method. We concluded that this is due to the comprehensive differences between the two platforms. These differences require migration methods to perform abstractions on a conceptual level in order to be effective. This is hard to generalize as it requires program comprehension. As a result, we observed that companies started redeveloping their systems from scratch, due to missing knowledge on how to develop a situation-specific migration method.

Our framework addresses this problem in two ways: on the one hand, the contents of the method base are based on Model-Driven Engineering (MDE) principles. By the project we were able to demonstrate that the proposed method base supports the migration between environments that are significantly different. The benefits of using model-driven principles have also been acknowledged by the Oracle community[6]. On the other hand, the proposed method engineering process provides useful guidance for the development of situation-specific migration methods. We conclude this, based on our experience with constructing the method for the project. During intensive discussions with the migration expert of our project partner, the use of concepts and patterns essentially enabled a systematic development.

We want to point out that our framework is centered around expert knowledge by design. This is highlighted by the fact that we do not predict, i.e.,

---

[6] http://www.oracle.com/technetwork/de/community/forms/overview/.

quantify, the efficiency and effectiveness of method patterns in advance, but rely on the estimations of experts. We consider that making a reliable prediction is hard, requiring profound, technology-specific knowledge. Instead, we aim to enable a systematic exploration of the context to make informed and traceable decisions, possibly enabling quantification in subsequent projects.

6   Related Work

The related work can be separated into two areas. First, we classify method engineering approaches based on their degree of situation-specific adaptivity [7]. Second, as migration methods are reengineering methods, we discuss frameworks that support reengineering tasks.

Most approaches define *fixed* methods, which can be seen as an edge case as they do not foresee situation-specific adaptation. Examples being the methods described in [6,17], they conform to the *Conceptual Migration* pattern. In the latter one, platform-independent user interface models, namely *Rapid Application Development (RAD)* models, are extracted to migrate user interfaces. The method described in [10] is also fixed but conforms to the *Concept Recognition-Based Language Migration* pattern. In this work, the information to which architectural layer a code block belongs is represented by a PIM. After the PIM had been restructured to conform to a specific architectural style, the M-PSM is derived by transforming the L-PSM. This transformation is parameterized over the information contained in the PIM.

For fixed methods, the assumed situational context is often described implicitly. If it is made explicit, it allows to define an approach to *select* the most suitable one, which can be seen as a way to perform situation-specific adaptation. An example for an approach of this category is the SOA migration framework (SOA-MF) [18]. It enables to select a method based on knowledge that is available or shall be generated. However, the resulting method is still fixed.

Approaches that specify adaptable methods provide a higher degree of flexibility to perform situation-specific adaptation by *configuring* variation points or by performing *tailorings*. Examples being REMICS [1] and ARTIST [2]. They have been developed to guide migrations towards *Service Oriented Architectures (SOA)* or *cloud platforms*. While configuration only enables adaptation to a foreseen context, tailoring can enable to perform arbitrary changes. However, in general, such approaches fall short in guiding the tailoring, i.e., a method engineering process is often missing.

Reengineering frameworks can be used to define migration methods, too. However, they have been developed with the focus on tool support, examples being CORUM [12] and MoDisco [3]. The former work introduced the horseshoe model with the intention to integrate existing tools. This is achieved by defining a schema that includes different abstraction levels and a corresponding process on how to instantiate it. However, the horseshoe is only used as a whole, adaptation is not discussed. In addition, the method does not use models as primary artifacts of the migration, while MoDisco does. However, MoDisco does not specify a migration method but provides a set of tools that can be freely assembled. In general, reengineering frameworks are useful to implement tools but fall short in providing guidance on how to systematically construct migration methods itself.

7 Conclusion and Future Work

We introduced a method engineering framework for the development of situation-specific, model-driven migration methods. The framework consists of two main constituents, namely a method engineering process and a method base.

We described the content of the method base which contains predefined building blocks of migration methods. On the one hand, it contains a set of atomic building blocks called method fragments. On the other hand, it contains a set of method patterns which encode migration strategies.

We introduced the method engineering process of the framework and described the first two activities in detail. They are concerned with the identification of the situational context of a migration project: First, concepts realized within a legacy system are identified. Second, the efficiency and effectiveness of the proposed method patterns, i.e., the migration strategies, are estimated by experts involved. This is essential to perform informed and traceable decisions when subsequently constructing a migration method.

We evaluated the framework by applying it in an industrial context. In particular, we constructed and enacted a migration method to transform a legacy system from the domain of real estates.

As future work, we plan to develop tool support for the activities of the proposed framework, e.g., to support the modeling of the situational context. In addition, we aim to define quality criteria for the assessment of constructed methods, e.g., to determine its completeness or correctness.

References

1. Barbier, F., Mohagheghi, P., Berre, A.J., et al.: Reuse and migration of legacy systems to interoperable cloud services - the REMICS project. In: 4th Workshop on Modeling, Design, and Analysis for the Service Cloud (2010)
2. Bergmayr, A., Bruneliere, H., Canovas Izquierdo, J.L., et al.: Migrating legacy software to the cloud with ARTIST. In: 17th European Conference on Software Maintenance and Reengineering, pp. 465–468 (2013)
3. Brunelière, H., Cabot, J., Dupé, G., et al.: MoDisco: a model driven reverse engineering framework. Inf. Softw. Technol. **56**(8), 1012–1032 (2014)
4. Chikofsky, E.J., Cross, J.H.I.: Reverse engineering and design recovery: a taxonomy. IEEE Softw. **7**(1), 13–17 (1990)
5. Fazal-Baqaie, M., Luckey, M., Engels, G.: Assembly-based method engineering with method patterns. In: Software Engineering 2013 Workshopband, pp. 435–444 (2013)
6. Fleurey, F., Breton, E., Baudry, B., Nicolas, A., Jézéquel, J.-M.: Model-driven engineering for software migration in a large industrial context. In: Engels, G., Opdyke, B., Schmidt, D.C., Weil, F. (eds.) MODELS 2007. LNCS, vol. 4735, pp. 482–497. Springer, Heidelberg (2007)

7. Grieger, M., Fazal-Baqaie, M.: Towards a framework for the modular construction of situation-specific software transformation methods. In: 17th Workshop Software-Reengineering and Evolution, pp. 41–42 (2015)
8. Grieger, M., Fazal-Baqaie, M., Klenke, M., Sauer, S.: A method to systematically improve the effectiveness and efficiency of the semi-automatic migration of legacy systems. In: 16th Workshop Software-Reengineering and Evolution, pp. 77–78 (2014)
9. Grieger, M., Sauer, S., Klenke, M.: Architectural restructuring by semi-automatic clustering to facilitate migration towards a service-oriented architecture. In: 2nd Workshop Model-Based and Model-Driven Software Modernization, pp. 44–45 (2014)
10. Heckel, R., Correia, R., Matos, C., et al.: Architectural transformations: from legacy to three-tier and services. Software Evolution, pp. 139–170. Springer, Heidelberg (2008)
11. Henderson-Sellers, B., Ralyté, J., Ågerfalk, P.J., Rossi, M.: Situational Method Engineering. Springer, Heidelberg (2014)
12. Kazman, R., Woods, S.G., Carrière, S.J.: Requirements for integrating software architecture and reengineering models: CORUM II. In: 5th Working Conference on Reverse Engineering, pp. 154–163 (1998)
13. Kozaczynski, W., Ning, J., Engberts, A.: Program concept recognition and transformation. IEEE Trans. Software Eng. **18**, 1065–1075 (1992)
14. Niere, J., Schäfer, W., Wadsack, J., Wendehals, L., Welsh, J.: Towards pattern-based design recovery. In: 24th International Conference on Software Engineering, pp. 338–348 (2002)
15. OMG: Architecture-Driven Modernization: Abstract Syntax Tree Metamodel (ASTM) (2011). http://www.omg.org/spec/ASTM/1.0/
16. OMG: Architecture-Driven Modernization: Knowledge Discovery Meta-Model (KDM) (2011). http://www.omg.org/spec/KDM/1.3
17. Ramón, Ó.S., Cuadrado, J.S., Molina, J.G.: Model-driven reverse engineering of legacy graphical user interfaces. In: 25th International Conference on Automated Software Engineering, pp. 147–150 (2010)
18. Razavian, M., Lago, P.: A systematic literature review on soa migration. J. Softw. Evol. Process **27**(5), 337–372 (2015)
19. Sneed, H.M.: Estimating the costs of a reengineering project. In: 12th Working Conference on Reverse Engineering, pp. 111–119 (2005)
20. Ulrich, W.M., Newcomb, P.: Information Systems Transformation: Architecture-Driven Modernization Case Studies. Morgan Kaufmann Publishers, San Francisco (2010)
21. Zimmermann, O.: An architectural decision modeling framework for service-oriented architecture design. Ph.D. thesis (2009)

Leveraging Feature Location to Extract the Clone-and-Own Relationships of a Family of Software Products

Manuel Ballarin, Raúl Lapeña, and Carlos Cetina[✉]

SVIT Research Group, San Jorge University, Zaragoza, Spain
{mballarin,rlapena,ccetina}@usj.es

Abstract. Feature location is concerned with identifying software artifacts associated with a program functionality (features). This paper presents a novel approach that combines feature location at the model level with code comparison at the code level to extract Clone-and-Own Relationships from a family of software products. The aim of our work is to understand the different Clone-and-Own Relationships and to take advantage of them in order to improve the way features are reused. We have evaluated our work by applying our approach to two families of software products of industrial dimensions. The code of one of the families is implemented manually by software engineers from the models that specify the software, while the code of the other family is implemented automatically by a code generation tool. The results show that our approach is able to extract relationships between features such as Reimplemented, Modified, Adapted, Unaltered, and Ghost Features, thus providing insight into understanding the Clone-and-Own relationships of a family of software products. Furthermore, we suggest how to use these relationships to improve the way features are reused.

Keywords: Feature location · Software variability extraction · Clone-and-own extraction

1 Introduction

Feature location is concerned with identifying software artifacts associated with a program functionality (features). Feature location is one of the most important and common activities performed by developers during software maintenance and evolution [1]. Most of the approaches carry out feature location at the code level [1–3], but in recent years feature location at the model level is gaining momentum [4–6].

This work has been partially supported by the Ministry of Economy and Competitiveness (MINECO), through the Spanish National R+D+i Plan and ERDF funds under The project Model-Driven Variability Extraction for Software Product Lines Adoption (TIN2015-64397-R).

G.M. Kapitsaki and E. Santana de Almeida (Eds.): ICSR 2016, LNCS 9679, pp. 215–230, 2016.
DOI: 10.1007/978-3-319-35122-3_15

This paper presents the first approach that combines the recent techniques on feature location at the model level with code comparison at the code level. We combine both to extract Clone-and-Own Relationships from a family of software products where the software has been specified through models, and implemented either in a manual or in an automatic way. The extracted Clone-and-Own Relationships reflect how features have been reused throughout the development of the family of software products.

In order to combine both techniques, we used the information that the techniques on feature location provide to develop an algorithm that isolates features at the model level. Then, our approach uses that information to guide code comparisons at the code level. This enables us to isolate features at the code level and retrieve their source code. Finally, we make one-to-one comparisons of the source code of a feature isolated in a product with the source codes of the different isolations of the same feature in other products.

We have evaluated our approach in the industrial domain of Induction Hobs (IH) over two families of IH products. On one of them, the firmware code of the products was implemented manually from the models. On the other, the firmware code of the products was implemented in an automatic way.

The results show that it has been possible to identify several different Clone-and-Own Relationships between features such as Reimplemented, Modified, Adapted, Unaltered, and Ghost Features. These relationships are then used to suggest improvements on how features are reused. In the case of automatic implementation, extracted relationships are used to analyze whether it is necessary to carry out changes over the model-to-code transformation. In the case of manual implementation, extracted relationships are used to detect reuse impediments, to analyze cost-benefit and to detect opportunities to improve the reuse maturity.

The rest of the paper is structured as follows: Sect. 2 presents our approach and shows how to apply our approach to a simple example. Section 3 shows the evaluation of our work. Section 4 comprehends the work related to this paper. Section 5 summarizes the conclusions of our work.

2   Clone-and-Own Extraction Approach

The aim of our approach is to extract Clone-and-Own Relationships that enable us to understand and improve how features are reused among the products. The input of our approach is a family of software products where the software has

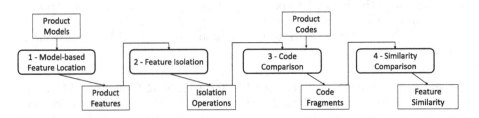

Fig. 1. Stages of the approach

been specified through models. The models are translated into code by humans or in an automatic way using a model-to-text transformation [7]. Our Clone-and-Own Extraction approach builds up on feature location at the model level and code comparisons. The main stages of our approach are: Model-based feature location, Feature Isolation, Code Comparison and Similarity Comparison. Figure 1 depicts the inputs and outputs of these stages, which are described in the following subsections.

We use a running example in order to illustrate our approach. The Linked List Example is based on a family of software products where the variability is not formalized. The products have associated models, from which the code of the products has been manually implemented by a human (see left side of Fig. 2). The products are lists, which can be singly or doubly linked lists. Each list has a different combination of added functionality: sorting functionality (using the bubble method), functionality that enables calculating the number of elements of the list, and functionality that prints the elements of the list.

2.1   Model-Based Feature Location

The first stage of our approach extracts the features from the products at the model level by using already existing techniques that identify features given a set of models. Feature location consists of identifying a fragment in the source code or software model that corresponds to a specific functionality. It is one of the most frequent maintenance activities undertaken by developers because it is a part of the incremental change process [1].

There are several research efforts in existing literature towards feature location from a set of models [5,6,8]. For this stage we have adopted Conceptualized Model Patterns to feature location (hereinafter CMP-FL) [9], which identify model patterns by human-in-the-loop (domain experts and application engineers become part of the decision-making process) and conceptualize the extracted patterns as reusable model fragments. We have adopted CMP-FL because the authors show CMP-FL improves the results obtained with previous approaches, providing features that are more recognizable by the engineers.

In CMP-FL, the elements that differ between the product models are extracted as alternatives for a feature. The elements that do not have a counterpart in the rest of the models are extracted as optional features. As a result, the models will be divided into reusable model fragments. Each of the reusable fragments will correspond with one of the features of the family of software products. The output of our first stage is a list for each product, that contains the features of the product which have been located at the model level by CMP-FL.

The Linked List Example (see 1 Model-based Feature Location of Fig. 2) tags the products with the located features. In the figure, the products, their features, and the names associated with the features are shown. In this example, five features are identified in the product family.

Current techniques used to locate features at the model level [5,6,8,9] do not provide meaningful names, only synthetic names (F1, F2, etc.). We have decided to add more meaningful names to the features in order to improve understanding

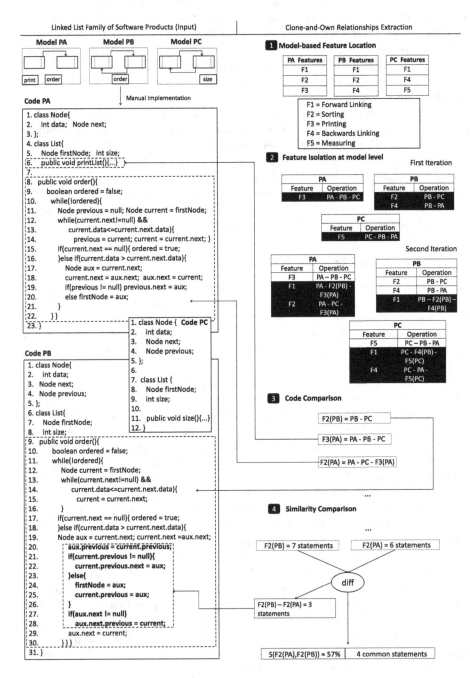

Fig. 2. Clone-and-own relationships extraction applied to the linked list example

of the example: F1, (Forward Linking), F2 (Sorting), F3 (Printing), F4 (Backwards Linking) and F5 (Measuring).

In the first product (PA), features F1, F2 and F3 have been detected. In the second product (PB), features F1, F2, and F4 have been detected. Finally, in the third product (PC), features F1, F4, and F5 have been detected.

Notice that some of the features are present in more than one product. For instance, F2 is present in both product PA and product PB. In order to avoid ambiguity in feature names through this example, a feature FN that belongs to a product PX will be referred to as FN(PX).

2.2   Feature Isolation

This stage performs subtractions between the different products at the model level to identify the features that can be potentially isolated in code. We developed an algorithm that performs the second stage. The algorithm's input is a list of the existing products and their features. The result of the algorithm is the list of the features that can be isolated at the model level, accompanied by one operation per feature which expresses the code subtractions that need to be carried out between products in order to isolate the mentioned feature. The implementation of the algorithm is described as follows:

- The algorithm creates an empty list to store the features that it is able to isolate.
- For each feature (FN) of every product (PX), the algorithm calculates the Complementary Feature Set (CFS). A CFS is a product, combination of products, or combination between products plus already isolated features which contains all the features in PX except for FN. A CFS is valid even if it contains features that are not present in PX. Subtracting the found CFS to PX results in isolating FN. The isolation operation becomes FN(PX) = PX - CFS (e.g.: F1(P7) = P7 - P6 - F3(P4)).
- The isolated features and their isolation operations are added to the list. The addition of new features to the list of isolated features enables for new CFS, hence new feature isolations, so we make iterations while new isolated features are added to the list.

The first iteration of the algorithm will include into the list those features that can be isolated by a CFS composed only of a product or combination of products. Isolation operations found in the first iteration constitute the base cases of our algorithm. Following iterations will use combinations between products plus already isolated features to calculate the CFS. Isolation operations found this way constitute the recursive cases of our algorithm.

The Linked List Example (see 2 Feature Isolation at model level of Fig. 2) shows the application of our feature isolation algorithm as follows.

- **First Iteration:** For all the features in PA, the feature isolation algorithm searches for the CFS that can isolate them. It is not possible to calculate the CFS for F1 nor F2, but it is possible to calculate it for F3. Subtracting PB and PC from PA, we eliminate from PA the code from F1, F2, F4, and F5. Eliminating F1 and F2 from PA leaves us with F3. We have found the first isolation operation. Notice that it would be enough to subtract PB from PA to achieve the same result, but we follow the criteria of eliminating the maximum possible CFS expression to get a purer result.

The feature isolation algorithm performs the same search in the rest of the products. In PB, it is possible to isolate its F2 by eliminating F1 and F4 from PC, and it is also possible to isolate its F4 by disposing of F1 and F2 via PA. In PC, we can isolate F5 in a similar fashion as F3 from PA.

At this point, the feature isolation algorithm has gone through all the features of the product family, so the iteration ends. In this iteration, the feature isolation algorithm has calculated the isolation operations for F3(PA), F2(PB), F4(PB), and F5(PC). As there are still features that lack an isolation operation and we have unlocked new isolation operations, the feature isolation algorithm makes a new iteration.

- **Second Iteration:** For all the features in PA that lack an isolation operation, the feature isolation algorithm searches for the CFS that can isolate them. In order to isolate F1, we need to eliminate both F2 and F3. In the first iteration, our algorithm located F2(PB) and F3(PA). They conform the CFS for F1(PA). We can isolate F2(PA) by subtracting PC and F3(PA).

We can repeat the same steps in both PB and PC. By combining the different products and the features that we isolated in the first iteration, it is possible to get all the isolation operations for the features that lacked them in the previous step (F1(PB), F1(PC), F4(PC)).

The second iteration has calculated the isolation operations for F1(PA), F2(PA), F1(PB), F1(PC), and F4(PC). At the end of the second iteration, the feature isolation algorithm has isolated all the features, so no more iterations are needed.

As the output of the Stage 2 of the Linked List Example, three tables are returned. Each one of these tables contains the product name, the features that belong to it, and the isolation operations found by the feature isolation algorithm.

2.3 Code Comparison

The third stage runs the code comparisons specified by the operations in order to isolate the features in the source code of the products. In a family of software products, the newest products are implemented by carrying out increments or decrements of the previous products in the family. Version control software has become really popular, and there is a wide amount of tool support that calculates differences between two source codes available. Apart from this, code comparison techniques have been used successfully for large scale systems [10,11], proving the computational cost of the operation to be affordable should we scale up our approach. For all these reasons, we use textual code comparison techniques (diff) to execute the code comparisons dictated by the operations given by the second step of our approach.

The Linked List Example (see 3 Code Comparison of Fig. 2) shows how features are isolated. In our approach, all the features isolated at the model level in the second stage are isolated at the code level in the third stage. Due to space restrictions, this example isolates only two features: F2(PB), and F2(PA). According to the operations, F2(PB) can be automatically isolated by subtracting the code belonging to PC from PB. In this example, subtracting the code results in eliminating from PB the inner class Node and the variable declaration section (PB, lines 1 to 8). Therefore, the approach isolates the Sorting Feature from PB (PB, lines 9 to 30).

In order to isolate F2(PA), we must first isolate F3(PA). We subtract both PB and PC to PA, and after eliminating the corresponding code, the approach isolates the Printing Feature (PA, declaration at line 6). We can now isolate F2(PA) by removing from PA the code that is common between PA and PC, and disposing of the F3(PA) code that we just isolated. By doing this, the approach isolates the Sorting Feature from PA (PA, lines 8 to 22). The third stage concludes when the features are isolated in code. The output of the third stage is, for each FN(PX), the code that isolates the feature.

2.4   Similarity Comparison

In this stage, the isolated pieces of code that implement the features that belong to more than one product are compared one to one in order to calculate the similarity between them. In order to calculate the similarity between the same feature in two different products, our approach performs a diff between them.

Diff returns the equal parts and the differences in the code of the two features. We discard the code differences and retain the parts of the code that are equal between them. Similarity between features is then measured in terms of the Total Number of Statements (TNOS) [1], which is a size metric for measuring code size. TNOS counts the number of statements (e.g. for, if, return, switch, while) in each method for assessing the entire code size. This size metric is not dependent on the coding style of programmers, unlike the Lines Of Code metric.

The Linked List Example (see 4 Similarity Comparison of Fig. 2) compares F2(PB) and F2(PA). From the lines of code present in the figure, it can be appreciated that the two order methods, while very similar, do not have the exact same code (notice the marked changes from line 20 to line 28 on PB). It is reasonable, as PA implements a singly linked list and PB implements a doubly linked list. Even if the sorting technique is the same (bubble sort), it cannot be implemented the same way with a different number of links between elements. In fact, F2(PA) has 6 statements and F2(PB) has 7 statements. Considering that 4 of the 7 statements are equal and represent the same conditions in the code, the similarity percentage between F2(PA) and F2(PB) is around the 57 %. From this example, we can conclude that some sort of modification has occurred to the feature since it was first implemented on PA until its appearance on PB.

Summarizing, our approach is applied to a family of software products where variability is not formalized. The first stage identifies the features from the products at a model level, tagging the products with them. Then, in the second stage, the operations to isolate the features are calculated. After that, in the third stage, the approach executes the code comparisons dictated by the operations. Finally, in the fourth stage, the approach quantifies the degree of similarity between the features that appear in more than one product. Our approach returns, for the different features in the family, the feature isolation at the code level and the degree of similarity between the features that appear in more than one product.

3   Evaluation

We have evaluated the presented ideas with our industrial partner (BSH group). Their induction division has been producing induction hobs (under the brands Bosch and Siemens among others) over the last 15 years.

3.1   The Induction Hobs Domain

The newest Induction Hobs (IHs) include full cooking surfaces, where dynamic heating areas are automatically calculated and activated or deactivated depending on the shape, size, and position of the cookware placed on top. In addition, there has been an increase in the type of feedback provided to the user while cooking, such as the exact temperature of the cookware, the temperature of the food being cooked, or even real-time measurements of the actual consumption of the IH. All of these changes are being possible at the cost of increasing the software complexity.

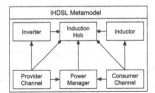 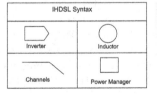 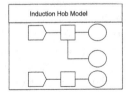

Fig. 3. IHDSL metamodel, syntax and model

The Domain Specific Language used by our industrial partner to specify the Induction Hobs (IHDSL) is composed of 46 meta-classes, 74 references among them and more than 180 properties. However, in order to gain legibility and due to intellectual property rights concerns, in this paper we use a simplified subset of the IHDSL (see Fig. 3). The main concepts of IHDSL are: Inverter, Induction Hob, Inductor, Provider Channel, Power Manager and Consumer Channel. The firmware code of each IH is implemented in ANSI C and includes about four hundred thousand TNOS.

In order to gain legibility and due to intellectual property rights concerns, in the following lines, we explain a subset of IHDSL to present the IH domain, although in the evaluation, the complete models have been used. The main concepts of IHDSL are: Inverter, Induction Hob, Inductor, Provider Channel, Power Manager and Consumer Channel.

Inverters are in charge of converting the input electric supply to match the specific requirements of the Induction Hob. Specifically, the amplitude and frequency of the electric supply needs to be precisely modulated in order to improve the efficiency of the IH and to avoid resonance. Then, the energy is transferred to the hotplates through the channels. There can be several alternative channels, which enable different heating strategies depending on the cookware placed on top of the IH at run-time. The path followed by the energy through the channels is controlled by the power manager.

Inductors are the elements where the energy is transformed into an electromagnetic field. Inductors are composed of a conductor that is usually wound into a coil. However, inductors vary in their shape and size, resulting in different power supply needs in order to achieve performance peaks. Inductors can be organized into groups in order to heat larger cookware while sharing the user interface controllers. Each group of inductors can have different particularities; for instance, some of them can be divided into independent zones while others can grow in size adapting to the size of the cookware being placed on top of them. Some of the groups of inductors are made at design time, while others can form at run-time (depending on the cookware placed on top).

3.2   Extracted Clone-and-Own Relationships

We have applied our Clone-and-Own approach to two families of products of our industrial partner. The first family of products was specified using IHDSL. After the specification, the IH's firmware was manually implemented (MI) in ANSI C by software engineers. This family of products contains a total of 46 products. Since this family of products uses IHDSL and manual implementation we refer to this family as IHDSL+MI. The second family of products was also specified using IHDSL. After the specification, the IH's firmware was automatically implemented (AI) using m2t (model-to-text) transformation. This transformation was produced by Acceleo [12]. This family is composed by a total of 66 products. Since this family of products uses IHDSL and automatic implementation we refer to this family as IHDSL+AI.

The IHDSL+MI family has a total of 81 different features. On the other side, the IHDSL+AI family contains a total of 47 features. After applying our Clone-and-Own Relationship extraction approach to both families of products we were able to isolate a total of 49 features belonging to IHDSL+MI and a total of 34 features belonging to IHDSL+AI. As a result, we detected five types of Clone-and-Own Relationships. Given the extracted code of FN(PX) and FN(PY), being product (PX) previous in time to product (PY), and being the same feature (FN) present in both products, we have identified the following feature relationships (see top part of Fig. 4).

- **Reimplemented Feature**, FN(PX) and FN(PY) do not share code between them. The implementations of these features are entirely different.
- **Modified Feature**, it exists shared code between both features. The part of code from FN(PX) which is present in FN(PY) is referred to as Legacy.

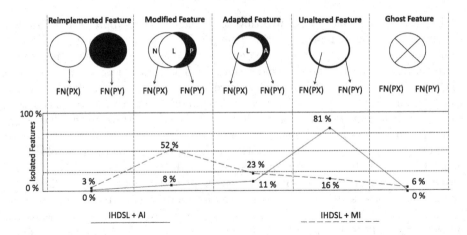

Fig. 4. Clone-and-own relationships extraction applied to both family of products

The differences between FN(PX) and the Legacy are referred to as Negative modifications. The differences between FN(PY) and the Legacy are referred to as Positive modifications.

- **Adapted Feature**, FN(PY) includes all code from FN(PX), and additional code which is not present in FN(PX). The part of FN(PX) is referred to as Legacy. Adapter represents the difference between FN(PY) and the Legacy.
- **Unaltered Feature**, the code of FN(PX) and FN(PY) is strictly the same.
- **Ghost Feature**, FN(PY) is specified at the model level but the extraction approach reveals that the code is missing.

We have the intuition that another type of relationship exists, Non-documented Features. Non-documented Features are those features that are not present at the model level, but they are at the code level. Software engineers reported that sometimes they implemented new code in later stages of the development without updating the corresponding IHDSL models. However, the full set of features of neither software family was completely isolated. The unclassified code may belong to either *Non-isolated Features* or *Non-documented Features*. Therefore, we have not evidence that this feature genuinely exists in IHDSL+MI or IHDSL+AI.

3.3   Clone-and-Own Relationships for Automatic Implementation

In the IHDSL+AI family our approach extracted the following relationships: 0 % Reimplemented, 8 % Modified, 11 % Adapted, 81 % Unaltered and 0 % Ghost. The presence of Modified and Adapted Features reveals that the implementation code of those features was refined (Modified Feature) or extended (Adapted Feature) by hand after the execution of the m2t transformation. Each feature classified as Unaltered Feature exhibits the same implementation code across all the members of the family that implement that particular feature. Unaltered Features suggest that the code of those features was not altered by software engineers after the execution of the m2t transformation.

In IHDSL+AI, the presence of Unaltered Features (81 %) surpasses the presence of both Modified and Adapted Features (19 %). This indicates that the m2t transformation actually saves implementation time to software engineers. Furthermore, the size of Positive modifications is smaller than the size of the Legacy feature on average (Modified Features) and the size of the Adapter is smaller than the Legacy feature on average (Adapted Features). These evidence contributes to concluding that the m2t transformation requires little human intervention.

We suggest that the Modified Feature and Adapted Feature relationships are useful to analyze whether it is necessary to carry out changes over the model-to-code transformation. If it is determined that it is necessary to update it, then the information provided by the occurrences of these relationships can be used to refine the metamodel and the code transformation rules.

In the IHDSL+AI family, modified features enabled to adjust the transformation rules. Negative parts of modified features reflected eliminated code introduced by obsolete transformation rules, and positive parts of modified features reflected manual code additions. The information provided by analyzing both the negative and positive parts enabled the company to update transformation rules with recurring changes that were predicted to keep occurring in the future.

3.4   Clone-and-Own Relationships for Manual Implementation

In the IHDSL+MI family our approach extracted the following relationships: 3 % Reimplemented, 52 % Modified, 23 % Adapted, 16 % Unaltered and 6 % Ghost. The presence of Modified and Adapted Features reveals that the implementation code was reused from another product as source and then refined to meet the particularities of the target product. F2(PA) and F2(PB) of the Linked List example (see Fig. 2) are instances of the Modified Feature relationship. On one hand, both F2(PA) and F2(PB) implement the same functionality (sorting the lists using the bubble method). On the other hand the implementation details of F2(PA) are different than those of F2(PB) to accommodate a feature (F4 = Backwards Linking) of PB which is not a feature of PA.

Unaltered Features were copied from previous products and used directly in new products. It turns out, Unaltered Features are reused among different products without requiring refinements on part of the engineer to accommodate the rest of the features of the product.

In IHDSL+MI, Unaltered, Adapted and Modified Features (91 %) reveal reuse opportunities identified by the software engineers. The presence of Reimplemented Features (3 %) indicates that software engineers did not realize former implementations of the feature. The implementation of these features was done from scratch, revealing missed reuse opportunities. Finally 6 % of isolated features were cataloged as Ghost Features. Ghost Features reveal inconsistencies between the model specification and the implemented code. The model specification should be updated to keep software engineers from failing to locate the code of those features.

We suggest that Reimplemented Feature relationships are useful to detect feature reuse impediments. In IHDSL+MI, for instance, they were useful to detect that a developer had left the company without performing knowledge transfer, and that the new developer in his place eventually reimplemented some code from scratch. Apart from detecting the situation, now we have awareness of both implementations, therefore widening the reuse possibilities.

We propose that Modified Feature and Adapted Feature relationships are useful for analyzing cost-benefit payoffs of reusing code fragments against reimplementing them. In IHDSL+MI, for instance, 12 cases were found where it had become more costly to create adapters that allowed reusing the legacy part of a feature than to reimplement the feature as needed.

We propound that Unaltered Feature relationships are useful to detect the opportunities to improve the reuse maturity of a family of software products. In IHDSL+MI, for instance, they were useful to build an implementation framework that has been used in further developments.

3.5 Limitations

There are some limitations that must be acknowledged. To begin with, there are companies that implement the code directly from the software requirements. This leads to software product families implemented without models. In such an scenario, our approach is not applicable. Developing and using techniques that permit to carry out feature location at the requisites level would widen the scope of our approach.

Second, depending on the configuration of the products in the software family, it is possible for our feature isolation algorithm to not find the isolation operations for every feature in every product. In the future, our approach might suggest the addition of products to the family with specific feature configurations that would allow the algorithm to isolate non-isolated features.

In addition, determining the kind of Clone-and-Own Relationships between products entails some degree of uncertainty. Specifically in the cases of reimplementation and feature modification, the current criteria is very rigid. This results in reimplemented features that, due to having low amounts of common code, are incorrectly classified as modified ones.

Finally, inspecting the isolated features with domain experts, we detected that in some cases, not all the lines of code provided in an isolated piece of code belong to the isolated feature and, in some other cases, some lines that do belong to the isolated feature are missing. Nevertheless, we have confirmed that the isolated code is a good heuristic for feature location, and domain experts have validated that the behavior detected by the described Clone-and-Own Relationships is the right one at the code level.

4 Related Work

Approaches related to the one presented in this paper can be distinguished into two areas: feature location at the model level and feature location at the code level. First we introduce the state-of-the-art of feature location at the code level and secondly, the state-of-the-art of feature location at the model level.

4.1 Feature Location at the Code Level

Some works apply type systems to extract relevant information when constructing the variability model. For instance, Typechef [13] provides an infrastructure to analyze the variability with the #ifdef directives. In [14] the authors extend Typechef in order to support the variability at run-time.

Text similarity techniques are based on mathematical methods to determine the similarity in a collection of texts. As an example, Latent Semantic Indexing (LSI) [15] takes into account the number of occurrences in a set of words in large texts. LSI can be used to obtain similarity measurement metrics between features and the code used to implement them. These similarity can be represented by Vector Space Models (VSM). On some occasions text similarity techniques are combined with dynamic analysis [16].

Other works focus on applying reverse engineering to the source code to obtain the variability model [3,17]. In [3] the authors use propositional logic which describes the dependencies between features. In [18] Typechef and propositional logic are used to extract conditions among a collection of features.

Several approaches [19,20] apply Program Dependence Analysis (PDA) to locate features. PDA can be represented by Program Dependence Graphs (PDG) where the nodes represent functions or global variables and the edges represent function calls or accesses to global variables.

Trace analysis is a run-time technique used to define a variability model through relevant information. When the technique is executed, it produces traces indicating which parts of code have been executed. Some approaches [21] are based on traces analysis. There are also works that combine dynamic analysis and static analysis as is the case of LSI [22], PDA [21] or VSM [2].

Compared to the above works, our approach introduces software models as a new source of knowledge for feature location at the code level. Furthermore, our approach not only isolates the implemented code of the features but it also extracts Clone-and-Own Relationships among these features. These relationships are used to better understand how features are reused, and to suggest improvements on the way they are reused.

4.2 Feature Location at the Model Level

In [5], the authors propose a framework for mining legacy product lines and automating their refactoring to contemporary feature-oriented SPLE approaches. They compare the elements of the input with each other, matching those whose similarity is above a certain threshold and merging them together. In [8], the authors propose a generic approach to automatically compare products and extract the variability among them in terms of Common Variability Language (CVL) [23,24]. In [9] an approach to automate the formalization of variability in a given family of models is presented. The model commonalities and differences are specified as placements over a base model and replacements in a model library. The resulting Software Product Line (SPL) enables the derivation of new product models by reusing the extracted model fragments. In [6] the authors propose another approach based on comparisons to extract the variability of any kind of asset. These works focus on formalizing the variability in a SPL. Finally, [4] identifies model patterns in a set of models and conceptualizes the extracted patterns as reusable model fragments.

The above approaches limit their application to finding fragments of a model which represent features in order to formalize the variability in a SPL. In contrast, our approach combines feature location at the model level with code comparison in order to isolate the implemented code of the features. Furthermore, our work identifies several different Clone-and-Own Relationships among the located features. These relationships enable us to make improvement suggestions based on the knowledge gathered on the way features are reused.

5   Conclusions

To keep pace with the increasing demand for custom-tailored software systems, companies often apply the clone-and-own practice, through which a new product in a software product family is built by copying and adapting code from other products in the family.

In this work, we show our approach, which leverages feature location to identify and extract the Clone-and-Own Relationships from a family of software products. We have proposed an approach that extracts the features at the model level and, with that information, calculates isolation operations that enable to isolate the features at the code level. This work allows us to isolate the features of the different products in the code. With the achieved code isolation, features are compared at the code level in order to define the relationships between them.

We have evaluated the approach with our industrial partner, extracting the Clone-and-Own Relationships presented in two product families of induction hob models. One of the families had its code implemented manually and the other one, in an automatic way.

A total of five different relationships have been extracted. These relationships entitle Reimplemented, Modified, Adapted, Unaltered, and Ghost Features. The results of our approach provide insight into understanding the Clone-and-Own relationships of the features in a family of software products. These relationships are then used to suggest improvements on how features are reused.

In the case of families where automatic code generation is applied, the Modified and Adapted Features are used to analyze whether it is necessary to carry out changes over the model-to-code transformation. If it is determined that it is necessary to improve it, then the information provided by the occurrences of these relationships can be used to refine the metamodel and the code transformation rules.

In the case of families where the code is manually implemented, Reimplemented Features are used to detect feature reuse impediments; Modified and

Adapted Features are used for analyzing cost-benefit payoffs of reusing code fragments against reimplementing them; and Unaltered Features are used to detect opportunities to improve the reuse maturity of a family of software products.

References

1. Dit, B., Revelle, M., Gethers, M., Poshyvanyk, D.: Feature location in source code: a taxonomy and survey. J. Softw. Evol. Proc. **25**, 53–95 (2013). doi:10.1002/smr. 567
2. Eaddy, M., Aho, A.V., Antoniol, G., Guéhéneuc, Y.G.: CERBERUS: tracing requirements to source code using information retrieval, dynamic analysis, and program analysis. In: Krikhaar, R.L., Lämmel, R., Verhoef, C. (eds.) The 16th IEEE International Conference on Program Comprehension, ICPC, Amsterdam, The Netherlands, 10–13 June 2008, pp. 53–62. IEEE Computer Society (2008)
3. Czarnecki, K., Wasowski, A.: Feature diagrams and logics: there and back again. In: Software Product Lines, 11th International Conference, SPLC, Proceedings, Kyoto, Japan, 10–14 Sept 2007. IEEE Computer Society (2007)
4. Font, J., Ballarín, M., Haugen, Ø., Cetina, C.: Automating the variability formalization of a model family by means of common variability language. In: Schmidt, D.C. (ed.) Proceedings of the 19th International Conference on Software Product Line, SPLC 2015, Nashville, USA, 20–24 July 2015, pp. 411–418. ACM (2015)
5. Rubin, J., Chechik, M.: Combining related products into product lines. In: de Lara, J., Zisman, A. (eds.) Fundamental Approaches to Software Engineering. LNCS, vol. 7212, pp. 285–300. Springer, Heidelberg (2012)
6. Martinez, J., Ziadi, T., Bissyandé, T.F., Klein, J., Traon, Y.L.: Bottom-up adoption of software product lines: a generic and extensible approach. In: Schmidt, D.C. (ed.) Proceedings of the 19th International Conference on Software Product Line, SPLC 2015, Nashville, TN, USA, 20–24 July 2015. ACM (2015)
7. Selic, B.: The pragmatics of model-driven development. IEEE Softw. **20**(5), 19–25 (2003). http://dx.doi.org/10.1109/MS.2003.1231146
8. Zhang, X., Haugen, Ø., Møller-Pedersen, B.: Model comparison to synthesize a model-driven software product line. In: de Almeida, E.S., Kishi, T., Schwanninger, C., John, I., Schmid, K. (eds.) Software Product Lines - 15th International Conference, SPLC, Munich, Germany, 22–26 Aug 2011, pp. 90–99. IEEE (2011)
9. Font, J., Arcega, L., Haugen, O., Cetina, C.: Building software product lines from conceptualized model patterns. In: Proceedings of the 19th International Conference on Software Product Line, SPLC 2015. ACM, New York (2015)
10. Kamiya, T., Kusumoto, S., Inoue, K.: CCFinder: a multilinguistic token-based code clone detection system for large scale source code. IEEE Trans. Software Eng. **28**(7), 654–670 (2002)
11. Li, Z., Lu, S., Myagmar, S., Zhou, Y.: CP-Miner: finding copy-paste and related bugs in large-scale software code. IEEE Trans. Softw. Eng. **32**(3), 176–192 (2006)
12. Kästner, C., Giarrusso, P.G., Rendel, T., Erdweg, S., Ostermann, K., Berger, T.: Variability-aware parsing in the presence of lexical macros and conditional compilation. In: Proceedings of the 2011 ACM International Conference on Object Oriented Programming Systems Languages and Applications, OOPSLA 2011, pp. 805–824. ACM, New York (2011). http://dx.doi.org/10.1145/2048066.2048128

13. Kästner, C., Giarrusso, P.G., Rendel, T., Erdweg, S., Ostermann, K., Berger, T.: Variability-aware parsing in the presence of lexical macros and conditional compilation. In: Lopes, C.V., Fisher, K. (eds.) Proceedings of the 26th Annual ACM Conference on Object-Oriented Programming, Systems, Languages, and Applications, 2011. ACM (2011)

14. Kästner, C., Ostermann, K., Erdweg, S.: A variability-aware module system. In: Leavens, G.T., Dwyer, M.B. (eds.) Proceedings of the 27th Annual ACM Conference on Object-Oriented Programming, Systems, Languages, and Applications, USA, 21–25 Oct 2012. ACM (2012)

15. Landauer, T.K., Psotka, J.: Simulating text understanding for educational applications with latent semantic analysis: introduction to LSA. Interact. Learn. Environ. (2000)

16. Asadi, F., Penta, M.D., Antoniol, G., Guéhéneuc, Y.G.: A heuristic-based approach to identify concepts in execution traces. In: Capilla, R., Ferenc, R., Dueñas, J.C. (eds.) 14th European Conference on Software Maintenance and Reengineering, CSMR, March 2010, Madrid, Spain. IEEE Computer Society (2010)

17. She, S., Lotufo, R., Berger, T., Wasowski, A., Czarnecki, K.: Reverse engineering feature models. In: Taylor, R.N., Gall, H.C., Medvidovic, N. (eds.) Proceedings of the 33rd International Conference on Software Engineering, ICSE 2011, Waikiki, Honolulu, HI, USA, 21–28 May 2011. ACM (2011)

18. Nadi, S., Berger, T., Kästner, C., Czarnecki, K.: Mining configuration constraints: static analyses and empirical results. In: Jalote, P., Briand, L.C., van der Hoek, A. (eds.) 36th International Conference on Software Engineering, ICSE 14, Hyderabad, India, 31 May – 07 June 2014, pp. 140–151. ACM (2014)

19. Walkinshaw, N., Roper, M., Wood, M.: Feature location and extraction using landmarks and barriers. In: 23rd IEEE International Conference on Software Maintenance (ICSM 2007), Paris, France, 2–5 Oct 2007. IEEE (2007)

20. Trifu, M.: Improving the dataflow-based concern identification approach. In: Winter, A., Ferenc, R., Knodel, J. (eds.) 13th European Conference on Software Maintenance and Reengineering, CSMR 2009, Architecture-Centric Maintenance of Large-SCale Software Systems, Kaiserslautern, Germany, 24–27 Mar 2009. IEEE Computer Society (2009)

21. Eisenberg, A.D., Volder, K.D.: Dynamic feature traces: finding features in unfamiliar code. In: 21st IEEE International Conference on Software Maintenance (ICSM), Budapest, Hungary, 25–30 Sept 2005, pp. 337–346. IEEE Computer Society (2005)

22. Poshyvanyk, D., Guéhéneuc, Y.G., Marcus, A., Antoniol, G., Rajlich, V.: Feature location using probabilistic ranking of methods based on execution scenarios and information retrieval. IEEE Trans. Softw. Eng. **33**(6), 420–432 (2007). doi:10.1109/TSE.2007.1016

23. Haugen, Ø., Møller-Pedersen, B., Oldevik, J., Olsen, G.K., Svendsen, A.: Adding standardized variability to domain specific languages. In: Software Product Lines, 12th International Conference, SPLC 2008, Proceedings, Limerick, Ireland, 8–12 Sept 2008, pp. 139–148. IEEE Computer Society (2008)

24. Svendsen, A., Zhang, X., Lind-Tviberg, R., Fleurey, F., Haugen, Ø., Møller-Pedersen, B., Olsen, G.K.: Developing a software product line for train control: a case study of CVL. In: Bosch, J., Lee, J. (eds.) SPLC 2010. LNCS, vol. 6287, pp. 106–120. Springer, Heidelberg (2010)

AIRES: An Architecture to Improve Software Reuse

Rosana T. Vaccare Braga[✉], Daniel Feloni, Karen Pacini,
Domenico Schettini Filho, and Thiago Gottardi

Institute of Mathematics and Computer Sciences (ICMC),
University of Sao Paulo (USP),
P.O. Box 668, Sao Carlos, Sao Paulo 13.566-590, Brazil
{rtvb,dfeloni,karenr,domenico,gottardi}@icmc.usp.br
http://www.icmc.usp.br

Abstract. Among the several challenges still faced by Software Engineering, software reuse can be listed as a potential solution towards improving productivity and quality, through the utilization of previously produced artifacts that can leverage development activities. Among these artifacts we can mention not only code, but also requirements' documents, analysis and design models, test cases, documentation, and even development processes that achieved success in the past and could be reused again and again. However, the diversity of methods, processes and tools for software engineering make it difficult to turn reuse into a systematic activity. Considering this context, the present paper aims at presenting an architectural model that encompasses the main elements needed to support software reuse in a large scale. This model, named AIRES, allows reuse to be realized intrinsically to the development process life cycle, providing mechanisms to facilitate a variety of processes and artifacts representation and a Service-Oriented Architecture (SOA) to make assets available to other software engineering environments or tools. The AIRES model is being implemented using open source platforms and will be available within the cloud.

Keywords: Software reuse · Reuse tools · Reuse environments

1 Introduction

Reuse techniques can be used to improve productivity and quality in software development processes, as they allow to take advantage of previous development efforts where several reusable assets have been produced. It is essential that computational support to reuse is provided since the very beginning, including reuse of the process itself, and then moving to reuse of artifacts of several process phases that occur before implementation, and finally with the reuse of code and test cases. This is not a trivial task, especially when we consider the great variety of representations for reusable processes and artifacts, as well as the ever-changing development platforms and tools that are not easily integrated.

© Springer International Publishing Switzerland 2016
G.M. Kapitsaki and E. Santana de Almeida (Eds.): ICSR 2016, LNCS 9679, pp. 231–246, 2016.
DOI: 10.1007/978-3-319-35122-3_16

Also, we can say that recent advances in Software Engineering, which could potentially offer solutions to these problems, are rarely used to build existing tools, as for example service-oriented architectures (SOA). SOA is an architectural style to build software applications taking advantage of services available in a network [2,10,11]. A typical SOA has three types of participants: a service provider, a service repository, and a service consumer (client). A service implements a well-defined business function that can be used by clients of different applications in different business processes. A service has a public interface that is available and interoperable, and it can dynamically connect to other services. Clients can be both final user applications (e.g., web pages or desktop applications) or application modules belonging to other business processes (e.g., other services) [10]. Therefore, the use of SOA is appropriate in distributed software development environments like AIRES, in which the integration among different tools is required, preferably in a transparent way.

A number of techniques and tools are used nowadays to facilitate reuse, but they are generally focused on specific forms of reuse. Indeed, the development of environments to support software reuse has been focused on the requirements of specific groups of developers, as shown by Mahmood and others [9]. Nine reuse environments were analyzed in their work in order to propose an analysis framework. Each of them focused on a specific artifact type (for example, UML class diagram, sequence diagram, feature model, etc.). Additionally, in a recent systematic mapping of the literature conducted by our group, it was identified that software engineering tools aiming at reuse are too specific (e.g. software product line tools, components and/or code repositories, patterns, etc.). Among examples of reuse tools, Eclipse provides the reuse of components and patterns; Peonia [1] allows the reuse of processes, software patterns and respective requirements tests; OdysseyShare [19] allows the reuse of conceptual models, software architectures and implementation models for a certain domain; and Pure::variants [17] allows the derivation of products of a software product line based in its feature model and implementation assets. On the other hand, we envision a more complete architecture to allow the integration of different types of software reuse tools, which we propose by employing SOA and RAS.

Moreover, software developers often employ more than one way of reuse, so they would need to manage different environments, tools, processes, and techniques. Without an unified support, this could lead to difficulties in integrating the resulting artifacts of different projects, as they were developed in different formats. Also, using an isolated tool for each reuse attempt can inhibit organizations towards reuse, because they know the difficulties of integration with existing development tools. In parallel to this, processes themselves could be reused to take advantage of successful experiences obtained in previous projects.

In this context, the use of SOA (or at least services) would be important to make available artifacts in different levels of abstraction, so that they could be shared by different projects of different organizations. It is also important to provide mechanisms to facilitate the storage and retrieval of assets, as for example by using a standard for asset representation and interchange.

Notice that SOA is only employed as a mechanism to ease the retrieval of reusable assets. The actual assets may have different types, including Web services themselves, as well as source code. This retrieval is done by software engineers during the development of new applications or maintenance of existing applications that can benefit from reuse, which is different from reusing Web services during run-time by invoking them on a Web Server (task done by the running application). Of course, after the Web Service is retrieved for reuse, its invocation will be placed in the source code and it will be invoked during run-time, which is the final result of reuse.

Therefore, the contribution of this paper is to propose an integrated architectural model that helps leveraging software reuse while complying to standards. It should be customized according to the particular needs of software engineers, who are the main target users. The main motivation of this proposal is to help organizations to implement a reuse approach, as well as to provide means to encourage the development of computational support that follows the proposed architectural model.

This paper includes a proposal of an architectural model, named AIRES (ArchItecture for REuse using Services), whose main goal is to allow software reuse in large scale, making use of services. It is aimed at organizations distributed in different locations and with different needs regarding reuse: from process reuse to different levels of software reuse, such as documents, models, code, test cases, etc.

The proposed architecture comprises several views of its components, their interfaces and the rationale involved in their design. Use cases are also provided to better illustrate how the architecture can be used to produce different reuse environments. To allow a standardization of assets storage and retrieval, AIRES adopts the Reusable Assets Specification (RAS) [14], from the Object Management Group (OMG). If other models are necessary, specific services to translate them to RAS, and vice-versa, can be implemented.

The remainder of the paper is organized as follows. In Sect. 2, an overview of the AIRES architecture is presented. In Sect. 3, all elements that compose AIRES are explained in detail. The evaluation of AIRES is reported in Sect. 4. Related work is discussed in Sect. 5. Finally, the conclusions, as well as future work, are discussed in Sect. 6.

2   AIRES Overview

AIRES was firstly conceived from one of the author's experience in the reuse domain for more than two decades. Several systematic mappings and reviews have been done during the last years related to the software reuse domain, and the results have indicated a lack of reuse environments that take advantage of SOA.

Therefore, the motivations for proposing AIRES came from different assumptions: (1) the importance of easing software development through reuse methodologies that can leverage both productivity and quality; (2) the relevance of having adequate computational support for reuse since the initial phases until the final development phases, including reuse of processes themselves; (3) the diversity of methods, processes, and tools used by software engineers along the development life cycle, with a great number of representation formats to processes and reusable assets; (4) the variety of development platforms, often proprietary or difficult to access, accompanied by tools with different visions and goals, which produce/consume artifacts in different formats and abstraction levels, being also difficult to integrate in the several development phases; and (5) the potential of service-oriented architectures to solve some of the problems mentioned. Therefore, AIRES architectural model contains all the necessary elements to support reuse considering assumptions 1 to 4, as well as taking advantage of SOA as mentioned in assumption 5.

By integrating reuse tools, AIRES intends to allow reuse intrinsically in the whole software development life cycle. To solve the problem of difficult access to reuse supporting tools, services should be provided and made available in the cloud. This makes it easier to build applications that consume these services, as well as facilitates integration with existing tools. To allow different representations of processes and reusable assets, AIRES uses standards as input to invoked services, which process them and produce the expected results. Considering that AIRES can be instantiated by different institutions, geographically distributed in different locations and operating independently, new services can be developed in the future to integrate these different instances.

It is important to notice that AIRES is not only intended to integrate asset repositories: it is also focused on leveraging reuse by allowing the construction of applications that benefit from its infrastructure to fulfill other more specific reuse requirements. In this sense, two different applications are being built based on AIRES, one to improve reuse in software product lines and another to allow the reuse of processes in the context of Software Process Improvement (SPI) and Software Process Assessment (SPA). Other applications can be developed in the future, as its SOA-based characteristics make it easier to add new services whenever they are necessary.

The possibility of integrating assets in different abstraction levels and establishing the relationships among artifacts enables reuse of as many assets as possible. For example, if the user searches for a source code in the telecommunications domain, (s)he would be able to also reuse the corresponding test cases, as well as other higher abstraction models of the same domain, if they exist.

3   AIRES Elements Detailing

In this section, we provide a detailed description of AIRES elements, from requirements to conceptual model. We also describe its development process and identified results.

3.1   Requirements - Use Cases Overview

One of the first activities in the AIRES definition was use case modeling. We have done several meetings with stakeholders, where several actors have been identified, as listed in Table 1, followed by use case modeling. Figure 1 presents a partial view of the use case diagram. Due to space restrictions, we have simplified the diagram to show only the main use cases for the three most important actors. The complete diagram can be found in the project documentation[1], where we also provide a detailed description of the intent of each use case.

Table 1. Actors identified during AIRES use case modeling

Actor name	Description
General user	Common User System. Main interests are to create an account, log in and log out of the system, search for groups, search for assets, create groups, request access to private assets and respond to requests to participate in groups
Asset owner	User with rights to include its own assets
Asset reviewer	Responsible for assessment and review of the asset. This is an optional actor
Group member	Member of a group. The main interest is to actively participate in a community of users, sharing and evaluating assets
Group leader	Member of the group responsible for managing it
System	Administrative routines are performed automatically by the system through scheduling

We propose the inclusion of the *Asset Reviewer* as an optional actor, as we believe that each asset owner is responsible for the assets he includes, independently of whether or not they are validated. It is therefore an alternative choice to have a reviewer for validating the assets. If we forced this role as mandatory, we could end with a model that is difficult to be implemented due to the lack of reviewers.

The evaluation performed by the *Asset Reviewer* would assess the applicability of the asset proposed by the *Asset Owner*, validating some requirements such as: (i) the asset is applicable to the group context; (ii) the asset has potential for reuse; (iii) there is not another similar asset in the groups library. If the asset meets the requirements set by the *Group Leader* then it can be added to the groups portfolio and shared with its members and other groups if so desired.

Additionally, it is a complex task to establish the validation criteria and AIRES managers would be overloaded if they needed to take the responsibility for all the assets they include. We agreed, together with the stakeholders, that the most acceptable solution to this problem is to make assets available as soon as they fulfil the minimum requirements to be included in AIRES, and users willing to reuse them are totally aware that they need to validate them before reusing. After the assets have been successfully reused, we can provide a way to register this in AIRES so that other users can benefit from this information.

---

[1] http://www.icmc.usp.br/~rtvb/Aires_doc/.

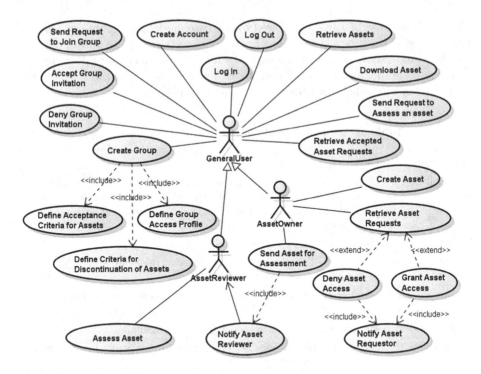

Fig. 1. AIRES - part of use case diagram for the three main actors.

On the other hand, for organizations where the control of assets needs to be done in a more systematic way, the role of the *Asset Reviewer* can be fully employed.

3.2 Architecture Overview

After defining the use cases, an architectural model for AIRES has been developed, according to the assumptions discussed in the beginning of Sect. 2. Figure 2 illustrates this model.

As mentioned in Sect. 1, AIRES adopts the Reusable Assets Specification (RAS) [14], from the Object Management Group (OMG), to store the assets in a repository, so any type of reusable asset is allowed, as for example requirements, analysis models, design models, source code, test cases, and processes. RAS allows a common approach to be used by developers when storing reusable assets. RAS contains a basic structure (CORE), but can be extended by the creation of extension modules to customize it to the particular needs of each project. The RAS specification is available via XSD (XML Schema Definition) and XMI (XML Metadata Interchange) files and its usage is defined by profiles. Another advantage of adopting RAS is to ease the interoperability with other tools that use it, as well as having the benefits of all the knowledge embodied in the specification itself.

Similarly to the specification, AIRES is an architecture designed with a *Core* layer, which serves as a foundation for every other layer. The *Core* represents the central modules, which include a module to allow unique identity for objects (*UUIds Manager*), a module to ensure the correct authentication of users (*AuthenticationManager*), another to manage the authorization of users to available services (*Authorization Manager*), a module to manage the reusable assets (*Assets Manager*), and a module to provide an interface to read and export assets as RAS in addition to translate from simple model (provided by AIRES) to RAS. (*RAS Interface*). For example, if a client application adopts a different asset representation, this module takes a simple modulated input and performs its translation to RAS, so client applications do not need to understand RAS to use the repository.

The persistence of objects related to users and authorization is done in a specific database (*AIRES Core*), and assets in another one (*Assets Repository*). Other possibilities exist, as for example the client application can have its own authorization/authentication services and use AIRES only to search for reusable assets, and not for managing them.

In AIRES, it is considered that assets can have private or public visibility. If an asset is private, only the owner can have writing access to it, while members of the owner group have reading access. On the other hand, public assets can be viewed by any users (writing access is also allowed only to the asset owner). As AIRES is based on SOA, the access (reading or writing) is done through specific services.

The *private services* layer offers services to access the *Core* layer. They can be invoked by the *Applications* layer, which contains external applications that interact with AIRES. Examples of such applications are Software Product Lines Manager and Certification Manager, but other applications can be added as required. Private services can also be invoked by Public services. This allows that modules belonging to the *Clients* layer or other external custom applications interact with the *Core* layer.

The access to modules of the *Applications* layer is also done through public services, which can be invoked both by the *Clients* layer and by custom applications. As mentioned before, public services can, in turn, invoke services from the *Private Services* layer, which provide access to more basic core functions. This avoids unauthorized access to private services and, at the same time, makes publicly available only relevant services required by applications. All services provided by AIRES have been documented through the detailed specification of their interfaces, i.e., the inputs required to invoke them, as well as the outputs they generate.

The *Clients* layer provides a graphical user interface to AIRES assets manager or other applications. The *AIRES Manager Frontend* aims at providing a Web application through which developers who do not have their own reuse tools can initiate a reuse program. This allows them to search for reusable assets and include their own assets, which can optionally be shared with the software community. Special mechanisms of quality control can be implemented to avoid the inclusion on undesired assets in the repository.

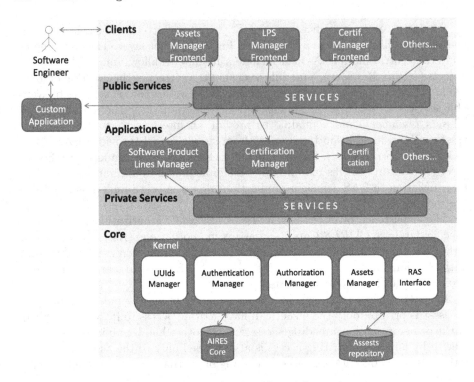

Fig. 2. AIRES - architectural model overview.

The *Software Product Lines Manager/LPS Manager Frontend* and *Certification Manager/Certification Manager Frontend* are examples of possible applications that can be built based on AIRES. The *SPL Manager* allows a SPL domain or application engineer to manage software product lines, since the inclusion of the SPL reusable assets until the management of derived products, as well as the documentation of the SPL development processes used by the organization. The *Certification Manager* aims at facilitating the reuse of process and conformance analysis by organizations that pursue the certification of their development processes against existing maturity models, but do not have supporting tools for that. They can include their current development processes and receive as output the conformance report. It should be observed that this requires that the maturity models are previously fed into the AIRES, as well as the transformation rules that allow the comparison to executed processes. These applications are being built in the context of ongoing Master projects at ICMC.

In Appendix A we provide a list of the available services provided in the *Private Services* layer, describing the service method signature, its parameters (input and output) and a brief description of its behaviour.

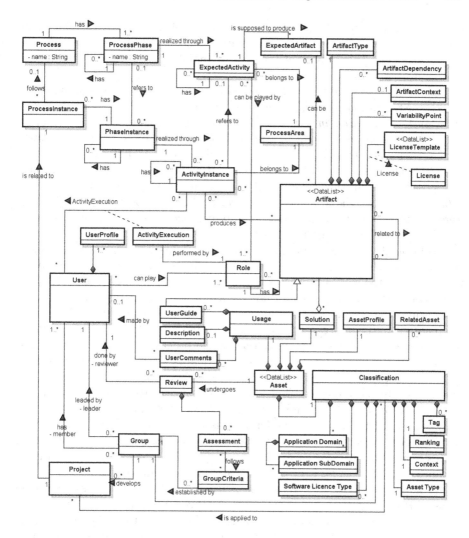

Fig. 3. AIRES conceptual model.

3.3 Conceptual Model

Figure 3 presents AIRES conceptual model. Its model follows SPEM, which is the most used standard for software process modeling, according to [4]. This makes it easier to integrate AIRES with software improvement approaches that also adopt SPEM. For example, if the software engineer wants to analyse the process employed in his organization against well-known standards, the architecture could export the current process to serve as input to conformance analysis tools that also follow SPEM.

The classes of the conceptual model related to SPEM are: *Process*, *ProcessPhase*, *ExpectedActivity*, and *ExpectedArtifact*. There are also classes or relationships to represent the dependencies among phases or activities (for example, a phase that follows another, or that is done in parallel to another). The classes just mentioned represent the process template as specified by standards or organizations [15].

Related to these classes, we have another set of classes corresponding to the process instantiation to a particular project. They are: *ProcessInstance*, *PhaseInstance*, *ActivityInstance* and *Artifact*. Note that there is a many-to-many relationship between *ActivityInstance* and *User*. This means that an activity can be performed by one or more users, and a user can perform one or more activities. This association derives an association class (*ActivityExecution*) where it is possible to link the execution of the activity to a specific role. An *ActivityInstance* can be related or not to an *ExpectedActivity*, because activities that were not predicted in the process template can occur in a concrete instance of the process, and they must be registered by the system.

Additionally, the *ExpectedActivity* and *ActivityInstance* classes has an association to the *ProcessArea* class, that represents the software engineering disciplines used in the software process development, such as requirements management, configuration management, quality assurance, among others.

It is important to notice that this model is used to represent both the process template (i.e., the process model as defined by its authors) and the process instance, which is derived by instantiating the process template for particular purposes [15]. A process instance refers to a template but has its own elements, according to the process execution. This is important because we may want to reuse not only the templates, but also the instances that were successful in a particular context and thus can be recommended when similar situations occur. For example, RUP is a process model (template) that can be reused in a concrete development project, resulting in a process instance. Later, when a new project begins in a similar context, instead of reusing RUP, we might want to reuse the instance instead, because it is already customized to that context.

As mentioned before, to represent reusable assets (*Asset* class), the main parts of RAS have been incorporated to AIRES conceptual model, with some adaptation. This aims at facilitating interoperability with tools that also employ RAS, besides taking advantage of the reuse knowledge embedded in the specification itself. All classes from RAS Core are related to Asset structure as shown in Fig. 3 (some minor classes are hidden due to lack of space). Basically, an *Asset* includes a *Solution*, a *Profile*, a *Usage*, and a *Classification*. Optionally, it can include one or more *Related Asset*. The *Solution* refers to one or more *Artifacts* that contain references to the concrete artifacts to be reused. An artifact can be classified into types (e.g., source code, model, text, template, feature, etc.). It can also have dependencies, a context and variability points. The *Usage* refers to *Description*, usage manual, installation guide, comments and other information relevant to the asset. The *Classification* aggregates several objects to ease the retrieval of the object by using different types of keys to classify it.

The remaining classes of the conceptual model were included to fit other needs of the stakeholders. For example, the *UserProfile* enables a user to assume several different profiles, both related to playing different roles in process activities, and having different positions regarding the asset management (reviewer, group leader, etc.). The *Group* is used to describe the group of users, allowing closed sharing of assets by defining their own rules of assessment and privacy. The *Project* holds all information about the project itself like title, estimate time and budget, so on. Another addition to the conceptual model was *Review*, which represents the optional functionality of allowing an asset to be included provisionally, and depending on the reviews received it will be included definitely. A Review is composed by several assessments about the asset, according to the criteria established by the group.

Another feature provided by the RAS metamodel is to add usage (class *Usage*) information to help on the usability of the assets stored by it. The *UserComments* class represents the users feedback about their experience on using the assets available in the repository. This feedback can be used by the *AssetOwner* or *GroupLeader* to improve the asset functionality.

3.4 AIRES Asset Life Cycle

An asset can be in different states within the development process, which we refer as *Asset Life Cycle*, as represented in Fig. 4. Firstly, by creating an asset, the creator is automatically defined as its owner. Therefore, any user could have permission to become an asset owner. As soon as the asset is created, it is defined as "Under Elaboration". After the asset is set as complete by the owner, it evolves to the "Complete" state. Then, the owner can submit the asset for review, performed by the *AssetReviewer*. Therefore, it would be in "Under Review" state. The *AssetReviewer* may either approve or reject the asset. In case of approval, the asset is moved into "Approved" state. In case of disapproval, there are two alternatives: if the asset is considered useless, it goes to the "Removed" state; otherwise, it needs to suffer modifications and be resubmitted for approval, thus it is moved back into "Under Review" state. After being moved to the "Approved" state, the asset can be submitted to periodic reviews, performed to evaluate its acceptance and reuse index. In this stage, an asset can be moved to the "Discontinued" state, indicating that it is no longer active in the repository and will not receive any improvements or bug fixes. Another possible scenario is that the asset is not being reused or it depends on platforms that became obsolete, so the *AssetOwner* or *GroupLeader* might decide to flag it as discontinued. Notice that, as mentioned before, reviews are optional. Once the asset candidate is moved to the "Complete" state, the review stages of the life cycle can be set as optional in an AIRES environment instance and, in this case, the assets will have an internal visibility to the institution that manages the repository instance.

4 AIRES Evaluation

AIRES has been evaluated using the Architecture Trade-off Analysis Method (ATAM) [7]. ATAM aims to identify how well an architecture satisfies the expected quality goals, as well as how these goals interact with each other.

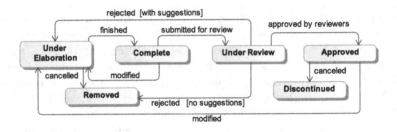

Fig. 4. Asset life cycle.

In the first step, a group of researchers and professionals interested in software reuse have been presented to ATAM. The group consisted of two experienced professionals, two graduate students with professional experience in software reuse, and one graduate student with no professional experience, but having deep knowledge about reuse tools. They have evaluated the business drivers that involve software reuse. In summary, after discussing the several challenges involved, they have reached a consensus that a considerable part of developers do not invest on software reuse because they do not have the adequate support to do that, not only in terms of processes and tools, but due to the lack of organizational support.

Therefore, the main business drivers that should be considered are: usability - it should be easy both to share new assets and to retrieve them, not only considering the computational support, but the organizational process involved in publishing new assets; flexibility - the system should be able to manage any kind of reusable asset, independently of its representation; and availability - the system should allow the retrieval of assets at any time. If these business drivers are achieved, the proposed architecture could serve as a means to leverage software reuse. In this sense, computational support is essential to encourage organizations to adopt a reuse program.

Next, AIRES architecture overview was presented to the team, with an explanation of each layer and corresponding components. Additionally, the use cases have been presented and discussed by the team, which lead to several modifications both to use cases and architecture. After refinements, the resulting models have been updated. The architecture shown in Fig. 2, as well as the use case diagram partially presented in Fig. 1 exemplify the results.

In a subsequent step, the team has established quality attributes relative to each business driver, indicating how each business driver would be dealt with by the architecture. For example, to achieve flexibility, RAS has been adopted as a way to represent reusable assets; to achieve usability, we have defined a process with mandatory and optional activities that can be adapted to each possible scenario; and to achieve availability, we have designed the architecture based on SOA principles. Cloud computing could be also considered to enhance availability, specially by adopting Platform as a Service to host AIRES instances.

Finally, different architectural approaches have been analyzed, and the team agreed that the proposed architecture was adequate according to the requirements defined in the previous step. Phase 2 of ATAM consists of extending the evaluation with the help of a larger stakeholder group and is planned as future work.

5 Related Work

There are a number of ways to build a RAS repository. The very RAS specification document offers some guidelines for searching, browsing and retrieving assets by using services [14]. It is possible to build them both as independent web services or as part of a larger product, which is the case of AIRES.

The use of RAS to represent processes has been explored in the work of Pacini and Braga [15]. The paper shows how to map RAS elements to each process element in order to ease the reuse of process phases, activities, artifacts, etc. This mapping is used in assets translation to RAS on *RAS Interface* module.

Another example of RAS application is proposed by Nianjun Zhou *et al.* [20]. In their approach, they present a legacy reuse analysis and integration method to support modeling legacy assets in a SOA context. To store the assets extracted by their approach, they use the IBM Rational Asset Manager Repository (RAM), which is typically used for storage of unstructured assets (jar, war and ear) and documents specified using RAS.

There are also other online repositories based on RAS in the web. One example is LAVOI, created by Moura [13] and OpenCom created by Ren Hong-min et al. [5]. Both extended the RAS profile to adapt it to a wide range of types of assets and to facilitate assets classification, search and use. However they only provide the repository, and it works for specific types of assets. On the other hand, AIRES proposes a complete architecture to build an integrated environment to manage and leverage reuse.

In Feloni and Braga [3], a systematic mapping was elaborated to identify the different approaches used to obtain software process certification (through maturity and process quality models). In particular, two research gaps were listed in the context of methodologies to assist process assessment and improvement regarding reuse: (1) the reuse of certified processes; and (2) the reuse of artifacts produced in software process execution in a large scale within the software engineering community. A concept still little explored is the reuse of the processes and quality models as a hole, such as the activities executed, roles performed and work products consumed/produced in its execution [3]. The creation of repositories to persist the created artifacts was also an approach used in some papers, but they limited the access to those artifacts for the company members only, eradicating the possibility for reuse outside the company. We claim that it should be available to more software engineers [12,16,18], which is the idea behind AIRES.

Lee et al. [8] propose the integration of Web Services technology into an environment, also proposed by them, where components could be integrated. This environment is developed in three parts: a Provider, a Consumer and a Component Repository. The Provider subsystem stores components and its attributes into a repository. The Consumer subsystem helps the client application to find the desired component in the repository. The Component repository stores in a relational database the components attributes and where they could be found for future sharing with the client. They proposed the use of Web Services to expand the interoperability between components and clients and to ease the access to these components.

Hongmin et al. [6] proposed a lightweight open framework for sharing assets repository based on SOA, whose main system is the Software Asset Repository Management System (SARMS). It is a set of software systems that control the creation, maintenance and use of the assets repository. The Asset Sharing Service Subsystem (ASSS) provides five categories of sharing services: User Management Service, Asset Management Service, Authorization Management Service, Facet Management Service and Meta Data Service. As future work, the authors claimed to explore the sharing asset repositories, developing an experimental system based on the open architecture proposed. However, we did not find any published works that proceeded with the implementation of the proposed architecture.

6   Conclusions and Future Work

In this paper, we have presented AIRES, an architectural model that intends to leverage software reuse initiatives. This architecture can be the basis for the implementation of different reuse environments according to the particular needs of software engineers. A RAS repository server has been developed and is functional. We have also devised user access modules to control authentication and authorization. We are currently developing clients for the server modules, including clients with graphical user interface, which is being tested for the Asset Manager component. In addition, we have also defined all the modeling of the Software Product Line and Certification components, and a Web Services generator based on class diagrams that will ease the creation of the services layer.

As future work, we intend to make available, in an open-source repository, all the artifacts produced so far as accessible assets by using our own proposal. We believe that by sharing these artifacts we can speed up the development of a global repository for software assets that can benefit all the software community.

A   Private Services Interface Definition

As defined in Subsect. 3.2, in this Appendix, we list the specification of private services that are used for accessing AIRES integration layer. Therefore, Table 2 consists of a subset of the services provided in the *Private Services* layer. In each row of the table, we provide the service signature and its description.

Table 2. Specification of Private Services - some examples

Service signature and Description
authenticate(String username, String passwd): String tokenID
Returns a token valid for a certain period of time if the username and passwd corresponds to a valid user. Otherwise, returns a null token
authorize(String tokenID, String operation): Boolean okResponse
Returns a boolean corresponding to the authorization of the user to perform a specific operation in the system
newAsset(Asset asset, String tokenID): String assetID
Includes a new asset in the repository. When the server executes this insertion, the validation rules are checked according to RAS specifications about structure, cardinality, and so on. Allowed only if the tokenID refers to an authenticated and authorized user. Returns the UID of the new generated asset
updateAsset(Asset asset, String assetID, String tokenID): Boolean okResponse
Updates an existing asset of the repository. Allowed only if the tokenID refers to an authenticated and authorized user.
removeAsset(String assetID, String tokenID): Boolean okResponse
Removes an existing asset of the repository. Allowed only if the tokenID refers to an authenticated and authorized user.
retrieveAsset(String assetID, String tokenID): Asset asset
Retrieves an existing asset based on its UID. Allowed only if the tokenID refers to an authenticated and authorized user.
retrieveAssetParents(String assetID, String tokenID): AssetList assetList
Retrieves a list with zero or more assets that correspond to the parents of the asset whose UID was supplied as parameter. Allowed only if the tokenID refers to an authenticated and authorized user.
retrieveAssetChildren(String assetID, String tokenID): AssetList assetList
Retrieves a list with zero or more assets that correspond to the children of the asset whose UID was supplied as parameter. Allowed only if the tokenID refers to an authenticated and authorized user.

References

1. Braga, R.T.V., Chan, A.: Peony: A web environment to support pattern-based development. In: ICWE, pp. 358–361. IEEE (2008)
2. Erl, T.: Principles of Service Design. Practice Hall, USA (2008)
3. Feloni, D., Braga, R.T.V.: Methodologies for evaluation and improvement of software processes in the context of quality and maturity models: a systematic mapping. In: XVIII Ibero-American Conference on Software Engineering (CIbSE), pp. 1–14 (2015)

4. Garcia-Borgonon, L., Barcelona, M., Garcia-Garcia, J., Alba, M., Escalona, M.: Software process modeling languages: A systematic literature review. Inf. Softw. Technol. **56**(2), 103–116 (2014)
5. Hong-Min, R., Zhi-Ying, Y., Jing-Zhou, Z.: Design and implementation of ras-based open source software repository. In: 6th International Conference on Fuzzy Systems and Knowledge Discovery (FSKD), vol. 2, pp. 219–223. IEEE (2009)
6. Hong-Min, R., Jin, L., Jing-Zhou, Z.: Software asset repository open framework supporting customizable faceted classification. In: 2010 IEEE International Conference on Software Engineering and Service Sciences (ICSESS), pp. 1–4 (2010)
7. Kazman, R., Klein, M., Clements, P.: Atam: Method for architecture evaluation. Technical report CMU/SEI-2000-TR-004, Software Engineering Institute, Carnegie Mellon University, Pittsburgh, PA (2000). http://resources.sei.cmu.edu/library/asset-view.cfm?AssetID=5177
8. Lee, R., Kim, H.K., Yang, H.S.: An architecture model for dynamically converting components into web services. In: 11th Asia-Pacific Software Engineering Conference, 2004, pp. 648–654 (2004)
9. Mahmood, S., Ahmed, M., Alshayeb, M.: Reuse environments for software artifacts: Analysis framework. In: Proceedings of the 12th International Conference on Computer and Information Science (ICIS), pp. 35–40. IEEE Computer Society (2013). http://dblp.uni-trier.de/db/conf/ACISicis/ACISicis2013.html#MahmoodAA13
10. Mahmoud, H.: Service-oriented architecture (soa) and web services: The road to enterprise application integration (eai) (2005)
11. Michael, M.P., Georgakopoulos, D.: Srveice-oriented computing. Commun. ACM **46**, 25–28 (2003)
12. Montoni, M., et al.: Taba workstation: supporting software process deployment based on CMMI and MR-MPS.BR. In: Münch, J., Vierimaa, M. (eds.) PROFES 2006. LNCS, vol. 4034, pp. 249–262. Springer, Heidelberg (2006)
13. Moura, D.d.S.: Software Profile RAS: extending RAS and building an asset repository. Master's thesis (2013). http://www.lume.ufrgs.br/handle/10183/87582
14. OMG: Reusable asset specification, November 2005. http://www.omg.org/spec/RAS/2.2/
15. Pacini, K.D.R., Braga, R.T.V.: An approach for reusing software process elements based on reusable asset specification: a software product line case study. In: Proceedings of the Tenth International Conference on Software Engineering Advances (ICSEA), pp. 200–206. IEEE, IARIA XPS Press, Barcelona, Spain (2015)
16. Park, E., Kim, H., Lee, R.Y.: Software repository for software process improvement. In: Lee, R., Kim, H.-K. (eds.) Computer and Information Science. SCI, vol. 131, pp. 51–64. Springer, Heidelberg (2008)
17. Pure-systems: [On-Line] PURE: : VARIANTS (2009). http://www.pure-systems.com/purevariants.49.0.html
18. Von Wangenheim, C.G., McCaffery, F., Hauck, J.C.R., Lacerda, T.C., Buglione, L., Vieira Da Cruz, R.F.: Building a maturity & capability model repository. In: ACM International Conference Proceeding Series, pp. 2–5 (2011)
19. Werner, C., Mangan, M., Murta, L., Pinheiro, R., Mattoso, M., Braga, R., Borges, M.: Odyssey-Share: An Environment for Collaborative Component-Based Development. Las Vegas, USA (2003)
20. Zhou, N., Zhang, L.J., Chee, Y.M., Chen, L.: Legacy asset analysis and integration in model-driven soa solution. In: IEEE International Conference on Services Computing (SCC), pp. 554–561. IEEE (2010)

Pragmatic Software Reuse in Bioinformatics: How Can Social Network Information Help?

Xiaoyu Jin[1], Charu Khatwani[1], Nan Niu[1(✉)],
Michael Wagner[2], and Juha Savolainen[3]

[1] Department of EECS, University of Cincinnati, Cincinnati, OH 45221, USA
{jinxu,khatwacu}@mail.uc.edu, nan.niu@uc.edu
[2] Division of Biomedical Informatics, Cincinnati Children's Hospital Medical Center,
Cincinnati, OH 45229, USA
michael.wagner@cchmc.org
[3] Head of Software Architecture, Roche Diagnostics, 6343 Rotkreuz, Switzerland
juha.savolainen@roche.com

Abstract. Little is known about the specific kinds of questions that bioinformatics programmers ask during pragmatic software reuse tasks and how well development online social networks help answer those questions. To fill the gap, we report an empirical study involving 20 biomedical software developers performing reuse tasks. A key contribution of our study is the discovery of 31 questions needed to be addressed, which we further classify into 5 categories along a software-architecture-centric and problem-domain-centric spectrum. Our study further provides evidence for the positive effect of social network information on pragmatic reuse tasks. Our work can lead to enhanced tool support so as to improve biomedical software reuse in practice.

Keywords: Pragmatic software reuse · Architecture-centric reuse · Biomedical software · Information needs · Social network information

1 Introduction

Software is a critical enabler to advance our understandings and make innovative discoveries in biomedicine. In fact, the software engineering challenges have grown so immense that, in the United States, for example, the primary biomedical and health-related funding agency — the National Institutes of Health (NIH) — began investigating ways to better discover software, namely to greatly facilitate the biomedical research community to locate and reuse software [5].

An essential challenge here is *pragmatic software reuse* that uses the software artifacts which were not necessarily developed with reuse in mind [25]. In contrast to pre-planned software reuse such as product line engineering [29], pragmatic reuse recognizes the opportunistic and exploratory nature of reuse decisions manifested in practices like copy-paste-modify code. A unique aspect in this domain is that the programmers are often researchers whose principal

© Springer International Publishing Switzerland 2016
G.M. Kapitsaki and E. Santana de Almeida (Eds.): ICSR 2016, LNCS 9679, pp. 247–264, 2016.
DOI: 10.1007/978-3-319-35122-3_17

training area is not software engineering but biomedical related fields. In the daily work of these bioinformatics researchers, pre-planned software reuse may not be instrumented or enforced, leaving pragmatic reuse the only feasible option.

Current approaches to pragmatic reuse attempt to support the developer's explicit recording of a reuse plan and automatically enact certain steps of the plan [19], define metrics to indicate the effects of reuse on project performance [21], and assist in the reusable component extraction by iteratively analyzing the structural complexity of code [14]. In addition, various kinds of code search and recommendation mechanisms are proposed [18,20,24,27,28], focusing on white-box reuse where existing code needs internal modifications so as to fit the target system. Despite the contemporary support, pragmatic software reuse remains a difficult endeavor. Among the salient challenges are the dependencies surrounding the reusable code and the breakdowns experienced when the code is integrated into the target system [25].

Such issues can be regarded as instances of *architectural mismatch* [16] representing a persistent difficulty in software reuse [17]. Architectural mismatch stems from the incompatible assumptions that each part of reuse had made about its operating environment. Although pragmatic reuse is often labeled *ad hoc* [19], we believe it should not be performed without explicit architectural considerations. Existing pragmatic reuse approaches, however, have not thoroughly examined the role of software architecture in pragmatic reuse.

To fill the gap, we investigate in this paper the kinds of architectural knowledge involved in pragmatic reuse. We conduct a controlled experiment to elicit the information needs from the bioinformatics programmers carrying out software reuse tasks. Our results drawn from 20 participants suggest 31 specific questions, which we group along a software-architecture-centric and problem-domain-centric spectrum. Furthermore, we test the extent to which development online social networks support the needs of the reuse tasks.

The contributions of our work lie in the discovery and codification of the information needs in pragmatic software reuse, as well as the positive evidence gained on the use of social network information to satisfy those needs. In what follows, we review related work in Sect. 2. Section 3 presents our study design, Sect. 4 analyzes the results, and finally, Sect. 5 discusses our work's implications and draws some concluding remarks.

2   Background and Related Work

2.1   Biomedical Software Discovery

Aimed to advance the understanding of human health and disease through harvesting the wealth of information in biomedical data, the NIH launched the Big Data to Knowledge (BD2K) initiative in 2012 [2]. While progresses in areas like data accessibility are made, challenges persist for the biomedical community to *discover software* in an effective and efficient manner. To tackle the problem, in May of 2014, about 40 people from government, academia, and industry participated in a workshop on biomedical software discovery and released a report [5].

In this report, software discoverability is defined as the ability to locate, cite, and reuse software. Although, in theory, every biomedical software is known and therefore discoverable, at least by its original developer(s), the improved software discoverability is much needed in practice by four specific stakeholders: (1) developers who face challenges measuring their software's adoption, (2) users who have difficulty in software reuse, (3) publishers who lack a consistent way to handle software citations, and (4) funders who struggle to make informed decisions about which software development projects to support.

The report then focuses mainly on proposing a global *indexing* solution. The solution is delineated as an automated, broadly accessible system allowing for comprehensive identification of biomedical software. Central to the solution is assigning each software tool with a unique identifier [5]. While such a proposal can facilitate how biomedical software is disseminated and cited, serious drawbacks are pointed out by the commenters shortly after the release of the report [4]. A common criticism is about scalability and argues against the development of a brand new indexing capability to cover a broad biomedical software spectrum.

Another major problem with the unique-identifier indexing proposal is the confusion between a software paper and the software itself [4]. In fact, some publishers began archiving papers describing research software. Elsevier, for instance, launched a new journal called SoftwareX in 2015 [6], aiming to disseminate software applications, tools, and libraries in various domains including medical and biological sciences. However, the unique identifier/index (e.g., a DOI linking to a SoftwareX article) captures rather the static metadata about the entire software (e.g., weblink to code repository, legal license, support email, etc.) than the dynamic usage information about specific part(s) of the software. In another word, what a global indexer [5] supports is black-box software *use* instead of white-box software *reuse*. Our objective is to tackle directly the pragmatic software reuse challenges faced by the biomedical community.

2.2   Pragmatic Software Reuse

Reuse attempts to improve software quality and developer productivity by leveraging existing artifacts and knowledge [23]. Two approaches can be distinguished in terms of how the reusable artifacts are created and used. Pre-planned approaches, such as object-oriented inheritance and product line engineering, explicitly build artifacts *for* reuse so that subsequent software product/system development can be carried out *with* reuse. In contrast, pragmatic approaches, such as code scavenging [23] and opportunistic programming [13], facilitate the reuse of software artifacts that were *not* necessarily designed for reuse [25]. While the distinction is not always clearcut, a key difference is that pre-planned approaches assume that a reusable part exists that either fits perfectly or that the target system can be adapted to make it fit whereas a pragmatic approach assumes that the reusable itself is a legitimate target for modification [19].

Maras *et al.* [25] identified 3 steps involved in pragmatic software reuse based on their experience of Web application development: locating the source code of an individual feature, analyzing and modifying the code, and integrating code into the target system. These steps are in line with the process model described by Holmes and Walker [19]. In [19], a tool named Gilligan was introduced to support Java developer's recording of a pragmatic reuse plan. Moreover, Gilligan helped automate simple cycles of the plan (e.g., copy a manually found element, paste it in a manually determined location, flag syntactic warnings, etc.). The experiments with 16 participants (2 undergraduates, 7 graduate students, and 7 industrial developers) using Gilligan showed that, compared to the location of reusable code, much difficulty occurred in analyzing the code, especially in resolving dangling dependencies to Java libraries, types, methods, and fields [19].

The difficult-to-resolve dependencies reflect incompatibilities at not only the source code level, but also the software architecture level. Architecture-centric reuse approaches date back at least to the work of Garlan et al. [16], who argued that a main reason why software architecture is important is because it lets designers exploit recurring architectural styles to reuse routine solutions for certain classes of problems. Drawing from their experience of failing to build a system from reusable parts, Garlan et al. [16] recognized a root cause being the conflicting assumptions among the parts and termed this phenomenon "architectural mismatch". Generally speaking, four categories of assumptions can lead to architectural mismatch: nature of the components, nature of the connectors, global architectural structure, and construction process.

Researchers have advanced architecture-centric reuse by trying to avoid or tolerate mismatch [30], to sustain evolutionary stability [32], and to catalog specialized solutions specific to a particular domain in a way that restricts the range of permissible components and their interactions [26]. Beyer et al. [10] reported a success story of introducing a product-line architecture to a small software team of 2 developers and 1 tester. During 4 iterations, an organization-specific software architecture was established, static architectural compliance checks were performed, and the reduced development effort was observed. In [10], the main benefit of the product-line architecture was to help communicate and negotiate the competing stakeholder concerns within the same organization. In our work, the focus is on examining the role of general software architectural styles in pragmatic code reuse without any organizational boundary.

2.3 Development Social Networks

Social interactions of software engineers have been studied from various technical and organizational aspects. For example, given a particular organization or project, people can "be friends" with the work items that they share [9], optimal group size can be determined by social information foraging principles [11], and latent sub-communities can be identified based on email exchanges [12].

What have recently emerged to shape software engineering practices are the *online* social networks where developers collaborate and exchange ideas and expertise. These technologies include community portals, Q&A sites, wikis, forums, and microblogs [8]. Reviewing feeds, watching projects, and following others are the most used social networking functionalities among today's software developers [15]. Surprisingly, little is known about how software reuse can utilize and even strengthen the online social networks. This lack of knowledge is especially prominent in pragmatic, white-box reuse tasks.

Exploiting online information to support software reuse, even before the social networking era, is not without problems. Hummel and Atkinson [20] pioneered the systematic investigation of the Web as a reuse repository; however, the web services that they deployed for white-box reuse experienced discontinuation and returned disappointing results. Happel *et al.* [18] found that most source code search engines focused on retrieving lines of code and often lacked the capability to help the re-user explore in-depth connected information. Zou and colleagues [35] proposed an automated approach to searching software reuse candidates and using the developer comments extracted from online social networks to perform sentiment analysis of the candidates. In sum, the support so far has been extensive on code search but not on the reuse *per se*. Understanding how social network information can help carry out the actual reuse task is precisely the focus of our research.

3 Study Design

Our work aims to answer two main research questions: what information is needed in pragmatic software reuse and how social networks can help meet those needs. Thus our inquiry is composed of two parts: first eliciting the information needs and then quantifying the effect of social networks. To address these research questions, we performed a lab experiment. The rest of this section details our experimental design and execution.

3.1 Participants

The population that our study intends to impact is the community of programmers who develop biomedical software; notably, most are bioinformatics researchers [5]. Twenty participants took part in our experiment (12 male and 8 female; 18 graduate students and 2 staff researchers). These participants were recruited from the Cincinnati local community via email invitations. To be eligible to participate in our experiment, each individual had to consider writing software as an essential (as opposed to accidental) part of their work, and consider that pragmatic code reuse (as opposed to pre-planned reuse) is common in their practice. We did not impose any criteria regarding research area, software development experience, or programming language, as we attempted to select a sample representative of developers across the broad biomedical domains. Our participants had a varied background: 13 had no professional software development experience, 1 had less than a year professional experience, 3 had 1–5 years, and 3 had more than 5 years. Table 1 overviews the demographics of the participants in our study. The data were collected through a pre-experimental, self-reported survey. Note that we performed two pilot trials before the actual

Table 1. Overview of participants and their self-reported pre-experimental survey data: "#" represents the number of participants, "Area" shows the participant's main research area, "PL" denotes one or more programming languages that the participant is familiar with, "SE Freq" classifies the software engineering (coding, debugging, etc.) frequency, and "Reuse Freq" indicates the frequency of pragmatic software reuse.

Area	#	PL	#	SE Freq	#	Reuse Freq	#
Genomics	5	Python	16	Daily	12	Frequently	11
Gene regulatory networks	4	C/C++	7	Weekly	4	Sometimes	7
Biostatistics survival analysis	4	Matlab	5	Monthly	1	Rarely	0
Neuroimaging analysis	3	R	5	Others (as needed, project-driven, etc.)	3	Others (in-house maintenance, etc.)	2
Others (molecular biology, proteomics, etc.)	4	Others (C#, Java, etc.)	14				

experimentation to test instrumentation and solicit feedback. The results from these two pilots are excluded for the rest of the paper.

3.2 Tasks

The participants were asked to perform pragmatic software reuse tasks that have direct biomedical relevance. We explicitly considered software architecture when designing the tasks. Two architectural styles were chosen: plug-in architecture and event-driven architecture. For each architecture, an open-source software acted as the target system where the actual reuse was expected to take place. Next is a description of these two systems and their reuse tasks.

- ImageJ [1] is a Java image processing program whose author, Wayne Rasband, works at the NIH's Research Services Branch. We downloaded the latest version of ImageJ (v1.49) and ran it as a standalone application on a Windows lab machine. ImageJ provides extensibility via Java plug-ins. Some plug-in examples are automatically installed and can be accessed as shown in Fig. 1a. It is believed that user-written ImageJ plug-ins make it possible to solve almost any image processing or analysis problem [1]. The reuse task that we defined for our participants was inspired by protein quantification with ImageJ [3]. In particular, we pre-processed an image containing a variety of different proteins being separated on a gel. We stored the pre-processing results in 4 textual

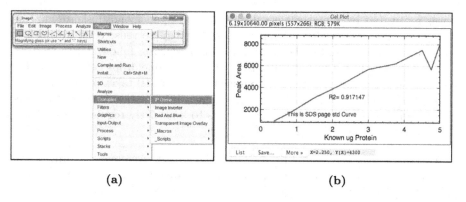

Fig. 1. ImageJ reuse task: **(a)** example plug-ins after installation, **(b)** sample output.

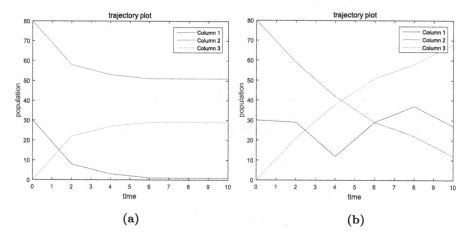

Fig. 2. StochKit task: **(a)** before reuse, **(b)** after reuse.

files, which were provided as inputs to the reuse task: Protein.txt defining the values on the x-axis and each of Result1.txt, Result2.txt, and Result3.txt giving rise to a protein sample. For each sample, the participant was asked to reuse code so as to draw the gel plot and perform linear regression of that plot. Figure 1b illustrates one sample curve and its linear regression result: R^2=0.917147. Biologically speaking, the best protein fit is the sample with the greatest R^2 value.

- StochKit [7] is a C++ biochemical reaction simulation program [31]. We installed its latest version (StochKit v2.0.10) on the same lab machine as ImageJ. StochKit utilizes event-driven architecture to achieve fine-grained control of the reaction process and to simulate real-time response. Event triggers are discrete changes in the system state or parameter value typically used to mimic biological processes or to recreate experimental conditions [31]. Figure 2 simulates the reaction: Blue + Red → Green. The reuse task here was motivated by a mathematical model of an open monosubstrate enzyme reaction [33]. Specifically, we asked the participant to reuse code so that the enzyme reaction could be better controlled, namely, to follow [33] to increase Blue's volume under two conditions: (i) when its value drops below 5, and (ii) at time units 2 and 8. If the two conditions interact, (i) takes precedence over (ii). The StochKit task illustrates that human intervention is essential, especially when the amount of reactants needs to be strictly regulated to achieve a stable biochemical reaction environment.

To circumvent the unfamiliarity with the target systems, we provided a few *seed elements* [19] to assist in participant's investigation. For the ImageJ task, the participants were pointed to the "Example_Plot implements PlugIn" class and the "PlotWindow(..)" constructor. For the participants tasked with StochKit, 3 files' names were given: \src\model_parser\Input_events.ipp, \src\solvers\SSA_Direct.ipp, and \src\solvers\SSA_Direct_Events.ipp. These seeds were provided to the participants on the printed hard copy of the task descriptions and were provided only as *structural* elements without any hint of runtime behavior [19].

While the seed elements were available to every participant, our independent variable was the social network information that we wanted to test in a controlled manner. To instrument such a treatment, two researchers manually searched for useful online resources and jointly finalized a set of links for each task. Tables 2 and 3 list these links pointing to portals (e.g., ImageJ #11), wikis (e.g., ImageJ #3), forums (e.g., StochKit #7), Q&A sites (e.g., StochKit #5), etc. These links are by no means complete. Our intention is to raise the participant's awareness of online social network information and offer a set of specific links to encourage them to take advantage of the information during their reuse tasks. In this sense, the links in Tables 2 and 3 should be treated as hints that provide shortcuts to potentially useful information for carrying out the pragmatic reuse tasks. We grouped these "shortcuts" in the experimental computer's web browser's bookmark — one bookmark folder per reuse task. To avoid participant's unintentional inference about the resources' importance, we ordered the links inside each bookmark folder alphabetically, as shown in Tables 2 and 3. For the remaining of the paper, we use "pre-selected SNI" to refer to the social network information presented in Tables 2 and 3.

3.3   Procedure

The participants worked individually in a lab and began by signing the consent form and completing a background survey (cf. Table 1). Each participant received a randomly assigned experimental ID and followed the corresponding block assignment to perform the two reuse tasks. Table 4 shows our block design, in which both SNI-treatment order and task order are counterbalanced. Thus, each participant performed one task with SNI and the other without the pre-instrumented SNI support. Similar to [19], our design is best understood as within-(participants plus SNI treatment) and between-(participants plus order).

Table 2. Social network information (SNI) provided for the ImageJ reuse task.

#	Title	Link
1	Data Analysis-Linear Regression	http://introcs.cs.princeton.edu/java/97data/
2	Development - ImageJ	http://imagej.net/Develop
3	Gel electrophoresis - Wikipedia	https://en.wikipedia.org/wiki/Gel_electrophoresis
4	gel quantification analysis [ImageJ Documentation Wiki]	http://imagejdocu.tudor.lu/doku.php?id=video:analysis: gel_quantification_analysis
5	image - Live vertical profile plot in ImageJ - Stack Overflow	http://stackoverflow.com/questions/19016991/ live-vertical-profile-plot-in-imagej
6	Java read file and store text in an array - Stack Overflow	http://stackoverflow.com/questions/19844649/ java-read-file-and-store-text-in-an-array
7	Java Read Files With BufferedReader, FileReader	http://www.dotnetperls.com/bufferedreader
8	Linear Regression	http://stattrek.com/regression/linear-regression.aspx
9	Linear regression - Wikipedia	https://en.wikipedia.org/wiki/Linear_regression
10	Plot issues in Jython script for ImageJ	http://stackoverflow.com/questions/26400563/plot-issues- in-jython-script-for-imagej-reference-sources-welcome
11	Plugins (ImageJ)	http://rsb.info.nih.gov/ij/plugins/index.html
12	Protein Electrophoresis | Applications &Technologies |	http://www.bio-rad.com/en-us/applications-technologies/ introduction-protein-electrophoresis
13	Read Text file in string array Java	http://www.technical-recipes.com/2011/ reading-text-files-into-string-arrays-in-java/

A researcher explained the first reuse task to the participant. The task description was printed on a hard copy which was presented throughout the task period for easy reference. The researcher then introduced the target

Table 3. Social network information (SNI) provided for the StochKit reuse task.

#	Title	Link
1	abs - C++ Reference	http://www.cplusplus.com/reference/cmath/abs/
2	C Program: Solving Simultaneous Equations in Two Variables	http://www.thelearningpoint.net/computer-science/ c-program-solving-simultaneous-equations- in-two-variables
3	C++ - Difference between .ipp extension and .cpp extension files	http://stackoverflow.com/questions/19147208/difference- between-using-ipp-extension-and-cpp-extension-files
4	Equations for 2 variable Linear Regression - Stack Overflow	http://stackoverflow.com/questions/459480/ equations-for-2-variable-linear-regression
5	Event Driven Programming? - Programmers Stack Exchange	http://programmers.stackexchange.com/questions/ 230180/event-driven-programming
6	Global Variables - C++ Forum	http://www.cplusplus.com/forum/windows/115425/
7	How do you make C++ solve equations? - C++ Forum	http://www.cplusplus.com/forum/beginner/34039/
8	java - Creating a simple event driven architecture	http://stackoverflow.com/questions/13483048/ creating-a-simple-event-driven-architecture
9	Solving a system of 2 Linear Equations using C++	http://stackoverflow.com/questions/14594240/ solving-a-system-of-2-linear-equations-using-c
10	visual studio - How to declare a global variable in C++	http://stackoverflow.com/questions/9702053/ how-to-declare-a-global-variable-in-c

system, as well as the seed elements by emphasizing their structural aspects. If the first task was with the SNI treatment, then the participant was made aware of the task-specific bookmark folder that the researcher pre-ported to the lab computer. For the instrumentation to be uniform, the researcher configured

Table 4. Experimental block assignments.

ID (Block name)	First task	Second task
A	ImageJ-without-SNI	StochKit-with-SNI
B	ImageJ-with-SNI	StochKit-without-SNI
C	StochKit-without-SNI	ImageJ-with-SNI
D	StochKit-with-SNI	ImageJ-without-SNI

all the 3 browsers' bookmarkings of the computer in the same way: Internet Explorer, Mozilla Firefox, and Google Chrome. If the first task was in the control group receiving no SNI treatment, then the researcher would make sure no task-related bookmarks existed in the browsers. The participant was then asked to perform the first reuse task and was encouraged to "think aloud" to verbalize their rationales, decision, strategies, and tactics being employed. Note that the participant was allowed to access the entire internet for completing the reuse task, independent of whether pre-selected SNI was present. Informed by our pilot trials, we set the expected task completion time to be 20 min and communicated such an expectation to the participant prior to the task. The participant was reminded around 20 min into the task but was not forced to terminate until a natural stop point was signaled by the participant himself or herself. The researcher then conducted an informal interview with the participant to collect feedback, and if the first task was treated with SNI then the usefulness of the pre-selected SNI was also surveyed verbally. The participant was given a break if desired, and then continued with the second reuse task in the same manner.

4   Results and Analysis

4.1   Information Needs in Pragmatic Software Reuse

Understanding the needs of software developers is a prerequisite for researchers and tool builders to better answer those needs. For software evolution tasks, Sillito et al. [34] identified 44 specific questions programmers ask and further classified those questions into 4 groups: (1) finding focus points, (2) expanding focus points, (3) understanding a subgraph, and (4) understanding groups of subgraphs. Ko et al. [22] abstracted from 17 Microsoft developers' daily practices into 21 types of information needs, emphasizing the communication and coordination demands in collocated software teams. The needs in pragmatic software reuse tasks, to the best of our knowledge, have not been thoroughly explored.

The participants in our study asked a variety of questions which we group into 5 categories. The data extraction was done manually and jointly by two researchers. Figure 3 positions the categories along a software-architecture-centric and problem-domain-centric spectrum. The specific questions are presented below, annotated with 'I' (relevant to ImageJ), 'S' (relevant to StochKit), or 'B' (relevant to both).

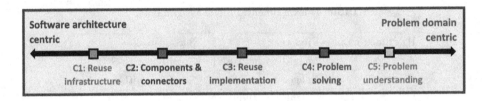

Fig. 3. Categories of information needs in pragmatic software reuse.

Reuse infrastructure (C1) touches upon the critical issues of the architectural style underpinning the target system, and if not addressed properly, will likely cause serious architectural mismatch [16, 17] thereby hampering pragmatic reuse.

1. Where is the starting point that kind of likes a main function? [B]
2. How does this software know that I am writing a plugin class? [I]
3. What is the control structure/flow in an event-driven architecture? [S]
4. Where is an event triggered and/or captured? [S]
5. How to reuse the seeds to realize simple functions like 'Hello World'? [B]

Components and connectors (C2) are at the heart of software architecture. Understanding the computation, the interface, the decomposition, and the interdependency is key to arrive at a successful reuse implementation.

6. How to name the plug-in class and what must be imported? [I]
7. Where should I save the plugin class in the file system? [I]
8. How do different events relate to each other? [S]
9. Where to specify precedence of multiple events? [S]
10. How can I customize the data to fit into the function being reused? [B]
11. How to initialize suitable variables to be applicable for a function? [B]
12. What is the linkage between the computation units (methods, procedures, etc.) and/or between the encapsulates (classes, templates, etc.)? [B]

Reuse implementation (C3) is where the two ends of Fig. 3 meet. Solving the needs in this category will facilitate the completion of the pragmatic reuse task in an architecturally compatible way.

13. Where can I see the compilation information? [B]
14. Is this software capable of printing things out to help me debug? [B]
15. Where are the input files located and how to change the values related to the reuse task in the (input) files? [B]
16. How to resolve the dangling references of a reused code fragment? [B]
17. How to output string with a numeric value together? [I]
18. How is the visualization for trajectories done? [S]

Problem solving (C4) shifts the information needs toward the functionalities that the reuse task dictates. Here the programmers search for reuse candidates written in same programming language as the target system.

19. Is there existing Java implementation that I can import (reuse) to calculate linear regression as well as curve plotting? [I]
20. Can I find existing code to read data from text files in Java? [I]
21. Is there available C++ code online to solve the linear equations? [S]
22. What might be the existing implementation for a specific function (variable type conversion [I], absolute value calculation [S], etc.)? [B]
23. How to initialize member variables and vectors in Java or C++? [B]
24. Are there unit tests to be reused together with code? [B]

Problem understanding (C5) helps the developers to clarify the conceptual questions about the reuse task. Formulating an appropriate task context is important to search and evaluate reuse candidates.

25. Why use linear regression in this task? [I]
26. What is the original gel sample: human or other species? [I]
27. How is the protein separated from the gel and what is the expected error rate of the given input files as this can affect the kinds of (linear) regression that I do? [I]
28. Do I have to plot three curves in a single figure or in 3 separate figures? [I]
29. What does species mean in a biochemical reaction? [S]
30. Are those values (time units 2 and 8, volume below 5) arbitrary or do they follow certain properties? [S]
31. What is the biomedical significance of the task? [B]

4.2 Supporting the Needs with Social Network Information

Having elicited the specific questions and characterized them, we now examine how the SNI supports pragmatic reuse needs. The support is analyzed both qualitatively and quantitatively. Figure 4 presents our qualitative analysis result, in which the mappings between the SNI links and the information-need categories are established. For each category, we present three statistics per task: the support from pre-selected SNI links (cf. Tables 2 and 3), the pre-selected links followed by the participants, and the additional online SNI that the participants accessed during pragmatic reuse.

A couple of observations can be made from Fig. 4. First, most pre-selected SNI links were actually followed. This indicates that the developers perceived the SNI as helpful hints which they were willing to spend time investigating. Second, for a category whose pre-selected SNI links were actively followed, more additional links were sought. This implies that the developers, once made aware of SNI support, were motivated to pursue more links, which in turn increased the likelihood of devising a reuse solution, as opposed to starting from scratch.

The usage data of Fig. 4 increased our confidence in the magnitude of the impact that SNI had on pragmatic reuse. In another word, if little SNI were followed, the impact would be trivial. To quantify such an impact, we assessed 2 variables: time to task completion and success of reuse solution. The comparisons were made between the control groups (participants who did not receive pre-selected SNI links) and the treatment groups (those who did).

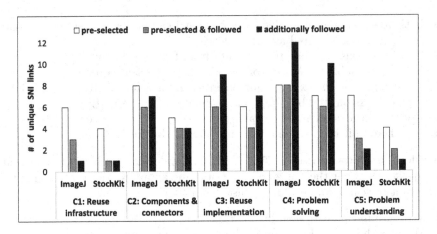

Fig. 4. SNI usage by tasks and information-need categories.

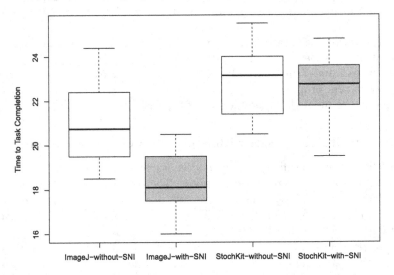

Fig. 5. Comparison of task completion time.

Figure 5 compares the time required for completing the reuse task in different settings. Generally speaking, developers spent less time on the ImageJ task than the StochKit task. This indicates that ImageJ's architecture, namely the plug-in architecture, is more extensible. By conforming to basic architectural constraints and the construction process (e.g., importing the necessary libraries, storing the new class file in the plug-in folder, etc.), the developers were able to quickly extend the functionality of ImageJ. When the median completion time is compared, pre-selected SNI links facilitated both tasks to be finished faster. However, the effect is statistically significant only on the ImageJ task (Wilcoxon signed rank test: $p=0.0098$, $\alpha=0.05$) but not on the StochKit task (Wilcoxon

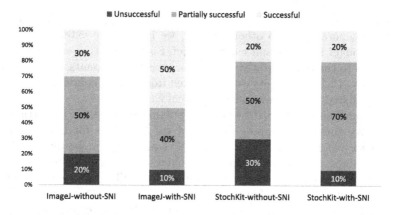

Fig. 6. Comparison of reuse solution success.

test: $p=0.2357$, $\alpha=0.05$). We speculate this may be caused by the more effort in understanding StochKit's event-driven architecture as well as in locating the feature where pragmatic reuse would interact with [25]. Testing this hypothesis requires further research.

In general, a (pragmatic) reuse task can have multiple, equally valid solutions. Thus we assessed the participants' reuse solutions on an individual basis without a pre-determined 'gold standard' answer. Two researchers jointly judged all the solutions and qualified them into 3 categories: successful (fulfilled functionality with the reuse done conforming to the underlying software architecture), unsuccessful (unfulfilled functionality or solution developed from scratch), and partially successful (things in between). Figure 6 shows the distributions. For the ImageJ task, when provided with SNI, the developers could better complete the reuse in that the successful rate increased from 30 % to 50 % and the unsuccessful rate decreased from 20 % to 10 % in Fig. 6. For StochKit, SNI's help seemed rather limited by shifting some unsuccessful reuse solutions to partially, but not completely, successful ones.

It is evident based on our observation and our interviews with the participants that, for the two tasks, developers preferred reuse over devising a solution from scratch. The preference was predominant. In addition, the support that the developers received from the SNI — either pre-selected, additionally followed, or both — is indisputable. In fact, all the participants in our study showed significant reliance on SNI that some went on using Google to confirm and even refine the pre-selected links prepared by us. In sum, our results suggest the positive impact of SNI on answering developers' needs and completing the pragmatic reuse tasks with speed and quality.

4.3 Threats to Validity

Our results about bioinformatics software developers' information needs in pragmatic reuse are clearly influenced by the types of architectural styles and particular systems adopted in our experiment. While the 31 specific questions may not be generalizable to other settings, we believe the external validity is relatively stronger for our result categories (cf. Fig. 3). Another external validity threat relates to the representativeness of our study participants. While we tried to be inclusive, the participants were recruited from a local community and were primarily affiliated with a university's medical campus.

For our analysis about SNI's effect on pragmatic reuse, an important construct validity threat is the pre-selection of the SNI links for both tasks. We attempted to avoid repetitiveness in our SNI preparation; however, different researchers might select different online resources. Nevertheless, the usage data reported in Fig. 4 show that any SNI preparation will be unavoidably incomplete. As a result, we argue that the main purpose of the SNI is not to present to the developers all the links, but to encourage them to engage in an active information seeking and knowledge acquisition process.

5   Conclusions

For the biomedical community, reusing software in a pre-planned manner is often infeasible. Pragmatic software reuse, therefore, is key to bioinformatics programmer's success in practice. This paper makes two major contributions: (1) a classification of 31 information needs elicited during pragmatic reuse tasks, and (2) a controlled experiment revealing the positive impact that development online social networks have on meeting the information needs and on completing the reuse tasks.

Our study's results have several direct implications for tool building. First of all, architecture decisions should be central to the identification and evaluation of reuse candidates. Moreover, when the code is reused and integrated into the target system [25], architectural conformance should be checked and violations should be managed. Last, but certainly not the least, social network information should be seamlessly incorporated into the entire process of pragmatic software reuse: ranging from understanding the reuse infrastructure to implementing a successful reuse solution. It is hoped that our work illuminates a systematic way to tackle architectural mismatch [17] in biomedical software reuse.

Acknowledgments. *This research is partially supported by the U.S. National Science Foundation (Award CCF-1350487) and the National Natural Science Foundation of China (Fund No. 61375053).*

References

1. ImageJ: Image Processing and Analysis in Java. http://imagej.nih.gov/ij/. Accessed March 2016
2. NIH Big Data to Knowledge. http://bd2k.nih.gov. Accessed March 2016
3. Protein Quantification Using ImageJ. http://openwetware.org/wiki/Protein_Quantification_Using_ImageJ. Accessed March 2016

4. Software Discovery Index: Request for Comments. https://nciphub.org/resources/888/download/Software_Discovery_Index_Meeting_Report_with_comments.pdf. Accessed March 2016
5. Software Discovery Meeting Report. https://nciphub.org/resources/885/supportingdocs. Accessed March 2016
6. SoftwareX: An Elsevier Journal. http://www.journals.elsevier.com/softwarex/. Accessed March 2016
7. StochKit: Stochastic Simulation Kit. http://www.engineering.ucsb.edu/~cse/StochKit/StochKit_whatis.html. Accessed March 2016
8. Begel, A., Bosch, J., Storey, M.-A.: Bridging software communities through social networking. IEEE Softw. **30**(1), 26–28 (2013)
9. Begel, A., Khoo, Y., Zimmermann, T., Codebook: discovering and exploiting relationships in software repositories. In: ICSE, pp. 125–134 (2010)
10. Beyer, H.-J., Hein, D., Schitter, C., Knodel, J., Muthig, D., Naab, M.: Introducing architecture-centric reuse into a small development organization. In: Mei, H. (ed.) ICSR 2008. LNCS, vol. 5030, pp. 1–13. Springer, Heidelberg (2008)
11. Bhowmik, T., Niu, N., Wang, W., Cheng, J.-R., Li, L., Cao, X.: Optimal group size for software change tasks: a social information foraging perspective. IEEE Trans. Cybern. (to appear)
12. Bird, C., Pattison, D., D'Souza, R., Filkov, V., Devanbu, P.: Latent social structure in open source projects. In: FSE, pp. 24–35 (2008)
13. Brandt, J., Guo, P., Lewenstein, J., Dontcheva, M., Klemmer, S.: Opportunistic programming: writing code to prototype, ideate, and discover. IEEE Softw. **26**(5), 18–24 (2009)
14. Constantinou, E., Naskos, A., Kakarontzas, G., Stamelos, I.: Extracting reusable components: A semi-automated approach for complex structures. Inf. Process. Lett. **115**(3), 414–417 (2015)
15. Dabbish, L., Stuart, H., Tsay, J., Herbsleb, J.: Leveraging transparency. IEEE Softw. **30**(1), 37–43 (2013)
16. Garlan, D., Allen, R., Ockerbloom, J.: Architectural mismatch: why reuse is so hard. IEEE Softw. **12**(6), 17–26 (1995)
17. Garlan, D., Allen, R., Ockerbloom, J.: Architectural mismatch: why reuse is still so hard. IEEE Softw. **26**(4), 66–69 (2009)
18. Happel, H.-J., Schuster, T., Szulman, P.: Leveraging source code search for reuse. In: Mei, H. (ed.) ICSR 2008. LNCS, vol. 5030, pp. 360–371. Springer, Heidelberg (2008)
19. Holmes, R., Walker, R.: Systematizing pragmatic software reuse. ACM Trans. Softw. Eng. Methodol. **21**(4), 20 (2012)
20. Hummel, O., Atkinson, C.: Using the web as a reuse repository. In: Morisio, M. (ed.) ICSR 2006. LNCS, vol. 4039, pp. 298–311. Springer, Heidelberg (2006)
21. Kakarontzas, G., Constantinou, E., Ampatzoglou, A., Stamelos, I.: Layer assessment of object-oriented software: A metric facilitating white-box reuse. J. Syst. Softw. **86**(2), 349–366 (2013)
22. Ko, A., DeLine, R., Venolia, G.: Information needs in collocated software development teams. In: ICSE, pp. 344–353 (2007)
23. Krueger, C.: Software reuse. ACM Comput. Surv. **24**(2), 131–183 (1992)
24. Lemos, O.A.L., Bajracharya, S.K., Ossher, J., Masiero, P.C., Lopes, C.V.: A test-driven approach to code search and its application to the reuse of auxiliary functionality. Inf. Softw. Technol. **53**(4), 294–306 (2011)
25. Maras, J., Štula, M., Crnković, I.: Towards specifying pragmatic software reuse. In: ECSAW, Article No. 54 (2015)

26. Niu, N., Easterbrook, S.: Exploiting COTS-based RE methods: An experience report. In: Mei, H. (ed.) ICSR 2008. LNCS, vol. 5030, pp. 212–216. Springer, Heidelberg (2008)
27. Niu, N., Jin, X., Niu, Z., Cheng, J.-R., Li, L., Kataev, M.: A clustering-based approach to enriching code foraging environment. IEEE Trans. Cybern. (to appear)
28. Niu, N., Mahmoud, A., Bradshaw, G.: Information foraging as a foundation for code navigation. In: ICSE, pp. 816–819 (2011)
29. Niu, N., Savolainen, J., Niu, Z., Jin, M., Cheng, J.-R.: A systems approach to product line requirements reuse. IEEE Syst. J. **8**(3), 827–836 (2014)
30. Niu, N., Yang, F., Cheng, J.-R., Reddivari, S.: Conflict resolution support for parallel software development. IET Softw. **7**(1), 1–11 (2013)
31. Sanft, K., Wu, S., Roh, M., Fu, J., Lim, R., Petzold, L.: StochKit2: software for discrete stochastic simulation of biochemical systems with events. Bioinform. **27**(17), 2457–2458 (2011)
32. Savolainen, J., Niu, N., Mikkonen, T., Fogdal, T.: Long-term product-line sustainability through planned staged investments. IEEE Softw. **30**(6), 63–69 (2013)
33. Sel'Kov, E.: Self-oscillations in glycolysis. Eur. J. Biochem. **4**(1), 79–86 (1968)
34. Sillito, J., Murphy, G., De Volder, K.: Asking and answering questions during a programming change task. IEEE Trans. Softw. Eng. **34**(4), 434–451 (2008)
35. Zou, Y., Liu, C., Jin, Y., Xie, B.: Assessing software quality through web comment search and analysis. In: Favaro, J., Morisio, M. (eds.) ICSR 2013. LNCS, vol. 7925, pp. 208–223. Springer, Heidelberg (2013)

Software Reuse Tools

Feature Location Benchmark for Software Families Using Eclipse Community Releases

Jabier Martinez[1,2(✉)], Tewfik Ziadi[2], Mike Papadakis[1],
Tegawendé F. Bissyandé[1], Jacques Klein[1], and Yves Le Traon[1]

[1] SnT, University of Luxembourg, Luxembourg, Luxembourg
{jabier.martinez,mike.papadakis,tegawende.bissyande,
jacques.klein,yves.letraon}@uni.lu
[2] LiP6, Sorbonne Universités, UPMC Univ Paris 06, Paris, France
tewfik.ziadi@lip6.fr

Abstract. It is common belief that high impact research in software reuse requires assessment in realistic, non-trivial, comparable, and reproducible settings. However, real software artefacts and common representations are usually unavailable. Also, establishing a representative ground truth is a challenging and debatable subject. Feature location in the context of software families is a research field that is becoming more mature with a high proliferation of techniques. We present EFLBench, a benchmark and a framework to provide a common ground for this field. EFLBench leverages the efforts made by the Eclipse Community which provides real feature-based family artefacts and their implementations. Eclipse is an active and non-trivial project and thus, it establishes an unbiased ground truth. EFLBench is publicly available and supports all tasks for feature location techniques integration, benchmark construction and benchmark usage. We demonstrate its usage and its simplicity and reproducibility by comparing four techniques.

Keywords: Feature location · Software product lines · Benchmark · Static analysis · Information retrieval

1 Introduction

Software reuse is often performed by industrial practitioners mainly to boost productivity. One such case is the *copy-paste-modify* which is performed when creating product variants for supporting different customer needs [9]. This practice may increase the productivity in a short term period but in the long run it becomes problematic due to the complex maintenance and further evolution activities of the variants [4]. To deal with these issues, Software Product Line (SPL) engineering has developed mature techniques that can support commonality and variability management of a whole product family and the derivation of tailored products by combining reusable assets [4].

Despite the advantages provided by SPLs, their adoption still remains a major challenge because of organizational and technical issues. To deal with

© Springer International Publishing Switzerland 2016
G.M. Kapitsaki and E. Santana de Almeida (Eds.): ICSR 2016, LNCS 9679, pp. 267–283, 2016.
DOI: 10.1007/978-3-319-35122-3_18

it, software reuse community proposed the so-called *extractive* or *bottom-up* approaches. Among the various bottom-up processes, in this paper we focus on feature location. A feature is defined as a prominent or distinctive user-visible aspect, quality, or characteristic of a software system or systems [15]. As pointed out in the surveys of Rubin *et al.* and Assunção *et al.* [5,24], feature location is an important and challenging problem of these bottom-up processes towards systematic reuse. Many approaches have been proposed and there is a progression in the number of research work conducted every year [5]. Thus, it can be stated that there is an increasing interest on the topic by the research community [19].

Comparing, evaluating and experimenting with feature location techniques is challenging due to the following reasons:

- Most of the research prototypes are either unavailable or hard to configure.
- Performance comparison requires common settings and environments.
- Most of the tools are strongly dependent on specific artefact types that they were designed for, e.g., programming language, design models, etc.
- Effectiveness of the techniques can vary according to different implementation element types, e.g., Abstract Syntax Tree (AST) nodes, software components, etc., that are to be located.

Common case study subjects and frameworks are in need to foster the research activity [30]. In this direction, we identified a set of requirements for such frameworks in feature location:

A standard case study subject. Subjects that are real, non-trivial and easy to use are mandatory. This includes: (1) A list of existing features; (2) For each feature, a group of elements that implements it. (3) A set of real product variants accompanied by the information of which features are included.

A benchmarking framework. In addition to the standard subjects, a full implementation that allows a common, quick and intensive evaluation is needed. This includes (1) available implementation with a common abstraction for the product variants to be considered by the case studies, i.e., as unified structured elements; (2) easy and extensible mechanisms to integrate feature location techniques to support the experimentation and (3) sets of predefined evaluation metrics to draw comparable results.

This paper proposes a framework, called **Eclipse Feature Location Benchmark (EFLBench)**, that fulfils the requirements identified above. We propose a standard and a realistic case study for feature location and an integrated benchmark using the packages of Eclipse releases, their features and their associated plugins. We also propose a full implementation to support benchmarking within Bottom-Up Technologies for Reuse (BUT4Reuse) [21] that is an open-source, generic and extensible framework for bottom-up approaches which allows a quick integration of feature location techniques.

The rest of the paper is structured as follows: Sect. 2 provides background information about feature location techniques and the Eclipse project. In Sect. 3 we present Eclipse as a case study subject and then in Sect. 4 we present the

EFLBench framework. Section 5 presents different feature location techniques and the results of EFLBench usage. Section 6 presents related work and Sect. 7 concludes and presents future work.

2   Background

In order to provide a better understanding for the following sections of this paper, we provide details about feature location and about the Eclipse project.

2.1   Feature Location

Bottom-up approaches for SPL adoption are mainly composed of the following processes: *Feature identification, feature location* and *re-engineering* [21]. While feature identification is the process that takes as input a set of product variants and analyses them to discover and identify features, the feature location is the process of mapping features to their concrete implementation in the product variants. Therefore, compared to the feature identification process, the assumption in feature location is that the features are known upfront. Feature location processes in software families also use to assume that feature presence or absence in the product variants is known upfront. However, what is unknown is where exactly they are implemented inside the variants. Finally, feature re-engineering is the process that includes a transformation phase where the artefact variants are refactored to conform to an SPL approach. This includes extracting, for each feature, reusable assets from the artefact variants.

As already mentioned, the objective of feature location approaches is to map features to their concrete implementation parts inside the product variants. However, depending on the nature of the variants, this can concern code fragments in the case of source code [2,11,23,34], model fragments in the context of models [12,20] or software components in software architectures [1,14]. Therefore, existing techniques are composed of the following two phases: (1) *Abstraction*, where the different product variants are abstracted and represented as implementation elements; (2) *Location*, where algorithms analyse and compare the different product variants to create *groups of implementation elements*. These groups are to be associated with the sought features. Despite these two phases, feature location techniques differ in the following three aspects:

– **The way the product variants are abstracted and represented.**
   Indeed, each approach uses a specific formalism to represent product variants. For example AST nodes for source code [11], Atomic-Model-Element to represent model variants [20] or plugins in software architectures [1]. In addition, the granularity of the sought implementation elements may vary from coarse to fine [16]. Some use fine granularity using AST nodes that cover all source code statements while others use purposely a little bit bigger granularity using object-oriented building elements [2] like Salman *et al.* that only consider classes [25].

- **The proposed algorithms.** Each approach proposes its own algorithm to analyse product variants and identify the groups of elements that are related to features. For instance, Fischer *et al.* [11] used a static analysis algorithm. Other approaches use techniques from the field of Information Retrieval (IR). Xue *et al.* [33] and Salman *et al.* [26] proposed the use of Formal Concept Analysis (FCA) to group implementation elements and then, in a second step, the IR technique Latent Semantic Indexing (LSI) to map between these groups and the features. Salman *et al.* used Hierarchical Clustering to perform this second step [25].
- **The used case studies to evaluate and experiment the proposed technique.** The evaluation of each technique is often performed using its own case study and with its own evaluation measures.

2.2   The Eclipse Project

The Eclipse community, with the support of the Eclipse Foundation, provides integrated development environments (IDE) targeting different developer profiles. The project IDEs cover the development needs of *Java, C/C++, JavaEE, Scout, Domain Specific Languages, Modeling, Rich Client Platforms, Remote Applications Platforms, Testing, Reporting, Parallel Applications* or for *Mobile Applications*. Following Eclipse terminology, each of the customized Eclipse IDEs is called an Eclipse **package**.

As the project evolves over time, new packages appear and some other ones disappear depending on the interest and needs of the community. For instance, in 2011 there were 12 packages while the next year 13 packages were available with the addition of one targeted to *Automotive Software* developers.

Continuing with Eclipse terminology, a *simultaneous release* (**release** hereafter) is a set of packages which are public under the supervision of the Eclipse Foundation. Every year, there is one main release, in June, which is followed by two service releases for maintenance purposes: SR1 and SR2 usually around September and February. For each release, the platform version changes and traditionally celestial bodies are used to name the releases, for example Luna for version 4.4 and Mars for version 4.5.

The packages present variation depending on the included and not-included **features**. For example, Eclipse package for Testers is the only one that includes the Jubula Functional Testing features. On the contrary, other features like the Java Development tools are shared by most of the packages. There are also common features for all the packages, like the Equinox features that implement the core functionality of the Eclipse architecture. The online documentation of each release provides a high-level information of the features that each package provides[1].

It is important to mention that in this work we are not interested in the variation among the releases (version 4.4, 4.5 and so on), known as *variation in time*, because this is related to software maintenance and evolution. We focus on

---

[1] https://eclipse.org/downloads/compare.php?release=kepler.

the variation of the different packages of a given release, known as *variation in space*, which is expressed in terms of included and not-included features. Each package is different in order to support the needs of the targeted developer profile by including only the appropriate features.

Eclipse is feature oriented and based on **plugins**. Each feature consists of a set of plugins that are the actual implementation of the feature. Table 1 shows an example of feature with four plugins as implementation elements that, if included in an Eclipse package, adds support for a versioning system based on CVS. At technical level, the actual features of a package can be found within a folder called *features*. This folder contains meta-information regarding the installed features including the list of plugins associated to each of the features. Each feature has an id, a name and a description as written by the feature providers of the Eclipse community. A plugin has an id and a name written by the plugin providers but it does not have a description.

Table 2 presents data regarding the evolution of the Eclipse releases over the years. In particular, it presents the total number of packages, features and plugins per release. To illustrate the distribution of packages and features in the project, Fig. 1 depicts a matrix of the different Eclipse Kepler SR2 packages.

Table 1. Eclipse feature example

Feature
id: org.eclipse.cvs
name: Eclipse CVS Client
description: Eclipse CVS Client (binary runtime and user documentation).

Plugin id	Plugin name
org.eclipse.cvs	Eclipse CVS Client
org.eclipse.team.cvs.core	CVS Team Provider Core
org.eclipse.team.cvs.ssh2	CVS SSH2
org.eclipse.team.cvs.ui	CVS Team Provider UI

Table 2. Eclipse releases and their number of packages, features and plugins

Year	Release	Packages	Features	Plugins
2008	Europa Winter	4	91	484
2009	Ganymede SR2	7	291	1,290
2010	Galileo SR2	10	341	1,658
2011	Helios SR2	12	320	1,508
2012	Indigo SR2	12	347	1,725
2013	Juno SR2	13	406	2,008
2014	Kepler SR2	12	437	2,043
2015	Luna SR2	13	533	2,377

Fig. 1. Eclipse Kepler SR2 packages and a mapping to their 437 features

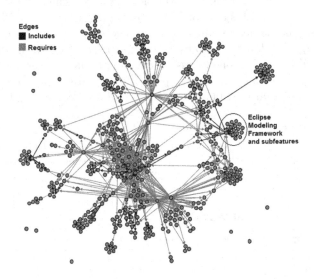

Fig. 2. Features of Eclipse Kepler SR2 and their dependencies

In this figure, a black box denotes the presence of a feature (horizontal axis) in a package (vertical axis). We observe that some features are present in all the packages while others are specific to only few, one or two, packages. The 437 features are alphabetically ordered by their id and, for instance, the feature *Eclipse CVS Client*, tagged in Fig. 1, is present in all of the packages except in the *Automotive Software* package.

Features, as in most of the feature oriented systems, have dependencies among them. *Includes* is the Eclipse terminology to define subfeatures and *Requires* means that there is a functional dependency between the features. Figure 2 shows the dependencies between all the features of Eclipse Kepler SR2. We tagged in Fig. 2 some features and subfeatures of the Eclipse Modeling Framework. Functional dependencies are mainly motivated by the existence of dependencies between the plugins of one feature with the plugins of other features.

Both Feature and Plugin dependencies are explicitly declared in their metadata. Figure 3 shows a very small excerpt of the dependency connections of the 2043 plugins of Eclipse Kepler SR2. Concretely, this excerpt shows the dependencies of the four CVS plugins presented in Table 1.

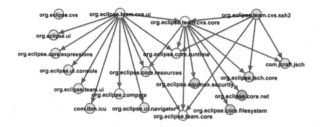

Fig. 3. Excerpt of plugin dependencies focusing on the dependencies of CVS plugins

3   Eclipse as a Standard Case Study Subject

Eclipse packages are an interesting candidate as a standard case study for a feature location benchmark. First, as mentioned in Sect. 1, it fulfils the requirement of providing the needed data to be used as ground truth. This ground truth can be extracted from features meta-information. Apart from this, Eclipse packages present other characteristics that make this case study interesting and challenging. This section aims to discuss these characteristics.

The relation between the number of available packages in the different Eclipse releases and the number of different features is not balanced. In fact, the number of available product variants has been shown to be an important factor for feature location techniques [11]. The limited number of packages and the big amount of features make the Eclipse case study challenging. The granularity of the implementation elements (plugins) is very coarse if we compare it with source code AST nodes, however, the number of plugins is still reasonably high. In Eclipse Kepler SR2, the total of plugins with different ids is 2043 with an average of 609 plugins per Eclipse package and a standard deviation of 192.

Eclipse feature and plugin providers have created their own natural language corpora. The feature and plugin names (and the description in the case of the features) can be categorized as meaningful names [24] enabling the use of several IR techniques. Also, the dependencies between features and dependencies between implementation elements have been used in feature location techniques. For example, in source code, program dependence analysis has been used by exploiting program dependence graphs [7]. Acher *et al.* [1] also leveraged architecture and plugin dependencies. As presented in previous section, Eclipse also has dependencies between features and dependencies between plugins enabling their exploitation during feature location.

There are properties that can be considered as "noise" that are common in real scenarios. Some of them can be considered as non-conformities in feature specification [31]. A case study without "noise" should be considered as a very optimistic case study. In Eclipse Kepler SR2, 8 plugins do not have a name and different plugins from the same feature have also exactly the same names. There are also 177 plugins which are associated to more than one feature. Thereby the features' plugin sets are not completely disjoint. These plugins are mostly related to libraries for common functionalities that they were not included as required plugins but as a part of the feature itself. In addition, 40 plugins present in some of the variants are not declared in any feature. Also, in few cases, feature versions are different among packages of the same release.

Apart from the official releases, software engineering practitioners have created their own Eclipse packages. Therefore, also researchers can use their own packages or create variants with specific characteristics. Interest of analysing plugin-based or component-based software system families to exploit their feature variability has been shown in previous works [1,14,29]. For instance, experiences in an industrial case study were reported by Grünbacher et al. [14] where they performed manual feature location in Eclipse packages to extract an SPL that involved more than 20 package customizations per year.

4   Eclipse Feature Location Benchmarking Framework

EFLBench is aimed to be used with any set of Eclipse packages. The benchmark can be created from any set of Eclipse packages that can have additional features which are not part of any official release. However, to set a common scenario for research we recommend and propose the use of Eclipse Community releases.

Figure 4, in the top part, illustrates the mechanism for constructing the benchmark taking as input the Eclipse packages and automatically producing two outputs, (a) a Feature list with information about each feature name, description and the list of packages where it was present, and (b) a ground truth with the mapping between the features and the implementation elements which are the plugins.

Once the benchmark is constructed, the bottom part of Fig. 4 illustrates how it can be used through BUT4Reuse [21] where feature location techniques can be integrated. The Eclipse adapter, which is responsible for the variants abstraction phase, will be followed by the launch of the targeted feature location techniques. This process takes as input the Eclipse packages (excluding the *features* folder)

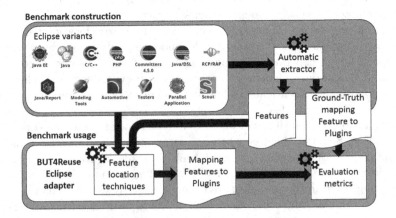

Fig. 4. EFLBench: Eclipse package variants as benchmark for feature location

and the feature list. The feature location technique produces a mapping between features and plugins that can be evaluated against the ground truth obtained in the benchmark construction phase.

The following subsections provide more details on the two phases.

4.1   Benchmark Construction

We implemented an automatic extractor of features information. The implementation elements of a feature are those plugins that are directly associated to this feature. From the 437 features of the Eclipse Kepler SR2, each one has an average of 5.23 plugins associated with. The standard deviation is 9.67. There is one outlier with 119 plugins which is the feature *BIRT Framework* present in the Reporting package. From the 437 features, there are 19 features that do not contain any plugins, so they are considered *abstract* features which are created just for grouping other features. For example, the feature *UML2 Extender SDK* (Software Development Kit) groups *UML2 End-User Features*, *Source for UML2 End-User Features*, *UML2 Documentation* and *UML2 Examples*.

Reproducibility is becoming quite easy by using benchmarks and common frameworks that launch and compare different techniques [30]. This practice, allows a valid performance comparison with all the implemented and future techniques. BUT4Reuse public repository includes EFLBench and its automatic extractor.

4.2   Benchmark Usage

During the product abstraction phase, the implemented Eclipse adapter decomposes any Eclipse installation in a set of plugins by visiting and analysing the Eclipse installation file structure. The plugin elements contain information about their id, name as well as their dependency to other plugin elements.

At technical level, BUT4Reuse provides an extension point and interface to easily include feature location techniques[2]. After feature location, it calculates the *precision* and *recall* for each feature location technique which are classical evaluation metrics in IR studies (e.g., [25]). We explain precision and recall, two metrics that complements each other, in the context of EFLBench. A feature location technique assigns a set of plugins to each feature. In this set, there can be some plugins that are actually correct according to the ground-truth, those are *true positives* (TP). TPs are also referred to as *hit*. On the set of plugins retrieved by the feature location technique for each feature, there can be other plugins that do not belong to the feature, those are *false positives* (FP) which are also referred to as *false alarms*. Precision is the percentage of correctly retrieved plugins from the total of retrieved plugins by the feature location technique. A precision of 100 % means that the ground truth of the plugins assigned to a feature and the retrieved set from the feature location technique are the same and no "extra" plugins were included. The formula of precision is as follows:

---

[2] Instructions to integrate feature location techniques in BUT4Reuse: https://github.com/but4reuse/but4reuse/wiki/ExtensionsManual.

$$precision = \frac{TP}{TP + FP} = \frac{plugins\,hit}{plugins\,hit\,+\,plugins\,false\,alarm}$$

According to the ground truth there can be some plugins that are not included in the retrieved set, meaning that they are *miss*. Those plugins are *false negatives* (FN). Recall is the percentage of correctly retrieved plugins from the set of the ground-truth. A recall of 100 % means that all the plugins of the ground-truth were assigned to the feature. The formula of recall is as follows:

$$recall = \frac{TP}{TP + FN} = \frac{plugins\,hit}{plugins\,hit\,+\,plugins\,miss}$$

Precision and recall are calculated for each feature. In order to have a global result of the precision and recall we use the mean of all the features. Finally, BUT4Reuse reports the *time* spent for the feature location technique. With this information, the time performance of different techniques can be compared.

5   Example of EFLBench Usage

This section aims at presenting the possibilities of EFLBench by benchmarking four feature location techniques. The four techniques are using Formal Concept Analysis (FCA) and three of them are using natural language processing (NLP). Before enumerating the four techniques, we briefly present FCA and the used NLP algorithms.

5.1   Background Algorithms

For the four techniques we used FCA [13] for the identification of an initial set of groups of implementation elements. We will refer to the identification of this initial set as block identification [21]. FCA groups elements that share common attributes. A detailed explanation about FCA formalism in the same context of block identification can be found in Al-Msie'deen *et al.* [2] and Shatnawi *et al.* [29]. FCA uses a *formal context* as input. In our case, the entities of the formal context are the Eclipse packages and the attributes (binary) are the presence or not of each of the plugins. With this input, FCA discovers a set of *concepts*. The concepts which contain at least one plugin (non empty concept intent in FCA terminology) is considered as a block. For example, in Eclipse Kepler SR2, FCA-based block identification identifies 60 blocks with an average of 34 plugins per block and a standard deviation of 54 plugins. In Eclipse Europa Winter, with only 4 packages, only 6 blocks are identified with an average of 80 plugins each and a standard deviation of 81. Given the low number of Eclipse packages, FCA identifies a low number of blocks. The number of blocks is specially low if we compare it with the actual number of features that we aim to locate. For example 60 blocks in Kepler SR2 against its 437 features. The higher the number of Eclipse packages, the most likely FCA will be able to distinguish different blocks. At technical level, we implemented FCA for block identification using ERCA [10].

In the approaches where we use IR techniques, we did not make use of the feature or plugin ids. In order to extract the meaningful words from both features (name and description) and elements (plugin names), we used two well established techniques in the IR field:

- Parts-of-speech tags remover: These techniques analyse and tag words depending on their role in the text. The objective is to filter and keep only the potentially relevant words. For example, conjunctions (f.e. "and"), articles (f.e. "the") or prepositions (f.e. "in") are frequent and may not add relevant information. As example, we consider the following feature name and description: "*Eclipse Scout Project. Eclipse Scout is ~~a~~ business application framework ~~that~~ supports desktop, web ~~and~~ mobile frontends. ~~This~~ feature contains ~~the~~ Scout core runtime components.*". We apply Part-of-Speech Tagger techniques using OpenNLP [3].
- Stemming: This technique reduces the words to their root. The objective is to unify words for not to consider them as unrelated. For example "playing" will be stemmed to "play" or "tools" to "tool". Instead of keeping the root, we keep the word with greater number of occurrences to replace the involved words. As example, in the Graphiti feature name and description we find "*[...] Graphiti supports the fast and easy creation of unified **graphical** tools, which can **graphically** display[...]*" so graphical and graphically is considered the same word as their shared stem is *graphic*. Regarding the implementation, we used the Snowball steamer [22].

5.2   Feature Location Techniques

We explain the four examples of feature location techniques. Next Sect. 5.3 will be dedicated to present the results of using EFLBench.

FCA and Strict Feature-Specific (SFS) location: FCA is used for block identification. Then, for feature location we use *Strict Feature-Specific location* that consider the following assumptions: A feature is located in a block when (1) the block always appears in the artefacts that implements this feature and (2) the block never appears in any artefact that does not implement this feature. Using this technique, the implementation of a feature is located in the plugin elements of the whole block. The principles of this feature location technique is similar to locating distinguishing features using diff sets [23]. In the Eclipse packages case, notice that, given the low number of variants and identified blocks, a lot of features will be located for the same block. In Eclipse Kepler SR2, an average of 7.25 features are located for each of the 60 blocks with a standard deviation of 13.71 features.

FCA and SFS and Shared term: The intuition behind this technique is first to group features and blocks with FCA and SFS and then apply a "search" of the feature words inside the elements of the block to discard elements that may be completely unrelated. For each association between feature to a block, we keep, for this feature, only the elements of the block which have at least one meaningful name shared with the feature. In other words, we keep the elements which *term frequency* (tf) between feature and element (featureElementTF) is greater than 0. For clarification, featureElementTF is defined as follows being f the feature, e the element and *tf* a method that just counts the number of times that a given term appears in a given list of terms:

$$featureElementTF(f, e) = \sum_{term_i \in e.terms} tf(term_i, f.terms)$$

FCA and SFS and Term frequency: FCA is used for block identification and then SFS as in the previous approaches. Then, the intuition of this technique is that all the features assigned to a block competes for the block elements. The feature (or features in case of drawback) with higher *featureElementTF* will keep the elements while the other features will not consider this element as part of it.

FCA and SFS and tf-idf: FCA and SFS are used as in the previous approaches. The features also compete in this case for the elements of the block but a different weight is used for each word of the feature. This weight (or score) is calculated through the *term frequency - inverse document frequency* (tf-idf) value of the set of features that are competing. tf-idf is a well known technique in IR [27]. In our context, the intuition is that words that appear more frequent through the features may not be as important as less frequent words. For example "Core", "Client" or "Documentation" are maybe more frequent across features but "CVS" or "BIRT", being less frequent, are more relevant, informative or discriminating. As in the previous approach, the feature (or features) with higher *featureElementScore* will keep the elements while the other features will not consider them. The *featureElementScore* formula is defined as follows, being F the set of features that are competing for the block element.

$$featureElementScore(f, e, F) = \sum_{term_i \in e.terms} tfidf(term_i, f, F)$$

$$tfidf(term_i, f, F) = tf(term_i, f.terms) \times idf(term_i, F)$$

$$idf(term_i, F) = \log \left(\frac{|F|}{|\{f \in F : term_i \in f\}|} \right)$$

5.3   Results

We used the benchmark created with each of the Eclipse releases presented in Table 2. The experiments were launched using BUT4Reuse at commit ce3a002 (19 December 2015) which contains the presented feature location techniques. Detailed instructions for reproducibility are available[3]. We used a laptop Dell Latitude E6330 with a processor Intel(R) Core(TM) i7-3540M CPU@3.00 GHz with 8 GB RAM and Windows 7 64-bit.

After using the benchmark, we obtain the results shown in Table 3. *Precision* and *Recall* are the mean of all the features as discussed at the end of Sect. 4.2.

---

[3] https://github.com/but4reuse/but4reuse/wiki/Benchmarks

Table 3. Precision and recall of the different feature location techniques

Release	SFS		SFS+ST		SFS+TF		SFS+TFIDF	
	Precision	Recall	Precision	Recall	Precision	Recall	Precision	Recall
Europa Winter	6.51	99.33	11.11	85.71	12.43	58.69	13.07	53.72
Ganymede SR2	5.13	97.33	10.36	87.72	11.65	64.31	12.80	52.70
Galileo SR2	7.13	93.39	10.92	82.01	11.82	60.50	12.45	53.51
Helios SR2	9.70	91.63	16.04	80.98	25.97	63.70	29.46	58.39
Indigo SR2	9.58	92.80	15.72	82.63	19.79	59.72	22.86	57.57
Juno SR2	10.83	91.41	19.08	81.75	25.97	61.92	24.89	60.82
Kepler SR2	9.53	91.14	16.51	83.82	26.38	62.66	26.86	57.15
Luna SR2	7.72	89.82	13.87	82.72	22.72	56.67	23.73	51.31
Mean	*8.26*	*93.35*	*14.20*	*83.41*	*19.59*	*61.02*	*20.76*	*55.64*

The results in terms of precision are not satisfactory in the presented feature location techniques. This suggests that the case study is challenging. Also we noticed that there are no very relevant differences in the results of these techniques among the different Eclipse releases. As discussed before, given the few amount of Eclipse packages under consideration, FCA is able to distinguish blocks which may actually correspond to a high number of features. For example, all the plugins that correspond specifically to the Eclipse Modeling package, will be grouped in one block while many features are involved.

The first location technique (FCA + SFS) does not assume meaningful names given that no IR technique is used. The features are located in the elements of a whole block obtaining a high recall. Eclipse feature names and descriptions are probably written by the same community of developers that create the plugins and decide their names. In the approaches using IR techniques, the authors expected a higher increment of precision without a loss of recall but the results suggest that certain divergence exists between the vocabulary used at feature level and at implementation level.

Regarding the time performance, Table 4 shows, in milliseconds, the time spent for the different releases. *Adapt* time corresponds to the time to abstract the Eclipse packages into a set of plugin elements and get their information. The FCA time corresponds to the time for block identification. Then, the following columns show the time of the different feature location techniques. We can observe that the time performance is not a limitation of these techniques as they take around half a minute maximum.

It is out of the scope of the paper to propose innovative feature location techniques. The objective is to present the benchmark usage, show that quick feedback from feature location techniques can be obtained in the Eclipse releases case studies. In addition, we provide empirical results of four feature location techniques that can be used as baseline. Other block identification approaches can be used to further split the groups obtained by FCA as for example the

Table 4. Time performance in milliseconds for feature location

Release	Adapt	FCA	SFS	SFS+ST	SFS+TF	SFS+TFIDF
Europa Winter	2,397	75	6	2,581	2,587	4,363
Ganymede SR2	7,568	741	56	11,861	11,657	23,253
Galileo SR2	10,832	1,328	107	17,990	17,726	35,236
Helios SR2	11,844	1,258	86	5,654	5,673	12,742
Indigo SR2	12,942	1,684	100	8,782	8,397	16,753
Juno SR2	16,775	2,757	197	7,365	7,496	14,002
Kepler SR2	16,786	2,793	173	8,586	8,776	16,073
Luna SR2	17,841	3,908	233	15,238	15,363	33,518
Mean	*12,123*	*1,818*	*120*	*9,757*	*9,709*	*19,493*

clustering proposed by Salman *et al.* [25]. Other feature location techniques can make use of the available plugin and feature dependencies information as presented in Figs. 2 and 3. Other works can evaluate the filtering of non-relevant domain specific words for the IR techniques (f.e. "Eclipse" or "feature") or even make use of an Eclipse domain ontology to refine feature location. Finally, meta-techniques for feature location can be proposed inspired by *ensemble learning* from the data mining research field. These meta-techniques can use multiple feature location techniques, providing better results than using each of them alone.

6   Related Work

In SPL engineering several benchmarks and common test subjects have been proposed. Herrejon *et al.* proposed evaluating SPL technologies on a common artefact, a Graph Product Line [17], which variability features are familiar to any computer engineer. The same authors proposed a benchmark for combinatorial interaction testing techniques for SPLs [18]. Betty [28] is a benchmark for evaluating automated feature model analysis techniques, which has long history in software engineering research [6]. Feature location on software families is also becoming more mature with a relevant proliferation of techniques. Therefore, benchmarking frameworks to support the evolution of this field are in need.

Many different case studies have been used for evaluating feature location in software families [5]. For instance, ArgoUML variants [8] have been extensively used. However, none of the presented case studies have been proposed as a benchmark except the variants of the Linux kernel by Xing *et al.* [32]. This benchmark considers 12 variants of the Linux kernel from which a ground truth is extracted with the traceability of 2400 features to code parts. However, even if the Linux kernel can be considered as an existing benchmark, EFLBench is complementary to foster feature location research because (a) it maps to a project that is plugin-based, while Linux considers C code, and (b) the characteristics of the Eclipse natural language corpora is different from the Linux kernel corpora. This last point is important because it has a major influence on the IR-based feature location techniques. Finally, using the Linux kernel benchmark, the ground truth may be also constructed but there is no framework to support the experiment. EFLBench is associated with BUT4Reuse which integrates feature location techniques making easier to control and reproduce the settings of the studied techniques.

7   Conclusion

We have presented EFLBench, a framework and a benchmark for supporting research on feature location. The benchmark is based on the Eclipse releases and is designed to support research on software reuse in the context of software product lines. Existing and future techniques dealing with this problem can find a challenging playground that is: (a) real, (b) contains a valid ground-truth and (c) is directly reproducible. We also demonstrated example results of four approaches using the EFLBench.

As further work we aim to create a parametrizable generator for Eclipse packages. This generator will combine different features in order to use the benchmark in special and predefined characteristics. We also aim to generalize the usage of feature location benchmarks inside BUT4Reuse providing extensibility points for other case studies. Finally, we plan to use the benchmark in order to test and report existing and innovative feature location techniques while also encouraging the research community on using it as part of their evaluation.

Acknowledgments. Supported by the National Research Fund Luxembourg (FNR), under the AFR grant 7898764.

References

1. Acher, M., Cleve, A., Collet, P., Merle, P., Duchien, L., Lahire, P.: Extraction and evolution of architectural variability models in plugin-based systems. Softw. Syst. Model. **13**(4), 1367–1394 (2014)
2. AL-Msie'deen, R.F., Seriai, A., Huchard, M., Urtado, C., Vauttier, S., Salman, H.E.: Feature location in a collection of software product variants using formal concept analysis. In: Favaro, J., Morisio, M. (eds.) ICSR 2013. LNCS, vol. 7925, pp. 302–307. Springer, Heidelberg (2013)
3. Apache: Opennlp (2010). http://opennlp.apache.org
4. Apel, S., Batory, D.S., Kästner, C., Saake, G.: Feature-Oriented Software Product Lines - Concepts and Implementation. Springer, Heidelberg (2013)
5. Assunção, W.K.G., Vergilio, S.R.: Feature location for software product line migration: a mapping study. In: International Software Product Line Conference: Companion Volume for Workshop, Tools and Demo papers, SPLC, pp. 52–59 (2014)
6. Benavides, D., Segura, S., Cortés, A.R.: Automated analysis of feature models 20 years later: a literature review. Inf. Syst. **35**(6), 615–636 (2010)

7. Chen, K., Rajlich, V.: Case study of feature location using dependence graph, after 10 years. In: The 18th IEEE International Conference on Program Comprehension, ICPC 2010, Braga, Minho, Portugal, 30 June–2 July, pp. 1–3 (2010)
8. Couto, M.V., Valente, M.T., Figueiredo, E.: Extracting software product lines: a case study using conditional compilation. In: European Conference on Software Maintenance and Reengineering, CSMR 2011, pp. 191–200 (2011)
9. Dubinsky, Y., Rubin, J., Berger, T., Duszynski, S., Becker, M., Czarnecki, K.: An exploratory study of cloning in industrial software product lines. In: 17th European Conference on Software Maintenance and Reengineering, CSMR 2013, Genova, Italy, 5–8 March, pp. 25–34. IEEE Computer Society (2013)
10. Falleri, J.R., Dolques, X.: Erca - eclipse's relational concept analysis (2010). https://code.google.com/p/erca/
11. Fischer, S., Linsbauer, L., Lopez-Herrejon, R.E., Egyed, A.: Enhancing clone-and-own with systematic reuse for developing software variants. In: Proceedings of International Conference on Software Maintenance and Evolution (ICSME 2014), pp. 391–400 (2014)
12. Font, J., Ballarín, M., Haugen, O., Cetina, C.: Automating the variability formalization of a model family by means of common variability language. In: SPLC, pp. 411–418 (2015)
13. Ganter, B., Wille, R.: Formal Concept Analysis: Mathematical Foundations, 1st edn. Springer-Verlag New York Inc., Secaucus (1997)
14. Grünbacher, P., Rabiser, R., Dhungana, D., Lehofer, M.: Model-based customization and deployment of eclipse-based tools: Industrial experiences. In: International Conference on Automated Software Engineering (ASE), pp. 247–256 (2009)
15. Kang, K.C., Cohen, S.G., Hess, J.A., Novak, W.E., Peterson, A.S.: Feature-oriented domain analysis (foda) feasibility study. Technical report, Carnegie-Mellon University Software Engineering Institute (1990)
16. Kästner, C., Apel, S., Kuhlemann, M.: Granularity in software product lines. In: Proceedings of the 30th International Conference on Software Engineering (ICSE), pp. 311–320 (2008)
17. Lopez-Herrejon, R.E., Batory, D.: A standard problem for evaluating product-line methodologies. In: Dannenberg, R.B. (ed.) GCSE 2001. LNCS, vol. 2186, pp. 10–24. Springer, Heidelberg (2001)
18. Lopez-Herrejon, R.E., Ferrer, J., Chicano, F., Haslinger, E.N., Egyed, A., Alba, E.: Towards a benchmark and a comparison framework for combinatorial interaction testing of software product lines. CoRR abs/1401.5367 (2014)
19. Lopez-Herrejon, R.E., Ziadi, T., Martinez, J., Thurimella, A.K., Acher, M.: Third international workshop on reverse variability engineering (REVE 2015). In: Proceedings of the 19th International Conference on Software Product Line, SPLC 2015, Nashville, TN, USA, 20–24 July, p. 394 (2015)
20. Martinez, J., Ziadi, T., Bissyandé, T.F., Klein, J., Traon, Y.L.: Automating the extraction of model-based software product lines from model variants. In: ASE 2015, Lincoln, Nebraska, USA (2015)
21. Martinez, J., Ziadi, T., Bissyandé, T.F., Klein, J., Traon, Y.L.: Bottom-up adoption of software product lines: a generic and extensible approach. In: Proceedings of International Conference on Software Product Line, SPLC 2015, pp. 101–110 (2015)
22. Porter, M.F.: Snowball: A language for stemming algorithms, http://snowball.tartarus.org/. Accessed 19 Nov 2015

23. Rubin, J., Chechik, M.: Locating distinguishing features using diff sets. In: IEEE/ACM International Conference on Automated Software Engineering, ASE 2012, Essen, Germany, 3–7 September, pp. 242–245 (2012)
24. Rubin, J., Chechik, M.: A survey of feature location techniques. In: Domain Engineering, Product Lines, Languages, and Conceptual Models, pp. 29–58 (2013)
25. Salman, H.E., Seriai, A., Dony, C.: Feature location in a collection of product variants: combining information retrieval and hierarchical clustering. In: International Conference on Software Engineering and Knowledge Engineering, SEKE, pp. 426–430 (2014)
26. Salman, H.E., Seriai, A., Dony, C.: Feature-to-code traceability in a collection of software variants: combining formal concept analysis and information retrieval. In: International Conference on Information Reuse and Integration, IRI, pp. 209–216 (2013)
27. Salton, G., Wong, A., Yang, C.S.: A vector space model for automatic indexing. Commun. ACM **18**(11), 613–620 (1975)
28. Segura, S., Galindo, J.A., Benavides, D., Parejo, J.A., Cortés, A.R.: Betty: benchmarking and testing on the automated analysis of feature models. In: Proceedings of Sixth International Workshop on Variability Modelling of Software-Intensive Systems, Leipzig, Germany, 25–27 January, pp. 63–71 (2012)
29. Shatnawi, A., Seriai, A., Sahraoui, H.: Recovering architectural variability of a family of product variants. In: Schaefer, I., Stamelos, I. (eds.) ICSR 2015. LNCS, vol. 8919, pp. 17–33. Springer, Heidelberg (2014)
30. Sim, S.E., Easterbrook, S.M., Holt, R.C.: Using benchmarking to advance research: a challenge to software engineering. In: Proceedings of the 25th International Conference on Software Engineering, Portland, Oregon, USA, 3–10 May, pp. 74–83 (2003)
31. Souza, I.S., Fiaccone, R., de Oliveira, R.P., Almeida, E.S.D.: On the relationship between features granularity and non-conformities in software product lines: an exploratory study. In: 27th Brazilian Symposium on Software Engineering, SBES 2013, Brasilia, Brazil, 1–4 October, pp. 147–156 (2013)
32. Xing, Z., Xue, Y., Jarzabek, S.: A large scale linux-kernel based benchmark for feature location research. In: Proceedings of International Conference on Software Engineering, ICSE, pp. 1311–1314 (2013)
33. Xue, Y., Xing, Z., Jarzabek, S.: Feature location in a collection of product variants. In: Proc. of Working Conference on Reverse Engineering, WCRE 2012, pp. 145–154 (2012)
34. Ziadi, T., Henard, C., Papadakis, M., Ziane, M., Traon, Y.L.: Towards a language-independent approach for reverse-engineering of software product lines. In: Symposium on Applied Computing, SAC 2014, pp. 1064–1071 (2014)

Java Extensions for Design Pattern Instantiation

André L. Santos[(⊠)] and Duarte Coelho

Instituto Universitário de Lisboa (ISCTE–IUL), ISTAR, Av. Das Forças Armadas,
Edifício II ISCTE, 1649-026 Lisbon, Portugal
andre.santos@iscte.pt, duarte.goncalo.coelho@gmail.com

Abstract. Design patterns are not easily traceable in source code, leading to maintainability and comprehension issues, while the instantiation of certain patterns involves generalizable boiler-plate code. We provide high-level language constructs addressing design patterns that transform source code by injecting a substantial part of their implementation at compile time. We developed proof of concept extensions addressing widely used design patterns, namely Singleton, Visitor, Decorator, and Observer, using annotations as the means to extend Java. We describe our Java annotations to support these design patterns and the associated source code transformations, demonstrating that it is possible to significantly reduce the necessary code to instantiate a pattern through the use of high-level constructs.

1 Introduction

Design patterns are widely used in software development and became an essential element in software reuse. Design patterns are language-independent, but paradigm-dependent, since they rely on certain programming language constructs that often are available in certain programming paradigms only. The focus of our work is on object-oriented design patterns [8].

Design patterns are used to aid the design of systems, often driven by variability and extensibility requirements. Issues related to maintainability and evolution may occur given that pattern instantiations are interleaved with the system domain and "fade away" into the source code [15]. This implies that pattern instantiations are hard to trace, mainly because they have no first-class representation in the source code in terms of programming constructs. Further, the presence of design patterns in source code may hinder understandability [13]. Certain patterns require substantial boiler-plate code to be written, as for instance, the abstract decorator class role in the Decorator pattern [8] that delegates all the calls to an enclosing reference (highly generalizable code).

Apart from a few exceptions, languages do not have dedicated constructs for representing design patterns in the source code. As a counter-example, the Iterator pattern [8] is supported by the libraries of mainstream object-oriented languages, such as Java and C#. On the other hand, some patterns do not make sense in the context of certain programming languages, simply because the

G.M. Kapitsaki and E. Santana de Almeida (Eds.): ICSR 2016, LNCS 9679, pp. 284–299, 2016.
DOI: 10.1007/978-3-319-35122-3_19

language constructs provide the means for solving the problem directly (e.g., the Visitor pattern [8] is not relevant in a language with multiple method dispatch).

Some approaches assist developers in the instantiation of patterns either through external programming languages (e.g., [1,2,10]) or IDE-integrated tools to guide and automate the process of implementing them through code generation (e.g., [9]). The former require using other programming paradigms, whereas the latter do not address pattern representation given that the trace is lost after the pattern is instantiated in the source code. The fact that there are tools capable of generating code that instantiates design patterns evidences that patterns are generalizable into higher-level abstractions, including dedicated language constructs (see a debate in [6]).

In this paper we describe an approach for generalizing design pattern instantiations for Java, providing high-level programming language constructs for instantiating them using annotations. As a proof of concept, we implemented support for widely used patterns, such as Singleton, Visitor, Decorator, and Observer, relying on an existing open-source project called Lombok[1]. This project provides the infrastructure for extending Java with generative annotations that perform compile-time AST transformations to inject class members and statements. Lombok provides extensions that enable developers to write code in a terse manner, as for instance support for getter and setter method injections, as well as some design patterns such as Value Object [7] and Builder [8]. We build on the Lombok infrastructure to address other design patterns that were not previously addressed, developing an extension that we refer to as JEDI[2].

Although the idea of having language constructs for design patterns is not new (e.g., [2,6]), we are not aware of other approaches that address this problem relying only on object-orientation in Java, that is, with no resort to additional programming paradigms or external tools. We demonstrate the feasibility of the approach, showing that significant amounts of pattern-related code can be generated from simple declarations embodied in the form of annotations. These have the advantage of being dedicated language constructs that are traceable, while simultaneously serving the purpose of documentation. Empirical experiments have shown that documenting patterns in the source code is beneficial for system maintenance [14]. Therefore, besides facilitating pattern instantiation, the annotations also mitigate traceability and maintainability issues.

This paper proceeds as follows. Section 2 introduces a running example that is used throughout the paper. Section 3 presents project Lombok and briefly explains its infrastructure for transforming classes. Section 4 describes the Java extensions that we developed to support design patterns. Section 5 analyzes the transformations performed by our extensions. Section 6 discusses the benefits and limitations of our approach. Section 7 discusses related work, and Sect. 8 presents our conclusions.

---

[1] www.projectlombok.org.

[2] Java Extensions for Design pattern Instantiation. Available at github.com/andre-santos-pt/lombok-jedi.

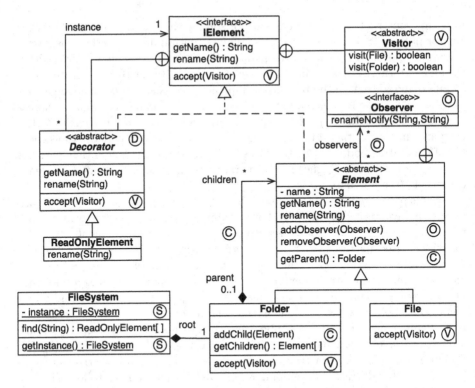

Fig. 1. UML class diagram describing the running example: a file system with files and folders. The operation compartments are divided according to the associated design pattern and the letter labels identify the pattern to which the types or members relate to (Singleton, Composite, Visitor, Decorator, Observer). Notation: $a \oplus \rightarrow b$ denotes that b is a nested classifier of a (in programming these are mapped to inner classes/interfaces).

2   Running Example

In order to illustrate our approach we introduce a small running example involving several design patterns (see Fig. 1), designed intentionally to be simple for clarity of presentation, and on the other hand, appropriate to demonstrate all of our Java extensions. Section 4 describes how our annotations are able to address the instantiation of each pattern, except for Composite, which we omit due to space constraints.

The example consists of a FileSystem that structures its Elements in a tree. The FileSystem class can only have a single instance (Singleton pattern), and holds a reference to the root Folder. The singleton property is ensured by having a static field instance that holds the unique instance, which can be obtained through the static operation getInstance() (there are no public constructors).

The class Folder is an Element that can have Files (leafs) and other Folders as children (Composite pattern). The methods for adding children and obtaining an Element's parent relate to the instantiation of this pattern.

The interface IElement is yet a more abstract representation of Element objects. The FileSystem tree is traversable to iterate over its Files and Folders (Visitor pattern), by providing a specialization of the abstract class IElement.Visitor. The instantiation of this pattern requires the accept method to be defined by every visitable node (File and Folder).

Elements may be wrapped in read-only views that disallow renaming (Decorator pattern) using the class ReadOnlyElement. The instantiation of this pattern, since there may be other kinds of decorator objects, involves the abstract class IElement.Decorator, which implements IElement and holds a reference to the decorated instance, delegating every call to it. Notice that the accept method pertaining to the Visitor pattern also had to be included here for interface compatibility. As an example of a concrete decorator, the class ReadOnlyElement overrides the rename(...) operation to throw a runtime exception (disallowed operation).

Finally, the Element objects are observable with respect to rename events (Observer pattern) through the registration of Element.Observer objects. The methods for adding and removing observers pertain to this pattern, as well has the association observers.

Notice that in this example the elements pertaining to the essence of the domain that the model is capturing (i.e. the file system structure) are clearly outnumbered by infrastructural elements that are necessary to implement the desired functionally and extensibility properties. The Composite pattern is the only pattern whose elements inherently pertain to the domain. This means that the remaining patterns "bloat" the design with several elements that are essentially technical (*accidents* in software engineering [3]).

3   Project Lombok and AST Transformations

Lombok is an open source project whose main aim consists of reducing the amount of boiler-plate code that writing Java programs often involves. The goal is achieved through annotations that work as language extensions. At compile time, Lombok annotation processors interfere with the AST of the classes where annotations are present in order to perform transformations, such as introducing members (fields, methods, types) or modifying existing ones. The transformed ASTs are in turn compiled normally. Lombok inspired our work and served as the infrastructure for the realization of our language extensions.

Figure 2 illustrates two of the simplest Lombok annotations. The annotation @Getter has the purpose of injecting getter methods based on attributes, whereas the @NonNull injects null pointer validations on parameters. Hereinafter, when presenting examples of transformations, we include a box with the code that the programmer writes followed by another shadowed box that contains the code that actually compiles after the AST transformation, highlighting the injected code with gray color. Note that the programmer does not manipulate the source

```
public class Element {
  @Getter
  private String name;

  public void rename(@NonNull String name) {
    this.name = name;
  }
}
```

```
public class Element {
  @Getter
  private String name;

  public String getName() {
    return name;
  }

  public void rename(@NonNull String name) {
    if(name == null)
      throw new NullPointerException("...");
    this.name = name;
  }
}
```

Fig. 2. Example of Lombok extensions: Getter method injection (@Getter) and null pointer validation (@NonNull).

code of the transformed version of the classes. The injected members cannot be edited and are not even visible to the programmer. However, the injected members are accessible to other classes at compilation time, and hence, one may write code that uses them as if they have been manually written.

One of the key advantages of this approach is that the annotated classes become significantly less bloated, with fewer lines of code. Furthermore, annotations capture programmer intent with a dedicated construct (the annotation). The given example is rather simple, and hence, the amount of injected code is not impressive. However, in other cases such as the annotation for addressing the Value Object pattern [7], Lombok transforms classes so that the number of injected lines of code outnumbers manually written code by a factor greater than five for classes with a few attributes.

As portrayed by the Lombok authors, the technical solution may be regarded as a "hack", since Java annotations were not meant to affect program semantics. However, there are other approaches that rely on annotations as the means to mark parts of programs that are transformed by a third-party. For instance, transformations to enhance the class with concurrency control (e.g., [5]) or to perform runtime verifications (e.g., [11]). Lombok was designed for extensibility, enabling third-party developers to contribute with additional annotations and their associated AST transformations. We have used this extensibility mechanism to implement our Java extensions.

4   Java Extensions

We developed JEDI, a proof of concept implementation of Java extensions for design patterns. JEDI comprises a set of annotations whose names (including participant names) resemble the ones described in [8]. So far, we successfully addressed the patterns Singleton, Composite, Visitor, Decorator, and Observer. In this paper, we omit the description of Composite due to space constraints. The purpose of our annotations is not to fully automate the instantiation of design patterns, but instead to aid in their instantiation by providing constructs for their generalizable aspects. For each provided annotation we developed a Lombok handler that transforms the annotated classes. The transformation may involve injection or modification of fields, methods, or inner types (classes or interfaces).

The following subsections describe in detail how JEDI annotations can be used and the code transformations that are performed when applying them, using the example of Sect. 2. In some situations the injected code makes use of the @NonNull annotation (illustrated in Sect. 3) that would further trigger additional transformations, but whose result we do not expand for clarity and brevity of presentation.

4.1   Pattern Instantiation Properties

Before illustrating our annotations and the associated AST transformations, this section explains certain properties of the pattern instantiations that are important with respect to the use of the annotations in software development.

Validations. The annotation processors perform validations to ensure that the annotations are applied correctly and guarantee the correctness of the injected code. Without the validations the annotation placements would be fragile, since the annotations would not feel like language extensions if errors are not emitted when they are used incorrectly. For instance, given that the Singleton pattern requires that the class has no public constructors, there is a validation for checking this issue that emits a compile-time error in case of violation.

Priorities. Each annotation handler has a fixed priority that determines the order in which the transformations pertaining to the different annotations are performed on the types. This aspect is relevant since some patterns inject elements that are of interest to other patterns, and hence, have an effect on the associated transformation. For instance, the Decorator pattern has a higher priority than the Visitor pattern, given that it requires the decorated interface to be complete (Visitor adds operations to interfaces), so that the transformation addresses all of its methods.

Identifiers. All the identifiers of injected elements (fields, methods, or types) have default values that are either constant of inferred from other related elements. However, since design patterns are abstract solutions that are made concrete in a variety of situations, JEDI annotations were designed to offer a reasonable degree of adaptability allowing programmers to override the values for identifiers through annotation parameters. For instance, the default name for the operation for registering observers in the Observer pattern is by default "addObserver", but this name can be set to other value. Throughout the paper, all the examples of annotation usage consider default values for identifiers.

Bidirectional Traceability. The elements that are injected in the AST are themselves annotated with an annotation for bidirectional traceability purposes, so that every injected element can unambiguously be traced back to the annotation pattern that generated it. For clarity and brevity of presentation we do not include these annotations in the transformed code of the given examples.

4.2 Singleton Pattern

The singleton pattern is a solution that guarantees that there is a single instance of a given class at runtime [8]. The pattern is typically applied by storing the unique instance in a static field of the class that is accessed through a static method (that performs lazy instantiation), while the class has no public constructors available. In the example given in Sect. 2, the FileSystem class illustrates the Singleton pattern. The static field instance stores the unique instance, which is accessed through the static method getInstance().

We provide the @Singleton annotation to aid on implementing the Singleton pattern (see Fig. 3). This annotation can only be used on classes, implying the injection of the following elements: (a) a static field to store the singleton instance with the same type as the class, (b) an empty private constructor to override the default public parameterless constructor if none is defined, and (c) a static method to retrieve the singleton instance (initializing (a) on the first call using the parameterless constructor). The annotation validation ensures that the class has no public constructors.

```
@Singleton
public class FileSystem {
  ...
}
```

```
@Singleton
public class FileSystem {
  private static FileSystem instance; // (a)

  private FileSystem() { // (b)
  }

  public static synchronized FileSystem getInstance() { // (c)
    if(instance == null) {
      instance = new FileSystem();
    }
    return instance;
  }
  ...
}
```

Fig. 3. Singleton pattern support and transformations (@Singleton).

4.3 Visitor Pattern

The Visitor pattern is a solution to separate operations from an object structure [8]. The pattern instantiation is achieved by defining an abstract class, whose compatible objects are referred to as *visitors*. This class contains methods, often named visit and typically overloaded, that receive multiple object types (the visitable nodes) to which the nodes provide their instance. In the example of Sect. 2, the file system elements take the role of visitable nodes (Folder and File), whereas the abstract class Visitor has the visitor role.

We provide three related annotations to address the visitor pattern (see Fig. 4). The @Visitor annotation is used to mark an interface that represents the set of visitable nodes. It injects an inner abstract class (a), that contains a method visit(...) returning true for each of the visitable node types (b), which are marked with the annotation @Visitor.Node. The annotation validation ensures that these types are compatible with a type annotated with @Visitor. By injecting each visit(...) method, we solve the problem of having to define manually each operation, which is one of the visitor's implementation negative consequences [8]. Additionally, an accept(...) operation declaration is injected into the interface (c) with a parameter of type equal to (a).

Visitable nodes may have child visitable nodes. The annotation @Visitor.Children is used to mark the visitor node fields that store the children nodes of the current node, so that the visitor traversal can be propagated to them. The annotation validation ensures that type of the visitor children fields must be either of a visitor node or of a collection of visitor nodes (compatible with java.util.Collection). On each visitable node type an accept(...) method is injected whose body contains a call to the visit(...) operation (d). In case a visitor node has children, the method body also includes a loop for invoking the accept(...) operation on each child (e).

4.4 Decorator Pattern

The decorator pattern [8] is an alternative solution to inheritance comprising an abstract class that represents *decorator* objects (that conform to a given interface), containing a reference to an object to which all the interface calls are delegated. In the example given in Sect. 2, the class IElement.Decorator represents decorators of IElement objects.

Figure 5 demonstrates the application of our @Decorator annotation on the IElement interface. The annotation validation ensures that it can only be used on interfaces. The annotation injects an abstract class representing the abstract decorator that implements the annotated interface (a), composed of: (b) an instance field for storing a reference to the decorated object, (c) a public constructor that receives the reference to the decorated object, and (d) an implementation of every method of the interface where the calls are delegated to the decorated object. By generating all the delegating calls, we significantly reduce the lines of code that otherwise would have to be written and maintained manually. Notice that in this case the injection is performed after the Visitor injections (priority issue explained previously), and hence, the accept(Visitor) operation is considered in the abstract decorator class.

We also provide the @Wrapper annotation that is a variant with a slightly different purpose than the decorator pattern. This annotation follows a more

```
@Visitor
public interface IElement {
  ...
}
```

```
@Visitor
public interface IElement {
  ...
  // (a)
  abstract class Visitor {
    public boolean visit(File node) { // (b)
      return true;
    }

    public boolean visit(Folder node) { // (b)
      return true;
    }
  }

  void accept(Visitor visitor); // (c)
}
```

```
@Visitor.Node
public class File extends Element {
  ...
}
```

```
@Visitor.Node
public class File extends Element {
  ...
  public void accept(@NonNull Visitor visitor) { // (d)
    visitor.visit(this);
  }
}
```

```
@Visitor.Node
public class Folder extends Element {
  ...
  @Visitor.Children
  @Composite.Children
  private List<Element> children;
}
```

```
@Visitor.Node
public class Folder extends Element {
  ...
  @Visitor.Children
  private List<Element> children;  // (e)

  public void accept(@NonNull Visitor visitor) { // (d)
    if(visitor.visit(this)) {
      for(Element child : children) { // (e)
        child.accept(visitor);
      }
    }
  }
}
```

Fig. 4. Visitor pattern support and transformations (@Visitor, @Visitor.Node, @Visitor.Children).

```
@Decorator
@Visitor
public interface IElement {
  String getName();
  void rename(String name);
}
```

```
@Decorator
@Visitor
public interface IElement {
  String getName();
  void rename(String name);
  void accept(Visitor visitor);

  // (a)
  abstract class Decorator implements IElement {
    private final IElement instance;  // (b)

    public Decorator(@NonNull IElement instance) {  // (c)
      this.instance = instance;
    }

    public String getName() { // (d)
      return instance.getName();
    }

    public void rename(String name) { // (d)
      instance.rename(name);
    }

    public void accept(@NonNull Visitor visitor) { // (d)
      instance.accept(visitor);
    }
  }
}
```

Fig. 5. Decorator pattern support and transformations (@Decorator). This example evolves the Visitor example presented in Fig. 4, demonstrating the effect of annotation processing priority. Given that Visitors precede decorators, the injected Decorator takes into account the previously injected accept method (dashed line).

flexible approach regarding method delegation. Instead of generating an abstract class, we can directly annotate the class that wraps the decorated object. This alternative requires the class whose objects we want to decorate to be defined in an annotation parameter (e.g., @Wrapper(classType=Collection.class)). The annotation injects a delegating method for each public method of the target class that is not manually defined.

4.5   Observer Pattern

The Observer pattern [8] is an effective way for objects (subjects) to communicate events of interest to other objects (observers) without depending directly on their classes. In the example of Sect. 2, the method rename(String) from the class Element (subject) illustrates an observable event notified through observer objects that are compatible with the Element.Observer interface.

Figure 6 illustrates the annotations for the Observer pattern on the method rename(String) of the class Element of the running example. We provide the

```
public abstract class Element implements IElement {
  ...
  @Observable
  public void rename(@Observable.Notify String name) {
    @Observable.Notify
    String oldName = name;
    this.name = name;
  }
}
```

```
public abstract class Element implements IElement {
  ...
  // (a)
  public interface Observer {
    void renameNotify(String name, String oldName);
  }

  // (b)
  private final List<Observer> observers = new ArrayList<>();

  public void addObserver(@NonNull Observer o) { // (c)
    observers.add(o);
  }

  public void removeObserver(@NonNull Observer o) { // (c)
    observers.remove(o);
  }

  @Observable                              // (d)
  public void rename(@Observable.Notify final String name) {
    @Observable.Notify
    final String oldName = this.name; // (d)
    this.name = name;
    for(Observer observer : observers) {  // (e)
      observer.renameNotify(name, oldName);
    }
  }
}
```

Fig. 6. Observer pattern support and transformations (@Observable and @Observable.Notify).

@Observable and @Observable.Notify annotations to aid on the instantiation. The former is used to annotate methods whose execution represents an event of interest that we want to enable observer objects to be notified of. The latter is used to mark the variables that hold the objects that we wish to include in the notification. We only support the implementation pertaining to the subject participant, given that the aspects related to observer objects are problem-specific and are not suitable for being generalized.

The purpose of the @Observable annotation is to create the elements for collaboration between the subject's event types and its observers, by generating the following elements in the subject class: (a) an inner interface representing the observable event, (b) a field that stores a collection of objects of type (a) to which the event notification is sent, and (c) methods to subscribe and unsubscribe the notification of the event. The structure of the injected interface is derived from the annotated elements. Each observable event has a corresponding operation in the interface, whose parameters are determined by variables annotated with @Observable.Notify (either parameters or local variable declarations). Each of these variables is augmented with the final modifier in order to guarantee their immutability (d). Finally, the body of the methods annotated with @Observable is augmented with the event notification to its subscribers (e).

We offer the possibility of using an existing interface, rather than having a newly injected one. If an inner interface already exists with the same name, such an interface is considered instead. The parameters of the @Observable annotation allow programmers to further customize the implementation of the observer pattern, namely with respect to point of notification (beginning or end of the method), interface to be used (existing or injected), and association of interface operations to events.

5 Analysis

In this section we analyze our running example with a focus on the amount of injected lines of code (LOC), and the relation between each Java extension and the transformed code. Table 1 presents the classes of the running example that were used as illustration throughout Sect. 4, in terms of manually written LOC, and LOC that were effectively compiled considering the transformations (manual plus injected code). The amount of injected LOC is decomposed, discriminating the LOC according to the design pattern they pertain to. Recall that the injected code resembles what otherwise would be written by hand when not using our extensions. Looking back to Fig. 1, notice that every element in the diagram labeled with a letter was obtained through a transformation. Although we omitted the description of our support for the Composite pattern, here we include the result of applying it in the running example.

Table 1. Overview of the number of lines of code in the running example classes, discriminating between manually written and injected code, decomposing the latter according to the related pattern.

	Manual	Injected	Compiled	Singleton	Composite	Visitor	Decorator	Observer
FileSystem	17	**10**	27 (159 %)	10	-	-	-	-
Element	26	**22**	48 (185 %)	-	8	1	-	13
Folder	14	**17**	31 (221 %)	-	10	7	-	-
File	7	**7**	14 (200 %)	-	4	3	-	-
IElement	7	**24**	31 (443 %)	-	-	9	15	-
Total	71	**80**	151 (213 %)	10	22	20	15	13

The effective number of LOC that define the classes is significantly higher than the manual code, more than twice in this example. This factor is by no means generalizable, given that the domain elements of the example were minimal, and hence, the weight of the injected code is high. Some of the transformations perform an injection whose size in terms of LOC is constant despite the elements where the annotations are applied, whereas the injected code of other transformations grows linearly with the size of the annotated elements. The latter are more powerful because they spare more effort when writing code, facilitate maintenance, and reduce the size of files significantly. The former are not as beneficial with this respect, but nevertheless, share the advantage of having a dedicated language construct that consists of an unambiguous representation of the pattern (traceability), which is guaranteed to be instantiated uniformly.

The Singleton extension is an example of a constant transformation, given that no matter how large is the annotated class, the injected code always has the same size. The value of 10 injected LOC for FileSystem will be the same in every other class. Both the Composite and Observer extensions fall into this category, too. On the other hand, the Visitor and Decorator extensions are cases where the larger the number of elements is (visitor nodes and interface operations, respectively), the larger the injected code. Notice the case of IElement where these two patterns were applied, resulting in an effective number of LOC than is more that four times larger than the manually written code. Therefore, these extensions are more powerful in terms of the transformation of source code.

6   Discussion

The novelty of our approach does not pertain to the form of instantiating design patterns, but instead in the automatization of their instantiation according to common idioms. Although we believe that our language constructs are a powerful abstraction, bringing the implementation of design patterns to the programming language level has some drawbacks, as pointed out by John Vlissides in a debate on the issue of having patterns as language constructs [6]. The more automation we aim at, the less flexible the pattern instantiation becomes, given that code generation approaches that bridge higher levels of abstraction to lower ones necessarily have to compromise flexibility to some extent. Even though we took into account the possibility of parameterizing pattern instantiations, our solutions will naturally not fit any context that a programmer might come up with. However, when certain patterns need to be instantiated in such a way that the annotations did not anticipate, programmers can always implement them manually without benefiting from the transformations.

We argue that the traceability benefit of having the annotations present in the source code consists of an important advantage, given that the documentation of design patterns in the code has revealed beneficial for system maintenance [14]. Annotations are types in the programming language, and the associated validations ensure that they are applied in the correct locations and obey to other constraints. In this way, annotations can be seen as a structured form of documentation and compliance verification, and hence, they also consist of a robust means to document and enforce design issues. This is an advantage when compared with unstructured documentation text present in source code comments, which is somewhat fragile and easily becomes outdated, or external artifacts such as design documents, which often suffer from the problem of architectural erosion [12].

Given that our annotations indicate the patterns and their roles we believe that they are easy to understand from a code reading perspective, since the programmer is basically attaching labels to code elements using a familiar construct (the annotations). Further, the existence of dedicated language constructs also promotes pattern learning and experimentation. However, we believe that the language extensions in some cases do not dismiss programmers of having to understand how the patterns actually work internally.

We demonstrated how some of the widely used patterns are suitable to be addressed in language extensions. Other potentially more specific patterns (e.g., concurrency, or related to a particular platform) could also be addressed with this mechanism. The implementation of our extensions was by no means technically trivial, given that it had to be based directly on the compiler API. A more friendly abstraction for writing transformations would make easier to define extensions. However, we envision that this kind of extensions would be developed by specialized programmers and packaged as if they were libraries, in order to have some degree of reliability and standardization.

7   Related Work

Previous works have proposed dedicated language constructs to address design patterns. Jan Bosch [2] proposed a design-level support for generating design pattern implementations. When the design is finished, the model is able to generate the equivalent C++ code. The problem with this approach is that it works as a code generation tool that only provides support at the design stage, and the generated code will resemble manual implementation. Since the C++ code does not keep up with the pattern instance specifications, as opposed to our approach, the problems of traceability and comprehension at the source code level are not addressed.

OpenJava [16] is a macro system for Java that offers a compile-time reflective means that can inject source code in a similar way as Lombok. Therefore, OpenJava could be an alternative means for implementing our approach for design pattern instantiation. However, it implies using syntax extensions to Java for the declaration of macro expansions, whereas Lombok does not (it relies on existing language constructs, the annotations).

FRED [9] is an environment that supports the implementation of design patterns in Java. The implementation of design patterns is aided through an incremental sequence of tasks until all the mandatory tasks are completed. A task is considered to be the creation of small elements like classes, methods and fields. This incremental process has to be done every time one wants to instantiate a pattern, which can be time-consuming. Since the pattern instantiation is supported by the environment, we have no assistance if we use the resulting code on another Java development environment.

Using a different strategy for implementing design patterns, AspectJ[3] was proposed as a suitable means [10] with modularity improvements that make possible to encapsulate pattern instantiations in independent modules – the *aspects*.

---

[3] www.eclipse.org/aspectj.

The main drawback of this approach is the fact that in order to instantiate the patterns programmers must have some technical skills with respect to AspectJ. As with our approach, the aspect-based pattern instantiations also address traceability at the source code level, because the pattern instantiations are given in well-defined entities (all the instantiations of a given pattern extend the same abstract aspect). However, issues pertaining to pattern inter-dependency and interaction might consist of an issue, as reported by a study on the scalability of pattern modularity using the aspect-based approach [4].

JavaStage [1] is an extension to Java that encompasses programming constructs to represent *roles*. The notion of role has a dedicated module that may define fields and methods that enhance the classes to which the role is bound (using a declarative-style primitive on their definition). The definition of the role modules have a similar purpose than the AST transformations in our approach, whereas the role binding primitives relate to our annotations. Defining extensions using roles is a more elegant and easy way in contrast to the AST transformations used in our approach. Namely, the authors illustrate their approach with the Observer pattern. However, complex cases that require enhancements across multiple types, e.g., as our Visitor pattern transformation, might not be possible to address using roles due to the transformation complexity.

8   Conclusions

In this paper we described a set of Java extensions addressing widely used design patterns, whose instantiation can be achieved partly through source code transformation. We conclude that at least the patterns we presented here are suitable to be addressed with dedicated language constructs, given the considerable amount of elements that can effectively be generalized, as demonstrated in the example instantiations. The provided annotations consist of powerful high-level language constructs, which besides automating parts of the pattern instantiation, also mitigate pattern traceability and comprehension issues, given that patterns instances are represented by first-class entities. Although the extensions were proven to work, research on their suitability to real projects still has to be carried out to evaluate if the balance between automation and flexibility is satisfactory. As future work, we plan to refactor an existing framework using our annotations for this purpose.

References

1. Barbosa, F.S., Aguiar, A.: Using roles to model crosscutting concerns. In: Proceedings of the 12th Annual International Conference on Aspect-Oriented Software Development, AOSD 2013, pp. 97–108. ACM, New York (2013)
2. Bosch, J.: Design patterns as language constructs. J. Object-Oriented Program 11(2), 18–32 (1998)
3. Brooks Jr., F.P.: No silver bullet - essence and accidents of software engineering. Computer 20(4), 10–19 (1987)

4. Cacho, N., Sant'Anna, C., Figueiredo, E., Garcia, A., Batista, T., Lucena, C.: Composing design patterns: a scalability study of aspect-oriented programming. In: Proceedings of the 5th International Conference on Aspect-Oriented Software Development, AOSD 2006, pp. 109–121. ACM, New York (2006)
5. Cachopo, J., Rito-Silva, A.: Versioned boxes as the basis for memory transactions. Sci. Comput. Program. **63**(2), 172–185 (2006)
6. Chambers, C., Harrison, B., Vlissides, J.: A debate on language and tool support for design patterns. In: Proceedings of the 27th ACM SIGPLAN-SIGACT Symposium on Principles of Programming Languages, pp. 277–289. ACM (2000)
7. Fowler, M.: Patterns of Enterprise Application Architecture. Addison-Wesley Longman Publishing Co., Inc., Boston (2002)
8. Gamma, E., Helm, R., Johnson, R., Vlissides, J.: Design Patterns: Elements of Reusable Object-Oriented Software. Pearson Education, Upper Saddle River (1994)
9. Hakala, M., Hautamäki, J., Koskimies, K., Paakki, J., Viljamaa, A., Viljamaa, J.: Architecture-oriented programming using FRED. In: Proceedings of the 23rd International Conference on Software Engineering, pp. 823–824. IEEE Computer Society (2001)
10. Hannemann, J., Kiczales, G.: Design pattern implementation in java and aspectj. In: Proceedings of the 17th ACM SIGPLAN Conference on Object-Oriented Programming, Systems, Languages, and Applications, OOPSLA 2002, pp. 161–173. ACM, New York (2002)
11. Nobakht, B., de Boer, F., Bonsangue, M., de Gouw, S., Jaghoori, M.: Monitoring method call sequences using annotations. Sci. Comput. Program. **94**, 362–378 (2014)
12. Perry, D.E., Wolf, A.L.: Foundations for the study of software architecture. SIGSOFT Softw. Eng. Notes **17**(4), 40–52 (1992)
13. Prechelt, L., Unger, B., Tichy, W.F., Brossler, P., Votta, L.G.: A controlled experiment in maintenance: comparing design patterns to simpler solutions. IEEE Trans. Softw. Eng. **27**(12), 1134–1144 (2001)
14. Prechelt, L., Unger-Lamprecht, B., Philippsen, M., Tichy, W.F.: Two controlled experiments assessing the usefulness of design pattern documentation in program maintenance. IEEE Trans. Softw. Eng. **28**(6), 595–606 (2002)
15. Soukup, J.: Implementing patterns. In: Coplien, J.O., Schmidt, D.C. (eds.) Pattern Languages of Program Design, Chap. Implementing Patterns, pp. 395–412. ACM Press/Addison-Wesley Publishing Co., New York (1995)
16. Tatsubori, M., Chiba, S., Killijian, M.-O., Itano, K.: OpenJava: a class-based macro system for java. In: Cazzola, W., Houmb, S.H., Tisato, F. (eds.) Reflection and Software Engineering. LNCS, vol. 1826, pp. 117–133. Springer, Heidelberg (2000)

Towards a Semantic Search Engine for Open Source Software

Sihem Ben Sassi[1,2(✉)]

[1] RIADI Laboratory, National School of Computer Sciences,
Manouba University, 2010 La Manouba, Tunisia
sihem.bensassi@isetcom.rnu.tn
[2] High Institute of Telecommunication, Technoparc ElGhazala,
2083 Ariana, Tunisia

Abstract. To be able to use or reuse an open source software, we must be aware of its existence and find it first. Existing search engines on the Web do not allow finding open source software satisfying given requirements while taking into account special semantics. In this paper, we propose a semantic search system for open source software allowing to identify and localize them. It relies on an ontology providing a mechanism to describe knowledge about open source software. Moreover, it can infer knowledge for semantic identification through some defined rules. Preliminary results are encouraging. The evaluation results compared to a non-semantic version of the same search engine confirm the added value of the consideration of the semantic aspect in search.

Keywords: Open source software · Ontology · Search engine · Semantic · FLOSS

1 Introduction

Open source software (OSS) adoption is growing up since it is an alternative to commercial software and it provides many benefits. In fact, recent surveys revealed that the number of OSS users is more than the double of what it was five years ago [1], and that the number of open source software projects is almost multiplied by three from 2011 to 2015 [2]. Organizations went open source software not only to save money as it was the case a decade ago, but also for its quality and flexibility features, and for agility and innovation needs [2,3].

OSS software is therefore not only used by end users as alternative to commercial software products, but also reused by developers as alternative to commercial off-the-shelf components (COTS) for the development of new systems. However, this type of development still faces some difficulties. As a matter of fact, commercial software vendors are investing to promote their products using several ways of advertisement, which could influence decision-makers and developers while searching for and choosing a software. This is also true for the Web which remains an important source of information. OSS products meeting the requirements of an organization or a system to develop may exist on the Web but they

© Springer International Publishing Switzerland 2016
G.M. Kapitsaki and E. Santana de Almeida (Eds.): ICSR 2016, LNCS 9679, pp. 300–314, 2016.
DOI: 10.1007/978-3-319-35122-3_20

are not (re)used due to the fact that decision-makers or developers are unaware of their existence. To find an open source software, the use of search engines is a must. Most effort spent in this field is devoted to code search. Several tools are proposed to mine code and retrieve relevant software asset from different repositories, many of them return snippets. Some tools return open source modules or "components" in the sens of method, function, class, etc. such as SPARS-J [4], JBender [5], Krugle [6], OpenHub [7], S6 [8], Merobase [9,10], Sourcerer [11] and Exemplar [12]. Some of these tools integrate semantic aspects by providing the possibility to specify the type of the searched asset (e.g. function definition, function call, method definition, interface, test case, etc.) and to specify the programming language if more than one is supported. Only few of them let the user specify the license of the searched code. Only very few of them return also the name of the originating project allowing the user identifying the OSS containing the fragment of code. These tools are rather programming task-oriented tools.

Another type of search engines, to which we are interested in this work, return software applications whose functionality match high-level requirements. Whether they are conventional such as Google or specific for software components such as open source software [13], the help they provide in the identification task is not as much as needed. As a matter of fact, they may return a large number of results that should be further studied and filtered. The more the candidate number is large the more the evaluation effort required is. Furthermore, this type of search engines do not take into account OSS features when searching like license or programming language.

On the other hand, it is known that the integration of semantics in the search process improves the relevance of the returned results and reduces the required effort by the user to identify the appropriate component satisfying his/her needs. This work proposes a semantic search system specific to open source software named Se2FLOSS. Returned results are open source software components that are unit of composition and can be independently deployed, that's to say they correspond to a given functionality therefore can be used as-is by end users, or can be reused to develop a new system. The semantic qualification stems from the ontology for open source software (OntoFLOSS) we elaborated and on which Se2FLOSS relies on. Since we are neutral between free software and open source software, we used the term FLOSS for free/libre open source software in the names chosen for the ontology and the search system i.e. OntoFLOSS and Se2FLOSS as it is recommended by Richard Stallman [14], but we keep using the term OSS in the description text.

The remainder of this paper is structured as follows. Section 2 deals with the OntoFLOSS ontology. Section 3 presents the architecture of Se2FLOSS with its two processes indexing and searching. Section 4 describes the experimentation. The paper ends with a conclusion and future work.

2   OntoFLOSS Ontology

An ontology defines the terms used to describe and represent some topic. It combines the basic concepts of that particular topic and the relationship between these concepts. It is therefore the specification of conceptualizations, used to help programs and humans share knowledge [15]. There are several methodologies to design ontologies such as Ontoclean [16], On-to-knowledge [17] and Methontology [18]. We used Archonte (Architecture for Ontological Elaborating) [19] which is a bottom-up approach for building ontology operating in three steps:

1. selecting relevant terms of the domain and specifying the semantic similarities normalization of relationships and differences between concepts;
2. formalizing knowledge by building a referential ontology and adding properties and annotations, and defining relationships domains and co-domains;
3. operationalizing the ontology using a knowledge representation language resulting in what is called computational ontology.

We present in this section OntoFLOSS standing for Ontology for Free/Libre Open Source Software through the three Archonte steps.

2.1 Semantic Normalization

Building any ontology should start by acquiring knowledge. We have studied software components description models in the literature as well as description models used by OSS editors or repositories on the Web. Gathered information is processed and structured in a description model as shown in Fig. 1.

In this model, there are five aspects of OSS software: the informational aspect, the relational aspect, the functional aspect, the use aspect and the quality aspect. Each of these includes a category of attributes to represent a particular view of the software.

Informational aspect provides general information about the software. An OSS software is defined by its "name", its functionality "description", the "languages" in which it is available, the "programming language" with which it was developed, the "operating systems" on which it can be used and "the target audience" to whom it is intended (e.g. developers, qualified engineers, system administrators, end users, etc.). It belongs at least to one subdomain which is a specific filed of a domain. A domain is defined by a list of terms. The OSS has one or more versions. Each version is characterized by its "name", "release date", total "size", "source code" file name and the total "number of downloads". Each version may have several features as it may be provided as binary format for different platforms. The characteristics of a version change with its "development state". The activity state of the software is captured through its "activity rate" and the "total number of downloads". Usually, this kind of software is published on the Web by its developers and registered in a software repository (such as SourceForge[1]) to allow its use and/or the OSS community contributing to its improvement. It may also be published in a specific Web page by the editing organization. An OSS software is generally distributed under one license, but it may sometimes be distributed under multiples licenses [20]. A license is characterized by its "name" and version. It can be one of three types: either strong

---

[1] http://sourceforge.net/.

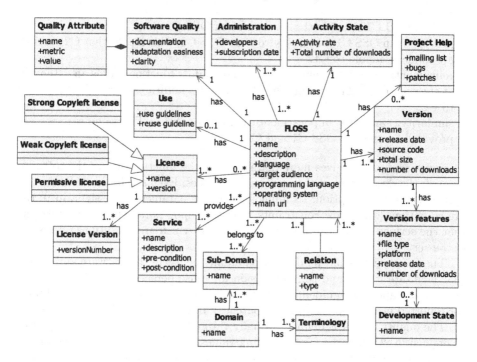

Fig. 1. Description model OSS components

copyleft, or weak copyleft or permissive [21, 22]. In fact, for free software licenses, the freedom to use and modify the software is unconditional as long as the software remains inside the organization. However, if the software is redistributed outside the organization, the type of the original license will decide for the final one.

1. Strong copyleft license type: the software redistributed with or without modification must always be under the original license. All new components associated are covered by the same license. As example, we cite GNU GPL v.3.0, GNU Affero GPL v3.0 and CeCILL v.2.
2. Weak copyleft license type: the software redistributed with or without modification must always be under the original license while the added components, features and code can be under another license. GNU LGPL v.2.1, Mozilla public license v.1.1, Eclipse public license and CeCILL-C are weak copyleft licenses.
3. Permissive license type: the software can be redistributed with or without modification under another license. BSD, Free BSD, Apache, MIT/X11 and CeCILL-B are permissive licenses.

The relational aspect represents the various relationships that an OSS may have with other ones. These, inspired from [23], may be one of the following:

- use: an OSS C1 requires the services of an OSS C2.
- provision: an OSS C1 uses a service of an OSS C2. This means that C2 services are made available to C1.
- refinement: an OSS C1 refines C2 if and only if its functionality is an extension of the one of C2. This means that C1 provides additional services comparing to C2.
- similarity: similarity implies identical functionalities. The same services are provided by the two OSS C1 and C2.

Functional aspect gives more details about the functionality of the software through the description of the services it provides. Each service is characterized by the name, a description, its input and output parameters (or signature), the pre-conditions which are constraints that the input parameters must meet so that the service can be run and post-conditions which are conditions on results of the service.

The use aspect includes information about the use of the software and means that facilitate its use and comprehension for reuse perspective. This is ensured through use and reuse guidelines. On the other hand, for each OSS, a list of bugs (or reported errors), corrections (or patches) and a mailing list are recorded.

The quality aspect is defined formally through OSS software quality metrics as defined in [24] and the corresponding values. In a less formal way, the model includes information about the documentation, adaptation easiness and clarity.

2.2 Knowledge Formalization

In this step, the referential ontology is built by transforming the acquired knowledge into concepts and relations between concepts; it is also question of adding properties and defining properties domains. Figure 2 illustrates, through a semantic network, an extract of determined concepts to capture knowledge about an OSS software. Some concepts are refined:

- either into more specific ones such as programming language which can be imperative, functional, object-oriented, prototype-oriented, aspect-oriented or specification language.
- or to handle more details such as operating system which has an architecture kernel representing a family of operating systems, having itself one or more distributions.

On the other hand, major instances of some concepts are determined, namely:

- strong copyleft, weak copyleft and permissive licenses,
- imperative, functional, object-oriented, prototype-oriented, aspect-oriented and specification programming language,
- development state, and
- operating system related concepts: kernel architecture, family and distribution.

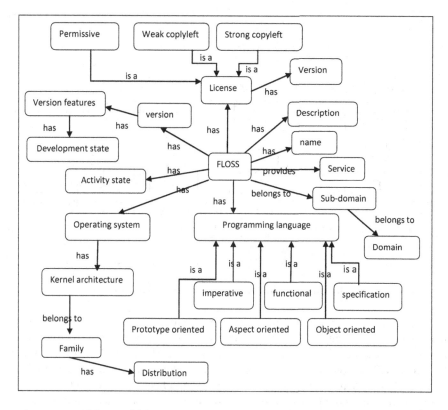

Fig. 2. OSS concept related to some of its concepts

Figure 3 shows license types and a sample of their instances with a sample of their versions. It is important to notice here that some licenses may be referred to by other names. We define synonyms for these ones. For example, original BSD license has as synonym BSD 4-clause, BSD old and old BSD. Modified BSD is also called new BSD, BSD-new, revised BSD and BSD 3-clause. Simplified BSD has as synonyms FreeBSD and 2-clause BSD.

As a sample of object-oriented programming language, we list Smalltalk, C++, Java, Eiffel, C#, Delphi, Ada, PHP5, Perl5 and Ruby. Agora, Cecil, JavaScript, R, ActionScript, Perl6 and TADS are a sample instances of prototype-oriented programming languages. Programming languages are also classified according to the type of applications they allow to build: real-time, Web or desktop application.

Development state instances are planning, pre-alpha, alpha, beta, mature, stable and inactive.

Regarding operating systems, there are two main architectures: Win32-based and kernel-based. As kernal, we may have smartphone (Android, IOS), GNU-Linux, UNIX and MAC-OS families. For GNU-Linux we have Redhat, Debian, Suse distributions, and so on.

After building the referential ontology and based on it, it is question to define some rules that will be used in order to improve the search results of OSS software.

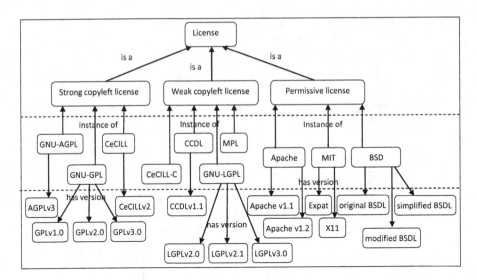

Fig. 3. Sample of instances related to License concept

Regarding license: when a user searches for an OSS having a given license, this latter is a specific license version of a license that belongs to one of the three licenses types. It is possible that no OSS of the given version satisfying the query will be found, or returned OSS with that version are considered not relevant. The user may therefore be interested to check alternative OSS. In this case and from license point of view, we estimate that it is interesting to include in the search results OSS with the same license but a higher version if any, OSS with the same license but a lesser version if any, OSS with licenses of the same type of the given one. To illustrate this rule, assume that the user searches for a software with a GPLv2.0 license. Based on Fig. 3, the search system should also return (1) OSS satisfying the other requirements with GPLv3.0 license, (2) those with GPLv1.0 and (3) those with CeCiLLv2 as well as AGPLv3 licenses.

The same idea is applied to have rules regarding operating systems knowing that OS families are incompatible and that 32 bits program can run over 32 or 64 bits system, but a 64 bits program can run only over a 64 bits system.

We apply the same principle to programming languages. For example, when searching for OSS written in Java, the search system returns also OSS written in Jee, Jsp.

Other rules relating programming language and operating system concepts are defined such as:

- If the programming language is Java than the OSS is operating system independent.
- If the programming language is .Net then the operating system is of Win32 architecture.

These rules are inter-conceptual ones, while the former are intra-conceptual rules.

2.3   Operationalization

In this step, the ontology should be transcribed in a formal and operational language to represent knowledge so that the machine can understand and manipulate it and infer new knowledge. For that purpose, we used OWL-DL language which is based on description logic and has desirable computational properties for reasoning. We used Protege2000 as ontology editor. The referential ontology is transformed into a computational ontology defined through classes, properties (object and datatype) instances and individuals. Inferring knowledge is performed through reasoning which is based on:

1. mechanisms provided by OWL and used to further specify properties, namely InverseOf and SymmetricProperty
2. specific rules defined during the knowledge formalization step (described in the preceding subsection). These rules are written using SWRL (Semantic Web Rule Language). The following is a rule example written in SWRL.

$$OSS(?o) \wedge hasProgrammingLanguage(?o, java) \rightarrow isOSIndependent(?o, true)$$

3   OSS Search System Description

Like any search engine Se2FLOSS is composed of modules handling the two main processes: the indexing process and the search process, described in the sequel.

3.1   The Indexing Process

To gather information about OSS components on the web, we coded a multi-threaded crawler that browses Web pages of each site. Crawlers explore a Web page, extract internal and external links on that page and then reiterate the same process on each found link. The coded crawler starts with a predefined URLs list of Web sites containing OSS and then manages internal or external URLs found. It classifies all URLs in a queue list which is updated as and when crawling URLs by eliminating incorrect ones as well as those that are already scanned. The crawler carries out two types of processing: a vertical one for major known OSS repositories such as SouceForge, and an horizontal one for the other sites/pages.

To decide if a Web page is representing an OSS, we define a method that is based on checking if a set of keywords are present on that page or not. For that purpose, we have carried out an empirical study on over 40 software components Web sites which let us determine the set of keywords and categorize them according to their location (URL, meta data or body) and importance (involvement in the decision).

After identifying an OSS page, the crawler indexes the OSS by extracting related information, processing it and saving it as an OntoFLOSS instance. In this version of the crawler, information related to quality and services is not considered as it requires to process the source code.

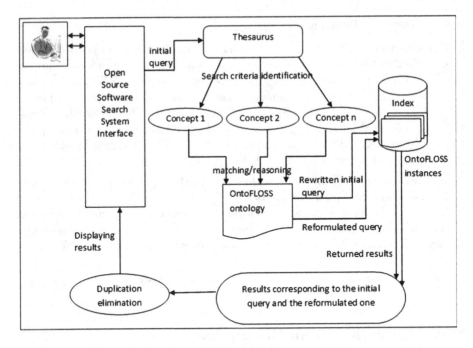

Fig. 4. The search process

3.2   The Search Process

The search process, illustrated in Fig. 4 relies mainly on the OntoFLOSS ontology and a thesaurus. We describe in the sequel how a query is processed.

The user enters a simple or compound query. A simple query contains keywords related to the name and or software functionality description while a compound query includes in addition words related to other characteristics such as license or operating system. For example: "download a PDF creator" is a simple query, and "download a PDF creator for Windows GPL" is a compound one. The thesaurus is used to:

- Remove stop words. In addition to standard stop words, we consider words such as download, license and free as stop ones since we focus on functionality related keywords and values of required features such as license value, programming language value and not on the words themselves.
- Identify terms/words related to the OSS name and/or description.
- Identify the other search criteria such as license, operating system, programming language.

A first search with the decomposed query is then performed on the index and a first result list is obtained. Afterward, it is question to match with concepts of OntoFLOSS in order to determine the rules and the inter-conceptual and intra-conceptual relations that will be used to reformulate the query. A second search with the reformulated query is performed and a second list is obtained. The final result presented to the user is composed of the first list to which is appended the second list, without duplication. The described process is illustrated through the following example:

User query: "download a PDF creator with GPLv2 license written in C"
Stop words: download, a, with, license, written, in
Software name/functionality: PDF creator
License: GPLv2
Programming language: C#
The first search is performed with the query: "PDF creator" to search in the name and/or description with GPLv2 as license and C# as programming language.
The ontology is used to find that:

- GPLv2 is a version of GPL license which has two other versions GPLv3 and GPLv1, and that GPL is a strong copyleft license like AGPL, CeCILL and Jabber OSL. OSS satisfying the other conditions and having one of the cited licenses are included in the result list.
- C# is an oriented programming language. However, it is not right to include any programming language before checking the operating system.

Using the rule programming language/operating system, it is found that the operating system type should be Win32, all Windows versions may apply. The object oriented programming languages that may be used is determined such as Java, dotNet, C++.
The second search is then performed with the new query:
Software name/functionality: PDF creator
License: GPLv2, GPLv3, GPLv1 AGPLv2, AGPLv3, CeCILLv2, Jabber OSLv1
Programming language: C#, C++, VB.Net, Java
Operating system: WindowsXP, Windows7, Windows8, Windows10.

4 Experimentation

We developed a prototype of the search system named Se2FLOSS (see Fig. 5 for a sample query results showing the identified knowledge.). After building an index by collecting information from the Web and in order to evaluate the effect of using the OntoFLOSS ontology, we carried out an experimentation by submitting a set of queries on one hand to Se2FLOSS, and on the other hand to a non-semantic version of it i.e. without using OntoFLOSS, working on a small index of 22233 OSS descriptions. We use the precision and the normalized recall metrics to evaluate the results.

- Precision is computed using the expression 1

$$precision = \frac{number\ of\ relevant\ OSS\ retrieved}{number\ of\ OSS\ retrieved} \tag{1}$$

- As it is impossible to know the total number of relevant OSS available on the Web, it does not make sense to user the standard recall metric. We use instead the normalized recall [25]. This latter introduces the rank of the relevant OSS on the returned results list and allows to limit the assessment to a given number of results N as shown by the expression 2.

$$Recall_{normalized} = 1 - \frac{\sum_{i=1}^{n} r_i - \sum_{i=1}^{n} i}{n(N-n)} \tag{2}$$

where n is the number of relevant OSS in the results list limited to N and r_i is the rank of the ith relevant document in that list.

We assessed the first 20 returned results. However, when the number of retrieved OSS is less than 20, precision and normalized recall are calculated over the number of retrieved OSS. Table 1 gives the mean values of the precision and the normalized recall obtained for both Se2FLOSS and Se2FLOSS without OntoFLOSS. We notice that Se2FLOSS performs better than the non semantic version thanks to the use of OntoFLOSS which improves both the precision and the normalized recall values by around 23 %.

Since no benchmark is available to compare results with other search systems, we carried out another experimentation based on a manually controlled collection. The built collection is composed of OSS descriptions gathered randomly using the domain specific language BOA [26] and completed by others

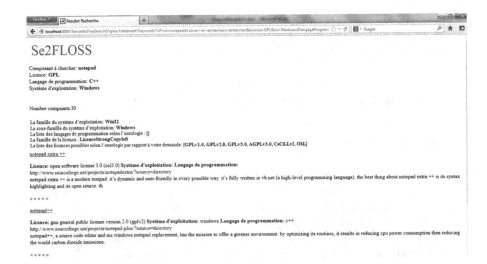

Fig. 5. A screenshot for a sample Se2FLOSS identified knowledge

Table 1. Mean precision and normalized recall for Se2FLOSS and effect of ONTOFLOSS

	Precision	Normalized recall
Se2FLOSS without ONTOFLOSS	0.423	0.35
Se2FLOSS	0.521	0.43
%improvement	23.16 %	22.85 %

gathered manually from OSS repositories, mainly SourceForge. A total of 2394 OSS are collected distributed as follows.

- regarding operating systems: about 36 % of OSS work on windows (all versions included), about 32 % work on linux and about 5 % work on FreeBSD. Among these ones, some are declared to work on all the preceding platforms meaning that they are OS independent. 16 % of OSS are explicitly declared OS independent.
- regarding programming languages: the most used ones are C++ and Java both around 18 %. C comes next with 15 %, followed by PHP which is used by about 11 % of gathered OSS. Python, Perl and C# are almost equally used each by around 5 % of OSS. Note that several OSS are developed using more than one programming language.
- regarding licenses: the most used license found in the collection is GPLv2 (about 55 %) followed by LGPLv2 (about 10 %) GPLv3 (6 %) and BSD license (5 %). Some OSS are released under more than one license.

While browsing OSS descriptions on the Web, it is easy to notice that OSS are not always fully described. Sometimes, important information such as the programming language, the operating system or the license is missing. The user should generally inspect OSS related files such as README and source code files for additional information. For the built collection, Table 2 gives the number of OSS for each missing information type.

Table 2. Number of OSS with missing information

	License	Programming language	Operating system
OSS number	29	16	112

Once the collection defined, we prepared a set of 20 queries. Each one is composed of a set of keywords to express the searched functionality and specific requirements. Types of queries along with their number and requirements are as follows:

- Type1: 2 queries without any specific requirements.
- Type2: 5 queries about OSS working on a given operating system.
- Type3: 5 queries about OSS released under a given license.

- Type4: 5 queries about OSS written with a given programming language.
- Type5: 3 queries about OSS written with a given programming language and released under a specific license.

It was then question of assessing the collection against the queries in order to know, for each query, which software is relevant as well as the total number of relevant OSS for that query. This process is carried out by three persons having a computer sciences background and bearing in mind not to consider linguistic semantics, mainly synonyms, while judging. The queries are afterward submitted to Lemur[2] along with the collection and the judgment files in order to perform a standard search and compute the precision for the 20 first returned results of each query. The baseline mean precision obtained is 0.735. Se2FLOSS do not perform better than Lemur regarding queries of Type1, Type4 and Type5. However, using rules defined in OntoFLOSS for licenses as well as those relating operating systems to programming languages, a part of missing information is deduced. Therefore, more relevant OSS are retrieved for queries of Type2 and Type3. Table 3 summarizes precision results and shows that rules within OntoFLOSS have improved the mean precision by 12 % and that the main improvement comes from queries with an operating system requirement. This latter has a good probability to be deduced when it is not initially specified in the OSS description. Indeed, for the whole collection and as it is mentioned in Table 2, 112 OSS descriptions do not explicitly include the operating system. Applying OntoFLOSS rules, operating system of 73 among the 112 are determined as follows: 57 OS independent, 13 Windows and 3 Unix. Therefore, derived knowledge allowed to fill about 65 % of missing information about operating system.

Table 3. Obtained precision compared to a baseline

	Overall mean pr.	Type2 mean pr.	Type3 mean pr.
baseline	0.735	0.58	0.82
with OntoFLOSS	0.828	0.88	0.89
improvement %	12.65	51.72	8.53

5   Conclusion

The aim of this work is to provide developers and end users with a semantic search engine for open source software. The system proposed uses an ontology elaborated in order to capture knowledge about OSS and allow reasoning to infer new knowledge. The OntoFLOSS ontology is used in the indexing process to unify open source software descriptions, and intervenes in the search process to expand the query. Reasoning is ensured through rules relating concepts together.

---

[2] http://www.lemurproject.org/.

Experimentation results show that the use of ONTOFLOSS improves the precision and recall of the system which means that the relevance of returned results is clearly increased. We plan to take into account during the search process the context of the user, especially when he/she is a developer. Preferences such as interest domain and programming language, as well as characteristics of the application being developed along with a ranking method would improve the relevance of the returned results.

Acknowledgments. Acknowledgment to Atef Charef and Raja Lagha for their participation during the elaboration of Se2FLOSS.

References

1. Survey Analysis: Open-Source Software Adoption and Governance-Worldwide-2014, February 2015. https://www.gartner.com/doc/2984418/survey-analysis-opensource-software-adoption
2. 2015 Future of Open Source Survey Results - Black Duck Software. http://fr.slideshare.net/blackducksoftware/2015-future-of-open-source-survey-results
3. Widespread Use of Open-Source Software Demands Strong and Effective Governance, August 2014. https://www.gartner.com/doc/2822619/widespread-use-opensource-software-demands
4. Inoue, K., Yokomori, R., Yamamoto, T., Matsushita, M., Kusumoto, S.: Ranking significance of software components based on use relations. IEEE Trans. Softw. Eng. **31**(3), 213–225 (2005)
5. Gysin, F.S.: Improved social trustability of code search results. In: 32nd ACM/IEEE International Conference on Software Engineering, Cape Town, South Africa, pp. 513–514. ACM Press (2010)
6. Krugle OpenSearch. http://opensearch.krugle.org
7. BlackDuck Open HUB. https://www.openhub.net
8. Reiss, S.P.: Semantics-based code search. In: 31st ACM/IEEE International Conference on Software Engineering, Vancouver, Canada, pp. 243–253. IEEE Computer Society (2009)
9. Merobase Source Code Search. http://www.merobase.com
10. Hummel, O., Janjic, W., Atkinson, W.: Code conjurer: pulling reusable software out of thin air. IEEE Softw. **25**(5), 45–52 (2008)
11. Linstead, E., Bajracharya, S., Ngo, T., Rigor, P., Lopes, C., Baldi, P.: Sourcerer: mining and searching internet-scale software repositories. Data Min. Knowl. Disc. **18**(2), 300–336 (2009)
12. McMillan, C., Grechanik, M., Poshyvanyk, D., Fu, C., Xie, Q.: Exemplar: a source code search engine for finding highly relevant applications. IEEE Trans. Softw. Eng. **38**(5), 1069–1087 (2012)
13. Open source software. http://opensource.ankerl.com
14. FLOSS and FOSS. http://www.gnu.org/philosophy/floss-and-foss.en.html
15. Gruber, T.: Ontology. In: Liu, L., Tamer Özsu, M. (eds.) Encyclopedia of Database Systems, pp. 1963–1965. Springer, Heidelberg (2009)
16. Guarino, N., Welty, C.: Evaluating ontological decisions with OntoClean. Commun. ACM **45**(2), 61–65 (2002)

17. Sure, Y., Studer, R.: On-to-knowledge methodology. In: Staab, S., Studer, R. (eds.) Handbook on Ontologies. Springer, Heidelberg (2003)
18. Gomez-Perez, A., Fernandez-Lopez, M., Corcho, O.: Ontological Engineering with Examples from the Areas of Knowledge Management, e-Commerce and the Semantic Web. Springer, London (2004)
19. Bachimont, B., Isaac, A., Troncy, R.: Semantic commitment for designing ontologies: a proposal. In: Gómez-Pérez, A., Benjamins, V.R. (eds.) EKAW 2002. LNCS (LNAI), vol. 2473, pp. 114–121. Springer, Heidelberg (2002)
20. Licences Libres. https://aful.org/ressources/licences-libres
21. Various Licenses and Comments about Them. http://www.gnu.org/licenses/license-list.en.html
22. Open Source Licenses Wars. http://www.shlomifish.org/philosophy/computers/open-source/foss-licences-wars/foss-licences-wars/index.html
23. Beltaifa, R.: Une infrastructure pour la rutilisation de composants logiciels. Ph.D. thesis, National School of Computer Sciences, Tunisia (2004)
24. Spinellis, D., Gousios, G., Karakoidas, V., Louridas, P., Admas, P.J., Samoladas, I., Stamelos, I.: Evaluating the quality of open source software. Electron. Notes Theor. Comput. Sci. **223**, 5–28 (2009)
25. Bollmann, P.: The normalized recall and related measures. In: 6th Annual International ACM SIGIR Conference on Research and Development in Information Retrieval, Maryland, USA, pp. 122–128. ACM Press (1983)
26. Dyer, R., Nguyen, H.A., Rajan, H., Nguyen, T.N.: Boa: a language and infrastructure for analyzing ultra-large-scale software repositories. In: 35th International Conference on Software Engineering, San Francisco, CA, USA, pp. 422–431. IEEE Press (2013)

Detecting Similar Programs
via The Weisfeiler-Leman Graph Kernel

Wenchao Li[1], Hassen Saidi[1], Huascar Sanchez[1], Martin Schäf[1(✉)],
and Pascal Schweitzer[2]

[1] SRI International, 333 Ravenswood Ave, Menlo Park 94025, USA
martin.schaef@sri.com
[2] RWTH Aachen University, Aachen, Germany
http://www.csl.sri.com/people/li/
http://www.csl.sri.com/people/saidi/
https://huascarsanchez.com/
http://www.csl.sri.com/people/schaef/
http://www.lii.rwth-aachen.de/~schweitzer/

Abstract. With the increasing availability of source code on the Internet, many new approaches to retrieve, repair, and reuse code have emerged that rely on the ability to efficiently compute the similarity of two pieces of code. The meaning of similarity, however, heavily depends on the application domain. For predicting API calls, for example, programs can be considered similar if they call a specific set of functions in a similar way, while for automated bug fixing, it is important that similar programs share a similar data-flow.

In this paper, we propose an algorithm to compute program similarity based on the Weisfeiler-Leman graph kernel. Our algorithm is able to operate on different graph-based representations of programs and thus can be applied in different domains. We show the usefulness of our approach in two experiments using data-flow similarity and API-call similarity.

1 Introduction

Over the past few years, we have seen a rapid increase in the amount of source code that is openly available on the Internet. Source code hosting platforms such as GitHub, BitBucket, or SourceForge and social media resources like StackOverflow have changed the way we program. This large amount of machine readable source code also has given rise to several interesting new research directions, such as code prediction [23], discovery of architectural patterns [20], using donor code for program repair [12,29], and more efficient ways to search for code [17,30].

Central to these new approaches is the ability to efficiently find *similar* code snippets in the wild. Unlike in traditional code clone detection, the notion of similarity depends heavily on the application. For automatic program repair, for example, it is important that code shares a similar data-flow, whereas for code

This work is funded in parts by AFRL contract No. FA8750-15-C-0010.

G.M. Kapitsaki and E. Santana de Almeida (Eds.): ICSR 2016, LNCS 9679, pp. 315–330, 2016.
DOI: 10.1007/978-3-319-35122-3_21

prediction, it is often sufficient if the code interacts with a certain API in a similar way. Hence, finding a generic approach to comparing code that can work with different representations and abstractions has the potential to be beneficial in a variety of fields.

To address this problem, we propose a new algorithm to compute a program similarity score based on a technique from graph isomorphism testing. Here, we use the term *program* as a shorthand for any piece of code, like a full program, isolated classes or methods, or just snippets.

Our algorithm consists of two parts. First, it turns a program into a labeled graph. Second, it computes a Weisfeiler-Leman kernel for this graph and compares it against the precomputed kernels of the graphs of other programs to identify the most similar ones.

The algorithm itself is agnostic to the graph representation of the program or the programming language and can be used with different graphs. To illustrate the usefulness of this approach, we introduce two graph representations of Java programs, a simplified inter-procedural data-flow graph (IDFG), and an API-call graph (ACG), and evaluate how these graphs can be used in combination with our algorithm to identify similar programs. The IDFG is a simplified version of the actual data-flow graph of a Java program and suitable to find programs that are algorithmically similar, while the ACG is a stripped-down version of an inter-procedural control-flow graph that only contains calls to a given API, which is suitable to find examples of API usage.

To evaluate the ability of our approach to identify similar programs, we conduct two experiments. For the first experiment, we choose a subset of the Google CodeJam[1] corpus as a benchmark. The corpus is a set of 4 algorithmic problems, each with hundreds of solutions given as small Java programs (in total 1,280 programs). Our goal is to show that, when picking any of these Java programs, our approach for finding similarities using the IDFG identifies similar programs that are in fact solutions to the same problem.

The programs in CodeJam are very algorithmic and make only limited use of API calls (e.g., for printing). Hence, this corpus is unfortunately not suitable to evaluate our approach in combination with the second graph representation, the ACGs. Thus, we perform a second experiment where we use the Apache commons-lang project as a benchmark. We compare the similarity between all pairs of methods in this application and evaluate manually if the reported similarities indicate similar API usage patterns.

Roadmap. In the following Section, we introduce the Weisfeiler-Leman algorithm to compute graph kernels for labeled graphs. In Sect. 3, we explain how we use these graph kernels to compute a similarity score between graphs. In Sect. 4, we introduce the two graph representations of Java programs (IDFG and ACG) that we use in our experiments. We evaluate our approach in Sect. 5, discuss the related work in Sect. 6, and propose future directions in Sect. 7.

---

[1] https://code.google.com/codejam.

2   Preliminaries

Our approach to measure the similarity between programs is based on a standard routing from graph isomorphism testing which we introduce in this section. More specifically, we use the 1-dimensional Weisfeiler-Leman algorithm, often also referred to as color refinement or naïve vertex classification. The procedure is for example employed in the currently fastest practical isomorphism solvers (such as Nauty and Traces [18], Bliss [11] and saucy [4]).

The algorithm repeatedly recolors the vertices of its inputs graphs. Starting with an initial coloring of the vertices which distinguishes them by their degree the algorithm proceeds in rounds. In each round the new color of a vertex encodes the previous color as well as the multiset of the colors of the neighbors. The k-dimensional variant, which we will not require in this work, colors k-tuples of vertices and can solve isomorphism on quite general graph classes (see [8]).

Next, we describe the one-dimensional variant more formally. If $G = (V, E, \chi_0)$ is a vertex colored graph, where χ_0 is a vertex coloring, we recursively define χ_{i+1} to be the coloring given by

$$\chi_{i+1}(v) := \left(\chi_i(v), \{\!\{ \chi_{i+1}(v') \mid \{v, v'\} \in E \}\!\} \right).$$

Here we use "$\{\!\{$" and "$\}\!\}$" to indicate multisets.

The process leads to an ever finer classification of the vertices. This process stabilizes at some point. In the context of graph isomorphism the histogram of the colors is used to distinguish graphs according to isomorphism.

However, for our purpose, the final colors are excessively descriptive, in the sense that they actually encode too much information. Indeed, by a result from [1], for almost all graph, each final color already encodes the isomorphism type of the graph.

Circumventing this problem we adopt the technique from [27] to only execute the algorithm for a few rounds and exploit the histograms of the colors that appear during the execution of the algorithm. In [27] these histograms are used to design a graph kernel which can then be applied in a machine learning fashion to perform for example graph classification. Said kernel captures similar information to other kernels that count subgraphs (see for example [9] or [28]). However, the Weisfeiler-Leman Kernel can be far more efficiently computed.

It is well known that the exact information captured by i iterations of naïve vertex classification can be precisely expressed in a certain type of logic (see [19]). However, it is difficult to grasp what the result means in terms of graph theoretic properties of the input graphs. While in a regular graph no information is generated at all, since all vertices have the same color in all iterations, in non-regular graphs typically the isomorphism type of a small neighborhood of a vertex is determined.

Concerning running time it is possible to perform h-iterations of the algorithm in $O(hm)$ time, where m is the number of edges of the input graph. To achieve such a running time, the labels have to be compressed to prevent label names from becoming excessively long. There are two options to do this, one

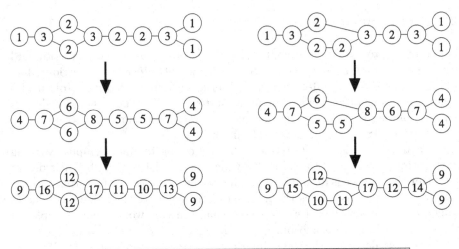

Fig. 1. The figure shows a left graph G_L and a right graph G_R to which the 1-dimensional Weisfeiler-Leman is being applied for 2 iterations. Here labels are hashed to smaller values. The renaming is as follows $4 := (1, \{\!\{3\}\!\}), 5 := (2, \{\!\{2,3\}\!\}), 6 := (2, \{\!\{3,3\}\!\}), 7 := (3, \{\!\{1,2,2\}\!\}), 8 := (3, \{\!\{2,2,2\}\!\}), 9 := (4, \{\!\{7\}\!\})$ and so on. The figure also shows the histograms of labels that appear in the two graphs highlighting their similarity.

employs techniques such as bucket sort, while the other one simply uses a hash function to compress the labels (see [27]). We adopt the latter approach and used the built-in hash function for strings in our implementation.

In our intended application, we benefit from the fact that the algorithm can take vertex-labeled graphs as input. Thus it is easy to introduce labeled nodes into the algorithm. In Sect. 4 we show how Java types (for IDFG) or method signatures (for the ACG) can be used as initial coloring χ_0 in the definition of the algorithm.

3   Similarities

Our goal is to design a similarity score $S(P, P')$ between programs P and P' with the following properties.

- All programs are 100 % similar to themselves, i.e. $S(P, P) = 1$.
- The score is symmetric, i.e. $S(P, P') = S(P', P)$.
- The score is normalized to a percentage number, i.e. $0 \le S(P, P') \le 1$.

A percentage score also has the advantage of being more easily interpreted by the user. We remark that an asymmetric score might be desired in some setting.

For example, the user may be interested in finding a similar program that is also of similar size.

Recall that the Weisfeiler-Leman kernel with h iterations for graphs G and G' is defined as follows [16]:

$$K_{WL}^{(h)}(G, G') = w_0 K(G_0, G_0') + w_1 K(G_1, G_1') + \ldots + w_h K(G_h, G_h') \quad (1)$$

where the G_is and G_i's are the graphs produced by successive recoloring of the original labeled graphs G_0 and G_0' (as shown in Fig. 1), and $K(G_i, G_i')$ is a graph kernel for graphs G_i and G_i'. $K_{WL}^{(h)}(G, G')$ is then constructed as a positive linear combination of the $K(G_i, G_i')$s using some positive weights w_is.

In each iteration of the Weisfeiler-Lehman algorithm, a histogram is produced which encodes certain structural information of the graph, as shown in Fig. 1. Treating these histograms as vectors, a natural candidate for K is the scalar product of two vectors. However, this can be problematic when the graph sizes are very different. Consider the scenario of two graphs G and G' where $|V| \ll |V'|$, and all the nodes in G' have an identical label l which exists somewhere in G. We presume G and G' correspond to either the API call graph or the inter-procedural data-flow graph generated from programs P and P' respectively. Observe that it is easy to have $K(G, G) < K(G, G')$. As a result, P' might be reported as a more similar program to P than P itself. Hence, we apply standard normalization using the lengths of the two vectors and use the angle between the vectors as our similarity measure.

Let $v(G_i)$ present the coloring vector (histogram) produced at the ith iteration of the Weisfeiler-Leman algorithm. Then $K(G_i, G_i') = v(G_i) \cdot v(G_i')/\|(v(G_i))\| \|(v(G_i'))\|$. Since we are interested in a percentage score, and $0 \leq K(G_i, G_i') \leq 1$ for each i, the weights w_is can be chosen appropriately to make $0 \leq K_{WL}^{(h)}(G, G') \leq 1$. In our experiments, we simply choose a uniform weight.

4   Graph-Based Program Representations

The ability of our algorithm to detect program similarity strongly depends on the graph representation of programs that we use when computing the graph kernels. Choosing a graph representation for programs is a trade off between precision and the ability to identify programs that serve a similar purpose but are structurally different. Using the precise control-flow graph of a program, for example, would be an efficient way to identify exact code clones but would reduce the chance to identify programs that are semantically similar but syntactically different.

In this paper, we search a balance between precision and flexibility by proposing two graph representations. We call our first graph *API Call Graph* (ACG) which is a stripped-down inter-procedural control-flow graph that only shows calls to a specific set of APIs. Our second graph is a (simplified) *inter-procedural data-flow graph* (IDFG) which tracks the flow of data between memory locations from a given program entry point.

```
1  public void reverseFile(String infile, String outfile)
       throws IOException {
2    String data = readFile(infile);
3    data = new StringBuilder(data).reverse().toString();
4    writeFile(outfile, data);
5  }
6
7  private String readFile(String fname) throws IOException
       {
8    byte[] encoded = Files.readAllBytes(Paths.get(fname));
9    return new String(encoded, Charset.defaultCharset());
10 }
11
12 private void writeFile(String fname, String data) {
13   try (Writer out = new BufferedWriter(
14       new OutputStreamWriter(new FileOutputStream(fname),
15         Charset.defaultCharset())); ) {
16     out.write(data);
17   } catch (Exception e) {
18     e.printStackTrace();
19   }
20 }
```

Fig. 2. Running example for our graph representation of programs. The method `reverseFile` is the entry point. It takes two file names as input. It reads the content from the first file to a String using the method `readFile`, reverses the String, and writes out the reverted String using `writeFile`.

Both graphs provide a certain level of abstraction. In the following we discuss the advantages and disadvantages of our design choices along the running example program in Fig. 2. This program has a (public) method `reverseFile` that takes the names of two files as input, calls `readFile` to read the contents of the first file into a string, reverses this string, and subsequently calls `writeFile` to write the resulting string to a file.

We now construct the graph representations for this program using Soot [31]. Soot first translates the program into an intermediate format called Jimple which provides us with a canonical form for expressions. For the graph construction, we extend Soot's flow analysis to collect the node and edges of our graph per method, where we keep placeholder nodes for method calls. Then, in a final step, we substitute the placeholder nodes for method calls by their corresponding graphs. We will discuss details and practical issues of the graph construction in more detail later on in the evaluation.

4.1 API Call Graph

The first graph that we construct is called API Call Graph which represents the order in which procedures of some given APIs can be called from a given entry point.

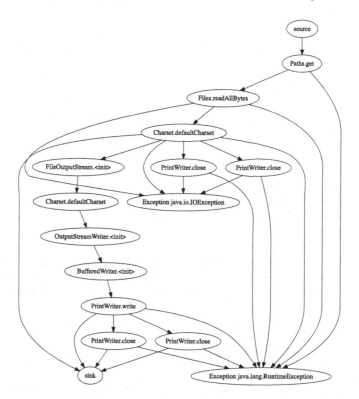

Fig. 3. ACG for our example from Fig. 2. The ACG approximates the possible sequences of calls to methods in `java.io.*` and `java.nio.*`. The labels are simplified for readability and usually also encode the types of parameters and return values.

The motivation for using an ACG for computing program similarity is our hypothesis that, in Java, programmers often achieve their goals by using external APIs. Programs that use the same API calls in the same order should have a similar objective, regardless of the statements in between. A programmer using our approach to find similar code might thus be interested in finding any code that shares the usage pattern of a specific subset of APIs.

For the construction of the ACG, we pick an entry point (e.g., `reverseFile` in our example) and the APIs that we are interested in (e.g., in our example we are interested `java.io.*` and `java.nio.*`). Then we follow the control-flow of the program starting from the entry point. Each time we encounter a call to a method that is declared in an API that we are interested in, we create a new node for this call. Figure 3 shows the ACG for our example from Fig. 2.

The ACG always has a unique source node but can have multiple sink nodes. One unique sink node always represents the normal termination of a procedure, other sink nodes may exist for exceptional returns. In Fig. 2 we have exceptional sinks for `RuntimeException` and `IOException`.

Each time we encounter a call to a method that is not part of an API that we are interested in, but for which we have code available, we inline the method

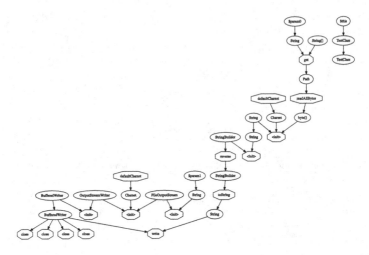

Fig. 4. IDFG for our example from Fig. 2. Vertices are labeled with variable types, edges represent data-flow. Octagon shaped vertices represent method calls. The actual operation are omitted from the edges since our algorithm ignores edge labels.

call. In Fig. 2, the method calls to `readFile` and `writeFile` have been inlined. Any call to methods defined in `java.io.*` and `java.nio.*` is represented by a single node, and all other calls (such as the calls to `reverse` and `toString` in Line 3) get ignored.

For resolving virtual calls, we use a static algorithm that is fast but imprecise. That is, the ACG only approximates the possible sequences of calls to methods from a certain API. For example, we do not perform a proper points-to analysis while constructing the graph and indirect control-flow such as library callbacks is not tracked (but can be provided by the user). We discuss various sources of imprecision specific to our implementation later on in the evaluation.

4.2   Inter-procedural Data-Flow Graph

Our second graph is an inter-procedural data-flow graph (IDFG). Data-flow graphs are frequently used in program analysis and compiler optimization. The graph captures the flow of data between program variables without taking the control-flow into account. Each node in this graph represents a program variable or memory location. A (directed) edge between two nodes represents that data from one source node flows into the variable associated with the sink node. This way, an IDFG groups variables together that interact with each other even if they are not immediately connected in the control-flow.

The motivation of using IDFGs for finding similar programs is that programs that perform similar algorithmic tasks such as sorting or searching in collections use a similar set of base types and perform similar operations on them. In contrast to the ACG which focuses on finding programs with similar API usage, the IDFG is used to find programs that use similar algorithms. That is, while we envision a typical scenario for ACG usage as a user trying to understand how to use a particular API, we think of the ICFG as a tool to find a method (in an API) that could be used to replace an algorithm in the user's program.

Figure 4 shows the IDFG for our example from Fig. 2. Each oval node corresponds to a program variable or a `new` expression, each octagon shaped node is a call to a procedure that could not be inlined (e.g., because it is a library call to which no source code is available). To obtain a more canonical representation, we label the nodes with the types of the program variables instead of the name. As an abstraction, we represent types that are not visible outside the current application with a question mark. We discuss possible ways of how to represent non-primitive Java types in the IDFG in the future work.

5   Evaluation

5.1   Evaluation of Code Similarity Using IDFG

We use the CodeJam dataset as a benchmark for evaluating our method of finding similar programs. This dataset consists of all the solutions to programming problems used in the Google Code Jam competition from 2008 to 2015. One advantage of using the CodeJam dataset is that the problem-solution setting acts as a free oracle for checking whether two programs are similar, since two solutions of the same problem must be input-output equivalent for the set of input test cases provided by Google (although several algorithms may exist as acceptable solutions). One downside of this dataset is that since the problems are highly algorithmic in nature (as opposed to large software design), many solution programs just operate on built-in datatypes and the only library classes that are frequently used are `String` and `StringBuffer`. This restricts our graph choices to IDFG instead of ACG. Another downside is that code quality is relatively low compared to well established open-sourced projects since the programs were produced in a competition environment with tight time constraints. An undesirable effect of this is that some programs could not be included in the experiments because of non-standard entry points (no `main` method), or other compilation issues (non-unicode characters in the source files).

Setup. We randomly selected four problems from the CodeJam dataset. There are 1280 Java programs in total in this subset. For each of the programs, we first create an inter-procedural data-flow graph as describe in Sect. 4 for its top-level entry point (usually the `main` method). Then, for each program, we use our graph kernel based method to find the top k most similar programs to it from the rest of the 1279 programs. Since these programs are known to solve one of these four problems, we consider a similar program found to be correct if it solves the same problem. Our goal of this experiment is to evaluate how well our method identifies the appropriate similar program.

Results. We first evaluate how accurately our method can find the most similar program. As a baseline comparison, a random guess would have an accuracy of 25 %. The accuracy of our method is 77.8 %. If we increase k to 2, i.e., consider the top 2 most similar programs found and check if any one of them is from the

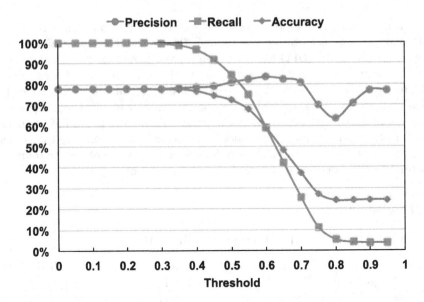

Fig. 5. Accuracy, precision and recall values plotted at different threshold values. Accuracy is the percentage times the program found is from the same problem and has a similarity score higher than the threshold, or it is from a different problem but is rejected because of a lower than threshold score. Precision is the percentage of correctly identified programs with a higher than threshold score over all programs with a higher than threshold score. Recall is the percentage of correctly identified programs with a higher than threshold score over all correctly classified programs that would have been returned without using the threshold.

same programming problem, then the accuracy increases to 87.9 %. In general, a larger k will produce better accuracy but at the expense of user experience and effort, since the user would have to spend more time reading these programs and some of them are irrelevant to her task.

We also consider using a threshold value on the similarity score for filtering the similar programs found. If the most similar program found still has a similarity score lower than the threshold, then the program is not shown to the user. Figure 5 shows the results of using different threshold values In our case, precision tops at a threshold of around 0.6. On the other hand, accuracy decreases monotonically with increasing threshold value.

Discussion. The experiments above show that our graph kernel based approach can effectively identify similar programs. However, to our surprise, a threshold value is not needed to achieve the highest accuracy (although one is needed for precision). This indicates that even a low similarity score may be sufficient to distinguish the kinds of programs, given the large space of possible implementations. We plan to include the rest of CodeJam for a more comprehensive evaluation in the future.

Threads to Validity. One internal threat to validity is the fact that several different algorithms may exist for the same programming problem, leading to widely different implementations. While IDFG encodes semantic information of the program as data-flow, it still follows closely the structure of the program. This means IDFG will likely fail to capture the fact that different algorithms and implementations are designed to solve the same problem. An external thread to validity is that we are only using four problems in our evaluation. We are currently working on evaluating our method on the whole CodeJam dataset. However, as mentioned earlier, these programs only represent codes that are highly algorithmic in nature and they still only constitute a tiny fraction of open-sourced programs.

5.2   Evaluation of ACG Similarity

Using the ACG to find similar programs on the CodeJam corpus turned out to be infeasible. The programs in CodeJam are of a very algorithmic nature and mostly operate on the built-in types of Java. The only library classes that are frequently used are `String` and `StringBuffer` which are used to log results. Hence, building ACGs for these programs did not produce any interesting results.

To evaluate the usefulness of the ACG for finding similar programs, we set up a different experiment where we compute ACGs for every method in the Apache project `commons-lang` which is a library that provides utilities for common tasks such as handling dates or serializing objects.

We choose `commons-lang` as a benchmark because it uses large parts of the Java packages `java.lang` and `java.util` which we can use in the ACG construction. Since we do not have an oracle to decide if two methods are similar like in the case of CodeJam, the moderate size of `commons-lang` helps us to examine the similarity results by hand.

The goal of this experiment is to evaluate whether methods considered similar based on ACG isomorphisms are indeed similar. To that end, we choose the following experimental setup: for each method in `commons-lang`, we compute an ACG for all calls to methods in `java.*` excluding `String` and `StringBuffer`. We inline calls to methods inside `commons-lang` up to depth four. Method calls that exceed this limit are dropped from the ACG. While running the experiments, we experimented with inlining depth up to ten which did not change the results significantly.

If the ACG of a method has less than four nodes (i.e., two calls to library methods and source and sink), we drop it since we are only interested in methods that make at least two library calls.

Results. In total, we processed 3017 methods. Out of these, 660 methods had an ACG with at least four nodes. For each constructed ACG we identify the two most similar methods (excluding the method itself) which results in a total of 1320 pairs of ACGs together with their similarity values.

In 686 of these 1320 cases we found a real isomorphism (with a similarity of 100 %). In 4 cases, we found a similarity between 99 and 80 %, in 8 cases a similarity between 79 and 60 %, in 24 cases between 59 and 40 %, and all other similarities were below 40 %.

The most notable part of our experimental result is the high number of real isomorphisms (over 50 %). To get an intuition where these isomorphisms come from, we investigated 40 methods by hand. In 27 of the 40 cases, the graphs were isomorphic because both methods only contained a single statement calling the same method. Hence, due to inlining, the ACGs were identical. In the remaining cases, the methods indeed used the same set of library calls such as iterators over collections or modifications of Date objects. We emphasize that this high number of isomorphisms is a result of our experimental setup and this would not be the case when searching for similar methods in a different code base.

In the four cases where methods had a similarity between 99 and 80 %, the methods were slightly different but shared a number of API calls. One example of this is the similarity between DateUtils.round and DateUtils.ceiling. The round method calls to another method that is almost identical to ceiling (this method and ceiling are in fact isomorphic).

In the similarity range between 79 and 60 %, we still find interesting results. Examples of similar procedures are pairs like FormatCache.getDateTime-Instance and FormatCache.getTimeInstance which, without going into the details of the code are understandably similar by looking at their names. Five of the eight similarities between 79 and 60 % were cases where one method called to other.

Similarities between 59 and 40 % were, for example, found in the StringUtils class between methods like endsWithAny and startsWithAny, or removeEndIgnoreCase and removeStartIgnoreCase which, as their naming suggests, perform very similar tasks. Other cases of 50 % similarity are different methods to find threads in ThreadUtil. These methods all iterate over a collection of Thread objects but use different methods to filter this set.

Even methods with a similarity below 40 % still were interesting in many cases. For example for the method LocalUtils.countriesByLanguage the most similar method was LocalUtils.languagesByCountry, or for Fraction.divideBy the most similar method (with 18 % similarity) was Fraction.multiply. Only when we reach a similarity of below 15 %, the results become less useful.

Discussion. This experiment shows that similarity based on the ACG is indeed useful to identify methods that serve a similar purpose. We emphasize that our experimental setup of finding similarities in the same code-base is certainly biased towards finding many isomorphic graphs, so the success rate of finding similar code with this approach can not be generalized from this experiment. What the experiment shows, however, is that methods with a similarity between 99 % and 20 % are still very similar even if they do not share code and that the approach hardly produces false alarms. For the method pairs that we inspected, there was no case where we could not spot the similarity.

Threats to Validity. Several threats to validity have to be discussed in this experiment. We already mentioned that searching for similar methods in the same code base is biased towards finding many isomorphic graphs. For a less biased experimental setup, we would need labeled data like in the case of CodeJam. We would need an oracle that can decide if methods are similar to measure how often our approach does not find a similar method where one exists. Unfortunately, we do not have such an oracle but it is part of our future work to build up a corpus to further evaluate our approach. Another thread to validity is the choice of java.* as an API and commons-lang as code base. In the future work we will experiment with more code bases and different APIs but within the scope of this paper we believe that this experiment is sufficient to convey our idea.

6   Related Work

The problem of finding similarities in source code is a known problem in software engineering. It crops up in many software engineering contexts as diverse as program compression [5], malware similarity analysis [3], software theft detection [14], software maintenance [7], and Internet-scale code clone search [25].

Previous research in program similarity has focused more on detecting syntactic similarity [24] and less on detecting semantic similarity, as the latter is generally undecidable. We can classify these different approaches into five categories: Text-based, Token-based, Tree-based, Semantic-based, and Hybrid.

In text-based solutions, the source code of a program is divided into strings and then compared against another. Under this type of solution, two programs are similar if their strings match [2]. In token-based solutions (lexical), the source code of a program is transformed into a sequence of lexical tokens using compiler style lexical analysis. The produced sequences are then scanned for duplicated subsequences of tokens. The representative work here is Baker's token based clone detection [2]. In tree-based solutions, the source code of a program is parsed in order to produce an abstract syntax tree (AST). The produced AST is then scanned for similar subtrees. The representative work here is Jiang's *Deckard* [10]. In semantic-based solutions, a source code is statically analyzed to produce a program dependency graph (PDG) [6]. Then, the program similarity problem is reduced to the problem of finding isomorphic graphs using program slicing [13]. In hybrid solutions, both syntactic and semantic characteristics are used to find similar code. The representative work here is Leitao's hybrid approach for detecting similar code. This hybrid approach combines syntactic techniques based on AST metrics, semantic techniques (call graphs), and specialized comparison functions to uncover code redundancies [15].

The approach presented in this paper can be seen as a hybrid solution as well. It identifies similar programs using graph similarity like semantic-based solutions but is agnostic to the kind of graph that is being used. For example our ACG is more of a syntactic representation and the IDFG more a semantic representation of the program.

When considering similarity measures of graphs one has to carefully distinguish between measures that are applied to labeled graphs and measure applied to unlabeled graphs. A labeled measure d may use information of the vertex names. For example the edit distance is usually defined for two graphs $G_1 = (V, E_1)$ and $G_2 = (V, E_2)$ over the same vertex set as $d(G_1, G_2) :=$

$|E_1 \setminus E_2| + |E_2 \setminus E_1|$. It captures the amount of edges/non-edges that need to be altered to turn the one graph into the other. In contrast to this, a measure for unlabeled graphs is not allowed to depend on the names of the vertices, that is for a permutation π of the vertices of G_2 we must have that $d(G_1, G_2) = d(G_1, \pi(G_2))$.

An overview over some graphs similarity measures is given in [26]. Labeled graph similarity measures are not suitable for our intended applications. Indeed, the names of the vertices of the IDFG and ACG do not seem to carry relevant information. (This is different for the labels that are assigned by the algorithm, which carry structural information, as discussed earlier.) The question remains which unlabeled graph similarity measures are suitable to capture code similarity? From a conceptual point it appears that the occurrence of substructures of certain kinds in a node's vicinity is related to the purpose of a code snippet containing said node. This is supported by the findings in [16, 20–22]. Guided by this insight, we chose the similarity based on Weisfeiler-Leman algorithm for our purposes. While it detects similar information as subgraph counts, it provides us with two significant advantages. On the one hand it is very efficiently computable, which not the case for subgraph detection, as also explained in [16, 22]. On the other hand it easily allows us to exploit the label information of different types of graphs generated from programs.

7   Conclusion

We have presented a generic algorithm to compute program similarity based on the Weisfeiler-Leman graph kernels. Our experiments suggest that the algorithm performs well for the IDFG and ACG representation of Java code that we proposed. However, we believe that our algorithm will also perform well with other graph-based models.

We see several interesting applications that we want to pursue as future work: one interesting property of graph kernels is that a combination of two graph kernels is again a graph kernel. In the case of the ACG, this would allow us to compute separate ACGs for different APIs (e.g., `java.lang` and `java.util`) and either use them in isolation or combine them, which would allow us to build more efficient search algorithms. Another interesting application would be to combine kernels from entirely different graphs, such as the ACG and the IDFG to experiment with new concepts of similarity.

Further, using graph kernels makes it easy to experiment with different graph representations. One could for example use a simplified version of a control-flow graph or use a more abstract labeling of the nodes to model different kinds of program similarity.

References

1. Babai, L., Erdős, P., Selkow, S.M.: Random graph isomorphism. SIAM J. Comput. **9**(3), 628–635 (1980)
2. Baker, B.S.: On finding duplication and near-duplication in large software systems. In: 2nd Working Conference on Reverse Engineering, WCRE 1995, Toronto, Canada, 14–16 July 2005, pp. 86–95 (1995)
3. Cesare, S., Xiang, Y.: Software Similarity and Classification. Springer Briefs in Computer Science. Springer, London (2012)
4. Darga, P.T., Liffiton, M.H., Sakallah, K.A., Markov, I.L.: Exploiting structure in symmetry detection for CNF. In: Malik, S., Fix, L., Kahng, A.B. (eds.), Proceedings of the 41th Design Automation Conference, DAC, San Diego, CA, USA, 7–11 June 2004, pp. 530–534. ACM (2004)
5. Evans, W.S.: Program compression. In: Koschke, R., Merlo, E., Walenstein, A. (eds.) Duplication, Redundancy, and Similarity in Software, 23–26 July 2006, vol. 06301 of Dagstuhl Seminar Proceedings. Internationales Begegnungs- und Forschungszentrum fuer Informatik (IBFI), Schloss Dagstuhl, Germany (2006)
6. Ferrante, J., Ottenstein, K.J., Warren, J.D.: The program dependence graph and its use in optimization. ACM Trans. Program. Lang. Syst. **9**(3), 319–349 (1987)
7. Godfrey, M.W., Zou, L.: Using origin analysis to detect merging and splitting of source code entities. IEEE Trans. Softw. Eng. **31**(2), 166–181 (2005)
8. Grohe, M.: Fixed-point definability and polynomial time on graphs with excluded minors. J. ACM **59**(5), 27 (2012)
9. Horváth, T., Gärtner, T., Wrobel, S.: Cyclic pattern kernels for predictive graph mining. In: Kim, W., Kohavi, R., Gehrke, J., DuMouchel, W. (eds.) Proceedings of the Tenth ACM SIGKDD International Conference on Knowledge Discovery and Data Mining, Seattle, Washington, USA, 22–25 August 2004, pp. 158–167. ACM (2004)
10. Jiang, L., Misherghi, G., Su, Z., Glondu, S.: Deckard: scalable and accurate tree-based detection of code clones. In: Proceedings of the 29th International Conference on Software Engineering, ICSE 2007, pp. 96–105. IEEE Computer Society Washington, DC, USA (2007)
11. Junttila, T.A., Kaski, P.: Engineering an efficient canonical labeling tool for large and sparse graphs. In: Proceedings of the Nine Workshop on Algorithm Engineering and Experiments, ALENEX, New Orleans, Louisiana, USA, 6 January 2007. SIAM (2007)
12. Ke, Y., Stolee, K.T., Le Goues, C., Brun, Y.: Repairing programs with semantic code search. In: Proceedings of the 30th IEEE/ACM International Conference on Automated Software Engineering (ASE), pp. 295–306, Lincoln, NE, USA, November 2015. doi:10.1109/ASE.2015.60, http://people.cs.umass.edu/brun/pubs/pubs/Ke15ase.pdf
13. Komondoor, R., Horwitz, S.: Using slicing to identify duplication in source code. In: Cousot, P. (ed.) SAS 2001. LNCS, vol. 2126, pp. 40–56. Springer, Heidelberg (2001)
14. Lancaster, T., Culwin, F.: A comparison of source code plagiarism detection engines. Comput. Sci. Edu. **14**(2), 101–112 (2004)
15. Leitão, A.M.: Detection of redundant code using R2D2. In: 3rd IEEE International Workshop on Source Code Analysis and Manipulation (SCAM 2003), Amsterdam, The Netherlands, 26–27 September 2003, pp. 183–192 (2003)
16. Lestringant, P., Guihéry, F., Fouque, P.-A.: Automated identification of cryptographic primitives in binary code with data flow graph isomorphism. In: Proceedings of the 10th ACM Symposium on Information, Computer and Communications Security, ASIA CCS 2015, pp. 203–214. ACM, New York (2015)

17. Mahmoud, A., Bradshaw, G.: Estimating semantic relatedness in source code. ACM Trans. Softw. Eng. Methodol. **25**(1), 10:1–10:35 (2015)
18. McKay, B.D., Piperno, A.: Nauty and traces user guide. https://cs.anu.edu.au/people/Brendan.McKay/nauty/nug25.pdf
19. Pikhurko, O., Verbitsky, O.: Logical complexity of graphs: a survey. CoRR, abs/1003.4865 (2010)
20. Pradhan, P., Dwivedi, A.K., Rath, S.K.: Detection of design pattern using graph isomorphism and normalized cross correlation. In: Parashar, M., Ramesh, T., Zola, J., Narendra, N.C., Kothapalli, K., Amudha, J., Bangalore, P., Gupta, D., Pathak, A., Chaudhary, S., Dinesha, K.V., Prasad, S.K. (eds.) Eighth International Conference on Contemporary Computing, IC3, Noida, India, 20–22 August 2015, pp. 208–213. IEEE Computer Society (2015)
21. Qiu, J., Su, X., Ma, P.: Library functions identification in binary code by using graph isomorphism testings. In: Guéhéneuc, Y., Adams, B., Serebrenik, A. (eds.) 22nd IEEE International Conference on Software Analysis, Evolution, and Reengineering, SANER, Montreal, QC, Canada, 2–6 March 2015, pp. 261–270. IEEE (2015)
22. Qiu, J., Su, X., Ma, P.: Using reduced execution flow graph to identify library functions in binary code. IEEE Trans. Softw. Eng. **42**(2), 187–202 (2015)
23. Raychev, V., Vechev, M., Krause, A.: Predicting program properties from "big code". In: Proceedings of the 42nd Annual ACM SIGPLAN-SIGACT Symposium on Principles of Programming Languages, POPL 2015, pp. 111–124. ACM, New York (2015)
24. Roy, C.K., Cordy, J.R., Koschke, R.: Comparison and evaluation of code clone detection techniques and tools: a qualitative approach. Sci. Comput. Program. **74**(7), 470–495 (2009)
25. Sajnani, H., Saini, V., Svajlenko, J., Roy, C.K., Lopes, C.V.: SourcererCC: scaling code clone detection to big code. CoRR, abs/1512.06448 (2015)
26. Schweitzer, P.: Isomorphism of (mis)labeled graphs. In: Demetrescu, C., Halldórsson, M.M. (eds.) ESA 2011. LNCS, vol. 6942, pp. 370–381. Springer, Heidelberg (2011)
27. Shervashidze, N., Schweitzer, P., van Leeuwen, E.J., Mehlhorn, K., Borgwardt, K.M.: Weisfeiler-lehman graph kernels. J. Mach. Learn. Res. **12**, 2539–2561 (2011)
28. Shervashidze, N., Vishwanathan, S.V.N., Petri, T., Mehlhorn, K., Borgwardt, K.M.: Efficient graphlet kernels for large graph comparison. In: Dyk, D.A.V., Welling, M. (eds.) Proceedings of the Twelfth International Conference on Artificial Intelligence and Statistics, AISTATS, Clearwater Beach, Florida, USA, 16–18 April 2009, vol. 5 of JMLR Proceedings, pp. 488–495. JMLR.org (2009)
29. Sidiroglou-Douskos, S., Lahtinen, E., Long, F., Rinard, M.: Automatic error elimination by horizontal code transfer across multiple applications. In: Proceedings of the 36th ACM SIGPLAN Conference on Programming Language Design and Implementation, PLDI, pp. 43–54. ACM, New York (2015)
30. Stolee, K.T., Elbaum, S., Dobos, D.: Solving the search for source code. ACM Trans. Softw. Eng. Methodol. **23**(3), 26:1–26:45 (2014)
31. Vallée-Rai, R., Co, P., Gagnon, E., Hendren, L., Lam, P., Sundaresan, V.: Soot - a java bytecode optimization framework. In: Proceedings of the Conference of the Centre for Advanced Studies on Collaborative Research, CASCON 1999, p. 13. IBM Press (1999)

Domain Analysis and Modelling

Metamodel and Constraints Co-evolution: A Semi Automatic Maintenance of OCL Constraints

Djamel Eddine Khelladi[1(✉)], Regina Hebig[2], Reda Bendraou[1], Jacques Robin[1], and Marie-Pierre Gervais[1]

[1] Sorbonne Universités, UPMC Univ. Paris 06, UMR 7606, 75005 Paris, France
{djamel.khelladi,reda.bendraou,jacques.robin,
marie-pierre.gervais}@lip6.fr
[2] Chalmers and University of Technology, Gothenburg, Sweden
hebig@chalmers.se

Abstract. Metamodels are core components of modeling languages to define structural aspects of a business domain. As a complement, OCL constraints are used to specify detailed aspects of the business domain, e.g. more than 750 constraints come with the UML metamodel. As the metamodel evolves, its OCL constraints may need to be co-evolved too. Our systematic analysis shows that semantically different resolutions can be applied depending not only on the metamodel changes, but also on the user intent and on the structure of the impacted constraints. In this paper, we investigate the reasons that lead to apply different resolutions. We then propose a co-evolution approach that offers alternative resolutions while allowing the user to choose the best applicable one. We evaluated our approach on the evolution of the UML case study. The results confirm the need of alternative resolutions along with user decision to cope with real co-evolution scenarios. The results show that our approach reaches 80 % of semantically correct co-evolution.

1 Introduction

In *Model-Driven Engineering*, metamodels are core components of a modeling language ecosystem [10]. They define the structural aspects of a business domain, i.e. the main concepts, their properties, and the relationships between them [4]. However, a metamodel alone is insufficient to capture all the relevant aspects and information of a domain specification [18]. To overcome this limitation, the Object Constraint Language (OCL) [21] is used to define constraints on top of the metamodel. For instance, the wide-spread Unified Modeling Language (UML) [23] in version 2.4.1 contains more than 750 OCL constraints expressing well-formedness rules to be enforced at the model instances level.

A challenge hereby arises when the metamodel is evolved causing the invalidation of some OCL constraints that need to be co-evolved (i.e. maintained to remain reusable [19]). For instance, the UML metamodel officially evolved 10 times in the past that led to manually adapting the OCL constraints.

© Springer International Publishing Switzerland 2016
G.M. Kapitsaki and E. Santana de Almeida (Eds.): ICSR 2016, LNCS 9679, pp. 333–349, 2016.
DOI: 10.1007/978-3-319-35122-3_22

Manual co-evolution is a tedious, time-consuming, and error-prone task, in particular when hundreds of OCL constraints exist. In such a context, it is crucial to support an automatic co-evolution.

Problem Statement. Automatically co-evolving OCL constraints remains challenging, mainly because of two issues: (1) *the existence of multiple and semantically different resolutions*, and (2) *a resolution can be applicable only to a subset of OCL constraints*. In the following we detail these issues.

(1) The impact of a metamodel change on an OCL constraint can be resolvable using resolutions that are syntactically and/or semantically different. For instance, the metamodel change *"multiplicity generalization of a property p from a single value to multiple values"* requires the OCL constraints to work on a collection of values, e.g. by introducing an iterator. Figure 1 gives an example of this change for the property *ref* with a simple OCL constraint.

Multiple resolutions can be applied here as depicted in Fig. 1, since multiple iterators with *different semantics* exist, e.g. forAll(), exists() etc. Proposing a unique resolution reduces the applicability of the co-evolution approach and limits its benefit. Final decision can only be specified by the user herself, to avoid unintended co-evolution changes.

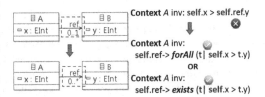

Fig. 1. Existence of multiple solutions

(2) A given resolution strategy is not always applicable for all OCL constraints. The complex nature of OCL requires different resolution strategies, each one applicable for only a subset of OCL constraints based on: *(a)* the *location* of the impacted part in an OCL constraint, and *(b)* its *context* (i.e. the metamodel element on which an OCL constraint is defined). Figure 2 illustrates this issue. It depicts an evolution of a metamodel where the property *depth* is deleted from the superclass **Component** and added to the subclass **Composite**, which fits the definition of a "push property" [9]. The first two constraints become invalid because *depth* is no more accessible in **Component**. The first constraint that uses the pushed property *depth* through the reference *component*, can be co-evolved by introducing an If expression that first checks whether *component* references an instance of the subclass **Composite** so that *depth* is accessible. In contrast, the second OCL constraint whose context is defined on the pushed property *depth*, is co-evolved differently by duplicating it for the subclass **Composite**. The original constraint is then removed as depicted in Fig. 2d. Note that the third constraint defined on the context of the subclass **Composite** that uses *depth* is not impacted. Clearly, a unique resolution strategy cannot be applied whatever the OCL constraint, for the three constraints in our example.

Consequently, it is crucial to consider the two above issues when co-evolving OCL constraints. However, existing approaches [5–7,13,16,17] propose a unique

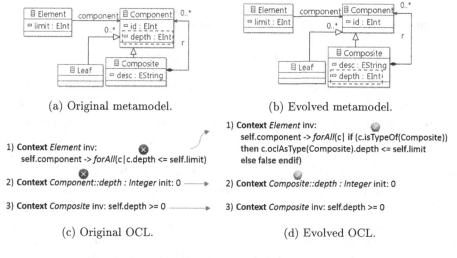

(a) Original metamodel.   (b) Evolved metamodel.

1) Context *Element* inv:
self.component -> *forAll*(c|c.depth <= self.limit)

2) Context *Component::depth : Integer* init: 0 ⟶

3) Context *Composite* inv: self.depth >= 0 ⟶

(c) Original OCL.

1) Context *Element* inv:
self.component -> *forAll*(c| if (c.isTypeOf(Composite))
then c.oclAsType(Composite).depth <= self.limit
else false endif)

2) Context *Composite::depth : Integer* init: 0

3) Context *Composite* inv: self.depth >= 0

(d) Evolved OCL.

Fig. 2. An evolution example of a composite pattern.

resolution per metamodel change. They neither consider the two above issues, nor interact with the user.

Contributions. We thus addressed these challenges by four contributions:

– First, we systematically investigated what are the *influencing factors* that lead to define alternative resolution strategies and when to apply them. Thus, we established that the metamodel changes alone are insufficient to propose the appropriate resolutions, and additional factors must be considered.
– Second, we propose an approach that considers multiple resolutions per impacted part of an OCL constraint based on the influencing factors. Thus, for a metamodel change, we propose various resolutions for different subsets of OCL constraints. It allows us to cover different alternatives of co-evolution.
– Third, we offer the user the option to choose the appropriate resolutions to be applied during co-evolution among the ones we propose. The user can also decide to not apply a resolution if it does not suit her needs. Involving the user greatly contributes to avoid applying unintended resolution strategies.
– Fourth, we evaluate our approach by comparing a set of manually co-evolved OCL constraints in practice against the same co-evolved ones with our tool. The evaluation confirms that alternative resolutions along with users final decision are required in practice for a correct co-evolution. The results on the UML Class Diagram case study show that our approach can handle a real case study, reaching 80 % of semantically correct OCL co-evolution.

For a better understanding of the current approach, this paper first discusses the factors that influence the application of the resolution strategies in Sect. 2. Section 3 then presents the overall approach introduces some of the proposed resolutions. Section 4 illustrates our implementation. The evaluation, results, discussion, and threats to validity are presented in Sect. 5. Finally, Sects. 6 and 7 present respectively the related work and the conclusion.

2 Factors Influencing the Resolution Strategies

In this section, we identify the factors that influence the choice of the resolution strategies. To illustrate the influencing factors we reuse the example of Fig. 2.

Factor 1. First of all, the metamodel change is fundamental to choose which resolution to apply, similarly as in model co-evolution (e.g. [15,25]). The impacts of a rename property and a push property cannot be fixed using the same resolution. Thus, the first influencing factor is: **the metamodel change**.

Factor 2. We further investigated which locations in an OCL constraint can influence the choice of a resolution. We identified two locations that have an influence: *navigation path* and *context*. For example, in Fig. 2 the two first OCL constraints need to be resolved differently since the pushed property *depth* is used in different locations. In the first constraint *depth* is located in the OCL expression (i.e. body) through a *navigation path*. Whereas, in the second constraint *depth* is located in the *context*. Thus, the second influencing factor is: **the location of the impacted metamodel element *e* in an OCL constraint**.

Factor 3. Finally, we found a third factor that is the *context* of the constraint, which can influence the choice of a resolution. In Fig. 2, the first constraint is co-evolved by introducing an If expression and not by duplicating the constraint to the subclasses where *depth* is pushed, as we did with the second constraint. This is due to the fact that the context of the first constraint is not the superclass Component. When changing the context, all accessible properties from the old context must remain accessible from the new context. If the context of the first constraint is changed from Element to Composite, the property *limit* will not be accessed anymore. For the third constraint which has the sub class Composite as context no resolution strategy is applied, since *depth* is still accessible. Therefore, the third influencing factor is: **the *context* of the impacted constraint**.

Our analysis of the state-of-the-art led us to identify the *factor 1*, only. To identify the additional *factors 2* and *3*, we systematically studied the different uses of the metamodel elements in the OCL language and we analyzed why a resolution can be applied to some constraints and not to others.

3 A Co-evolution Approach of OCL Constraints

This section presents our approach to co-evolve OCL constraints. Figure 3 depicts an overview of our approach. We first present the metamodel changes that we consider during an evolution and we present how they are identified [1]. After that, we discuss the identification of impacted OCL constraints, in particular the localization of the impacted parts in the constraints [2]. Then, we explain how we obtain the three influencing factors for each impacted OCL constraint. Finally, we show how alternative resolutions are proposed to the user [3] and how they are automatically applied [4].

3.1   Metamodel Changes During Evolution

During a metamodel evolution two types of changes are distinguished: (a) *Atomic changes* that are additions, removals, and updates of a metamodel element, and (b) *Complex changes* that consist in a sequence of atomic changes combined together. For example, *move property* is a complex change where a property is moved from one class to another via a reference. This is composed of two atomic changes: delete property and add property [9].

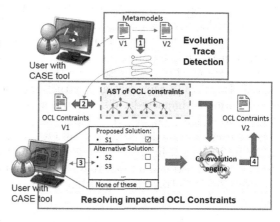

Fig. 3. Overall approach.

We consider the following set of atomic changes: *add, delete, and update* of metamodel elements. An *update*, changes the value of a property of an element, such as 'type', 'name', 'upper/lower bounds'. The metametamodel elements that are considered in this work are: *package, class, attribute, reference, operation, parameter, and generalization.* Those elements represent the core features of a metamodel in the EMF/Ecore [24] and the MOF [20] standards. In the literature, over sixty complex changes are proposed [9]. Among them, we focus on seven complex changes: *move property, pull property, push property, extract super class, flatten hierarchy, extract class, and inline class.* A study of the evolution of GMF[1] metamodel showed that these seven changes are the most used ones and constitute 72 % of the applied complex changes [8,14]. In our case study they constitute 100 % of the applied complex changes in the evolutions.

In our co-evolution approach we must first identify metamodel changes that led from version n to version $n + 1$, as shown by the step 1 in Fig. 3. This is a prerequisite for both impact analysis and automatic support of the co-evolution. We reuse our detection tool [11,12], an extension of the Praxis tool [1]. It first records at run-time all atomic changes applied by users within a modeling tool. The sequence of recorded atomic changes then serves as input for the detection of complex changes. Our tool [11,12] has been designed to detect all applied changes. This is confirmed in the evaluation results by always reaching a 100 % recall (i.e. all complex changes are detected) and a precision (i.e. correct detection) of 91 % and 100 %. Our tool [11,12] allows the user to confirm the list of complex changes that best reflect her intention during the evolution. Therefore, a final precise, complete, and ordered trace of both atomic and complex changes is computed. This trace is taken as input by our herein tool to co-evolve the OCL constraints.

---

[1] Graphical Modeling Framework http://www.eclipse.org/modeling/gmf.

3.2 Identification of Impacted OCL Constraints

The second step of our approach is to identify the OCL constraints impacted by metamodel changes during the evolution. In particular, we identify all the impacted parts of the OCL constraints that need to be co-evolved.

To run the impact analysis we need to access all the elements used in an OCL constraint. Thus, we first parse the OCL constraints to use the Abstract Syntax Tree (AST) representing a structured view of an OCL constraint. The identification of impacted OCL constraint is then performed on the generated AST. Before identifying where an AST is impacted, we first compute a table that lists for each metamodel element e, all OCL constraints using e with references to the AST nodes using e. Those references will be further used in the resolution step. Table 1 illustrates an example of our computed table. To build Table 1, we use pre-order tree traversal algorithm through the AST while filling the table.

Table 1. Impact identification on OCL constraints.

Metamodel elements	OCL constraints	References to AST nodes
e_1	$OCL_1, \dots$	$ref_1, ref_2, \dots$
...	...	...

For each metamodel change on a metamodel element e_i, we access the set of impacted OCL constraints and we access exactly the impacted AST nodes with the saved references. Note that a metamodel complex change can involve several elements $e_i \dots e_j$. Thus, the set of impacted OCL constraints are accessed naturally for each element e_k where $i \leq k \leq j$. During the co-evolution process Table 1 is also updated accordingly with the applied resolutions. For instance, when a rename element e occurs, it is also renamed in the table.

3.3 Obtaining the Influencing Factors

As discussed in Sect. 3.1 the metamodel changes are given as input from our detection [11,12]. The two last factors, i.e. location and context, are obtained from the impacted AST and AST nodes from Table 1. Each AST node has a type and information that we can use to determine the impacted location in the constraints as well as the context of a constraint. For the context, we further identify whether the impacted element is accessed from the level of its container, the sub classes, or the super class. At this point, once the three influencing factors for an impacted part of an OCL constraint are determined, we can propose a set of possible resolutions, as we will describe it in Sect. 3.5.

3.4 Resolution Strategies

In this section we present our resolutions and the influencing factors under which they are applied. As an example, we present the resolution strategies associated with the metamodel change *"generalize property multiplicity (GPM) from a single value to multiple values"* that is applied in Fig. 1.

This metamodel change requires the OCL constraint to work on a collection of values of a property p and not a single value anymore. Multiple solutions can be proposed all with a slightly different semantic.

Id : #S3. Context : n/a.

Location in the constraint : navigation path.

Description : An iterator *"forAll"* is added to access the property p, and the subexpression using the values of p is moved to the body of the *"forAll"* while replacing the access path with a temporary variable. The given semantic here is that the OCL constraint is satisfied if it is satisfied for all the values of p.

$$Exp.\boldsymbol{p}.restExp => Exp.\boldsymbol{p}_{->}\boldsymbol{forAll}(x|x.restExp)$$

Id : #S4. Context : n/a.

Location in the constraint : navigation path.

Description : An iterator *"exists"* is added to access the property p, and the subexpression using the values of p is moved to the body of the *"exists"* while replacing the access path with a temporary variable. The given semantic is that the OCL constraint is satisfied if at least it is satisfied for one value of p.

$$Exp.\boldsymbol{p}.restExp => Exp.\boldsymbol{p}_{->}\boldsymbol{exists}(x|x.restExp)$$

Table 2 presents the metamodel changes that have an impact on OCL constraint which can be automatically resolved, and their associated resolutions while specifying the two new influencing factors. As shown in Table 2, for 8 metamodel changes we propose 17 resolutions. Note that we do not attempt to define all possible resolutions. Indeed, there will always be a situation in which the user might apply a manual resolution or a particular refactoring. This is handled in our approach by the *ignore option* since we allow the user to not apply a specific resolution when desired. Description and examples of all our resolutions can be found in our companion web page[2].

3.5   Proposing Resolution Strategies

In our approach we define and we implement a set of fixed resolutions that can be applied during co-evolution. When defining the resolutions we already specify under which influencing factors each resolution is applied (see Sect. 3.4).

Figure 4 depicts our process of selecting the appropriate resolutions. It starts with all implemented resolutions and excludes a subset of resolutions based on the influencing factors. The final subset of applicable resolutions is then proposed to the user. The first factor we consider to exclude resolutions is the metamodel change that reduces the possible applicable resolutions (step 1). If we encounter a rename change we exclude the resolutions defined for other metamodel changes. After that, the impacted location is considered to also reduce the subset of the

---

[2] https://pages.lip6.fr/Djamel.Khelladi/ICSR2016/.

Table 2. Resolutions proposed in our co-evolution approach.

Metamodel change (Factor 1)	Location in the OCL constraint (Factor 2)	Context (Factor 3)	Resolution strategies	Total no of proposed resolutions
⋄ Rename element	n/a	n/a	#S1	1
⋄ Delete element	n/a	n/a	#S2	1
⋄ GPM from a single value to multiple values	navigation path	n/a	#S3 #S4 #S5 #S6 #S7	5
⋄ Move property	context	container	#S8	3
	navigation path	n/a	#S9 #S10	
⋄ Push property	context	container	#S11	3
	navigation path	container	#S12	
	navigation path	not via the subclasses	#S13	
⋄ Extract class	context	container	#S8	2
	navigation path	n/a	#S9	
⋄ Inline class	context	container	#S14	3
	navigation path	n/a	#S15 #S16	
⋄ Flatten hierarchy	n/a	container	#S17	1

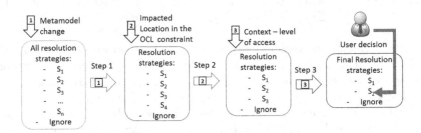

Fig. 4. Process of selecting the appropriate resolution strategies per impacted part of a constraint and per metamodel change.

possible applicable resolutions (step 2). Finally, the context of the impacted constraint allows us to further reduce the resolutions to a final subset (step 3) that is proposed to the user who decides which one to apply.

A constraint can be impacted in different parts, i.e. different AST nodes, by either the same or different metamodel changes. The process of Fig. 4 is applied for each impacted part of an OCL constraint, i.e. for each tuple of { impacted OCL constraint × impacted AST node}. Note that when a constraint is impacted by several metamodel changes, the resolutions are proposed and applied following the chronological order of the changes in the evolution trace. It ensures consistency in the co-evolution since the resolutions are applied in the order of their associated metamodel changes. To remain flexible and to not introduce unintended solutions, our approach also proposes the possibility to *ignore* (in Fig. 4) the proposed resolutions.

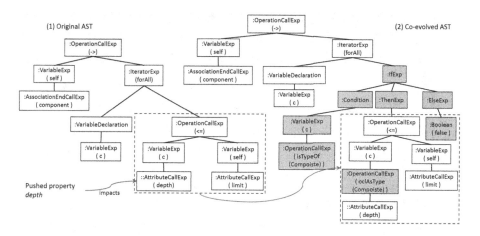

Fig. 5. AST of the original and co-evolved OCL constraint

3.6 Automated Application of the Constraints' Resolutions

At this stage, we can propose, for each impacted part of an OCL constraint, a set of resolution strategies among which the user can choose.

A resolution updates the AST by adding, removing, or updating nodes. Each resolution is implemented as a transformation function applied on the ASTs. Figure 5 depicts the co-evolution of the first constraint in Fig. 2c to the first constraint in Fig. 2d at the AST level. The identified impacted AST node by the push property *depth* is represented with an arrow labeled "impacts" in Fig. 5. Note that some resolutions can be applied directly on the impacted AST node such as for a *rename*. Other resolutions can be applied on a subtree composing the OCL subexpression that includes the impacted AST node. The resolution for the pushed property *depth* cannot be applied on the AST node `AttributeCallExp` of *depth* alone. To this end, the first OCL subexpression in the AST is identified on which the resolution strategy is applied locally. In Fig. 5, the subtree on which the resolution #S13 applies is surrounded by the dashed square. The resolution is represented by the gray nodes, and it consists in introducing an `If` expression that tests whether the current instance of the container is of type `Composite`. The `Then` branch contains the found subtree while introducing a conversion to `Composite` before to call the property *depth*.

4   Implementation

Our tool manipulates Ecore/EMF metamodels and OCL files for the constraints. After identifying the metamodel evolution trace with the detection tool [11,12]. Our tool runs the impact analysis on the OCL constraints and for each impacted part we propose alternative resolutions. The user can then choose the appropriate resolution among the proposed ones or can decide to apply none of them.

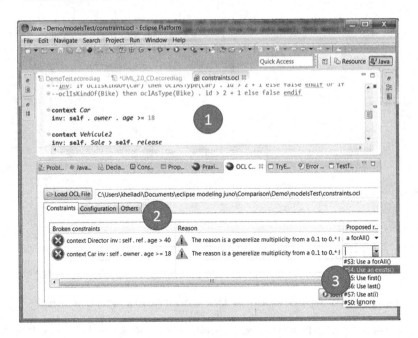

Fig. 6. Screenshot of the Eclipse plugin Tool.

Then, our co-evolution engine applies the chosen resolution for each impacted part of an OCL constraint at the AST level. The core functionalities of this component are implemented with Java and are packaged into an Eclipse plugin that is chained with the external plugins of Blanc et al. [1] and [11,12].

Figure 6 displays a screenshot of our tool. Window (1) shows the OCL constraints that are co-evolved. In window (2) we present the impacted constraints and the cause of the impact in a textual message (the metamodel change and the location of the used element). In Window (3) a set of resolutions is proposed in a dropdown menu to the user along with the *ignore* option. Then, each resolution is applied to each impacted part of an OCL constraint.

5   Evaluation

This section presents a qualitative evaluation of our approach by comparing for the same set of constraints how they are manually co-evolved in practice against how they are co-evolved by our tool. This allows us to measure the precision of our approach. We first present our dataset. Then, we present the co-evolution as it occurred in practice. After that, the co-evolution results of our approach are illustrated. Finally, we compare our results against the ones in practice. Time performances of the co-evolution are measured as well. The goals of this evaluation are the following:

#G1: Demonstrate that alternative resolutions are required in practice.

#G2: Show that our 17 resolutions are close to the user's needs.

#G3: Show that the set of initial metamodel changes we support already allows handling a realistic co-evolution scenario.

5.1   Dataset

We evaluate on a real evolution case study, namely: the UML Class Diagram (CD) metamodel from version 1.5 to 2.0 with their respective 73 and 110 OCL constraints. We collected the OCL constraints that are associated to the metamodel's versions 1.5 and 2.0. We put the constraints into a canonical form, e.g. by adding the keyword "self" to remove any ambiguity.

5.2   Co-evolution Results as Occurred in Practice

As a first step of our evaluation, we studied how the OCL constraints are co-evolved in practice in response to the metamodel evolution. To this end, we first studied the evolution of the UML CD from 1.5 to 2.0 to determine the atomic and complex changes. In order to study how the OCL constraints are co-evolved in practice, we followed the next procedure:

- Identify non-impacted constraints in the original version that are present in the new version.
- Identify non-impacted constraints in the original version that are deleted in the new version.
- Identify impacted constraints in the original version that should be co-evolved.
- For these impacted constraints, we systematically verify in the new version whether it exists a constraint that:
  - Has the same objective. We judge based on the comments describing the constraint's purpose (given in the specification). We also check returned type equality.
  - Has the same structure, using similar OCL operators, and/or using the same metamodel elements.
  - Final decision is made manually:
    1. If no constraint is found, we consider the impacted constraint as deleted.
    2. If a constraint is found, we consider it to be the co-evolved version of the impacted constraint.
- Identify new constraints added in the evolved version.

Our analysis' results of the co-evolution in practice are presented in Table 3.

Table 3. Co-evolution of the OCL constraints as they occurred in practice.

Co-evolution of OCL constraints in practice	UML CD 1.5 to 2.0
◇ Constraints that are not impacted	19
◇ Constraints not impacted and present in both versions	7
◇ Constraints not impacted and deleted in the new version	12
◇ Constraints impacted in the first version (to be co-evolved)	54
◇ Constraints co-evolved by deletion in the new version	35
◇ Constraints co-evolved and present in the new version	19
◇ New constraints in the new version	84

5.3 Co-evolution Results by Our Approach

We first detected with our tool [11,12] the evolution traces of the UML CD metamodel that is given as input to our co-evolution tool. In the experiment, the authors play the user role. We aimed at co-evolving the OCL constraints *as close as possible* to the co-evolution in practice while also avoiding the use of the ignore solution (for an objective comparison in the next section). The results of our applied co-evolution are presented in Table 4.

Table 4. Co-evolution of OCL constraints by our approach

Co-evolution of OCL constraints by our approach	UML CD 1.5 to 2.0
◇ Constraints that are not impacted	19
◇ Constraints impacted in the first version (to be co-evolved)	54
◇ Constraints co-evolved by deletion	28
◇ Constraints co-evolved by other resolution strategies	26

Several constraints are impacted by more than one metamodel change. Thus, more than one resolution is applied for several constraints. For instance, rename #S1 (see Table 2) is several times applied along with #S2, #S3, #S9 #S12, or #S13 on the same constraint. As mentioned previously, the resolutions are applied following the chronological order of the detected metamodel changes.

Performances. We ran our experiment on a PC VAIO with i7 1.80 GHz Processor and 8 GB of RAM with Windows 7 as OS. After selecting the resolutions to be applied among the proposed ones, all impacted OCL constraints were co-evolved in less than 1 s in each of the case studies.

5.4 Comparison of the Results:"Our Approach" VS "in Practice"

Following our procedure of Sect. 3.2 we were able to identify all the 54 impacted constraints.

Deleted constraints. Among those 54 constraints, 28 constraints are co-evolved by deletion. This is due to the fact that some properties and/or classes used in those 28 constraints are deleted during the metamodel evolution. Those 28 deleted constraints are also deleted in the real case study, i.e. they are included in the 35 deleted constraints in practice.

Undeleted constraints. In our approach we co-evolved 26 constraints with various resolutions. Among those 26 constraints, 19 constraints are co-evolved in our approach that correspond to the 19 co-evolved constraints in practice. Moreover, 7 constraints are co-evolved in our approach and correspond to the 7 impacted constraints that are deleted in practice.

Regarding the 19 constraints that are co-evolved with our tool, 11 co-evolved constraints are syntactically equal to 11 of the 19 constraints that resulted from the co-evolution in practice. Additional 4 constraints are not syntactically but are semantically equal to 4 of the 19 constraints that are co-evolved in practice, making 15 semantically correct co-evolved constraints with our tool.

However, the last 4 constraints are non-syntactically and non-semantically matching. They are refactored in practice with a different semantic. For example, one original constraint that checks absence of circular inheritance is impacted by the renaming of `GeneralizableElement` to `PackageableElement`. It is co-evolved by our approach as follows from (1) to (2) by applying the rename strategy #S1.

$$\text{context } \texttt{GeneralizableElement inv:} \quad (1)$$
$$\text{not self.allParents()} -> \text{includes(self)}$$
$$\text{context } \texttt{PackageableElement inv:} \quad (2)$$
$$\text{not self.allParents()} -> \text{includes(self)}$$

In practice the context of constraint (1) was changed to the subclass `Classifier` instead of or after applying the rename. Thus, the semantic is slightly changed by the manual co-evolution since the applicability scope of the new constraint is reduced to elements of type `Classifier`.

The rates of syntactically and semantically correct co-evolution are respectively 72 % and 80 %[3].

Maintained constraints. In our approach, 7 impacted constraints are co-evolved whereas they are deleted in practice $\boxed{A}$. We applied 8 times the rename strategy #S1 for six of the constraints and 1 time the strategy #S16 of an inline class for one constraint. Thus, only 35 % (19/54) of the impacted constraints are maintained in practice, while 48 % (26/54) of the impacted constraints are maintained in our approach. For example, constraint (3) is an operation defined on a `ModelElement` returning a set of all direct suppliers of the `ModelElement`; it is impacted by the rename of `ModelElement` to `NamedElement`. We co-evolved it to (4) simply by applying the rename strategy #S1.

$$\text{context } \texttt{ModelElement} \text{ def: supplier :} \quad (3)$$
$$\text{Set}(\textit{ModelElement}) = \text{self.clientDependency.supplier}$$

---

[3] % = ((deleted constraints + syntactically (respectively semantically) correct co-evolved constraints)/impacted constraints).

$$\text{context NamedElement def: supplier :}\qquad(4)$$
$$\text{Set}(NamedElement) = \text{self.clientDependency.supplier}$$

From our point of view, it is surprising to delete a constraint, whereas it would have been possible to rename the impacted element or to apply another resolution. One possible explanation is that the constraints became meaningless in the new version of the metamodel. Another arguable explanation is that the lack of a (semi) automated support for co-evolution was the cause of the loss of those constraints. Otherwise, they would have been easily maintained in the new version. Furthermore, it is also surprising to find deletion of 12 non-impacted constraints $\boxed{B}$. For example, constraint (5) expressing that an interface can only contain operations is deleted.

$$\text{context Interface inv:}\qquad(5)$$
$$\text{self.allFeatures()}->\text{forAll(f | f.oclIsKindOf(Operation))}$$

Similarly, a possible explanation is that those constraints are no more necessary. As a further investigation, we had a look at later versions of UML CD specifications (versions 2.1, 2.2, and 2.3), and the constraints are indeed missing.

5.5   Discussion and Threats to Validity

The preliminary evaluation shows that our approach is able to cope with real co-evolution of OCL constraints. In the following we discuss the observed results.

(1) First of all, as mentioned previously multiple resolutions are used in particular for the metamodel changes *push property* (#S12, #S13) and *inline class* (#S15, #S16). These results emphasize and confirm the necessity to propose alternative resolutions in order to cope with realistic scenarios of OCL constraints' co-evolution. Otherwise, the rates of automatic co-evolution would be lower than the ones in this paper, with a higher risk of introducing inappropriate solutions.

(2) Furthermore, the first 7 cases of maintained constraints $\boxed{A}$ underline the need to also propose the delete strategy #S2 whenever a constraint is impacted, and not always try to maintain the constraint. Moreover, the second 12 cases of deleted constraints $\boxed{B}$ emphasize the fact that even if all impacted constraints are correctly co-evolved, user intervention would still be needed to decide whether to keep or to remove some of the non-impacted constraints.

(3) Finally, the cases of the semantically not matching constraints in UML CD (e.g. constraint (3)) underline the need to let the user *ignore* a proposed co-evolution. By not applying a particular resolution, the user can manually co-evolve it and further refactor it w.r.t. her intent.

We now discuss threats to validity (internal, external, and conclusion) after Wohlin et al. [26] w.r.t. our three evaluation goals #G1, #G2, and #G3.

Internal Validity. During the analysis of the co-evolution of the OCL constraints in practice, it is possible that we could have missed a correspondence between an original constraint and a co-evolved constraint when the latter is subject to a strong refactoring. To reduce this risk, in the procedure of our analysis for each impacted constraint, we investigated the constraints of the new versions one by one to avoid missing any correspondence. Moreover, other complex changes than the 7 ones we considered may occur in the evolution requiring additional resolutions that are not in our 17 resolutions. However, in our evaluation the 7 complex changes we considered as well as the 17 resolutions were sufficient in our case studies. Therefore, this threat is acceptable here.

External Validity. We evaluated our tool on a case study of metamodels and its OCL constraints. However, it is difficult to generalize our obtained results for other metamodels and OCL constraints. Nonetheless, the UML CD case study provided a representative and a complex evolution trace that had a significant impact on the OCL constraints.

Conclusion Validity. Our evaluation gives promising results demonstrating that alternative resolutions are used in real cases. The results also indicate that our 17 resolutions are semantically close to the user need during the co-evolution. Thus, our evaluation results meet our goals #G1 and #G2. However, we cannot estimate the quality of the resolutions only based on our UML CD case study. Third goal #G3 is also met since our tool covers all metamodel changes that occurred in the UML CD evolution. Yet, more experiments are necessary to retrieve a more precise measure of the resolutions' quality, their occurrence frequency, and the benefit of the ignore option in practice.

6   Related Work

In contrast to models and transformations co-evolution where many works exist (e.g. [15,25]), co-evolution of OCL constraints has received little attention so far. Demuth et al. [5,6] proposed an approach for OCL co-evolution based on templates. They provided 11 templates that define a fixed structure for OCL constraints. Thus, the co-evolution in this case is a re-instantiation of the templates to update the constraints. However, their approach is not applicable for arbitrary OCL constraints, and is limited to 11 templates only. They do not handle metamodel changes that impact the structure of the constraints.

Hassam et al. [7] proposed to co-evolve OCL constraints using QVT [22] a transformation language. Similarly, Markovic et al. [16,17] proposed to refactor, based on QVT, OCL constraints annotated on UML class diagrams when these last evolve. Kusel et al. [13] discussed the impact of metamodel evolution on OCL expressions and proposed to resolve impacted expressions. However, they do not consider an OCL constraint as a whole. In particular, the context is ignored whereas it can be the impacted part that requires a resolution.

Cabot et al. [3] focused on the metamodel change delete element. In particular, they aimed at removing only a sub part of the OCL constraint that is using the deleted element. However, the approach is applicable only to OCL constraints written in the form of Conjunctive Normal Form (CNF). Buttner et al. [2] discussed the impact of changing the multiplicity of a property on OCL constraints. In our approach we also address this issue in our resolution (#S3-7).

All existing approaches [2,3,5–7,13,16,17] consider only the metamodel change as a factor to propose a resolution. Thus, they define for each metamodel change only a unique resolution. In contrast, we identified two additional factors that lead to propose alternative resolutions.

To the best of our knowledge, we are the first to consider these issues and to show that multiple resolutions are needed in practice. We therefore are the first to propose alternative resolution strategies while considering the metamodel change, the impact location in an OCL constraint, and the context.

7   Conclusion and Future Work

In this paper, we addressed the topic of metamodel and OCL constraints co-evolutions and proposed a semi-automatic approach with alternative resolution strategies. We identified two new *factors* that lead us to propose alternative resolutions to the user to chose from. This has the advantage to co-evolve OCL constraints w.r.t. the user intent and to avoid applying unintended resolutions. We evaluated our approach on a big-medium sized case study: the UML CD metamodel with its OCL constraints. The results show that our approach is suitable to handle complex co-evolution scenarios of metamodels and OCL constraints. It reached 72 % of 80 % of syntactically and semantically correct co-evolution.

Although we focused on the co-evolution of OCL constraints defined on top of metamodels, our approach can also handle the co-evolution of OCL constraints defined on top of object-oriented models in general. Thus in future work, we first aim to evaluate our approach on other applications of OCL constraints such as OCL queries, or OCL scripts that express model transformations. We further plan to explore the possibility to allow the user to import external resolutions in particular to be used along with the *ignore* option.

Acknowledgment. The research leading to these results has received funding from the industrial innovation Project MoNoGe under grant FUI - AAP no. 15.

References

1. Blanc, X., Mounier, I., Mougenot, A., Mens, T.: Detecting model inconsistency through operation-based model construction. In: ACM/IEEE 30th ICSE 2008, pp. 511–520 (2008)
2. Buttner, F., Bauerdick, H., Gogolla, M.: Towards transformation of integrity constraints and database states. In: DEXA, pp. 823–828 (2005)
3. Cabot, J., Conesa, J.: Automatic integrity constraint evolution due to model subtract operations. In: Wang, S., et al. (eds.) ER Workshops 2004. LNCS, vol. 3289, pp. 350–362. Springer, Heidelberg (2004)
4. Cabot, J., Gogolla, M.: Object constraint language (OCL): a definitive guide. In: 12th SFM, Bertinoro, Italy, pp. 58–90 (2012)
5. Demuth, A., Lopez-Herrejon, R., Egyed, A.: Automatically generating and adapting model constraints to support co-evolution of design models. In: 27th IEEE/ACM ASE, pp. 302–305 (2012)

6. Demuth, A., Lopez-Herrejon, R.E., Egyed, A.: Supporting the co-evolution of metamodels and constraints through incremental constraint management. In: MODELS, pp. 287–303, January 2013
7. Hassam, K., Sadou, S., Gloahec, V.L., Fleurquin, R.: Assistance system for OCL constraints adaptation during metamodel evolution. In: CSMR, pp. 151–160. IEEE (2011)
8. Herrmannsdoerfer, M., Ratiu, D., Wachsmuth, G.: Language evolution in practice: the history of GMF. In: Brand, M., Gašević, D., Gray, J. (eds.) SLE 2009. LNCS, vol. 5969, pp. 3–22. Springer, Heidelberg (2010)
9. Herrmannsdoerfer, M., Vermolen, S.D., Wachsmuth, G.: An extensive catalog of operators for the coupled evolution of metamodels and models. In: Malloy, B., Staab, S., van den Brand, M. (eds.) SLE 2010. LNCS, vol. 6563, pp. 163–182. Springer, Heidelberg (2011)
10. Hutchinson, J., Whittle, J., Rouncefield, M., Kristoffersen, S.: Empirical assessment of MDE in industry. In: Proceedings of the 33rd International Conference on Software Engineering, pp. 471–480. ACM (2011)
11. Khelladi, D.E., Bendraou, R., Gervais, M.-P.: Ad-room: a tool for automatic detection of refactorings in object-oriented models. In: The 38th ICSE (2016)
12. Khelladi, D.E., Hebig, R., Bendraou, R., Robin, J., Gervais, M.-P.: Detecting complex changes during metamodel evolution. In: Zdravkovic, J., Kirikova, M., Johannesson, P. (eds.) CAiSE 2015. LNCS, vol. 9097, pp. 263–278. Springer, Heidelberg (2015)
13. Kusel, A., Etzlstorfer, J., Kapsammer, E., Retschitzegger, W., Schoenboeck, J., Schwinger, W., Wimmer, M.: Systematic co-evolution of OCL expressions. In: 11th APCCM 2015, vol. 27, p. 30 (2015)
14. Langer, P., Wimmer, M., Brosch, P., Herrmannsdorfer, M., Seidl, M., Wieland, K., Kappel, G.: A posteriori operation detection in evolving software models. J. Syst. Softw. **86**(2), 551–566 (2013)
15. Mantz, F., Taentzer, G., Lamo, Y., Wolter, U.: Co-evolving meta-models and their instance models: a formal approach based on graph transformation. Sci. Comput. Program. **104**, 2–43 (2015)
16. Markovic, S., Baar, T.: Refactoring OCL annotated UML class diagrams. In: MODELS, pp. 280–294 (2005)
17. Markovic, S., Baar, T.: Refactoring OCL annotated UML class diagrams. Softw. Syst. Model **7**(1), 25–47 (2008)
18. Mezei, G., Levendovszky, T., Charaf, H.: An optimizing OCL compiler for metamodeling and model transformation environments. In: Sacha, K. (ed.) Software Engineering Techniques: Design for Quality, vol. 227, pp. 61–71. Springer, New York (2006)
19. Morisio, M., Ezran, M., Tully, C.: Success and failure factors in software reuse. IEEE Trans. Softw. Eng. **28**(4), 340–357 (2002)
20. OMG. Meta object facility (MOF) (2011). www.omg.org/spec/MOF/
21. OMG. Object constraints language (OCL) (2015). www.omg.org/spec/OCL/
22. OMG. Query/views/transformations (QVT) (2015). www.omg.org/spec/QVT/
23. OMG. Unified modeling language (UML) (2015). www.omg.org/spec/UML/
24. Steinberg, D., Budinsky, F., Merks, E., Paternostro, M.: EMF: Eclipse Modeling Framework. Pearson Education, Upper Saddle River (2008)
25. Wachsmuth, G.: Metamodel adaptation and model co-adaptation. In: Ernst, E. (ed.) ECOOP 2007. LNCS, vol. 4609, pp. 600–624. Springer, Heidelberg (2007)
26. Wohlin, C., Runeson, P., Höst, M., Ohlsson, M.C., Regnell, B., Wesslén, A.: Experimentation in Software Engineering. Springer, Heidelberg (2012)

A Model Repository Description
Language - MRDL

Brahim Hamid[(⊠)]

IRIT, University of Toulosue, 118 Route de Narbonne,
31062 Toulouse Cedex 9, France
`hamid@irit.fr`

Abstract. Repository-based development of software systems has gained more attention recently by addressing new challenges such as security and dependability. However, there are still gaps in existing modeling languages and/or formalisms dedicated to define model repositories and the way how to reuse them in the automation of software development. Thus, there is a strong requirement for defining a model repository description language not only as a modeling approach, but also as a suitable instrument to support system and software engineers in the activity of search and retrieval of appropriate models beyond keyword-based search. Moreover, modeling approaches allow using tools for the specification and the exploitation of the designed artifacts (e.g. analysis and evaluation). The goal of this paper is to advance the state of the art in model repository description for software and systems engineering. In particular, we have designed a flexible and extensible modeling language, by means of an OMG style metamodel, to specify model repositories for modeling artifacts, and we have defined an operational architecture for development tools. In particular, we show the feasibility of our own approach by reporting some preliminary prototype providing a model-based repository of security and dependability (S&D) pattern models.

Keywords: Model repository · Metamodel · Model-driven engineering · Software system engineering

1 Introduction

Our society has become increasingly dependent on software-intensive systems, such as Information and Communication Technology (ICT) systems, not only in safety-critical areas (e.g., defense, transportation, nuclear power generation, space exploration), but also in areas such as finance, medical information management and systems that use web applications (e.g., cloud computing systems). ICT systems are a type of socio-technical systems, which include not only technical systems but also operational processes and the people who use and interact with those technical systems. However, the shift from traditional computer systems toward the Internet of Things, i.e., devices connected via the Internet,

© Springer International Publishing Switzerland 2016
G.M. Kapitsaki and E. Santana de Almeida (Eds.): ICSR 2016, LNCS 9679, pp. 350–367, 2016.
DOI: 10.1007/978-3-319-35122-3_23

wireless communication or other interfaces, requires a reconsideration of software system engineering processes. As a result, new recommendations should be considered to develop novel methods capable of handling the complexity and reducing the cost of the development of these systems. We believe that the specification and packaging of software modeling artifacts can provide an efficient means of addressing these problems, improving industrial efficiency and fostering technology *reuse* across domains (the reuse of models at different levels), thus reducing the time and effort required to design a complex system [1,2].

During system development lifecycles, modeling artifacts may be used in various forms such as domain models, design patterns, component models, code modules, test and code generators [3–5]. Repositories of modeling artifacts have recently gained increased attention as a means of encouraging reuse in software engineering. In fact, repository-centric development processes are more widely adopted in software system development than are other approaches, such as architecture-centric or pattern-centric development processes. According to Bernstein and Dayal [6], a repository is a shared database of information regarding engineered artifacts. These authors note that a repository possesses (1) a *Manager* for modeling, retrieving, and managing the objects in the repository; (2) a *Database* to store the data; and (3) *Functionalities* to enable interaction with the repository. In our work, we go one step further: we conceptualize a model-based repository to support the specifications, definitions and packaging of a set of modeling artifacts. This paper addresses the challenges of creating a flexible repository of modeling artifacts and managing the models in that repository while providing assistance with the selection of appropriate modeling artifacts in the various stages of the system engineering lifecycle. We propose an abstract syntax, by means of an OMG-style metamodel, for constructing the modeling language for model repository models, build in an incremental approach. The abstract syntax is based on the requirements for the model repository modeling language, describing various concerns, such as engineering concepts, repository interactions, modeling artifact management and reuse. To specify model repositories conforming to the proposed metamodel, we develop a concrete syntax. In addition to this task, several services dedicated to repository features are developed. The objective is to integrate multiple features through model-based repository engineering coupled with Model-Driven Engineering (MDE) technology, making it possible to leverage the reuse of model building blocks from the repository.

The remainder of this paper is organized as follows. Section 2 describes several previous approaches to repository building and to system development based on repositories. In Sect. 3, we describe our approach to designing a model repository for software system engineering. Then, Sect. 4 presents the design process of a model-based repository. Section 5 describes the architecture of the tool suite and an example of the implementation of a repository. Finally, Sect. 6 presents our conclusions and suggests possible directions for future work.

2   Related Work

Several methodologies use repositories for the storage of reusable artifacts. In general, these approaches rely on repositories to resolve code dependencies during the development process. The usage of such repositories (of code, code libraries, or binaries) is widespread in development and deployment processes. Code or code library repositories are used for dependency management. For example, the available repositories in the Java domain include Ivy [7] and Maven [8], and recently emerging approaches such as Gradle [9] or Bundler [10] for Ruby are prominent representatives of the usage of these repositories. One example of repositories for binaries (e.g., deployable components) is the Eclipse Platform, which uses the Equinox p2 repositories [11]. Code, code library and binary repositories are generally developed in close collaboration with the tools through which they are accessed. Maven and other Java-based tools may use software repositories such as Apache Archiva or Sonatype Nexus, for example.

In Model-Driven Development (MDD), model repositories [6, 12–15] are used to facilitate the exchange of models through tools for managing modeling artifacts. In the field of biology, the CellML Model Repository [16] provides free access to over 330 biological models. The CellML Model Repository provides versioning capabilities and stores the version information at the model level. When a model is modified, a new version is created and added to the repository. Model repositories are often built as a layer on top of existing technologies (for instance, databases). To facilitate querying of the repository, metadata can be added to assist in the selection of the desired artifacts. Therefore, certain repositories exist that are composed solely of metadata. For instance, as presented in the ebXML standard [17] and in the ebXML Repository Reference Implementation [18], a service repository can be regarded as a metadata repository that contains metadata about location information to assist in finding a service.

In [14], the authors propose a reusable architecture decision model for establishing model and metadata repositories. Their purpose is the design of data model and metadata repositories. In addition, several helpful tools are included in the product to assist in the selection of a basic repository technology, appropriate repository metadata, and suitable modeling levels for the model information stored in the repository. In [19], the authors propose a repository implementation with support for artifact storage and management. The supported types of artifacts are metamodels, models, constraints, specifications, transformation rules, code, templates, configuration or documentation information, and their associated metadata.

Another issue of concern is the generation of graphical modeling tools, as studied in the GraMMi project [20]. In this project, the repository is based on three levels of abstraction (meta-metamodel, metamodel and model). The repository stores both metamodels (notation definitions) and models (instantiation definitions). The repository is accessed through a self-provided interface. GraMMi's kernel permits the management of persistent objects. Thus, the purpose of this kernel is to convert the objects (models) into an understandable form for the user via the graphical interface.

Gomes et al. [21] have proposed a centralized knowledge base that can be used through case-based reasoning, a paradigm for reusing past knowledge stored in the form of cases. In this context, a case is a UML diagram that is enriched with certain identifiers. WordNet is used as a common-sense ontology to provide a classification of software projects described in UML. Searches are performed based on similarity metrics, which consider the relationships between the UML elements (packages, classes, interfaces, attributes, methods and relationships) and WordNet elements. Different metrics must exist, one for each type of UML element, and the use of the ontology allows more relaxed matching to be performed. The proposed framework cannot be used with any metamodels; only UML class models are supported.

The ReMoDD (Repository for Model-Driven Development) project [15] focuses on MDD to reduce the effort involved in the development of complex software by raising the level of abstraction at which software systems are developed. This approach is based on a repository that contains artifacts that support research and education in MDD. The ReMoDD platform provides a set of tools with which to interact with the repository. Concretely, ReMoDD artifacts include documented MDD case studies, examples of models that reflect good and bad modeling practices, modeling exercises and problems that can be used to develop classroom assignments and projects.

Moogle [22] is a model search engine that uses a UML or DSL metamodel to create indexes that facilitate the evaluation of complex queries. Its key features include the ability to search through different kinds of models, as long as their metamodels are provided. The index is built automatically, and the system attempts to present only the relevant portion of the results, for example, to remove the XML tags or other unreadable characters to improve readability. The model element types, the model attributes and the hierarchy among model elements can be used as search criteria. Models are searched by using keywords (Simple Search), by specifying the types of model elements to be returned (Advanced Search) and by using filters organized into facets (Browse). To properly use such advanced search engines, the user must have knowledge of the metamodel elements. Moogle uses the Apache SOLR ranking policy for its results. The most important information contained in the results is highlighted for clarity to the user.

ModelBus [23] provides a framework for model storage and transformation as well as a directory of model services. Similarly, the MORSE project [24] offers a Model-Aware Service Environment repository to facilitate dynamic, reflective model searches. MORSE addresses two common problems in MDD systems: traceability and collaboration. The model repository is the main component of MORSE and was designed with the intent of abstraction from specific technologies. MORSE focuses on runtime services and processes and on their integration and interaction with the repository.

The technique described in [25] is a general-purpose approach that uses graph query processing to search a repository of models represented as graphs. First, the repository models are translated into directed graphs. Then, the system receives a query that conforms to the considered DSL metamodel. To reduce the matching problem to one of graph matching, the submitted query is also transformed into a graph. Matches are calculated by finding a mapping between the query graph and the project graphs or sub-graphs, depending on the granularity. The results are ranked based on the graph edit distance metric using the A-Star algorithm. The prototype addresses the case of the domain-specific WebML language.

Most process model repositories are linked to business process management systems and business process editors. In addition to these systems, APRO-MORE [26] is an Advanced Process Model Repository supported by a tool infrastructure that integrates a set of features for the analysis, management and use of process models. The work presented in [27] provides a survey of business process model repositories and their related frameworks. This work addresses the management of large collections of business processes that use repository structures and provide common repository functions such as storage, search capabilities and version management. It targets the process model designer to facilitate the reuse of process model artifacts. A comparison of process model repositories is presented to highlight the degree of reusability of artifacts.

Repository-centric engineering implies multiple kinds of interactions with repositories, e.g., management, population and access, to assist in software system development through reuse. To our knowledge, there are no existing methodological tools to support the definition and description of these interactions in repository-based approaches. The workflows, especially those for the development of systems with dependency resolutions and the deployment of components, are well documented. However, the ability to describe these approaches in MDE is lacking, and there is also a shortage of available approaches to the use of models that possess integrated model management functionalities. Our work aims to provide a new engineering approach to facilitate the reuse of these solutions (infrastructures and approaches). Regarding compliance with a specific repository, the approach described in this paper, including the description languages and the methodology, may be used to specify the management and use of several of the aforementioned types of repositories. Finally, our approach focuses not on implementation but rather on the methodology for the development and use of model repositories. We have used EMF and a repository based on the Eclipse Connected Data Objects (CDO) framework to implement the structure and interfaces of a prototype repository. However, other existing platforms for repository implementation may also be targeted using our proposed approach.

3   Conceptual Model of a Model-based Repository

The proposed model-based repository will effectively support reuse and the integration of the processes of model specification and system development using models. The resulting modeling framework reduces the time/cost of understanding and analyzing system artifact descriptions by virtue of its abstraction mechanisms and reduces the cost of the development process by virtue of its generation mechanisms. Concretely, a repository system is a structure that stores specification languages as well as models and the relationships among them, coupled with a set of tools to manage, visualize, export and instantiate these artifacts for use in engineering processes. In this section, we introduce the requirements for a repository system and how they influence the design decisions regarding the specification language of the model-based repository.

3.1 Requirements

Here, we address the set of requirements involved in the design of a model repository description language. These requirements are primarily focused on defining the engineering process for the development of repository-based applications (the definition, integration, transformation, and validation of a modeling artifact for use in an application). Additionally, these requirements identify ways in which the engineering process may serve the engineer in the implementation of this process and, finally, identify the restrictions that must be considered in the specification of a model repository.

The following is a list of high level requirements which were established by the Semco Project [28] and the TERESA Project [29] and which also target lacks in existing model repository building processes. The following set of requirements does not represent a complete set of requirements for any arbitrary model-based repository, as such a set depends on the application domain. As we will demonstrate, these requirements are identified based on an analysis of the challenges that the repository should address and range from the top-down specification of the repository structure to its implementation and deployment with the intent of facilitating reuse in the process of model-based system and software engineering. As we will see, the metamodel proposed in this paper tries to fulfill most, if not all, of the requirements elicited during the projects. The requirements elicited are categorized into five categories (Table 1) and are outlined in Table 2.

Table 1. Categories of requirements for the metamodel

Category	Abbreviation
Repository content and organization	RC
Populating the repository	PR
Managing the repository	MR
Accessing the repository	AR
Specification of the repository structure and interfaces	SR
Implementing the repository software system	IR

3.2 System and Software Artifact Repository Conceptual Model (SARM)

An analysis of the identified requirements leads to the definition of a set of concepts on which to base the modeling languages. We have identified three main concepts for this purpose, as shown in Fig. 1.

Table 2. List of requirements - overview

Category	Requirement	Description
IR	R-01. Repository construction	-Domain-independent vs. domain-specific repository construction
RC	R-02. Repository organization	-Domain-independent vs. domain-specific repository organization
SR	R-03. Artifact description	-Repository-compliant description of artifacts -Support for multiple types of artifacts
PR	R-04. Artifact publication	-Support for the artifact insertion operation - Support for the incomplete artifact description insertion operation
AR	R-05. Artifact retrieval	-Domain-independent vs. domain-specific artifact retrieval -Domain- and role-based artifact searching -Support for the artifact search function
MR	R-06. Dependencies	-Support for dependencies between artifacts -Assurance of consistency in artifact dependencies
AR	R-07. Artifact visualization	-Support for the visualization of artifacts -Support for the visualization of the internal structure of the repository (browsing) -Role-dependent visualization of the content of the repository -Adaptation of the visualization mode depending on the user role
AR	R-08. Repository interaction	-Guidelines for easy interaction with the repository -Multiview support for domain- and actor-specific knowledge -Multiview support for domain- and actor-specific tools
MR	R-09. User access control	-Mechanisms to support access control for artifacts -Mechanisms to support access control for dependencies
MR	R-10. Administration	-Support of administrative functions -Support of maintenance and reorganization of the repository content

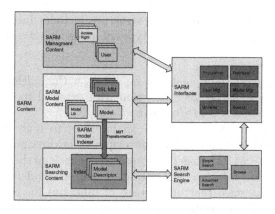

Fig. 1. SARM architecture

(1) SARM content. The repository structure includes a storage space that is used to describe multiple storage targets, in which different types of content are stored. The repository is model-based, and its main content consists of models and their related libraries. The remainder of the repository content is used to store necessary elements for the functioning of the repository.

- *SARM Model Content.* To store models, the repository structure requires a dedicated storage space for model content, including models, metamodels and model libraries.
- *SARM Search Content.* To facilitate model searching, the repository must store metadata for both models and metamodels. To create such metadata, an indexer component examines models from the repository and extracts all information needed for the search.
- *SARM Management Content.* The repository must also store data regarding its users. The SARM Management Content stores user profiles and the associated access rights.

(2) SARM search engine. The repository structure includes a search engine, which is used to search the contents of the repository. The search engine uses metamodeling information and indexing mechanisms to enable the performance of more sophisticated queries. The SARM repository offers three modes of searching for models: Simple Search, Advanced Search and Browsing.

- *Simple Search.* Designed to perform general-purpose queries using keywords. This type of search is best suited to earlier stages of development, when the developer is looking for models related to domain concepts.
- *Advanced Search.* Designed to perform more complex queries. In this case, the user can specify the types of model elements to be returned.
- *Browsing.* Similar to Advanced Search but without the need to specify keywords to be searched. Instead, all elements matching the specified filters are shown. The user can select one or more filters and combine them for more precise browsing results.

(3) SARM interfaces. The repository structure includes interfaces (APIs) to enable interaction with its content. Six types of necessary interfaces can be identified.

- *Populating interface.* To populate the repository with models, SARM provides a set of interfaces (APIs) for interaction with external tools. This interface interacts with the *SARM Model Content.*
- *Retrieval interface.* SARM provides an interface to search for, select and instantiate models within a specific development environment. This interface interacts with the *SARM Model Content* and depends on the *Search interface.*
- *Model Management interface.* For management of the models, SARM provides an interaction interface that offers a set of functions for incorporating new metamodels into the repository, specifying relationships between models, and adding other information. This interface interacts with the emphSARM Model Content.
- *User Management interface.* For user management in the repository, SARM provides an interaction interface that offers a set of functions for managing user data. This interface interacts with the *SARM Management Content.*
- *Search interface.* SARM offers a search interface that uses the *SARM Search Engine* to search for models in the repository.
- *Browse interface.* SARM offers a browsing interface that uses the *SARM Browsing* functionality of the search engine to browse models.

3.3   Metamodel of the Repository Structure

We propose an abstract syntax, by means of an OMG-style metamodel, for constructing the MRDL modeling language for model repositories build in an incremental approach. The abstract syntax is based on the previous requirements (Table 2), describing various concerns, such as engineering concepts, repository interactions, artifact-based engineering and reuse. We specify our model repository modeling language using the Meta Object Facility (MOF) constructs [30], a Object Management Group (OMG) standard for describing modeling languages such as the Unified Modeling Language (UML) [31], and using the open-source Eclipse Modeling Framework (EMF) [32] environment. EMF provides an implementation of EMOF (Essential MOF), a subset of MOF, called Ecore[1]. EMF offers a set of tools to specify metamodels in Ecore and to generate other representations of them. The principal classes of the metamodel of the repository are described using Ecore notation in Fig. 2. Greater detail is provided below with regard to the meanings of the principal concepts used to specify the structure of the repository.

- SarmRepository. The core element used to define the repository.
- SarmModelContent. Represents the model content, including models, metamodels and model libraries.

---

[1] Ecore is a meta-metamodel.

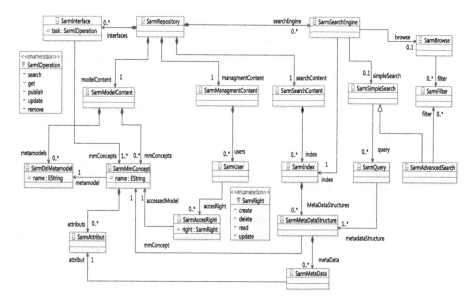

Fig. 2. SARM - Structure

– **SarmDslMetamodel.** Represents the specification languages (metamodels) for the modeling artifacts.
– **SarmMmConcept.** Represents a specific concept from a specific metamodel. In general, a concept represents a modeling artifact that will be stored in the repository.
– **SarmAttribut.** Defines a property of a specific concept.
– **SarmManagementContent.** Represents the management content, including user data.
– **SarmUser.** Used to define user profiles.
– **SarmAccesRight.** Used to define characteristics regarding access rights to the repository and its contents.
– **SarmSearchContent.** Represents search contents, including the model metadata for indexing.
– **SarmIndex.** A structured collection of data used to store a list of model descriptors. The index is used by SarmSearchEngine to perform model searches.
– **SarmMetaDataStructure.** Used to describe each stored model. This class defines all information to be searched and all metadata used for the Advanced Search functionality.
– **SarmMetaData.** Used to define specific metadata with regard to a model.
– **SarmInterface.** Provides a specification of the interfaces (APIs) for visualizing the contents of the repository and for repository management.
– **SarmSearchEngine.** Uses metamodeling information and indexing mechanisms to enable the performance of more sophisticated queries.

4   Definition of a Repository Model

The objective of this step is to specify the repository structure in accordance with the conceptual model defined in Sect. 3.3. To create model instances of the proposed metamodel, we choose to use a tree-structured concrete syntax provided by Eclipse Modeling Framework Technology (EMFT)[2]. It provides graphical, but not-diagrammatic notations, to specify Ecore models. It allows to represent a model as a nested, collapsible structure with composite and leaf elements having text labels and/or symbols. A concrete syntax for the SARM language supports to instantiate the SARM metamodel to create the model of the repository comprising the creation of the metamodel compartments, the modeling artifact compartments, the user list, the interfaces, the search engines, and so on.

In addition, other features are supported, such as the specification of views of the repository according to its interfaces, its organization and the needs of the targeted system engineering processes. The structure of the repository and its interfaces can then be made available (1) to modelers for populating and managing the repository and (2) to access tools for reusing the repository's content. Thus, we provide an EMF-based tree editor for specifying repository models, as visualized in Fig. 3.

Fig. 3. Example of a repository model

---

[2] https://eclipse.org/modeling/emft/.

In our example, we define *SemcoRepository* as an instance of SarmRepository: a model- based repository of S&D patterns and their related property models. To support these S&D pattern models and property models, we use *SEPM* and *GPRM*, as instances of SarmDslMetamodel, which uses a set of instances of Sarm-MmConcept to store the pattern modeling language and property modeling language concepts, respectively. The Generic PRoperty Metamodel (GPRM) [33], which is described using Ecore notation in Fig. 4, is a metamodel that defines a new formalism (i.e., language) for describing property libraries, including units, types and property categories. For instance, S&D attributes [34] such as authenticity, confidentiality and availability are defined as categories. These categories require a set of measure types (degree, metrics,...) and units (Boolean, float,...). These models are used as external model libraries to type the properties of the patterns.

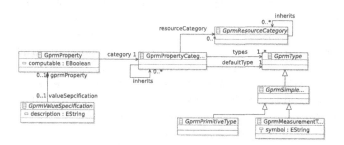

Fig. 4. The (simplified) GPRM

The System and Software Engineering Pattern Metamodel (SEPM) [35] is a metamodel that defines a new formalism for describing S&D patterns and constitutes the basis of our pattern modeling language. Here, we consider patterns to be subsystems that provide access to services (via interfaces) and manage S&D and resource properties (via features), offering a unified means of capturing meta-information related to a pattern and its context of use. Figure 5 describes the principal concepts of the SEPM using Ecore notation.

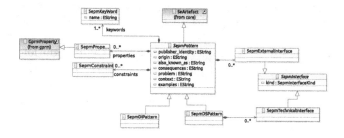

Fig. 5. The (simplified) SEPM

In addition to the repository structure, we define a model of the interfaces used to visualize and manage the contents of the repository. For instance, *Patternsearch* and *Patternpublish* are defined as instances of SarmInterface for pattern search and publication, respectively.

5   Tool Support

In this section, we propose an MDE tool chain to support the proposed approach and hence assist the developers of Model-based Repository Software Systems. As we will see, the proposed tool chain is designed to support the proposed metamodels, and hence, the tool chain and the remainder of the activities involved in the approach may be developed in parallel. Appropriate tools for supporting our approach must fulfill the following key requirements:

- Enable the creation of the UML class diagrams used to describe metamodels in our approach.
- Support the model-based repository development process.
- Enable the creation of modeling artifacts and the publication of the results into the repository using the appropriate repository interface.
- Enable the creation of model libraries for artifact classification.
- Enable the creation of model libraries for the classification of the relationships between artifacts.
- Support the administration of the repository.
- Enable the creation of visualizations of the repository to facilitate its access.

To satisfy the above requirements, we define four integrated sets of software tools:

- *Tool set A* for populating the repository,
- *Tool set B* for retrieval from the repository,
- *Tool set C* to serve as the repository software and
- *Tool set D* for managing the repository.

There are several environments that can be used to build an MDE tool chain. In the context of our work, we have chosen to use EMFT to build the support tools for our approach. All metamodels used are specified using EMF. The design tools were semi-automatically generated from these metamodels. Several enhancements have been added to the generated code, such as creation wizards, to guide the modeling artifact designer in populating the repository. Visual enhancements have been added to facilitate the recognition of different concepts, as a first step toward a future visual syntax. To describe the model transformations, the QVT Operational language[3] is used. The structure of the repository is derived from the repository structure model and implemented using Java and the Eclipse CDO[4] framework.

---

[3] http://www.omg.org/spec/QVT/.

[4] http://www.eclipse.org/cdo/.

We have successfully applied our approach in the context of the FP7 TERESA (Trusted computing Engineering for Resource constrained Embedded Systems Applications) project by applying the approach to Pattern-Based System Engineering (PBSE). Specifically, we have developed SEMCOMDT[5] (SEMCO Model Development Tools) as an MDE tool chain to support all steps of our approach. As visualized in Fig. 6, SEMCOMDToffers the following features:

- *Gaya* as a repository platform (structure and interfaces) that conforms to *SARM*,
- *Tiqueo* for specifying models of S&D properties that conform to *GPRM*,
- *Arabion* for specifying patterns that conform to *SEPM*,
- *Admin* for repository management,
- *Retrieval* for repository access.

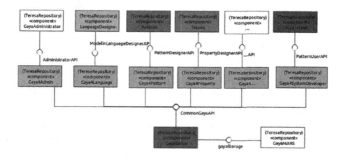

Fig. 6. An overview of the tool components

The server portion of *Gaya* consists of two components: (1) *GayaServer*, which provides the implementation of the common API, and (2) *GayaMARS*, which provides the storage mechanisms. The client portion of *Gaya* provides interfaces, such as *Gaya4Pattern* (which implements API4PatternDesigner), *Gaya4Property* (which implements API4PropDesigner), *Gaya4Admin* (which implements API4Admin) and *Gaya4SystemDeveloper* (which implements API4PatternUser).

For populating the repository, we have built two design tools: (1) the property design tool (Tiqueo), to be used by a property designer, and (2) the pattern design tool (Arabion), to be used by a pattern designer. Arabion (resp. Tiqueo) interacts with the Gaya repository for publication purposes through the *Gaya4Pattern* (resp. *Gaya4Property*) API. Furthermore, Arabion includes mechanisms for verifying the conformity of the pattern with the *SEPM* metamodel and for publishing the results to the repository.

For management of the repository by a repository manager, the *Admin* features provide a set of tools for the organization and usage and usage of the

---

[5] http://www.semcomdt.org/.

Fig. 7. Access tool/pattern tailoring

repository through the *Gaya4Admin* API. We also provide basic features such as user and artifact management. Moreover, we provide features to support the management of the relationships among artifact specifications and between artifact specifications and their complementary models.

For access to the repository by a system engineer, the Retrieval tool provides a set of functionalities to assist in the search, selection and sorting of patterns. The access tools interact with the Gaya repository through the *Gaya4SystemDeveloper* API. For instance, as shown on the right-hand side of Fig. 7, the tool offers assistance in selecting appropriate patterns through key word searches and lifecycle stage searches. The results are displayed in the search result tree as System, Architecture, Design and Implementation patterns. The tool includes features for export and tailoring using dialogs, primarily based on model transformation techniques, to adapt pattern models to the target development environment. Moreover, the tool includes dependency-checking mechanisms. For example, a pattern cannot be tailored when a property library is missing; an error message will be thrown.

6   Conclusion and Future Work

The promoted model-based approach for software application development relies on a repository of models and focuses on the problem of software system engineering through a design philosophy that fosters reuse. The primary purpose of such a repository is to share expertise in a manner that interacts with existing engineering processes to facilitate the construction of applications for various domains. The proposed framework for building a repository is based on meta-modeling techniques that enable the specification of the repository structure and interfaces, on content in the form of modeling artifacts, and on model transformation techniques for the purposes of generation. We begin by specifying a conceptual model of the desired model-based repository and proceed by designing modeling languages that are appropriate for the content. The results of these efforts are then used to specify and build the repository. Furthermore, we propose an operational architecture for a tool suite to support the proposed approach. We have successfully applied our approach in a case study of PBSE. Specifically, we have developed a tool suite, named SEMCOMDT, was built using EMFT and a CDO-based repository and is currently provided in the form of Eclipse plugins. In addition, the tool suite promotes the separation of concerns during the development process by distinguishing the roles of the stakeholders. Primarily, access to the repository is customized with regard to the development phases and the stakeholders' domain and system knowledge.

In our future work, we plan to complete the case study and assess whether domain experts agree on the benefits of adopting the our specification language in a real industrial context. This requires an instantiation of the full software engineering tool and method and an evaluation across the experiences of many users across many domains. We intend to validate the feasibility and effectiveness of the proposed specification and design frameworks - how our approach may significantly reduce the cost of engineering a system compared to current practice. In addition, we will study the automation of the model search and tailoring tasks, and a framework to allow the simpler specification of constraints would be beneficial. Our vision is for modeling artifacts to be inferred from the browsing history of users and constructed from a set of already developed applications. In addition, we will study the customization of the tool suite, primarily the access tool, with regard to the development phases and the stakeholders' domain and system knowledge. We would also like to study the integration of our tools with other MDE tools. Concurrently, more sophisticated techniques to manage artifacts relationships at a metamodel level can be implemented.

References

1. McClure, C.: Software Reuse Techniques: Adding Reuse to the System Development Process. Prentice-Hall Inc, Upper Saddle River (1997)
2. Agresti, W.: Software reuse: developers' experiences and perceptions. J. Softw. Eng. Appl. 4(1), 48–58 (2011)
3. Krueger, C.: Software reuse. ACM Comput. Surv. 24(2), 131–183 (1992)
4. Morisio, M., Ezran, M., Tully, C.: Success and failure factors in software reuse. IEEE Trans. Softw. Eng. 28(4), 340–357 (2002)
5. Frakes, W., Kang, K.: Software reuse research: status and future. IEEE Trans. Softw. Eng. 31(7), 529–536 (2005)
6. Bernstein, P.A., Dayal, U.: An overview of repository technology. In: Proceedings of the 20th International Conference on Very Large Data Bases, VLDB 1994, pp. 705–713. Morgan Kaufmann Publishers Inc. (1994)

7. Apache Software Foundation, Ivy (2015). http://ant.apache.org/ivy/
8. Apache Software Foundation: Maven (2015). https://maven.apache.org/what-is-maven.html
9. GRADLE INC., Gradle (2015). https://gradle.org/why/robust-dependency-management/
10. Bundler Core Team, Bundler (2015). http://bundler.io/
11. Berre, D.L., Rapicault, P.: Dependency management for the eclipse ecosystem: eclipse p2, metadata and resolution. In: Proceedings of the 1st International Workshop on Open Component Ecosystems, pp. 21–30. ACM (2009)
12. Sriplakich, P., Blanc, X., Gervais, M.: Supporting transparent model update in distributed CASE tool integration. In: Proceedings of the ACM Symposium on Applied Computing, SAC 2006, pp. 1759–1766. ACM, New York (2006)
13. Kramler, G., Kappel, G., Reiter, T., Kapsammer, E., Retschitzegger, W., Schwinger, W.: Towards a semantic infrastructure supporting model-based tool integration. In: Proceedings of the International Workshop on Global Integrated Model Management, GaMMa 2006, pp. 43–46. ACM, New York (2006)
14. Mayr, C., Zdun, U., Dustdar, S.: Reusable architectural decision model for model and metadata repositories. In: de Boer, F.S., Bonsangue, M.M., Madelaine, E. (eds.) FMCO 2008. LNCS, vol. 5751, pp. 1–20. Springer, Heidelberg (2009)
15. France, R.B., Bieman, J., Cheng, B.H.C.: Repository for model driven development (ReMoDD). In: Kühne, T. (ed.) MoDELS 2006. LNCS, vol. 4364, pp. 311–317. Springer, Heidelberg (2007)
16. Lloyd, C.M., Lawson, J.R., Hunter, P.J., Nielsen, P.F.: The CellML model repository. Bio./Comput. Appl. Biosci. **24**, 2122–2123 (2008)
17. ebXML: Oasis Registry Services Specification v2.5 (2003)
18. freebXML: Oasis ebxml registry reference implementation project (2007). http://ebxmlrr.sourceforge.net/
19. Milanovic, N., Kutsche, R.-D., Baum, T., Cartsburg, M., Elmasgünes, H., Pohl, M., Widiker, J.: Model & metamodel, metadata and document repository for software and data integration. In: MoDELS, pp. 416–430 (2008)
20. Sapia, C., Blaschka, M., Höfling, G.: GraMMi: Using a standard repository management system to build a generic graphical modeling tool. In: Proceedings of the 33rd Hawaii International Conference on System Sciences, HICSS 2000, vol. 8, p. 8058. IEEE Computer Society (2000)
21. Gomes, P., Pereira, F., Paiva, P., Seco, N., Carreiro, P., Ferreira, J., Bento, C.: Using wordnet for case-based retrieval of UML models. AI Commun. **17**, 13–23 (2004)
22. Lucrédio, D., de M. Fortes, R.P., Whittle, J.: MOOGLE: A model search engine. In: Czarnecki, K., Ober, I., Bruel, J.-M., Uhl, A., Völter, M. (eds.) MODELS 2008. LNCS, vol. 5301, pp. 296–310. Springer, Heidelberg (2008)
23. Hein, C., Ritter, T., Wagner, M.: Model-driven tool integration with modelbus. In: Workshop Future Trends of Model-Driven Development, pp. 50–52 (2009)
24. Holmes, T., Zdun, U., Dustdar, S.: MORSE: A model-aware service environment. In: APSCC (2009)
25. Bislimovska, B., Bozzon, A., Brambilla, M., Fraternali, P.: Graph-based search over web application model repositories. In: Auer, S., Díaz, O., Papadopoulos, G.A. (eds.) ICWE 2011. LNCS, vol. 6757, pp. 90–104. Springer, Heidelberg (2011)
26. Rosa, M.L., Aalst, H.R.W.V.D., Dijkman, R., Mendling, J., Dumas, M., García-Bañuelos, L.: APROMORE: An advanced process model repository. Expert Syst. Appl. **38**(6), 7029–7040 (2011)

27. Yan, Z., Dijkman, R.M., Grefen, P.: Business process model repositories - framework and survey. Inf. Softw. Technol. **54**(4), 380–395 (2012)
28. Hamid, B.: SEMCO Project (System and software Engineering for embedded systems applications with Multi-COncerns support). http://www.semcomdt.org
29. TERESA: TERESA Project (Trusted Computing Engineering for Resource Constrained Embedded Systems Applications). http://www.teresa-project.org/
30. OMG: MetaObject Facility 2.4.2, Specification (2014). http://www.omg.org/spec/MOF/2.4.2/
31. OMG: OMG Unified Modeling Language (OMG UML), Superstructure, August 2011. http://www.omg.org/spec/UML/2.4.1
32. Steinberg, D., Budinsky, F., Paternostro, M., Merks, E.: EMF: Eclipse Modeling Framework 2.0, 2nd edn. Addison-Wesley Professional, Boston (2009)
33. Ziani, A., Hamid, B., Trujillo, S.: Towards a unified meta-model for resources-constrained embedded systems. In: 37th EUROMICRO Conference on Software Engineering and Advanced Applications (SEAA), pp. 485–492. IEEE (2011)
34. Avizienis, A., Laprie, J.-C., Randell, B., Landwehr, C.: Basic concepts and taxonomy of dependable and secure computing. IEEE Trans. Depen. Secur. Comput. **1**, 11–33 (2014)
35. Hamid, B., Gurgens, S., Jouvray, C., Desnos, N.: Enforcing S&D pattern design in RCES with modeling and formal approaches. In: Whittle, J., Clark, T., Kühne, T. (eds.) MODELS 2011. LNCS, vol. 6981, pp. 319–333. Springer, Heidelberg (2011)

Reverse-Engineering Reusable Language Modules from Legacy Domain-Specific Languages

David Méndez-Acuña[1]([⊠]), José A. Galindo[1], Benoit Combemale[1],
Arnaud Blouin[1], Benoit Baudry[1], and Gurvan Le Guernic[2]

[1] INRIA and University of Rennes 1, Rennes, France
{david.mendez-acuna,jagalindo,benoit.combemale,arnaud.blouin,
benoit.baudry}@inria.fr
[2] DGA Maîtrise de l'Information, Bruz, France
gurvan.le-guernic@intradef.gouv.fr

Abstract. The use of domain-specific languages (DSLs) has become a
successful technique in the development of complex systems. Nevertheless, the construction of this type of languages is time-consuming and
requires highly-specialized knowledge and skills. An emerging practice
to facilitate this task is to enable reuse through the definition of language modules which can be later put together to build up new DSLs.
Still, the identification and definition of language modules are complex
and error-prone activities, thus hindering the reuse exploitation when
developing DSLs. In this paper, we propose a computer-aided approach
to (i) identify potential reuse in a set of legacy DSLs; and (ii) capitalize
such potential reuse by extracting a set of reusable language modules
with well defined interfaces that facilitate their assembly. We validate
our approach by using realistic DSLs coming out from industrial case
studies and obtained from public `GitHub` repositories.

1 Introduction

A domain-specific language (DSL) is a software language whose expressiveness is
limited to a well-defined domain. A DSL offers the abstractions (a.k.a., *language
constructs*) needed to describe an aspect of a system under construction. For
example, we find DSLs to build graphical user interfaces [22] and to specify
security policies [15]. The use of DSLs has become a successful technique to
achieve separation of concerns in the development of complex systems [7].

Naturally, the adoption of such a language-oriented vision relies on the availability of the DSLs necessary to describe all the aspects of the system [3]. This
implies the development of many DSLs, which is a challenging task due the specialized knowledge it demands. The ultimate value of DSLs has been severely
limited by the cost of the associated tooling (i.e., editors, parsers, etc.) [13].

To improve cost-benefit when using DSLs, the research community in software languages engineering has proposed mechanisms to increase reuse during

G.M. Kapitsaki and E. Santana de Almeida (Eds.): ICSR 2016, LNCS 9679, pp. 368–383, 2016.
DOI: 10.1007/978-3-319-35122-3_24

the language development process. The idea is to leverage previous engineering efforts and minimize implementation from scratch. In particular, there are approaches that take ideas from Component-Based Software Engineering [4] in the construction of DSLs (e.g., [17,24]). Language constructs are grouped into interdependent *language modules* that can be later integrated as part of the specification of future DSLs. Current approaches for the modular development of DSLs are focused on providing foundations and tooling that allow language designers to specify dependencies among language modules as well as to provide the composition operators needed during the subsequent assembly process.

In practice, however, reuse not necessarily achieved through monolithic processes where language designers define language modules while trying to predict that they will be useful in future DSLs. Contrariwise, the exploitation of reuse is often an iterative process where reuse opportunities are discovered in the form of replicated functionalities during the construction of individual DSLs. Those functionalities can be extracted in reusable language modules. For example, many DSLs offer expression languages with simple imperative instructions, variables management, and mathematical operators. Xbase [1] is a successful experiment that shows that, using compatible tooling, such replicated functionality can be encapsulated and (re)used in different DSLs.

A major complexity of this reuse process is that both, the identification of replicated functionalities and the extraction of the corresponding language modules are manually-performed activities. Language designers must compare DSL specifications to identify replicated language constructs, and then, to perform a refactoring process to extract those replications in language modules. Due the large number of language constructs defined within a DSL, and the dependencies among them, this process is tedious and error-prone [9]. As a result, modularization approaches are often discarded, and non-systematic reuse practices such as simple copy&paste are still quite popular in DSLs development processes. This type of solutions produce many code clones within DSLs' specifications thus replicating bugs and increasing maintenance costs [26].

In this paper, we propose the use of reverse-engineering techniques to automatically extract reusable language modules from a given set of legacy DSLs. To this end, we define some comparison operators that allow the identification of replicated language constructs. These operators take into account not only the names of the constructs but also the inter-constructs relationships and the semantics. Then, we extract replicated constructs as interdependent language modules whose dependencies are expressed through well-defined interfaces. Those language modules can be later assembled among them to build up new DSLs. The approach presented in this paper is implemented in a language workbench on top of the Eclipse Modeling Framework.

The validation of our approach is twofold. Firstly, we apply the reverse-engineering strategy to a case study, deeply explained by Crane et al. [8], and composed of a set of DSLs for finite state machines. Secondly, we explore public GITHUB repositories in search of insights that indicate how common is the phenomenon of specification clones in DSLs development process.

The reminder of this paper is organized as follows: Sect. 2 introduces a set of preliminary definitions/assumptions that we use all along the paper. Section 3 presents a motivation to the problem by introducing a concrete development scenario. Section 4 describes the proposed approach. Section 5 presents the validation. Section 6 discusses the related work. Section 7 concludes the paper.

2   Background: Domain-Specific Languages in a Nutshell

We use this section to introduce some basic definitions intended to establish a unified vocabulary that facilitates the comprehension of the ideas presented in the rest of the paper.

DSLs Specification. Like general purpose languages, domain specific languages are defined regarding three implementation concerns: abstract syntax, concrete syntax, and semantics [11]. The *abstract syntax* refers to the structure of the DSL expressed as the set of concepts that are relevant to the domain and the relationships among them. The *concrete syntax* relates language concepts to a set of symbols that facilitate the usage of the DSL. These representations are usually supported by editors acting as the user interface of the DSL. Finally, the *semantics* of a DSL assigns a precise meaning to each of its language constructs. More precisely, *static semantics* constrains the sets of valid programs while *dynamic semantics* specifies how they are evaluated.

Technological Space. There are diverse technological spaces available for the implementation of the aforementioned concerns [18]. The abstract syntax can be specified using context-free grammars or metamodels. The concrete syntax can be either textual or graphical. The static semantics can be expressed through diverse constraint languages. Finally, the dynamic semantics can be defined operationally, denotationally, or axiomatically [20].

In this paper, we are interested in executable domain-specific modeling languages (xDSMLs) where the abstract syntax is specified by means of *metamodels*, and dynamic semantics is specified operationally as a set of *domain-specific actions* [5]. Domain-specific actions are weaved on the metaclasses of a metamodel [12]. The concrete syntax and static semantics are out of the scope of this paper.

Example: A DSL for Finite State Machines. Figure 1 shows a DSL for finite states machines. In that case, the metamodel that implements the abstract syntax contains three metaclasses: StateMachine, State, and Transition. There are some references among those metaclasses representing the relationships existing among the corresponding language constructs.

The domain-specific actions at the right of the Fig. 1 introduce the operational semantics to the DSL. In this example, there is one domain-specific action for each metaclass. In executable metamodeling, the interactions among domain-specific actions can be internally specified in their implementation by means of the *interpreter pattern*, or externalized in a model of computation [5].

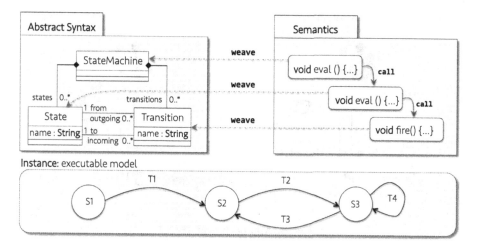

Fig. 1. A simple DSL for finite state machines

3   Motivating Scenario

Suppose a team of language designers working on the construction of the DSL for finite state machines presented in Sect. 2. During that process, language designers implement the constructs typically required for expressing finite state machines: states, transitions, events, and so on. Besides, a constraint language that allows final users to express guards on the transitions should be provided, as well as an expression language for the specification of actions in the states.

After language designers release the DSL for state machines, they are required to build another DSL. The new DSL is intended to manipulate the traditional Logo turtle, which is often used in elementary schools for teaching the first foundations of programming [21]. Instead of states and transitions, Logo offers some primitives (such as Forward, Backward, Left, and Right) to move a character (i.e., the turtle) within a bounded canvas. Still, Logo also requires an expression language to specify complex movements. For example, final users may write instructions such as: forward (x + 2).

At this point, language designers face the problem of reusing the expression language they already defined for the state machine DSL. Because this expression language was not implemented separately from the DSL for state machines, the typical approach is to copy&paste its corresponding specification segment in the second DSL. In doing so, language designers introduce specification clones all along the project. This practice is repeated in the construction of each new DSL where some reuse is needed. For example, if our language designers team is required to build a third DSL such as a flowchart language that uses not only expressions but also constraints, they will (again) copy&paste the corresponding specification segments. After some iterations, we obtain a set of DSLs with many specification clones, which is quite expensive to maintain.

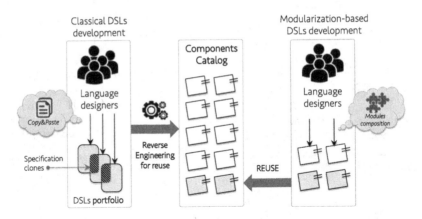

Fig. 2. Approach overview

4 Proposed Approach

We propose the use of reverse-engineering techniques to deal with the problem illustrated above. Our proposal, summarized in Fig. 2, starts from a classical language development process where a team of language designers develops a set DSLs (a.k.a., the DSLs portfolio) introducing specification clones by copy&paste repeated constructs. This portfolio is the input of a reverse-engineering strategy to extract a set of reusable language modules. Those modules are useful for two purposes. First, they can be assembled to build a new version of the portfolio that does not contain specification clones, thus reducing maintenance costs. Second, they can be used in the construction of future DSLs. In that case, language designers might have to build new language modules.

4.1 Principles of Reverse-Engineering for Language Reuse

Our reverse-engineering strategy is based on five principles that will be introduced in this section. Then, we explain how we use those principles to extract a catalog of reusable language modules.

Principle 1: DSL specifications are comparable. Hence, specification clones can be automatically detected. Two DSL specifications can be compared each other. This comparison can be either coarse-grained indicating if the two specifications are equal regarding both syntax and semantics, or fine-grained detecting segments of the specifications that match. The latter approach permits to identify specification clones between two DSLs and supposes the comparison of each specification element. In the case of the technological space discussed in this paper, specification elements for the abstract syntax are metaclasses whereas specification elements for the semantics are domain-specific actions.

For the case of **comparison of metaclasses**, we need to take into account that a metaclass is specified by a name, a set of attributes, and a set of references to other metaclasses. Two metaclasses are considered as equal (and so, they are clones) if all those elements match. Formally, comparison of metaclasses can be specified by the operator $\doteq$.

$$\doteq \; : MC \times MC \rightarrow bool \tag{1}$$

$$
\begin{aligned}
MC_A \doteq MC_B = true \implies \\
MC_A.name = MC_B.name \; \wedge \\
\forall a_1 \in MC_A.attr \mid (\exists a_2 \in MC_B.attr \mid a_1 = a_2) \; \wedge \\
\forall r_1 \in MC_A.refs \mid (\exists r_2 \in MC_B.refs \mid r_1 = r_2) \; \wedge \\
|MC_A.attr| = |MC_B.attr| \; \wedge \; |MC_A.refs| = |MC_B.refs|
\end{aligned}
\tag{2}
$$

In turn, for the case of **comparison for domain-specific actions** we need to take into account that –like methods in Java– domain-specific actions have a signature that specifies its contract (i.e., return type, visibility, parameters, name, and so on), and a body where the behavior is implemented. Two domain-specific actions are equal if they have the same signature and body.

Whereas comparison of signatures can be performed by syntactic comparison of the signature elements, comparison of bodies can be arbitrary difficult. If we try to compare the behavior of the domain-specific actions, then we will have to address the semantic equivalence problem, which is known to be undecidable [16]. To address this issue, we conceive bodies comparison in terms of its abstract syntax tree as proposed by Biegel et al. [2]. In other words, to compare two bodies, we first parse them to extract their abstract syntax tree, and then we compare those trees. Note that this decision makes sense because we are detecting specification clones more than equivalent behavior. Formally, comparison of domain-specific actions (DSAs) is specified by the operator $\doteq$.

$$\doteq \; : DSA \times DSA \rightarrow bool \tag{3}$$

$$
\begin{aligned}
DSA_A \doteq DSA_B = true \implies \\
DSA_A.name = DSA_B.name \; \wedge \\
DSA_A.returnType = DSA_B.returnType \; \wedge \\
DSA_A.visibility = DSA_B.visibility \; \wedge \\
\forall p_1 \in DSA_A.params \mid (\exists p_2 \in DSA_B.params \mid p_1 = p_2) \; \wedge \\
|DSA_A.params| = |DSA_B.params| \; \wedge \\
DSA_A.AST = DSA_B.AST
\end{aligned}
\tag{4}
$$

Principle 2: Specification clones are viewed as overlapping. If a DSL specification is viewed as sets of metaclasses and domain-specific actions, then specification clones can be viewed as intersections (a.k.a., overlapping) of those sets. Figure 3 illustrates this observation for the case of the motivation scenario introduced in Sect. 3. We use two Venn diagrams to represent both syntax and semantic overlapping. In that case, the fact that the expression language is used in all the DSLs is represented by the intersection in the center of the diagram where the three sets overlap the metaclass `Expression` (and its domain-specific actions). In turn, the intersection between the state machines DSL and Logo shows that they overlap the metaclass `Constraint` that belongs to the constraint language. Note that the identification of such overlapping is only possible when there are comparison operators (principle 1) that formalize the notion of equality.

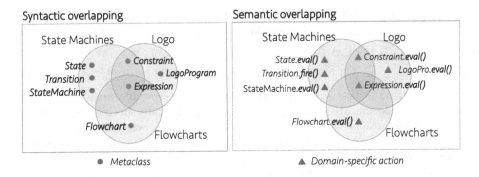

Fig. 3. Syntactic and semantic overlapping in a set of DSLs

Principle 3: Breaking down overlapping produces reusable language modules. According to principle 2, overlapping between two DSLs implies the existence of repeated metaclasses/domain-specific actions (i.e., specification clones). Those repeated elements can be specified once and reused in the two DSLs [25, pp. 60–61]. Hence, reusable language modules can be obtained by breaking-down the overlapping existing among DSL specifications as illustrated in Fig. 4; each different intersection is encapsulated in a different language module.

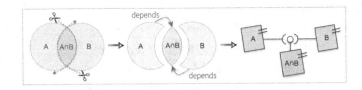

Fig. 4. Breaking down overlapping for obtaining reusable language modules

Principle 4: Abstract syntax first, semantics afterwards. As aforementioned, the abstract syntax of a DSL specifies its structure in terms of metaclasses and relationships among them. Then, the domain-specific actions add executability to the metaclasses. Hence, the abstract syntax is the backbone of the DSL specification, and so, the process of breaking down overlapping should be performed for the abstract syntax first. Afterwards, we can do the proper for the semantics. In doing so, we need to take into consideration the phenomenon of semantic variability. That is, two cloned metaclasses might have different domain-specific actions. That occurs when two DSLs share some syntax specification but differ in their semantics.

Principle 5: Metamodels are directed graphs. Hence, breaking down a metamodel is a graph partitioning problem. The metamodel that specifies the abstract syntax of a DSL can be viewed as a directed graph G.

$$G =< V, A >$$

where:

- **V**: is the set of vertices each of which represents a metaclass.
- **A**: is the set of arcs each of which represents a relationships between two meta-classes (i.e., references, containments, and inheritances).

This observation is quite useful at the moment of breaking down a metamodel to satisfy the principle 4. Breaking down a metamodel can be viewed as a graph partitioning problem where the result is a finite set of subgraphs. Each subgraph represents the metamodel of a reusable language module.

4.2   Reverse-Engineering Process: The 5 Principles in Action

The reverse-engineering strategy to produce a catalog of reusable modules is illustrated in Fig. 5. It is composed of two steps: identifying overlapping and breaking down.

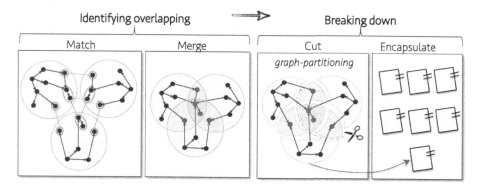

Fig. 5. Breaking down the input set by cutting overlapping

Identifying Overlapping: *match* and *merge*. To identify syntactic overlapping in a given set of DSLs, we start by producing a graph for each DSL according to the principle 5. Then, we identify specification clones (the matching phase)

using the comparison operators defined in principle 1. After that, we have a set of graphs (one for each DSL) and a set of matching relationships among some of the vertex. At that point we can proceed to create the overlapping defined in principle 2. To this end, we merge the matched vertex as illustrated in the second square of Fig. 5. This merging permits to remove cloned metaclasses.

To identify semantic overlapping, we check whether the domain-specific actions of the matched metaclasses are equal as well. If so, they can be considered as clones in the semantic specification, so there is semantic overlapping. In that case, these domain-specific actions are merged. If not all the domain-specific actions associated to the matched metaclasses are the same, different clusters of domain-specific actions are created, thus establishing semantic variation points.

Breaking Down: *cut* and *encapsulate*. Once overlapping among the DSLs of the portfolio has been identified, we extract a set of reusable language modules. This process corresponds to break-down the graph produced in the last phase using a graph partitioning algorithm. The algorithm receives the graph(s) obtained from the merging process and returns a set of vertex clusters: one cluster for each intersection of the Venn diagram. Arcs defined between vertices in different clusters can be considered as cross-cutting dependencies between clusters. Then, we encapsulate each vertex cluster in the form of language modules. Each module contains a metamodel, a set of domain-specific actions, and a set of dependencies towards other language modules.

Dependencies between language modules can be viewed through the classical required and provided roles in components-based software development illustrated in Fig. 6. There is a *requiring module* that uses some constructs provided by a *providing module*. The requiring module has a dependency relationship towards the providing one. To avoid direct references between modules, we introduce the notion of interfaces for dealing with modules' dependencies. The requiring language has a *required interface* whereas the providing one has the *provided interface*. A required interface contains the set of constructs required by the requiring module that are supposed to be replaced by actual construct provided by another module(s).

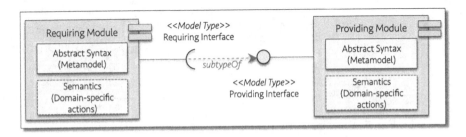

Fig. 6. Interfaces for language modules

We use *model types* [23] to express both required and provided interfaces. A module can have some references to the constructs declared in its required interface. In turn, the relationship between a module and its provided interface is *implements* (deeply explained in [9]). A module implements the functionality exposed in its model type. If the required interface is a subtype of the provided interface, then the provided interface fulfills the requirements declared in a required interface.

Implementation. The approach presented in this paper is implemented in the PUZZLE tool suite[1], which is developed on top of the Eclipse Modeling Framework (EMF). In that context, metamodels are specified in the Ecore language whereas domain-specific actions are specified as methods in Xtend. The mapping between metaclasses and domain-specific actions are specified through the notion of aspect introduced by Kermeta [12] and Melange [9].

5   Evaluation

The evaluation of our approach is twofold. First, we evaluate the *correctness* of the approach using a test oracle that consists of a well-documented case study where we exactly know the existing overlapping among the involved DSLs. We execute the reverse-engineering on the case study, and we check that the produced language modules are consistent with the known overlapping. Second, we evaluate *relevance* of our proposal. More concretely, we use empirical data to demonstrate that the phenomenon of specification clones actually appears in DSLs that we obtain from public GitHub repositories.

5.1   Evaluating *Correctness*: The State Machines Case Study

Test Oracle. To evaluate the correctness of our approach, we use the case study introduced by Crane et al. [8]. It is composed of three different DSLs for expressing state machines: UML state diagrams, Rhapsody, and Harel's state charts. These three DSLs have some commonalities since they are intended to express the same formalism. For example, all of them provide basic concepts such as StateMachine, State, and Transition. According to the development scenario we address in this paper, these commonalities will be materialized as clones in the DSL specifications. However, not all those DSLs are exactly equal. They have both syntactic and semantic differences.

Syntactic differences are reified by the fact that not all the DSLs provide the same constructs. There are differences in the support for transition's triggers and pseudostates. Whereas Rhapsody only supports atomic triggers, both Harel's statecharts and UML provide support for composite triggers. In Harel's statecharts triggers can be composed by using AND, OR, and NOT operators. In turn, in UML triggers can be composed by using the AND operator. In addition, whereas there are pseudostates that are supported by all the DSLs (Fork, Join,

---

[1] Puzzle's website: http://damende.github.io/puzzle/.

ShallowHistory, and Junction); there are two psueudostates i.e., DeepHistory and Choice that are only supported by UML. The Conditional pseudostate is only provided by Harel's state charts. Figure 7 shows a table with the language constructs provided by each DSL.

Language vs. Construct	StateMachine	Region	AbstractState	State	Transition	Trigger	NotTrigger	AndTrigger	OrTrigger	Pseudostate	InitialState	Fork	Join	DeepHistory	ShallowHistory	Junction	Conditional	Choice	FinalState	Constraint	Statement	Program	NamedElement	Total
UML	•	•	•	•	•	•	·	•	·	•	•	•	•	•	•	•	·	•	•	•	•	•	•	20
Rhapsody	•	•	•	•	•	•	·	·	·	•	•	•	•	·	•	•	•	·	•	•	•	•	•	18
Harel	•	•	•	•	•	•	•	•	•	•	•	•	•	•	•	•	•	·	•	•	•	•	•	22

Fig. 7. Oracle for evaluation of correctness

In turn, semantic differences are reified by the fact that not all the DSLs have the same behavior at execution time. For example, whereas Harel's statecharts attend simultaneous events in parallel, both UML and Rhapsody follow the run to completion principle. So, simultaneous events are attended sequentially [8]. Consequently, not all the domain-specific actions are the same. In particular, the domain-specific actions eval() and step() in the StateMachine metaclass are different in each DSL.

Results. Figure 8 presents the results produced by Puzzle for the first part of the analysis: identification of overlapping. The figure shows the Venn diagrams for both syntactic and semantic overlapping. In the case of the syntactic overlapping, the cardinalities of the intersections in the Venn diagram match the test oracle. In turn, the domain-specific actions eval() and step() associated to the StateMachine metaclass are correctly identified as different in each DSL.

Figure 9 presents the results for the second part of the approach: breaking down overlapping. There is a language module that contains all the constructs shared by the three DSLs. That is, the constructs existing in the intersection Harel∩UML∩Rhapsody. Note that the behavioral differences are materialized by several implementations of the semantics, i.e., semantic variation points.

Also, other language modules encapsulate pseudostates and triggers separately. This is because pseudostates and triggers are supported differently in the DSLs, so they should be specified in different language modules. In this way, language designers can pick the desired constructs to build a particular DSL. Particularly, to obtain the Harel's statecharts DSL, we need to compose the modules 1, 2, and 5. In turn, to obtain UML we need to compose modules 1, 3, and 4. Finally, to obtain Rhapsody we need to compose modules 1 and 5. The instructions to replicate this experiment are available online[2].

---

[2] Website for experiment 1: http://puzzlestatemachines.weebly.com/.

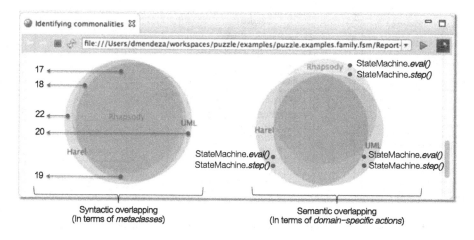

Fig. 8. Overlapping detected by Puzzle in the state machines case study.

5.2 Evaluating *Relevance*: Are Specification Clones a Real Phenomenon in DSLs Development Processes?

Although our experience indicates that copy&paste is a real practice in language development processes so it is normal to find specification clones, we still need to verify that it is a phenomenon that appears in other development teams, and industrial contexts. To answer that question, we explored public GitHub repositories in search of DSLs that are built on the same technological space that we used in our approach. The intention is to confirm the existence of specification clones among those DSLs. The results are presented in this section, and all the data and tooling needed to replicate these experiments are available on-line[3].

Data. We conducted an automatic search on GitHub repositories to find Ecore metamodels enriched with operational semantics written as Kermeta aspects in Xtend. As a result of this search, we obtained a data set composed **2423** metamodels. Nevertheless, because Kermeta 3 and its implementation in Xtend is a quite recent idea, we found very few data for the semantics part. Besides, all of them have been developed in our research team. We decided to conduct the analysis only in the metamodels since we consider that detection of specification clones at the level of the abstract syntax can give us a good insight about the existence of copy&paste practices in DSLs development processes.

Experiment. To identify specification clones in the metamodels from our data set, we performed a pair-wise comparison among all the metamodels (w.r.t. the $\doteq$ operator introduced in Sect. 4). Then, we compute the matrix $O(i,j)$ where each cell (i,j) contains the number of cloned metaclasses between the metamodels i and j. $O(i,j) = 0$ means that there is no cloned metaclasses between the metamodels i and j. We are interested in the cells (i,j) such that $O(i,j) \neq 0$

---

[3] Website for experiment 2: http://empiricalpuzzle.weebly.com/.

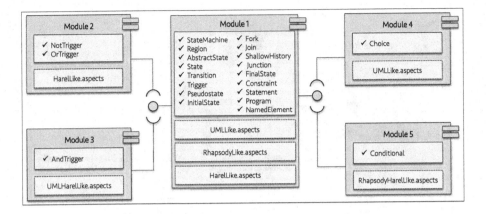

Fig. 9. Language modules extracted by Puzzle in the state machines case study.

and $i \neq j$. Those cells correspond to a pair of metamodels with some specification clones. Then, we analyze the matrix with two questions in mind: (1) how many metamodels have some specification clones among them?; and (2) how many classes are cloned from one metamodel to the other?

Results. Figure 10 shows two charts with the results to the experiment. The chart at the left is intended to answer the first question. In this chart, each entry x of the horizontal axis represents one metamodel of the data set. In turn, the vertical axis i.e., $y(x)$ shows the amount of metamodels with some specification clones for x. Formally, $y(x) = (+k|\ 0 \geq k \geq 2423 \wedge O(x,k) > 0 : 1)$. For example, the metamodel with ID **1.053** has some specification clones with **272** metamodels. Note that each point located up the zero line of the vertical axis represents a metamodel with some specification clones with one or more metamodels, thus suggesting that specification clones is a real phenomenon.

The chart at the right of the Fig. 10 is intended to answer the second question. In this chart, each entry x of the vertical axis represents one metamodel of the data set. The vertical axis i.e., $z(x)$ shows the average amount of cloned classes for x. Formally, $z(x) = 1/y(x) * (+k|\ 0 \geq k \geq 2423 : O(x,k))$ For example, the metamodel **1.928** shares, in average, **99.4** metaclasses with other metamodels. Note that there is an important amount of metamodels whose average overlapping size is between **0** and **100** metaclasses. Note also that there are four metamodels that share about **600** metaclasses. This case corresponds to a set of different versions of a metamodel for UML.

6   Related Work

Reuse in DSLs Development Processes. The research community in software language engineering has previously studied mechanisms to leverage reuse in the development of DSLs. In this context, languages modularization is probably

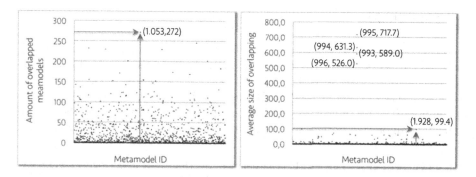

Fig. 10. Results for the evaluation of overlapping in GitHub metamodels

the most popular approach. We can find approaches supporting complex modularization scenarios such languages extension (e.g., [10]) applicable to diverse technological spaces such as metamodeling [24] or attribute grammars [17].

Another approach to leverage reuse in DSLs is the definition of domain-specific metamodeling languages [14, 26]. The idea is to define abstract language constructs that can be useful in several DSLs, and to provide mechanisms to specialize such abstract constructs to particular application contexts. For example, a language designer can define a DSL for finite state machines with an abstract behavior, and adapt it to several DSLs according to the needs of the final users.

More recent approaches are focused on facilitating the reuse process itself. For instance, Melange [9] is a tool-supported language that introduces some operators (such as slice, inheritance, and merge) intended to manipulate legacy DSLs in such a way that they can be easily integrated into new developments.

The main contribution of our approach is the advance towards the automation of the reuse process. We show that, under certain conditions, the process can be automated through reverse-engineering techniques. We exploit the reuse opportunities in the form of specification clones, thus reducing maintenance costs and facilitating the construction of future DSLs.

Déjà vu in Object-Oriented Programming? There is a symbiosis between executable metamodeling and object-oriented programming. Besides, there are several approaches intended to extract reusable modules from legacy object-oriented software systems (e.g., [6, 19]). Our approach, however, should not be viewed as yet another technique to extract reusable object-oriented components. Rather, we propose to take advantage of such symbiosis and use advances achieved in object-oriented programming to solve problems that also occur during the development of executable DSL. Indeed, there is still large room to exploit those ideas to improve reverse-engineering techniques in DSLs. In doing so, the central issue to consider is the separation of concerns in DSL specifications. That is, the fact that the syntax and semantics of the DSLs are usually specified separately, in many cases, using different metalanguages.

7   Conclusion

In this paper, we presented an approach to exploit reuse during the construction of DSLs. We show that it is possible to automate the reuse process by identifying specification clones in DSLs and automatically extracting reusable language modules that can be later used in the construction of new DSLs. We evaluated our approach in an industrial case study, and we demonstrate that there is an important amount of potential reuse in DSLs we obtain from public repositories.

Acknowledgments. This work is supported by the ANR INS Project GEMOC (ANR-12-INSE-0011), the bilateral collaboration VaryMDE between Inria and Thales, and the bilateral collaboration FPML between Inria and DGA.

References

1. Bettini, L., Stoll, D., Völter, M., Colameo, S.: Approaches and tools for implementing type systems in xtext. In: Czarnecki, K., Hedin, G. (eds.) SLE 2012. LNCS, vol. 7745, pp. 392–412. Springer, Heidelberg (2013)
2. Biegel, B., Diehl, S.: Jccd: a flexible and extensible api for implementing custom code clone detectors. In: Proceedings of the International Conference on Automated Software Engineering, ASE 2010, pp. 167–168, Antwerp, Belgium. ACM (2010)
3. Clark, T., Barn, B.S.: Domain engineering for software tools. In: Reinhartz-Berger, I., Sturm, A., Clark, T., Cohen, S., Bettin, J. (eds.) Domain Engineering: Product Lines, Languages, and Conceptual Models, pp. 187–209. Springer, Heidelberg (2013)
4. Cleenewerck, T.: Component-based DSL development. In: Pfenning, F., Macko, M. (eds.) GPCE 2003. LNCS, vol. 2830, pp. 245–264. Springer, Heidelberg (2003)
5. Combemale, B., Hardebolle, C., Jacquet, C., Boulanger, F., Baudry, B.: Bridging the chasm between executable metamodeling and models of computation. In: Czarnecki, K., Hedin, G. (eds.) SLE 2012. LNCS, vol. 7745, pp. 184–203. Springer, Heidelberg (2013)
6. Constantinou, E., Naskos, A., Kakarontzas, G., Stamelos, I.: Extracting reusable components: a semi-automated approach for complex structures. Inf. Process. Lett. **115**(3), 414–417 (2015)
7. Cook, S.: Separating concerns with domain specific languages. In: Lightfoot, D.E., Ren, X.-M. (eds.) JMLC 2006. LNCS, vol. 4228, pp. 1–3. Springer, Heidelberg (2006)
8. Crane, M., Dingel, J.: Uml vs. classical vs. rhapsody statecharts: not all models are created equal. Softw. Syst. Mod. **6**(4), 415–435 (2007)
9. Degueule, T., Combemale, B., Blouin, A., Barais, O., Jézéquel, J.-M.: Melange: a meta-language for modular and reusable development of dsls. In: Proceedings of the International Conference on Software Language Engineering, SLE 2015, pp. 25–36, Pittsburgh, PA, USA. ACM (2015)
10. Erdweg, S., Rieger, F.: A framework for extensible languages. In: Proceedings of the International Conference on Generative Programming, GPCE 2013, pp. 3–12, Indianapolis, USA. ACM (2013)
11. Harel, D., Rumpe, B.: Meaningful modeling: what's the semantics of "semantics"? Computer **37**(10), 64–72 (2004)

12. Jézéquel, J.-M., Combemale, B., Barais, O., Monperrus, M., Fouquet, F.: Mashup of metalanguages and its implementation in the kermeta language workbench. Softw. Syst. Mod. **14**(2), 905–920 (2015)
13. Jézéquel, J.-M., Méndez-Acuña, D., Degueule, T., Combemale, B., Barais, O.: When systems engineering meets software language engineering. In: Boulanger, F., Krob, D., Morel, G., Roussel, J.-C. (eds.) CSD&M 2014, pp. 1–13. Springer International Publishing, Heidelberg (2015)
14. de Lara, J., Guerra, E.: Domain-specific textual meta-modelling languages for model driven engineering. In: Vallecillo, A., Tolvanen, J.-P., Kindler, E., Störrle, H., Kolovos, D. (eds.) ECMFA 2012. LNCS, vol. 7349, pp. 259–274. Springer, Heidelberg (2012)
15. Lodderstedt, T., Basin, D., Doser, J.: SecureUML: a UML-based modeling language for model-driven security. In: Jézéquel, J.-M., Hussmann, H., Cook, S. (eds.) UML 2002. LNCS, vol. 2460, pp. 426–441. Springer, Heidelberg (2002)
16. Lucanu, D., Rusu, V.: Program equivalence by circular reasoning. In: Johnsen, E.B., Petre, L. (eds.) IFM 2013. LNCS, vol. 7940, pp. 362–377. Springer, Heidelberg (2013)
17. Mernik, M.: An object-oriented approach to language compositions for software language engineering. J. Syst. Softw. **86**(9), 2451–2464 (2013)
18. Mernik, M., Heering, J., Sloane, A.M.: When and how to develop domain-specific languages. ACM Comput. Surv. **37**(4), 316–344 (2005)
19. Mishra, S., Kushwaha, D., Misra, A.: Creating reusable software component from object-oriented legacy system through reverse engineering. J. Object Technol. **8**(5), 133–152 (2009)
20. Mosses, P.D.: The varieties of programming language semantics. In: Bjørner, D., Broy, M., Zamulin, A.V. (eds.) PSI 2001. LNCS, vol. 2244, pp. 165–190. Springer, Heidelberg (2001)
21. Olson, A., Kieren, T., Ludwig, S.: Linking logo, levels and language in mathematics. Educ. Stud. Math. **18**(4), 359–370 (1987)
22. Oney, S., Myers, B., Brandt, J.: Constraintjs: programming interactive behaviors for the web by integrating constraints and states. In: Proceedings of the Annual Symposium on User Interface Software and Technology, UIST 2012, pp. 229–238, Cambridge, Massachusetts, USA. ACM (2012)
23. Steel, J., Jézéquel, J.-M.: On model typing. Softw. Syst. Mod. **6**(4), 401–414 (2007)
24. Voelter, M.: Language and IDE modularization and composition with MPS. In: Lämmel, R., Saraiva, J., Visser, J. (eds.) GTTSE 2011. LNCS, vol. 7680, pp. 383–430. Springer, Heidelberg (2013)
25. Völter, M., Benz, S., Dietrich, C., Engelmann, B., Helander, M., Kats, L.C.L., Visser, E., Wachsmuth, G.: DSL Engineering - Designing, Implementing and Using Domain-Specific Languages. CreateSpace Independent Publishing Platform, Hamburg (2013). dslbook.org
26. Zschaler, S., Kolovos, D.S., Drivalos, N., Paige, R.F., Rashid, A.: Domain-specific metamodelling languages for software language engineering. In: van den Brand, M., Gašević, D., Gray, J. (eds.) SLE 2009. LNCS, vol. 5969, pp. 334–353. Springer, Heidelberg (2010)

A Framework for Enhancing the Retrieval of UML Diagrams

Alhassan Adamu[1,2(✉)] and Wan Mohd Nazmee Wan Zainoon[1]

[1] School of Computer Sciences, Universiti Sains Malaysia,
11800 George Town, Penang, Malaysia
kofa062@gmail.com, nazmee@usm.my
[2] Department of Computer Science,
Kano University of Science and Technology, Wudil, Kano 3422, Nigeria

Abstract. Software design is one of the demanding task that requires a lot of experience, expertise, and knowledge in many different design alternatives. Experience software designer's knowledge is considers as a vital asset to the software development company, especially in current competitive market environment. In order to benefit from the knowledge of experienced software designers, Software Company needs a tool to store these design knowledge for future use and retrieved those design from repository when needed, especially before developing a new system. This tool should complement the effort required to design a new system from scratch and be able to compare the requirement of a new project with the requirements of the old projects in the repository. This paper proposes a framework for reusing UML diagrams.

Keywords: Software reuse · UML · Retrieval · Pre-filtering · Meta-models

1 Introduction

Software development consists of mainly a few different phases: analysis, design, implementation, testing, and documentation. Each of these phases generate new knowledge that can be utilize by the organization for future system development. One kind of knowledge that is most valuable to the organization is the software design, which is usually being a modeled using UML (Unified Modeling Language) diagram. These diagrams are often the *de facto* used by many software engineers during the software design stage. This paper aim to propose an approach that could establish an efficient approach to navigate through the query and repository models for matching and retrieval of these diagrams.

2 Proposed Approach

The proposed UML diagrams retrieval approach is hinged around the fact that software in the same or similar domain has the same or similar requirements. For example, software in the banking domain may have some attributes like account name, account number, bank name, account type, and bank address which are usually common. Developing new

G.M. Kapitsaki and E. Santana de Almeida (Eds.): ICSR 2016, LNCS 9679, pp. 384–390, 2016.
DOI: 10.1007/978-3-319-35122-3_25

software from scratch will resulted in duplicated software artifacts, increased maintenance costs, and inefficient use of software specialists. Reusing of similar software design models to create a new software system can overcome these challenges.

This section discusses the architecture of the proposed reuse framework. The framework consists of three main modules: meta-model pre-processing, query processor, and similarity assessment module as shown in Fig. 1.

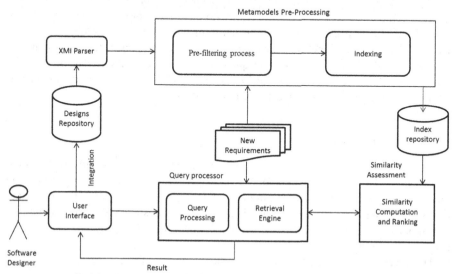

Fig. 1. Schematic Diagram of the proposed reuse system

2.1 Meta-models Pre-processing

The meta-model processing received a collection of models specified in XMI (XML Metadata Interchange) extract from repository as input data source. First, the XMI parser injects the structure of the entire projects. This is to propagate through the document and mine as much information about the structure of the existing projects so that information regarding metadata of the project can be extracted. The document are checked to make sure it conforms to XMI standard, if the file are well-formed then the parser identify UML model elements in the XMI document (e.g. classes, attributes, methods, etc.). Other elements to be found include structure relation in class diagram (e.g. association, aggregation, realization etc.) or message send or received in sequence diagrams.

2.2 Pre-filtering Process

The pre-filtering technique is aim at minimizing the retrieval time of models from repository. The aim is to select the subset of repository models that are potentially similar to the new requirement in a computationally inexpensive way. The subsets of the repository are then compared in a subsequent computationally expensive stage to ascertain the actual degree of similarity between query (**Q**) and repository (**R**) models. This process in return eliminate the need to load all the repository models into computer primary during retrieval, as such additional speed up can be achieved. We propose using three type of metadata which were previously obtained: conceptual data, functional data and metric data [1]. Both these set of metadata are automatically extracted from requirement specifications when new software are stored in the repository, and subsequently changes made to the existing software. Conceptual data is obtained based on the concepts contained in the new requirement with the aid of ontology. The concept here referred are class, method and attribute name in class diagrams, or object name in sequence diagram. The functional data represent the interaction between the system and its users [2]. Metric data provides the quantitative measures of software models, for example total number of classes, attributes, methods in class diagram, number of exchanges messages between object in sequence diagrams [3].

2.3   Query Processor

Query is one of the pre-requisite for software retrieval. The query stands as the initial draft of new software to be developed. It is a way of formulating a request that can select a number of diagrams as a result of satisfying some similarity criteria. To find the most similar diagram out of a set of previous UML diagrams from repository means the user should formulate a query and send the query to the repository for possible matching and retrieval.

The query processor module deals with the query input from the user interface, the query processing and retrieval. The query processing module index the query in exactly the same way repository diagrams was indexed. The retrieval module takes the query and performs the actual search for relevant diagrams with respect to the query. During the searching for the actual diagram, query expansion is performed by comparing the concepts (classifies') in query and repository diagrams. The concept expansion is done through the domain ontology, based on a threshold value $\alpha[0,1]$, with 1 indicating maximum similarity and 0 indicating optimal dissimilarity between concept. Table 1 adapted from [4] shows the level of similarity and dissimilarity between the diagrams (i.e. if the relationship connecting two class diagrams exist).

2.4   Retrieval Engine

Retrieval involves the process of matching the query and repository diagrams focusing on the most useful related to the problem at hand. A similarity measure has to be applied to allow the process of retrieving the most similar diagrams. The retrieved diagrams provide a solution to the new problem at hand. The retrieval engine consists of old problems and their solutions stored in the repository. The repository is a library system for storing and managing of software components for building business applications. It supports the storing, registration and management of all software artifacts produce during software development lifecycle, and support the reuse of those components. It can contain different information, depending on the scope of the system [5].

Table 1. Normalized diagrams relationship distance adapted from [4]

R Type	Ass	Agr	Com	Dep	Gen	Rea	Int
Ass	0	0.11	0.11	0.45	0.45	0.66	0.77
Agr	0.11	0	0.11	0.45	0.45	0.66	0.77
Com	0.11	0.11	0	0.45	0.45	0.66	0.77
Dep	0.49	0.49	0.49	0	0.28	0.21	0.32
Gen	0.49	0.49	0.49	0.28	0	0.49	0.6
Rea	0.83	0.83	0.83	0.34	0.62	0	0.11
Int	1	1	1	0.51	0.79	0.17	0

Ass: Association, Agr: Aggregation, Com:
Composition, Dep: Dependency, Gen: Generalization,
Rea: Realization, Int: Interface Realization.

2.5 Similarity Computation

In similarity computation, query and repository diagrams are retrieved based on measuring their similarity. The usefulness of a diagram is estimated based on the presence or absence of similar features between the query and repository. The similarity is access through numeric computation and reflected as a single value; for example weighted sum, which shows all aspect of the similarity. There are three similarity metrics to be used by the retrieval engine: Concept Similarity computation (CSim), Functional Similarity Computation (FSim) and Metric Based Similarity Computation (MBSim). Concept similarity computation is performed by comparing the concept name appearing in both query and repository models with the aid of WordNet ontology, details can be found in our earlier work [3].

If the concept appearing in query and repository are not a valid English word, the similarity computation can break since WordNet ontology is centered on the use of valid English words. In this case, N-Gram similarity is applied to compute the similarity based on the number identical substrings of length n contained in both strings.

The second approach of similarity computation is the Metric Based which computes the similarity between query and repository by comparing the metric values of both query and repository diagrams. It is expected that the corresponding metric for similar software should not differ significantly.

3 Case Study

To show how the retrieval and matching is performed in this framework, an example is presented in this section. Currently only class diagrams is considered, in the future we plan to extend it to other diagrams such as sequence and state machine diagrams.

Given a query **Q** containing classes in its diagram **cQ** and Repository containing four class diagrams **cR$_{1-4}$** shown in Fig. 2.

Firstly, words found in the query are extracted, such as the "class name". For example the class name "AccountType" is considered as two words (Account and Type) and then search for similar words in the repository diagrams. Table 2 shows the

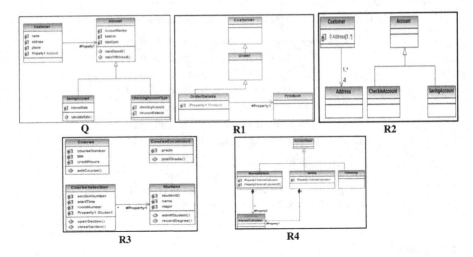

Fig. 2. Query and repository diagrams

truth table for the similarity function which is used to compute the similarity futures between the **Q** and **R** diagrams. The similarity function is defined as function S of any two diagrams D1 and D2 such that S(D1, D2) is defined as a tri-function such that D1 and D2 exist in either **Q** or **R** [6, 7].

Table 2. Similarity function truth table

D1	D2	Sim(D1,D2)
0	0	0
0	1	0
1	1	1

In Table 3 shows similarity matrix representing the dimensional matching between Q1 through R1 – R4.

The computation of similarity matching score in Table 3 was performed using the formula in (1) and (2). It is worth to note that the formula was adopted from [8], in which the similarity between use case diagrams was calculated (Table 4).

$$Total\ Matched\ (TM) = \sum_{i=1}^{n} 1 \tag{1}$$

$$Sim(Q,R) = \frac{TM}{\sum_{j=1}^{m} Q} \tag{2}$$

$$Sim(Q,Di) = \sum_{all\ similarity\ items,S} \alpha * (Sim(Q,R) + (1-\alpha) * Simrel(Q,R) \tag{3}$$

Table 3. Concept similarity computation

Query words	Diagrams matching				
	R1	R2	R3	R4	Q
Customer	1	1	0	0	1
Account	0	1	0	1	1
Saving	0	1	0	1	1
Checking	0	1	0	1	1
Type	0	0	0	0	1
Total matched	1	4	0	3	5
Sim(Q,R)	0.2	0.8	0	0.6	1

Table 4. Ranked list of similarity scoring

Dm%	Matched	Diagrams ranking				
		R2	R4	R1	R3	#Retrieved
100	5					0
80	4	0.8				1
60	3	0.8	0.6			2
40	2	0.8	0.6			2
20	1	0.8	0.6	0.2		3

Where Sim_{con} is the similarity between the concepts in Q and R, Sim_{rel} is the similarity between relationships (association, composition etc.), and α is the corresponding weight that affects the formula [4]. The similarity between relationship in Q and R is calculated as a distance between their topology with the aid of Table 1 as follows.

$$sim_{rel}(Q, R1) = (dist(Association, Generalization), dist(Association, Association),$$
$$dist(Generalization, Generalization), dist(Generalization, Association))$$

$$Sim_{rel}(Q, R1) = (0.11, 0, 0, 0.11) = 0.11$$

Table 5. Ranked diagrams

$S(Q,R_i)$			
R4	R2	R1	R3
0.825	0.625	0.325	0

From result in Table 5, the diagram R4 will be presented first to the reuser as the most relevant to the query.

4   Conclusion

This paper proposes a reuse approach based on UML, a modeling language widely used during the software design stage. The design stage of software development plays an important role in the area of software reuse, in which ability of matching and retrieving previous software design knowledge is a key factor for successful design reuse. A UML retrieval framework is presented, supported by multi similarity matching techniques.

This paper demonstrated the concept similarity computation by comparing the concept in query class diagram and that of repository (class diagram name). It also show how the retrieved diagrams can be ranked by similarity through computing the weighted sum of concept name similarity and relationship type similarity.

As our future work, we are currently working to fine-tune our matching approach to include other diagrams elements, such as attributes, operations and parameters.

Acknowledgments. The author would like to acknowledge the publication support for this paper from the Ministry of Higher Education (MOHE), Exploratory Research Grant Scheme No. 203/PKOMP/673140.

References

1. Adamu, A., Zainon, W.M.N.W., Salami, H.O.: Pre-filtering repository models. In: The 9th Malaysian Software Engineering Conference (MySec 2015), Kuala Lumpur, Malaysia, pp. 200–205 (2015). ISBN: 978-1-14799-5439-1
2. Ahmed, M.: Towards the development of integrated reuse environments for UML artifacts. In: ICSEA 2011, The Sixth International Conference on Software Engineering Advances (2011)
3. Salami, H.O., Ahmed, M.: A framework for reuse of multi-view UML artifacts. arXiv preprint arXiv:1402.0160 (2014)
4. Robles, K., et al.: Towards an ontology-based retrieval of UML Class Diagrams. Inf. Softw. Technol. **54**(1), 72–86 (2012)
5. Subedha, V., Sridhar, S.: Design of a conceptual reference framework for reusable software components based on context level. IJCSI Int. J. Comput. Sci. Issues **9**(1), 26–31 (2012)
6. Srinivas, C., Radhakrishna, V., Rao, C.: Clustering and classification of software component for efficient component retrieval and building component reuse libraries. Procedia Comput. Sci. **31**, 1044–1050 (2014)
7. Srinivas, C., Radhakrishna, V., Guru Rao, C.: Clustering software components for program restructuring and component reuse using hybrid XOR similarity function. AASRI Procedia **4**, 319–328 (2013)
8. Srisura, B., et al.: Retrieving use case diagram with case-based reasoning approach. J. Theor. Appl. Inf. Technol. **19**(2), 68–78 (2010)

Tool Demonstrations

Puzzle: A Tool for Analyzing and Extracting Specification Clones in DSLs

David Méndez-Acuña(✉), José A. Galindo, Benoit Combemale,
Arnaud Blouin, and Benoit Baudry

INRIA, University of Rennes 1, Rennes, France
{david.mendez-acuna,jagalindo,benoit.combemale,arnaud.blouin,
benoit.baudry}@inria.fr

Abstract. The use of domain-specific languages (DSLs) is a successful technique in the development of complex systems. Indeed, the construction of new DSLs addressing the particular needs of software projects has become a recurrent activity. In this context, the phenomenon of *specification cloning* has started to appear. Language designers often copy&paste some parts of the specification from legacy DSLs to "reuse" formerly defined language constructs. As well known, this type of practices introduce problems such as bugs propagation, thus increasing of maintenance costs. In this paper, we present PUZZLE, a tool that uses static analysis to facilitate the detection of specification clones in DSLs implemented under the executable metamodeling paradigm. PUZZLE also enables the extraction specification clones as reusable language modules that can be later used to build up new DSLs.

1 Introduction

A domain-specific language (DSL) is a software language whose expressiveness is limited to a well-defined domain. A DSL offers the abstractions (a.k.a., *language constructs*) needed to describe an aspect of a system under construction. The use of DSLs has become a successful technique to achieve separation of concerns in the development of complex systems [5].

Naturally, the adoption of such a language-oriented vision relies on the availability of the DSLs necessary to describe all the aspects of the system under construction [3]. As a result, the DSLs development has become a frequent activity in software projects [7]. In this context, the phenomenon of *specification cloning* has started to appear. Language designers often copy& paste some parts of the specification from legacy DSLs with the objective to "reuse" formerly defined language constructs. This practice might have some problems such as bug replications that increase maintenance costs [11].

Ideally, reuse should correspond to a systematic practice where the language constructs that are used in more than one DSL are defined in interdependent language modules that can be used as plug-in pieces during the DSLs development process. In this paper, we present PUZZLE, a tool to assist refactoring

© Springer International Publishing Switzerland 2016
G.M. Kapitsaki and E. Santana de Almeida (Eds.): ICSR 2016, LNCS 9679, pp. 393–396, 2016.
DOI: 10.1007/978-3-319-35122-3_26

processes intended to remove specification clones in a given set of legacy DSLs. More precisely, PUZZLE offers the following features:

Detection of Specification Clones. PUZZLE provides a set of comparison operators that enable automatic detection of specification clones in a given set of DSLs. These operators take into account not only the names of the constructs, but also the inter-constructs relationships and their semantics. Additionally, the implementation of PUZZLE is flexible enough to permit the definition of new comparison operators. Hence, the detection strategy can be easily improved or adapted to particular contexts.

Quantification of Potential Reuse. PUZZLE comes out with a set of metrics (inspired in [1]) to quantify the potential reuse emerging from the existing specification clones. The objective is to provide a mechanism that allows language designers to estimate (in an objective fashion) the benefit of a refactoring process intended to remove specification clones in a given set of DSLs. For example, PUZZLE measures the amount and percentage of language constructs cloned in a set of DSLs, as well as how different is a given DSL with respect to the others. All these metrics are presented in the form of charts implemented as HTML reports that can be easily shared and published.

Extraction of Reusable Language Modules. PUZZLE enables a reverse engineering process to extract reusable language modules from the detected specification clones [8]. This strategy is based on a principle illustrated in Fig. 1: if a DSL specification is viewed as a set of specification elements, then specification clones can be viewed as sets overlapping, and reusable language modules can be obtained by breaking down that overlapping [10]. The language modules resulting from this refactoring process can be later assembled in the construction of new DSLs.

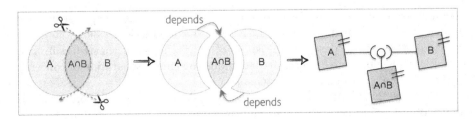

Fig. 1. Breaking down overlapping for obtaining reusable language modules

2   Puzzle

Technological Space. Like general purpose languages, DSLs are implemented in terms of syntax and semantics. Nowadays, there are diverse technological spaces available for the implementation of such implementation concerns [9]. PUZZLE supports DSLs such that the syntax is specified through metamodels whereas semantics is specified operationally through *domain-specific actions* [4].

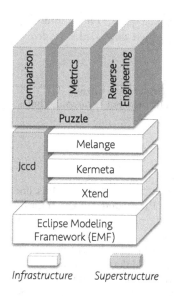

Fig. 2. Tool's architecture

Architecture. The architecture of PUZZLE is composed of two parts illustrated in Fig. 2: the infrastructure and the superstructure. The *infrastructure* is a set of plug-ins that enable the specification of DSLs according to the technological space described above. In turn, the *superstructure* is a set of plug-ins that provides analysis and reverse-engineering techniques on the DSLs specified on top of the infrastructure.

The PUZZLE's infrastructure is based on the Eclipse Modeling Framework (EMF). EMF provides a modeling language, called Ecore, which we use to specify metamodels. In turn, we use the notion of aspects provided Kermeta [6] to specify operational semantics. An aspect encapsulates a set of domain-specific actions that are weaved into a metaclass of the metamodel. The mapping between metamodels and aspects is specified in Melange[1].

In turn, the superstructure of PUZZLE corresponds to a set plug-ins that can be divided into three categories according to their functionalities: comparison, metrics, and reverse-engineering. Comparison plug-ins implement the comparison operators needed to detect specification clones at the level of abstract syntax and semantics (for the case of comparison of semantics, Puzzle uses JCCD [2]. The metrics plug-ins compute a set of metrics for the detected specification clones and present the results as a set of HTML reports that display those metrics in the form of charts. The reverse-engineering plug-ins implement the algorithms that extract reusable language modules from the detected specification clones.

Tool Demonstration. In the rest of this section, we provide three videos (available in the papers' website[2]) that show the way in which a set of DSL defined in the PUZZLE's infrastructure is analyzed by the PUZZLE's superstructure. The PUZZLE's source code is available in the project's website[3].

The input of PUZZLE is a Melange script that references a set of DSLs. The analysis starts by comparing the DSLs specifications (at the level of the abstract syntax and the semantics) and produces a first report indicating whether there are any specification clones or not. This report looks like a Venn diagram where each DSL is represented by a set, and intersections among sets indicate specification clones (*video 1: detecting specification clones*). Then, a set of metrics is computed from those specification clones. These metrics are intended to quantify the specification clones among the DSLs to objectively measure the associated potential reuse (*video 2: measuring specification clones*). Finally, a set of reusable

---

[1] Melange website: http://melange-lang.org/.

[2] **Tool demonstration:** http://puzzle-demo.weebly.com/.

[3] Puzzle's website: http://damende.github.io/puzzle/.

language modules is extracted from those specification clones. Those language modules can be later assembled among them to produce new DSLs (*video 3: Reverse-engineering reusable language modules*).

Acknowledgments. This work is supported by the ANR INS Project GEMOC (ANR-12-INSE-0011), the bilateral collaboration VaryMDE between Inria and Thales, and the bilateral collaboration FPML between Inria and DGA.

References

1. Berger, C., Rendel, H., Rumpe, B., Busse, C., Jablonski, T., Wolf, F.: Product line metrics for legacy software in practice. In: Workshop Proceedings of the International Software Product Lines Conference, SPLC 2010, pp. 247–250, Jeju Island, South Korea. Springer (2010)
2. Biegel, B., Diehl, S.: JCCD: A flexible and extensible API for implementing custom code clone detectors. In: Proceedings of the International Conference on Automated Software Engineering, ASE 2010, pp. 167–168. ACM, Antwerp, Belgium (2010)
3. Clark, T., Barn, B.S.: Domain engineering for software tools. In: Reinhartz-Berger, I., Sturm, A., Clark, T., Cohen, S., Bettin, J. (eds.) Domain Engineering: Product Lines, Languages, and Conceptual Models, pp. 187–209. Springer, Heidelberg (2013)
4. Combemale, B., Hardebolle, C., Jacquet, C., Boulanger, F., Baudry, B.: Bridging the chasm between executable metamodeling and models of computation. In: Czarnecki, K., Hedin, G. (eds.) SLE 2012. LNCS, vol. 7745, pp. 184–203. Springer, Heidelberg (2013)
5. Cook, S.: Separating concerns with domain specific languages. In: Lightfoot, D.E., Ren, X.-M. (eds.) JMLC 2006. LNCS, vol. 4228, pp. 1–3. Springer, Heidelberg (2006)
6. Jézéquel, J.-M., Combemale, B., Barais, O., Monperrus, M., Fouquet, F.: Mashup of metalanguages and its implementation in the kermeta language workbench. Softw. Syst. Model. **14**(2), 905–920 (2015)
7. Jézéquel, J.-M., Méndez-Acuña, D., Degueule, T., Combemale, B., Barais, O.: When systems engineering meets software language engineering. In: Boulanger, F., Krob, D., Morel, G., Roussel, J.-C. (eds.) Complex Systems Design & Management, pp. 1–13. Springer, Heidelberg (2015)
8. Méndez-Acuña, D., Galindo, J.A., Combemale, B., Blouin, A., Baudry, B.: Reverse-engineering reusable language modules from legacy domain-specific languages. In: Kapitsaki, G., Santana de Almeida, E. (eds.) ICSR 2016. LNCS, vol. 9679, pp. 368–383. Springer, Heidelberg (2016)
9. Mernik, M., Heering, J., Sloane, A.M.: When and how to develop domain-specific languages. ACM Comput. Surv. **37**(4), 316–344 (2005)
10. Völter, M., Benz, S., Dietrich, C., Engelmann, B., Helander, M., Kats, L.C.L., Visser, E., Wachsmuth, G.: DSL Engineering - Designing, Implementing and Using Domain-Specific Languages (2013). http://dslbook.org
11. Zschaler, S., Kolovos, D.S., Drivalos, N., Paige, R.F., Rashid, A.: Domain-specific metamodelling languages for software language engineering. In: van den Brand, M., Gašević, D., Gray, J. (eds.) SLE 2009. LNCS, vol. 5969, pp. 334–353. Springer, Heidelberg (2010)

FeatureIDE: Scalable Product Configuration of Variable Systems

Juliana Alves Pereira[1(✉)], Sebastian Krieter[1], Jens Meinicke[1,2],
Reimar Schröter[1], Gunter Saake[1], and Thomas Leich[2]

[1] University of Magdeburg, Magdeburg, Germany
`juliana.alves-pereira@ovgu.de`
[2] METOP GmbH, Magdeburg, Germany

Abstract. In the last decades, variability management for similar products is one of the main challenges in software systems. In this context, feature models are used to describe the dependencies between reusable common and variable artifacts, called features. However, for large feature models it is a complex task to find a valid feature combination as product configuration. Our Eclipse plug-in FEATUREIDE provides several mechanisms, such as information hiding and decision propagation, which support the configuration process to combine the reusable artifacts in various manners. We illustrate the applications of these mechanisms from a user's point of view.

1 Introduction

Variable software systems are essential to fulfill the individual requirements of several users. Such systems are commonly based on reusable but interdependent artifacts represented by a set of features that can be combined to form custom products [7]. Feature models are a common notation to define features and their interdependencies [3]. As feature models specify the set of valid products (i.e. a selection of features that fulfills all interdependencies), they form the basis of the product configuration process.

In industry feature models often define several thousand features. Hence, it is impractical for the user to keep track of all features and their dependencies during the configuration process. On the one hand, it may be difficult for a user to specify a valid configuration, especially since also features of no interest need to fulfill their dependencies. On the other hand, the user can unintentionally introduce conflicts by specifying mutually exclusive features. However, the user can be guided to configure valid products using specialized tool support.

In this paper, we present the configuration support of our tool FEATURE IDE [4,8]. With a close connection to FEATUREIDE's feature-model editor, the configuration editor can provide several mechanisms that guide the user. With automated decision propagation, we ensure that any partially configured product is in accordance to the feature model so that the result only describes valid

---

Demo Video. https://youtu.be/zM9K3wqUiVE.

G.M. Kapitsaki and E. Santana de Almeida (Eds.): ICSR 2016, LNCS 9679, pp. 397–401, 2016.
DOI: 10.1007/978-3-319-35122-3_27

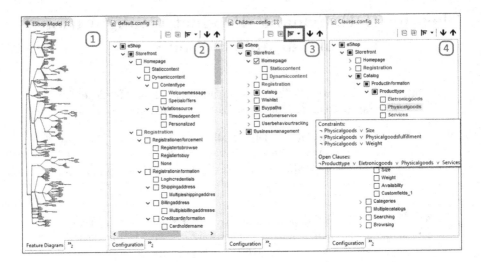

Fig. 1. An overview of FeatureIDE's configuration support: ① feature model editor, ②–④ configuration editor (② showing all features, ③ showing direct children, ④ finalizing configuration). (Colour figure online)

combination of reusable artifacts. Furthermore, we help the user with information hiding mechanisms that let them focus on the parts of the configuration that are of interest. Finally, we present how we guide the user to a valid configuration.

2   Preventing Conflicting Feature Combinations

Product configuration is a decision process to form a valid feature combination, where the interdependencies of all features are considered [7]. Especially when dealing with large feature models with complex feature dependencies, a configuration process without tool support is an error-prone and tedious task. Completely configuring products and checking validity afterwards is henceforth not advisable as at least one feature dependency is probably violated.

To ease the configuration process, FEATUREIDE provides an iterative strategy, which only allows feature selections that comply with the feature model's dependencies. Thus, similar to the tools SPLOT [5] and fmp [1], FEATUREIDE prevents the user to introduce conflicts in their configuration. This functional characteristic of FEATUREIDE is based on two concepts: (a) a close coupling between configurations and their feature models and (b) decision propagation.

Close Connection of Feature Models and Configurations. The feature model and the configuration editor of FEATUREIDE are closely connected and influence each other. On the one hand, the configuration editor of FEATUREIDE uses the same hierarchical structure as the corresponding feature model. Furthermore, the feature model influences configurations so that, for instance, a renaming of a feature also renames the feature in each configuration. On the other hand, each selection in a configuration forces a validity check considering the corresponding feature model. In addition, all implied and excluded features are automatically (de)selected and a change of their selection is forbidden. In Fig. 1①–②, we depict this functionality for the product line *EShop*. In Fig. 1①, the dependencies of the feature model are hard to resolve. However, the representation in the configuration editor (see Fig. 1②) allows an iterative selection of features according to the feature model.

Decision Propagation. Based on the close connection between feature models and configurations, FEATUREIDE's configuration editor prevents conflicts in each iteration of the configuration process using *decision propagation*. In detail, if a (de)selection of a feature forces the (de)selection of another feature, FEATUREIDE automatically adopts the implied configuration changes. For instance, if we select the feature *Welcomemessage* in the product line *EShop* (see Fig. 1②), all parent feature will be also selected.

3   Information Hiding

Configuring a product can be a difficult process as users usually do not know all features and their dependencies, especially for large feature models [2]. Consequently, showing all features (see in Fig. 1②) is impractical as a user can only focus on one part of the configuration at once. However, a user may already know their features of interest. To ease the configuration process, we provide information hiding mechanisms that focus the user's view on the relevant configuration space. The user can select one of these mechanisms via the configuration editor's menu bar (see the blue rectangle in Fig. 1③).

Focused View. FEATUREIDE aims to focus on the part of the configuration that is currently modified. Thus, it initially does not expand all features. When the user selects a feature, they are probably interested in its sub-features (e.g., fine-grained features of the same area). We provide a specialized expand algorithm that automatically expands and shows the sub-features after a feature is selected. This behavior is exemplary illustrated in Fig. 1③. Initially, only the feature *Storefront* is expanded. After the user selects the feature *Homepage*, the expand algorithm shows the sub-features *Staticcontent* and *Dynamiccontent*. With the focus on direct children only, we reduce the number of presented configuration options significantly and present only features that are of interest at the moment.

Finalize Partial Configurations. Decision propagation and specialized expand algorithms can only help to configure partial configurations. Still, a configuration needs to fulfill all dependencies defined in the feature model. Automatic selection of features is an efficient way to create a valid configuration based on the given partial configuration (e.g., the auto-completing mechanism presented by SPLOT [5]). However, such algorithms arbitrarily select features without considering the user's intentions. Thus, undesired features might be selected as well. In order to address this challenge, the tools VISIT-FC [6] and FaMa [9] introduce dependency visualization mechanisms to support the user in configuring products, but both tools present all features to the user. In contrast, FEATUREIDE provides a mechanism that guides the user to a valid configuration, reasoning from a smaller number of features. Based on unsatisfied clauses of the feature model's CNF-representation [2], its mechanism shows the user which decisions are necessary to finish the configuration process by highlighting the corresponding features. As each clause needs to be satisfied, the user can focus on one clause at a time. Thus, again the number of configuration options presented to the user is reduced to a minimum. We exemplary show this behavior in Fig. 1④. As shown, only the current open clause (displayed in the tooltip of *Physicalgoods*) is expanded. The feature *Producttype* was automatically selected by decision propagation. Thus, at least one of its children (highlighted with green) has to be selected to satisfy the open clause. A deselection of a feature might also satisfy a clause as shown in Fig. 1③ with a blue highlighting of the feature *Homepage*. After a clause is satisfied by the user's (de)selection, the focus will automatically change to the next unsatisfied clause. Using this mechanism, the user can efficiently finish the configuration process and simultaneously prevent undesired feature selections.

4   Conclusion

Feature models describe the dependencies between features in order to specify valid product configurations. However, the actual process of configuring products for large feature models is an error-prone and tedious task. In this paper, we illustrate FEATUREIDE's facilities to support this process by providing advanced configuration support, such as decision propagation and information hiding. This approach ensures a valid and complete configuration while simultaneously maintaining efficiency as the user can focus on their features of interest.

Acknowledgments. This work was partially supported by the CNPq grant (202368/2014-9) and the BMBF grant (01IS14017A, 01IS14017B).

References

1. Antkiewicz, M., Czarnecki, K.: FeaturePlugin: feature modeling plug-in for eclipse. In: Eclipse, pp. 67–72. ACM (2004)
2. Benavides, D., Segura, S., Ruiz-Cortés, A.: Automated analysis of feature models 20 years later: a literature review. Inf. Syst. **35**(6), 615–708 (2010)
3. Kang, K.C., Cohen, S.G., Hess, J.A., Novak, W.E., Peterson, A.S.: Feature-Oriented Domain Analysis (FODA) Feasibility Study. Technical report CMU/SEI-90-TR-21, Software Engineering Institute (1990)
4. Meinicke, J., Thüm, T., Schöter, R., Krieter, S., Benduhn, F., Saake, G., Leich, T.: FeatureIDE: Taming the preprocessor wilderness. In: ICSE. ACM (2016). (to appear)

5. Mendonça, M., Branco, M., Cowan, D.: S.P.L.O.T.: Software product lines online tools. In: OOPSLA, pp. 761–762. ACM (2009)
6. Nestor, D., Thiel, S., Botterweck, G., Cawley, C., Healy, P.: Applying visualisation techniques in software product lines. In: SoftVis, pp. 175–184. ACM (2008)
7. Pohl, K., Böckle, G., van der Linden, F.J.: Software Product Line Engineering: Foundations, Principles and Techniques. Springer, Heidelberg (2005)
8. Thüm, T., Kästner, C., Benduhn, F., Meinicke, J., Saake, G., Leich, T.: FeatureIDE: An extensible framework for feature-oriented software development. Sci. Comput. Program. **79**, 70–85 (2014)
9. Trinidad, P., Cortés, A.R., Benavides, D., Segura, S.: Three-dimensional feature diagrams visualization. In: SPLC, pp. 295–302 (2008)

Recalot.com: Towards a Reusable, Modular, and RESTFul Social Recommender System

Matthäus Schmedding[1], Michael Fuchs[2], Claus-Peter Klas[1(✉)], Felix Engel[1], Holger Brock[1], Dominic Heutelbeck[1], and Matthias Hemmje[1]

[1] Faculty for Mathematics and Computer Science, University of Hagen,
58084 Hagen, Germany
{matthaeus.schmedding,felix.engel,holger.brock,dominic.heutelbeck,
matthias.hemmje}@fernuni-hagen.de,
claus-peter.klas@gesis.org
[2] Wilhelm Büchner University of Applied Sciences, Darmstadt, Germany
michael.fuchs@ftk.de

Abstract. Many different recommender system (RS) frameworks have been developed by the research community. Most of these RS frameworks are designed only for research purposes and offline evaluation of different algorithms. A reuse of such frameworks in a productive environment is only possible with high effort. In this paper, we present a concept of a generic reusable RESTful recommender web service framework, designed to perform directly offline and online analysis for research and to use the recommender algorithms in production.

Keywords: Recommender systems · Web service · Modular development

1 Introduction

Many different approaches exist how recommendation can be computed and libraries that offer these functionalities. However, these RS libraries often focus on a special use cases and neglect other areas. Scientific libraries, like MyMediaLite [3], LenKit [2], recommender101 [8], or librec [5], are easily extendable and can perform different offline evaluations out-of-box. However, a productive usage or an online evaluation requires additional work and a specific knowledge about the library. On the other hand, commercial libraries, like factfinder[1], or epoq[2], can perform online evaluation and can be used productive, but are often closed-source and the underlying recommendation strategies are usually hidden. Within the portal of the EU-funded RAGE (Realising an Applied Gaming Eco-system) project[3], we developed a generic recommender system for web

---

[1] http://www.fact-finder.de/.
[2] http://www.epoq.de/de/.
[3] http://www.rageproject.eu/.

© Springer International Publishing Switzerland 2016
G.M. Kapitsaki and E. Santana de Almeida (Eds.): ICSR 2016, LNCS 9679, pp. 402–406, 2016.
DOI: 10.1007/978-3-319-35122-3_28

portals with a social data structure. Based on a requirement analysis we compared different RS libraries, but none matched our objectives. Thus, we decided to develop the RS framework[4], which provides the necessary functionality and can be used in varying environments.

2   Developing a RS Framework

Framework Requirements. There are several requirements we want our framework to meet (see Table 1). As we want to support multiple applications simultaneously and evaluate different RS approaches, our library needs to be able to manage different and several data sources at once. In addition, that data model needs to handle the entities users, items, relationships, ratings and the relations between these entities. Since, the framework should be able to process the information in the data model, it should contain RS approaches from the area Social RS [6], but also be able to compute approaches from the classic categories Collaborative Filtering, Content-based RS, and Hybrid RS [1]. Finally, as the framework should be used to compare recommendation algorithms, it is important to provide a wide range of these build in.

The usage of the framework can be distinguished into scientific and productive usage (as library/API). For the scientific usage, it is important that the framework can be easily extended, can perform off- and on-line evaluation [4]. For the productive usage, the library has to be fast, reliable, distributable, easily integrable and accessible. However, since the requirement 'speed' is strongly dependent on the running recommendation approach, we did not consider these requirements as part of our objectives. These can be overcome e.g. by distributing the algorithms over several computation nodes. However, the requirements integrability and accessibility play an important role for us and will be met by using a RESTful web service.

Table 1. Framework analysis according to our requirements

Library	Multiple Data Sources	Relationships Data Model	Collaborative Filtering	Content-based RS	Hybrid RS	Social RS	Context-Aware RS	Platform independent	Extendable	Offline Evaluation	Online Evaluation	RESTful Web Service
MyMediaLite[3]	x	x	x	x		x	x	x	x	x		
LensKit[2]	x		x					x	x	x		
LibRec[5]	x	x	x		x	x	x	x	x	x		
Apache Mahout[10]	x		x					x	x	x		x
PREA[9]	x	x	x			x	x	x	x	x		
Duine[12]	x		x					x	x	x		
easyrec[11]	x		x					x	x			x
Recommender101[8]	x		x	x				x	x	x		

---

[4] https://github.com/mys3lf/recalot.com.

Framework Evaluation. We analyzed existing open-source frameworks and libraries according to our requirements down to the source-code level, depicted in Table 1. None of these met our requirements, as they are focused on specific research agendas. Therefore we decided to implement our own framework, reusing the approaches of the existing systems and extending them into one generic framework.

Therefore, we identified frequently used open-source libraries and frameworks from scientific works and the open-source community. We examined LensKit [2] the library behind movielens.org, LibRec [5] that contains many current RS approaches, Mahout [10] from the Apache Software Foundation, MyMediaLite [3] that is written in C# and optimized for mono, PREA [9] the Personalized Recommendation Algorithms Toolkit, Duine [12] that had been developed by the Telematica Instituut / Novay, easyrec [11] a recommendation REST web service, and Recommender101 [8] that was developed by the Technical University of Dortmund.

As our framework needs to be easily extensible, platform independent and able to perform off- and online evaluations, we decided to rely on the modular development technology OSGi in its implementation on Apache Felix. To be integrated in existing frameworks, we will propagate the functionality via a full RESTful web service. The actual implementation will use Java EE and follow the software-as-a-service paradigm for easy deployment, also in the cloud for efficiency purposes. As displayed in Fig. 1, we distinguish between data-, recommendations-, and experiments components, as well as model-, view-, and controller components. Following the concepts of modular or component-based programming [7], each component is an independent and interchangeable module within the OSGi framework.

Framework Design and Development. In order to meet our needs and to develop an easily extensible system, which is platform independent, can perform off- and on-line evaluation, and will be deployed as a RESTful Web service, we opted for the modular development technology OSGi and the implementation Apache Felix.

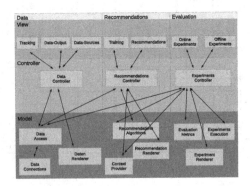

Fig. 1. Architecture of the generic recommender web service

We implement our framework by the usage of Java EE and by following the software-as-a-service paradigm, which allows to run the framework at a central location and to use it on multiple applications. Our architecture follows the MVC design pattern for the development of the RESTful RS web service. As displayed in Fig. 1, we distinguish between data-, recommendations-, and experiments components, as well as model-, view-, and controller components. Following the concepts of modular or component-based programming, each component is an independent and interchangeable module within the OSGi framework.

The modular design allows the usage of individual components without changing the entire framework. An extension of the framework is done by adding OSGi bundles with new functionality (e.g. recommender algorithms).

3   Conclusion and Outlook

In this paper we presented the rational and requirements why to implement our own RS framework. The main features are on- and offline evaluation, extentability and the use as a research framework and in productive environments. The framework is available at: https://github.com/mys3lf/recalot.com and we currently adding more RS algorithms and integrate it as recommender in different use cases.

4   Acknowledgements and Disclaimer

This publication has been produced in the context of the RAGE project. The project has received funding from the European Union's Horizon 2020 research and innovation programme under grant agreement No 644187. However, this paper reflects only the author's view and the European Commission is not responsible for any use that may be made of the information it contains.

References

1. Adomavicius, G., Tuzhilin, A.: Toward the next generation of recommender systems: a survey of the state-of-the-art and possible extensions. IEEE Trans. Knowl. Data Eng. **17**(6), 734–749 (2005)
2. Ekstrand, M.D., Riedl, J.T., Konstan, J.A.: Collaborative filtering recommender systems. Found. Trends Hum. Comput. Interact. **4**(2), 81–173 (2011)
3. Gantner, Z., Rendle, S., Freudenthaler, C., Schmidt-Thieme, L.: MyMediaLite: A free recommender system library. In: Proceedings of the 5th ACM Conference on Recommender Systems (RecSys 2011) (2011)
4. Gunawardana, A., Shani, G.: A survey of accuracy evaluation metrics of recommendation tasks. J. Mach. Learn. Res. **10**, 2935–2962 (2009)
5. Guo, G., Zhang, J., Sun, Z., Yorke-Smith, N.: Librec: A java library for recommender systems. In: Posters, Demos, Late-breaking Results and Workshop Proceedings of the 23rd Conference on User Modeling, Adaptation, and Personalization (UMAP 2015) (2015)

6. He, J.: A Social Network-based Recommender System. Ph.D. thesis, Los Angeles, CA, USA, AAI3437557 (2010)
7. Heineman, G.T., Councill, W.T.: Component-Based Software Engineering: Putting the Pieces Together. Addison-Wesley, Boston (2001)
8. Jannach, D., Lerche, L., Gedikli, F., Bonnin, G.: What recommenders recommend – an analysis of accuracy, popularity, and sales diversity effects. In: Carberry, S., Weibelzahl, S., Micarelli, A., Semeraro, G. (eds.) UMAP 2013. LNCS, vol. 7899, pp. 25–37. Springer, Heidelberg (2013)
9. Lee, J., Sun, M., Lebanon, G.: A Comparative Study of Collaborative Filtering Algorithms. ArXiv e-prints, May 2012
10. Owen, S., Anil, R., Dunning, T., Friedman, E.: Mahout in Action. Manning Publications Co., Greenwich, CT, USA (2011)
11. Surhone, L., Tennoe, M., Henssonow, S.: EASYREC. Betascript Publishing, Saarbrücken (2010)
12. van Setten, M., Reitsma, J., Ebben, P.: Duine Toolkit: User Manual. Telematica Instituut, 2.0.3rd edn. (2006)

CORPO-DS: A Tool to Support Decision Making for Component Reuse Through Profiling with Ontologies

Savvas Loumakos and Andreas S. Andreou[(✉)]

Department of Computer Engineering and Informatics, Cyprus University of Technology,
Lemesos, Cyprus
sp.loumakos@edu.cut.ac.cy, andreas.andreou@cut.ac.cy

Abstract. This paper introduces a software tool that supports the activities of a novel, reuse-based development framework, which focuses on assessing the suitability level of candidate components. The tool enables the creation of a specifications profile using a semi-formal natural language, which describes the desired functional and non-functional properties of the component(s) sought. It also offers the means to parse the profile automatically and translate it into instance values of a dedicated CBSE ontology. Finally, the tool performs matching between required and offered component properties at the level of ontology items and suggests the most suitable components to consider for integration based on a suitability ratio calculated.

Keywords: Components · Reuse · Matching · Software tool · Decision-Support

1 Introduction

The present paper introduces the CORPO-DS (COmponent Reuse through Profiling with Ontologies Decision Support) system, a web-based software tool that builds upon the notions of the approach in [1] and fully supports the process described therein for locating and retrieving the most appropriate software components according to functionality previously expressed as a set of properties. The main novelty of this tool is that it offers a user friendly and efficient decision support tool for CBSE that boosts the capabilities of reusers and helps them deal with trivial yet time consuming issues for determining the suitability of components for integration. To the best of our knowledge, existing tools do not offer such automated management and full support of components' reuse processes at the practical level.

Although the relevant literature for component search and retrieval is rich with studies reporting mechanisms for matching components, it lacks focus on tools that support and enhance the reuse process. A very brief report on relevant studies follows: Chen et al. [2] proposed a database management system that supports a suitable data modeling language and allowed automatic mapping of component specifications with goal specifications. Klein and Bernstein [3] presented an ontology-based approach for web-services (including component implementations) using characteristics from a process taxonomy, while Park [4] reports on a software component retrieval method using static sampling of components' input-output behavior based on concept analysis.

© Springer International Publishing Switzerland 2016
G.M. Kapitsaki and E. Santana de Almeida (Eds.): ICSR 2016, LNCS 9679, pp. 407–410, 2016.
DOI: 10.1007/978-3-319-35122-3_29

The present paper aspires to fill this gap in literature by offering a fully functional and easy to use software tool to support a certain reuse process.

2   The CORPO-DS Tool

The present paper introduces an efficient software tool that was developed to support the framework described in [1] for automatic matching of software components using semi-formal specifications supported by a CBSE ontology. This framework utilizes a specific profiling scheme and automatically delivers the most suitable components in three simple steps: The first step involves describing the desired functional and non-functional properties of the component(s) sought in a specifications profile using a semi-formal natural language. Each component is profiled with information revolving around three axes describing functional, non-functional and reusability properties. Component properties are expressed in the Extended Backus-Naur Form (EBNF). In the second step, the profile is automatically parsed and translated into instance values of a dedicated CBSE ontology. The third and final step performs matching between required and offered components' properties at the level of ontology items and a numerical suitability ratio is calculated that takes into account the nature of the properties a reuser seeks for, either mandatory (constraints) or desired. Two types of properties are supported, one of binary type (offered 'yes'/'no') and one of numerical type (e.g. price, response time). The suitability ratio essentially measures the distance of available components from the required one in terms of binary and numerical properties and finally suggests which components are considered more appropriate (closest matches) to consider for possible integration.

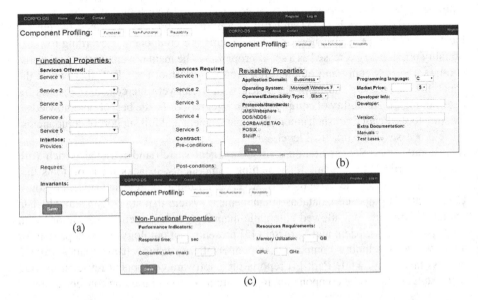

Fig. 1. Profiling information for (a) Functional, (b) Reusability, (c) Non-functional properties

As Fig. 1 shows, the profiling information is organized in three different categories-screens, one for each of the axes described earlier. A user is guided through drop-down lists and predefined values to describe certain properties, while in other cases she/he is quite flexible to define property descriptions through free text which is then parsed and analyzed semantically.

The Search process is depicted in Fig. 2. Using the form shown in Fig. 2(a), the user can search the database to find components based on the preferences inserted. Component characteristics are selected from dropdown lists and their type, either "constraint" (a property that the component sought for must possess) or "desired" (a property that if offered will raise its suitability ratio) is defined on the right. By selecting value "All" or "Any" for a specific characteristic the user instructs the system that this characteristic is indifferent and that matching of that property should return all values found in the database. When all properties have been filled in pressing the button "Search" triggers the matching process which searches the database, locates suitable candidates working at the level of ontology instances and calculates their suitability level, the latter being used to rank components and return them in the "Results" page presented in Fig. 2(b). The user may further filter the components appearing in the list by selecting one or more properties appearing on the left column which were declared as indifferent in the original search. If the user wishes to see more information about a particular component she/he may do so by pressing the "More Info" button. In such a case a popup window will show up, which contains more details on the functional characteristics of that component and the option to reveal its full profile along with a link to the vendor's page so that the user may proceed and purchase the component.

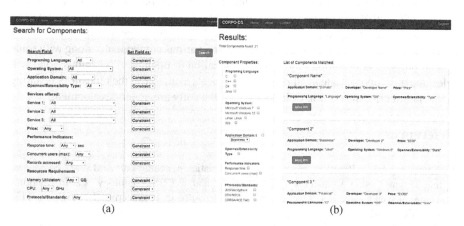

Fig. 2. Searching for components: (a) Property values are inserted on the left and their type on the right, (b) The most suitable components are returned appearing from top to bottom

The tool was initially released under an alpha version that was tested in a controlled environment using 1000 synthetic component instances which were generated to cover the needs of this testing stage, as well as those of the next (beta). The tool has successfully completed the first level of assessment and has moved on to its beta version. This version is already handed to a group of 25 subjects, 20 of which are graduate (master) students at the

Cyprus University of Technology and 5 are software practitioners. The students hold an undergraduate degree in Computer Science and/or Engineering that included courses in Software Engineering (SE) and presently follow an advanced SE course with emphasis on CBSE and reusability. The practitioners consist of software developers, 3 of which extensively make use of component reuse for the last 5 years and 2 produce components for internal reuse in their company for the last 3 years. All subjects underwent a short period of training (2 h) on the proposed approach (profiling scheme and semi-formal structures of the natural language used) and the functionality of the tool. The aim is to conclude the second stage correcting potential bugs prior to the final release of the tool that will make it freely accessible by the scientific community (http://seiis.cut.ac.cy/tools/corpo).

3   Conclusions

This paper presented an efficient web-based software tool that supports component-based development. The CORPO-DS tool enhances reuse by offering a user friendly way for locating and retrieving components stored in a repository easily and most importantly with high accuracy. CORPO-DS is based on a framework that expresses functional and non-functional component characteristics using a certain form of profile written in EBNF. The profile is transformed to instances of a dedicated component-based ontology developed to support the component specification matching activities. The latter transformation enables comparison at the level of ontology tree instances which is used to assess if hard constraints are violated (i.e., absolutely necessary properties required are not offered by candidates) and if not, to calculate a similarity metric that dictates the level of appropriateness of components for possible integration. Future work will concentrate on expanding the tool incorporating an "intelligent" engine which will receive multiple preferences of a reuser reflecting various components, along with some special-purpose information (e.g. cost minimization or openness constraints), and will select the most appropriate synthesis of components available in the repository resulting in the automatic construction of large parts of the software under development.

References

1. Andreou, A.S., Papatheocharous, E.: Automatic matching of software component requirements using semi-formal specifications and a CBSE ontology. In: International Conference on Evaluation of Novel Approaches to Software Engineering (ENASE), pp. 118–128. IEEE (2015)
2. Chen, P., Hennicker, C.R., Jarke, M.: On the retrieval of reusable software components. In: Software Reusability, Selected Papers from the Second International Workshop on Advances in Software Reuse, pp. 99–108. IEEE (1993)
3. Klein, M., Bernstein, A.: Searching for services on the semantic web using process ontologies. In: The Emerging Semantic Web (2001)
4. Park, Y.: Software retrieval by samples using concept analysis. J. Syst. Softw. 54(3), 179–183 (2000)

Author Index

Adamu, Alhassan 384
Alam, Omar 122
Ali, Shaukat 89
Amorim, Luiz 73
Ampatzoglou, Apostolos 149
Andreou, Andreas S. 407
Arcega, Lorena 39

Bagheri, Ebrahim 20
Ballarin, Manuel 215
Bashari, Mahdi 20
Baudry, Benoit 368, 393
Belloir, Nicolas 122
Ben Sassi, Sihem 300
Bendraou, Reda 333
Bibi, Stamatia 149
Bissyandé, Tegawendé F. 267
Blouin, Arnaud 368, 393
Braga, Rosana T. Vaccare 231
Brock, Holger 402

Cetina, Carlos 39, 215
Chatzigeorgiou, Alexander 149
Cleophas, Loek 63
Coelho, Duarte 284
Collet, Philippe 122
Combemale, Benoit 122, 368, 393

DeAntoni, Julien 122
Du, Weichang 20

Engel, Felix 402
Engels, Gregor 199

Fazal-Baqaie, Masud 199
Feloni, Daniel 231
Filho, Domenico Schettini 231
Font, Jaime 39
Fuchs, Michael 402

Galindo, José A. 368, 393
Gervais, Marie-Pierre 333
Gomaa, Hassan 181

Gottardi, Thiago 231
Grieger, Marvin 199

Hamid, Brahim 350
Haugen, Øystein 39
He, Keqing 106
Hebig, Regina 333
Hemmje, Matthias 402
Heutelbeck, Dominic 402
Hoch, Ralph 138

Jin, Xiaoyu 247

Kaindl, Hermann 138
Khatwani, Charu 247
Khelladi, Djamel Eddine 333
Kienzle, Jörg 122
Klas, Claus-Peter 402
Klein, Jacques 122, 267
Klenke, Markus 199
Krieter, Sebastian 397

Lapeña, Raúl 215
Le Guernic, Gurvan 368
Le Traon, Yves 267
Leich, Thomas 397
Li, Hongtao 106
Li, Wenchao 315
Lity, Sascha 3
Liu, Chao 89
Loumakos, Savvas 407

Männistö, Tomi 55
Martinez, Jabier 267
Meinicke, Jens 397
Méndez-Acuña, David 368, 393
Mendonça, Manoel 73
Morbach, Thomas 3
Mussbacher, Gunter 122
Myllärniemi, Varvana 55

Niu, Nan 247
Nyamsuren, Enkhbold 165

Pacini, Karen   231
Papadakis, Mike   267
Paschali, Maria-Eleni   149
Pathirage, Don   181
Peng, Zhenlian   106
Pereira, Juliana Alves   397
Popp, Roman   138

Raatikainen, Mikko   55
Robin, Jacques   333
Rumpe, Bernhard   122

Saake, Gunter   397
Saidi, Hassen   315
Sanchez, Huascar   315
Santos, André L.   284
Savolainen, Juha   247
Schaefer, Ina   3, 63
Schäf, Martin   315
Schmedding, Matthäus   402
Schöttle, Matthias   122
Schröter, Reimar   397

Schweitzer, Pascal   315
Seidl, Christoph   63
Shin, Michael   181
Stamelos, Ioannis   149

Thüm, Thomas   3
Tiihonen, Juha   55

van der Vegt, Wim   165

Wagner, Michael   247
Wang, Jian   106
Watson, Bruce W.   63
Westera, Wim   165

Yue, Tao   89

Zainoon, Wan Mohd Nazmee Wan   384
Zeidler, Christian   138
Zhang, Huihui   89
Ziadi, Tewfik   267

Printed in the United States
By Bookmasters